Essentials of Horary Astrology or Praśnapadavī

Essentials of Horary Astrology or Praśnapadavī

M. Ramakrishna Bhat

Assisted by

B.P. Nair

MOTILAL BANARSIDASS PUBLISHERS
PRIVATE LIMITED • DELHI

First Edition: Delhi, 1992
Reprint: Delhi, 1995, 2002

ISBN: 81-208-0888-6 (Cloth)
ISBN: 81-208-1012-0(Paper)

Also available at:
MOTILAL BANARSIDASS
236, 9th Main III Block, Jayanagar, Bangalore 560 011
41 U.A. Bungalow Road, Jawahar Nagar, Delhi 110 007
8 Mahalaxmi Chamber, Warden Road, Mumbai 400 026
120 Royapettah High Road, Mylapore, Chennai 600 004
Sanas Plaza, 1302 Baji Rao Road, Pune 411 002
8 Camac Street, Kolkata 700 017
Ashok Rajpath, Patna 800 004
Chowk, Varanasi 221 001

Printed in India
BY JAINENDRA PRAKASH JAIN AT SHRI JAINENDRA PRESS,
A-45 NARAINA, PHASE-I, NEW DELHI 110 028
AND PUBLISHED BY NARENDRA PRAKASH JAIN FOR
MOTILAL BANARSIDASS PUBLISHERS PRIVATE LIMITED,
BUNGALOW ROAD, DELHI 110 007

FOREWORD

"No sinner will creep into a place that is sanctified by the presence of a true astrologer. No person who studies and divines the course of destiny will ever be found in hell, but will reside permanently in the world of Brahman."

—VARĀHMIHIRA

Astrology, it has been rightly said, is the most systematic attempt to explain natural phenomena. The development of astrology at a popular level owes considerably to the new intellectual vitality of the applied sciences. Today there is no area of human experience which is not touched upon in some way or the other by astrology. Historical evidence supports the claim that astrology is a valid discipline with vast potential for enriching an understanding of all phases of life.

The literature of astrology is as vast as the history of man. No one scholar can possibly hope to untangle all of its intrinsically woven strands in the course of his life. He cannot read the extant works on the subject, let alone resolve its intrinsic patterns of thought. Astrology has been described as both a "Science" and an "Art". In short casting and interpreting horoscopes have been, for more than two thousand years, the focus of the science of astrology. Though widely discredited, especially in the west, it is an exacting art demanding considerable expertise of its techniques.

A sophisticated science of astrology that evolved among the Babylonians was taken over and modified by the Greeks and the Romans. In the second century A.D. the Egyptian astronomer Ptolemy reduced astrology to a clear set of laws—the basis of European Astrology for many centuries to come. In India, *Nakshatravidya*, the science of the stars, has been thought of as an intellectual attainment even in the Vedic literature. The vedic as well as pre-vedic literature including purāṇas contain innumerable references that show astrology to have been held in high esteem and referred to as the 'eye of knowledge'. It is an important limb of Hindu religion and philosophy, handed down from great seers who had amply sanctified the subject with their contributions.

This oldest of sciences has exercised a fascination over mankind, and the romance associated with the stars has inspired poets from all ages. Modern research tends to show that it had its origin in stellar worship, for, in ancient times the stars were believed to be the abode of the gods. Astrology, as in the case of other ancient arts which possessed the germs of truth, has gradually freed itself from the penumbra of superstitions to emerge as the true science of the heaven.

The development of this science of the stars however had its own vagaries. Some profane accretions and unscrupulous practices crept into the hoary science and probably the baser side of it began to manifest itself. It was for this reason, perhaps, Manu and later Kautilya denounced the use of astrology or its practice in ordinary life. Similar views have been expressed in *Gautama Dharma Sutra* and *Taittriya Upanished.* The famous astronomer-cum-astrologer Varāhamihira also characterised a bad astrologer as a sinner and one who defiles society. However, he pays extraordinary compliments to a worthy astrologer who, in his view, should know practically all branches of knowledge under the sun, and be a guide, philosopher and teacher to society. This hoary lore, according to Prof. Bhat, is to be practised not for selfish ends, but to guide the needy and the distressed, to remove the cause of their suffering and to turn their attention towards God. Though an astrologer cannot control the powers of the stars, he can harness it through "Elections" and so enhance the prospects of success in any undertaking or for any individual.

I had the unique privilege of going through the manuscript of over five hundred pages of this monumental work—"Essentials of Horary Astrology". Astrology by the deep rooted nature of its origins, spans many centuries, and hence has many sub-disciplines and specialities. In general, it has evolved in practice over the years into three broad areas. 'Prediction' relates to forecasting an individual's destiny from his nativity—a calculation of the state of the heavens at his birth. 'Election' denotes the process of choosing the most propitious moment when the influence of the planets would be most favourable for undertaking any action ranging from matters of State to the weaning of an infant. Finally 'Horary' resolves personal problems—

medical, moral and very often matrimonial—according to the state of the heavens at the instant the question is posed to the astrologer. It is this third branch of astrology that has immensely benefited from Prof. Bhat's work.

This book is intended to provide insights into the laws of consciousness whereby the reader can comprehend that he is but an integral unit of the larger framework of consciousness in which all of us unite. I was not only touched by the sensitivity, clarity, precision, and details of Prof. Bhat's treatment of the subject, but also enlightened by the vastness of this science and its compass over all human activities with detailed clarifications of their attributes.

Prof. Bhat's earlier work—*Fundamentals of Astrology*—first published in 1967 has subsequently seen two more editions and the third revision is now available. It has found favour with both students and practitioners in the east as well as the west. Since then he has authored a number of books, the most important of them being the translation of the Bṛhatsaṁhitā of Varāhamihira—a monumental encyclopaedia in Sanskrit of astrological and other subjects of human interest—with explanatory notes and comments. This work in two volumes has already run through two editions with wide appreciation. As a Sanskrit poet, he has a number of *kāvyas* to his credit; to mention a few, the Mahākāvya, "*Śrī Śivānanda Vilāsaḥ*", "*Kāvyamañjarī*" and "*Guru-Mahima-Stotra*" (a string of hymns in praise of the life and work of H.H. Sri Chandrasekharendra Saraswathi of Kānchī Kāmakoṭi Peetham).

In this volume Prof. Bhat presents his subject in a variety of ways and in different contexts. The lucid and clear manner of Prof. Bhat's work makes it pleasant to read. He has done a great service to Indian astrology in general, and to this branch in particular, by striving to remove the misconceptions about it. I am sure that a critical study of this work will greatly benefit the students and practitioners of this science. Prof. Bhat is a restless scholar always in relentless pursuit of knowledge. Even in his eighties now, he strives to disseminate his knowledge and experience through his writings.

Mere knowledge of this science, however deep and clear, does not take you to the level of predictive astrology and the practice there of, unless one has complete faith in God and His supreme grace. Thus Prof. Bhat has in abundance from Lord Śrī Siddhi Vināyaka of Madhupura. More than once he has admitted to vain efforts in the realizations of the results of his work; and in many cases with His grace of immediate success.

Prof. Bhat has been my friend, philosopher and guide in the true sense of the term. Our friendship spans over the last four decades and has been one of most agreeable and fruitful nature. It is a privilege and honour to be able to write a foreword for this excellent work of a unique speciality of astrological science--Horary Astrology or *Praśna-Śāstra.*

"May Lord Siddhi Vināyaka shower His grace and give Prof. Bhat many years of good health for the benefit of the field of astrology and its ardent students" is my fervant prayer.

Carbondale IL-62901 R.K. RANGAN
USA, Diwali,
October 28, 1989

CONTENTS

ABBREVIATIONS

A.K.	Akṣarakośa
A.L.S.	Abhilāṣa-Sphuṭa
A.V.	Aṣṭakavarga
Ba. S.	Bādhā-Sthāna
B.D.	Benefic Dots
B.S.	Bṛhat Saṁhitā
C.A.	Candrāvasthā
C.G.	Coragraha
C.K.	Candra-Kriyā
C.V.	Candra-Velā
D.A.	Daśādhyāyī
K.C.	Kāla-Cakra
K.H.	Kālahorā
M.A.	Mahābhicāra
M.J.	Mārkaṇḍeya Jyautiṣa
M.N.	Mahā-Nakṣatra
N. Asct.	Natal Ascendant
N.G.	Nakṣatra-Gocara
N.P.D.	Naṣṭapraśna-Dīpikā
N.S.	Natal Sign
P.G.	Pramāṇa-Gulika
P.J.	Praśna-Jñāna
P.M.	Praśna-Mārga
R.S.C.	Ravi-Sūla Cakra
S.C.	Sūrya-Cakra
S.C.S.	Santāna-Candra-Sphuṭa
S.J.	Santāna-Jīva
S.K.C.	Sūrya-Kālāgni-Cakra
S.R.S.	Santāna-Ravi-Sphuṭa
S.S.	Santāna-Śukra
Sa. Śa.	Sapta-Śalākā
S.T.	Santāna-Tithi
S.T.S.	Santāna-Trisphuṭa
S.Y.S.	Santāna-Yoga-Sphuṭa
T.S.	Trisphuṭa

V.S.A.	Vīrasiṁhāvaloka
Y.K.	Yamakaṇṭaka
Y.S.	Yāma-Śukra
Y.S.	Yoga-Sphuṭa

PREFACE

BOUNDLESS and spontaneous indeed is the grace of the Supreme Lord *Śrī Siddhi-Vināyaka* that has provided me, the humblest devotee of His, with inspiration to write this book on Horary Astrology. I am quite aware of my severe limitations to write a book of such magnitude and reputation as this at the fag end of my life. I, therefore, consider this as an opportunity granted to me by the Lord to serve the cause of astrology which reveals the subtle laws or powers of the Almighty in the form of the divine planets appointed to administer justice and bestow the fruits of *Karma* (action) on all beings living on this earth.

I have been consistently maintaining that the purpose of astrology is to wean humanity away from the path of *adharma* (evil deeds) resulting in misery and destruction, and to lead them towards the path of light and glorious life. The reader, I am sure, will find in this work enough opportunity to remind himself of the fact that he is suffering in his present existence, which is a continuation of the soul's journey (sojourn) towards the abode of perfection or self-realization, as a result of his own past misdeeds or sins, and that he can improve his lot and get over his infirmities by taking appropriate remedial measures through mind, word and deed. Ultimately, as Swami Vivekananda has declared, it would dawn on men that there is divinity in every one of them and it is their bounden duty to draw out that divinity and manifest it in all their thoughts, words and deeds.

I have tried to answer in this work the question regarding the relevance of this horary branch of astrology, which has been developed into a reputed branch of predictive astrology in Kerala, where there are some renowned families that practise this science with uncanny powers of foretelling, giving, especially the *Aṣṭamaṅgala Praśna* system which has attained unusual celebrity and acceptance in the West Coast of India. Sessions of this type of horary astrology are largely resorted to in cases of temple construction or renovation, calamities in a family or village etc. The *Praśna-Śāstra* (Query Science) is made use of in cases of theft, missing persons, lost horoscopes, serious diseases, suspected divine displeasure, black magic etc. It is also found useful in the case of *Muṣṭi-praśna* (query about what is held in the closed fist). In fact, the work Kṛṣṇīya of Kṛṣṇācārya, which is also called *Horāśāstra*, is otherwise known as Cintājñānam, meaning, Knowledge of what is in the querist's mind, "Science of Thought-reading". While admitting the prevalence of horary astrology in all parts of our ancient land right from Vedic times and that of Varāhamihira, his famous commentator and others, I should like to mention some of the special features of this Kerala system: (1) *Aṣṭamaṅgalapraśna*; (2) *Devapraśna*; (3) *Karmavipāka* (ripening of past deeds); (4) *Vīthi*, and *Chatra Rāśi*; (5) *Bhūtodaya* (rise of elements); (6) Duration of *Yāma* (watch); (7) Lordship of asterisms as per the *Vimśottarīdaśā* system; (8) Tastes allotted to planets in different contexts e.g. Venus rules over sweet, the Sun over salt and astringent, at a query about food eaten; (9) Letters of the alphabet are assigned to the elements; (10) *Cora* (thief) *Grahas*, (11) *Vittāya*, *Tīrtha* etc. in *A.V.*; (12) *Candragupti* chart for *water-divination*; (13) All planets exercise all the four types of aspect; (14) Significators of relatives, e.g. Mars stands for paternal cousin, Saturn for paternal uncle, Jupiter for maternal uncle; (15) Time represented by fixed, movable and dual signs as years, days and months respectively; (16) *Kṛṣṇīya* makes Mars a friend of Venus; (17) *Bādhāsthānas* (Houses of affliction); (18) Jupiter's number is 3, and the Moon's 7 as in modern numerology; (19) *Māndi's* greatest importance among minor planets; (20) Analysis of the nature of *Pretas* (Discarnate spirits); (21) *Ṛṇānubandha* (Antenatal bonds) between bride and groom; (22) *Navāmśa* calculation of the *Ārūḍha*; (23) The Sūtras such as *Sāmānya* and *Adhipa*; (24) *Yāma Śukra*; (25) *Abhilāṣa Sphuṭa* of the Moon; (26) *Māndi's Caturvarga*; (27) *Nava-Navāmśa* and *Navāmśa-Dvādaśāmśa*; (28) *Kāla-Cakra-Daśā*; (29) High and Low Tide signs; (30) *Pramāṇa-Gulika*; (31) *Sūryakālāgni-Cakra*; (32) Thief's movements from village to forest etc; (33) Many alternatives for arriving at the querist's natal Star; and (34) *Daśā* based on *Māndi's* Star. Another feature of this science is that the authors clinch an issue by means of many an argument and example.

I have drawn materials for this work from the *Praśnamārga*

(P.M.), *Kṛṣṇīya Horā*, *Praśnajñāna*, *Satpañcāśikā*, *Varāhamihira's Horā-Śāstra* and *Bṛhat Saṁhitā*, *Jātakapārijāta*, *Naṣṭapraśna-Dīpikā*, *Vīrasimhāvaloka*, *Jātakādeśamārga*, *Narapatijayacaryā*, *Daśādhyāyī* (*Naukā*) on the *Bṛhad-Jātaka*, *Vidyāmādhavīyā*, *Sārāvalī*, *Caraka*, *Suśruta* etc.

The illustrious author of the renowned *Praśna-Mārga* nowhere mentions explicitly his own name and date of composition of the work. However the tradition among the long line of the Kerala-astrologers is that he lived around Kollam year 825 (1649 A.D.) in a village named Eḍakkāḍ between Tellicherry and Cannanore. There is a Viṣṇu Temple about 2 km. to the north of the Eḍakkāḍ railway station. It is the deity of this temple that is invoked by the author. Mr. Krishnālayam Govindan Palluruthy (Kerala), Commentator of the P.M. in Malayālam, has come to the foregoing conclusion after studying and examining the traditions and as a result of the 'On the Spot' enquiries. He adds that the author was a Nambūdiri Brahmin, whose mother's name was Śrī and father's Mahādevan.[1] This work was the result of his teaching (*upadeśa*) the subject to his disciples that was written at their request. *It is possible that this Nambūdiri Brahmin was the Chief Priest or Tantrin at the Viṣṇu Temple* (Italics mine). Sri Govindan alludes in this connection to the opinions of the "Kerala Sāhitya-Caritam" by Mahākavi U.S.P. Iyer and another work of the same title by *Raja Raja Varma*, as well as "*Sarvavijñānakośam*", "*Viśvavijñānakośam*" etc. It is understood that the author's house of birth was known as *Panakkāḍ Illam*, which is no longer in existence for want of descendants of the family. This *Illam* (brahmin house) was close to the temple. The author's life-period was between 800 and 870 of the *Kollam* era (1624 and 1694 A.D.). In this connection I wish to express my humble opinion before the great astrological luminaries of Kerala and elsewhere in respect of the author's name, which was one of the synonyms of the name of the "*Spouse of the Daughter of the Milky Ocean*". Most probably his name was Viṣṇu Nambūdiri. For, the author has significantly used two synonyms of the name of his favourite deity, i.e.

1. Vide P.M. I-1 to 4 and XXXI-117.

Murahā[1] and Murāri, for suggesting the date of composition and his own name respectively: We have to interpret the word *Labdhodayaḥ* also as 'One who was obtained his name for the first time in a holy sacrament (*Nāmodayaḥ*) from Murāri'. For, a person is known in the world by his or her physical birth and Name (*Nāmarūpa*)—without a registered name a person is not recognized legally as a living entity. So the naming ceremony (*Nāmakaraṇa*) also represents an important birth. This type of birth also is to be understood in the present context.

It might be argued that should the author's name be a synonym of Nārāyaṇa, it could be any one of the following words—Kṛṣṇa, Mādhava, Govinda, Dāmodara, Hṛṣikeśa, Padmanābha, Murāri etc. and not Viṣṇu in particular. This argument could be successfully met by reading carefully and understanding the author's own metaphorical language which is pregnant with useful and pleasant information bearing on his name, which is suggested pretty openly while referring to the hostility of *Śaivas* (devotees of Śiva) towards Vaiṣṇavas (devotees of Viṣṇu). The reader should bestow some thought on the author's prayer about his detractors, wherein occur these two compounds viz. *Iśvara-pakṣapātam* and *Viṣṇu-Bhaktān* used apparently to highlight the rivalry between the two sects. If they do so, it would dawn on them that the clever author has suggested his own name, Viṣṇu, while referring to the rivalry between the disciples of his strong rival belonging to the Coḷa country, Īśvara Dikṣitar by name, who was also a reputed astrologer of that time. The word *Bhakta* means both devoted disciple and devotee (of God).

When the author has explicitly mentioned his rival's real name, and not any of its synonyms such as Śiva, Bhava and Hara, though in a simile, why should we not take the word Viṣṇu in its literal sense as his real name? His father, Mahādevan Nambūdiri, must have given his favourite deity's name (*Mahā*) Viṣṇu to his son.

1. Vide the Malayālam Commentary, *Uparatnasekha* Pt. II by Punnasseri N.N. Sarma—"*Kolambe Murahāsamkhye*", (Preface to Second Edition by C. Parameśvaran Mussathu, the commentator's pupil). Vide P.M. XXXII-17 and 131.

The author's first disciple, according to tradition, was a poet known as Kūkaṇiyāl, who belonged to the Kaniyār community[1] and lived in his family house, Kaniyān Kaṇḍiyil in Eḍakkāḍ, which is known to be still in existence. This poet has written an astrological work entitled *Praśna-Rīti*. We learn from the Preface mentioned above that the author of P.M. has himself written a Sanskrit commentary on his work, entitled "*Durgamārtha-Prakāśinī*" (that which reveals difficult or recondite subject-matters). We are told that another great scholar viz. Kaikulaṅgara Rāma Warrier, has written a commentary on the P.M. under the title *Ratnaśikhā* (Lustre of Gem). Punnaśśeri N. Nīlakaṇṭha Śarmā has written a Sanskrit commentary on the first part of this work. His Malayālam commentary is called *Uparatna-Śikhā* ("Lustre of Minor Gem").

Another Malayālam poet known as Machattilayathu was a Grand-disciple (*Praśiṣya*) of the author of the P.M. His pupil was the reputed astrologer. Ezhikara Nārāyaṇa Mūssathu, whose disciple was Kerala-Varma Unithiri. The last-mentioned astrologer was the *Guru* (teacher) of another famous scholar viz. Punnaśśeri Nīlakaṇṭha Śarmā (who was the Principal of Pattāmbi Sanskrit College, wearing a *Rudrākṣa* bead around his neck), whose uncle was E. Nārāyaṇa Mūssathu. His (Punnaśśeri's) disciple was C. Parameśvaran Mūssathu. This gentleman has provided us with information regarding the line of succession of pupils in his Preface to the Commentary of *Punnasseri N. Śarmā* (Kollam 1084, *Meṣa* 12th day). This line of succession could be understood clearly by means of the table given on next page.

Puliyūr P.S. Puruṣottaman Nambūdiri has echoed the abovementioned views in his Preface written in 1950.

In addition to the works mentioned above there are some English editions as well as one in Kannaḍa with the *Dīpikā* Commentary by Śrī Kabyāḍi Śrīnivāsācārya Jyotiṣi of Udupi, who states that he had studied this work under a *Guru* living at Tripuṇattura near Cochin. He says that there is some difference

1. Vide P.M. I-13. Though the author insists on brahmins alone to take up the study and practice of this science, still he is not averse to others seeking this knowledge provided they are endowed with superior virtues.

Viṣṇu Nambūdiri	Author of P.M.
Kūkaṇiyāl	I Disciple
Machathilayathu	II ,,
Ezhikara Nārāyaṇa Mūssathu (Uncle of No. V)	III ,,
Kerala-Varma Unithiri	IV ,,
Punnaśśeri Nilakaṇṭha Śarmā	V ,,
Parameśvaran Mūssathu	VI ,,

in the traditions of Kerala and South Kanara district in respect of *Daivas* and *Devas* (minor deities). This famous astrologer has rendered notable service to the people of Karnāṭaka by undertaking to write an exhaustive commentary with illustrative charts and half-a-dozen Appendices containing much useful information for the benefit of practising astrologers as well as students of astrology. However, I find divergence of interpretation of verse 33 of XXVI especially about the method of fixing the *Lagnarkṣa*. According to many eminent Kerala scholars it is a new place which is determined by the number of stars the Divasarkṣa is away from Āśvinī and by adding that number to the Divasarkṣa, whereas the Kannaḍa edition construes it as one got by calculation of Udayarkṣa already explained in verses 24 and 25 of the same chapter. I have adopted the interpretation of Kerala scholars like Punnaśśeri N. Śarmā, as they represent the author's intention through their contact with the original author by means of an unbroken teacher pupil tradition.

In the line of distinguished commentators including translators of this unique work viz. P.M., Dr. B.V. Raman, Editor of the Astrological Magazine, Bangalore, has made significant contribution to the science of astrology through his English translation with copious comments and explanations. I learn that Mr. J.N. Bhasin of Delhi has published his commentary on this work in English in three volumes. The foregoing description of commentaries and translations of the P.M. proves conclusively the great qualities of this work and outstanding merits as well as undisputed superiority of its methodology and indispensable nature as far as astrologers are concerned. It is a marvellous work indeed almost on a par with Varāhamihirā's *Bṛhat Saṁhitā*, which its author holds in very high esteem; and *Bṛhajjātaka*, which he compares to a beautiful necklace to be worn around the neck (i.e. to be studied with meticulous attention and understanding). He extols the Kṛṣṇīya Śāstra (*Horā*) and likens it to the *Maṅgala Sūtra* (auspicious string) worn by a *Sumaṅgalā* (auspicious, married woman), around her neck. So, in the opinion of the author of the P.M. the Kṛṣṇīya had already attained the status of a sacred work in the realm of astrology. The Editor of the Kṛṣṇīya, which was published as the 243rd work of the "Trivandrum Sanskrit Series" (1976), states in his scholarly and analytical Introduction: "The fact that many Kṛṣṇīya stanzas are found quoted in *Praśna-Mārga* and that numerous similar quotations are seen in Rudra's *Horā-Vivaraṇa* (Commentary on B.J.) abundantly bespeaks the unrivalled popularity enjoyed by Kṛṣṇīya. . . in the vast domain of *Praśna* and *Jataka*". Sri. K.V. Śarmā informs us that the earliest scholar who quoted him frequently is Govinda Bhaṭṭatiri of *Talakkulam* (A.D. 1237-95).[1] The above Editor is of opinion that Kṛṣṇācārya may be identical with that Kṛṣṇa, author of a commentary of *Varāha's Horā*. The unusual popularity of the Kṛṣṇīya could easily be inferred from the fact that a citation of *Kṛṣṇīya-Horā* is found in the *Malayālam Campū Kāvya* entitled *Uṇṇiyaccicaritam* (13th century A.D.).[2] It appears that in one of the manuscripts of this work the scribe's name is given as Atula. If this Atula is the same as the one who authored the *Mūṣakavamśa*, Kṛṣṇa's date may be prior to the 11th century A.D.[3] There is a Sanskrit commentary on the Kṛṣṇīya named *Caturasundarī*. Puliyūr Purushottaman Nambūdiri has written a Malayālam commentary on the Kṛṣṇīyahorā.

1. Vide "*A History of the Kerala School of Hindu Astronomy*" by K.V. Śarmā, V.V.R. Institute, Hoshiarpur, 1972, p. 47.
2. Vide Intro. p. iii and vi footnote.
3. Vide "Keralasāhityacaritram", Vol. I, p. 199.

Now we have to turn our attention to another work hailed by the author of the P.M., i.e. *Daśādhyāyī*[1] which has attained remarkable celebrity in the South, but nobody knows anything about its wonderful author. The greatness of this commentary, otherwise known as *Naukā* (boat), is vouchsafed by the author of the P.M., who has devoted three verses to panegyrize it.[2] He quotes a number of authorities such as Bādarāyaṇa, Parāśara, Yavaneśvara, Govinda, Mādhava, Vidyāmādhava, Śrīpati, Sārāvalī, Yātrā, Yukta(?)Bhaṭṭotpala, Saṁgrāmavijaya, Jātakasaṁgraha etc. The Govinda referred to by the author of the D.A. must be Govinda Bhaṭṭathiri mentioned above, who wrote a commentary on *Varāha's Horā*. When we know the dates of Kṛṣṇācārya for the upper limit and that of the Praśna-Mārga for the lower limit, we can fairly fix the chronology of the *Daśādhyāyī*. We have some references to Vidhyāmāḍhava[3] in this commentary which could bring down the upper limit. According to R. Shama Shastri, Curator, Government Oriental Library, Mysore, who wrote in his Preface to the first edition (1923) of the *Vidyāmādhavīya* with the Commentary, *Mūhūrta-dīpikā*, of Viṣṇu Śarmā the author's son that the latter flourished under the patronage of Mallappa, son of the Vijayanagara King, Bukkarāya", the date of Viṣṇu Śarmā is 1363 A.D. The lowest limit being the date of the P.M. which is known to be 1649 A.D. as shown above, the *D.A.* could be placed about 100 years prior to this, i.e. 1549 A.D. I presume that the author of the *D.A.* has not revealed his own name owing to his great modesty and inferiority complex, because in spite of his training in theory and practice in astrology, he must have thought that his scholarship of Sans-

1. Vide "*Daśādhāyī*" Pub. by Shri Venkateshwar Press, Bombay, 1912.
2. Vide P.M. I-30 to 32.
3. Vide the *Avatārikā* by Puliyur P.S. Purushottaman Nambūdiri to his Malayālam Commentary of Mādhavācārya's *Mādhaviyam* (22nd Edn. 1987). According to this writer the author was a Havyaka Brahmin of Guṇavante village near Gokarṇa. Later he came down to the village called Maṅki. There was a second Mādhava who wrote the commentary on the Sūtasaṁhitā named *Tātparyadīpikā*. There was a third Mādhava who wrote the *Praśna-Mādhaviyam*. There is yet another scholar of the same name, an astronomer, referred to in the work called *Sphuṭanirṇaya*. A Mādhava is referred to as his *Guru* by Melputtūr Bhaṭṭatiri.

krit grammar, prosody etc. was deficient. However, his erudition and creative intellect are clearly seen exhibited by his masterly exposition of the inner meanings of textual passages of the Horā.

It is surprising, however, that there is a strong belief among some Kerala astrologers regarding the authorship of the *Daśādhyāyī* and *Naukā*: They aver that the *D. A.* was written by Govinda Bhaṭṭatiri, while the *Naukā* is the Sanskrit Commentary on the former, the name of this commentator being unknown. This opinion is given by Dr. B.C. Balakrishnan, Editor, *Malayālam Lexicon*, Kerala University, in his Preface (1987) to the work entitled *Ahorātia-Daśādhyāyī* printed in Malayālam script and published by Dr. N. Gopala Panicker, Professor of Astrology (Retd.), Govt. Sanskrit College, Trivandrum (1988). This work consists of two parts, the First being a free Malayālam translation of the *D.A.* with Dr. Panicker's comments, and the Second containing prose order (*Anvaya*), meanings etc. This editor is of the definite opinion that the author of the *Daśādhyāyī* was Govinda Bhaṭṭatiri and the *Naukā*, only the Sanskrit Commentary on the *D.A.* by an unknown *Kerala* scholar.

I am, however, reluctant at this stage of my information to concur with the opinion that Govinda Bhaṭṭatiri wrote the *D.A.* an unusually brilliant commentary on the *Bṛhajjātaka* for ten chapters only. For, the Bombay edition of the *D.A.* (*Naukā*) that was edited by Pandit Hanuman Śarmā (1912) refers to Govinda more than ten times in the commentary as "Atrāha Govindaḥ" (on page 10). If this author were to write a commentary on the work of Goviṇda, why on earth should he repeatedly refer to him by name? On the other hand, he would have stated at the outset that he was commenting on Govinda's work. This shows that Govinda is not the author of the *Daśādhyāyī*, but a previous Commentator on Varāhamihira's Horā, to whom this scholarly Commentator refers very often approvingly. The Bombay edition of the *Naukā* contains eight benedictory verses in the beginning. Among them the seventh verse states "I am writing succinctly the meaning of the *Varāha-Horā* as understood by me for the instruction of my pupils". The next stanza too is revealing as it says, "This *Ṭīkā* named *Naukā* (boat) has been set sail on the ocean of inner meanings of *Varāha's Horā* for gathering gems in the form of true meanings". This too proves that the *Naukā* or *Daśādhyāyī* is a direct commentary on the *Horā* itself. In this connection the reader may remind himself of Varaha's statement, "*Śāstraplavaṁ prārabhe*".

He has also shown his wonderful memory-power by quoting almost all branches of Sanskrit and Vedic literature, both philosophical and secular[1] including all branches of astrology-cum-astronomy, except perhaps grammar and porsody. I shall content myself by quoting the author's own words in translation, occurring at the end of his commentary *Naukā*, just before his *Anuṣṭubh* verses numbering 14½ that clearly expound the methodology of writing Horoscopes: "However, as a result of my incompetence in exposition etc., inability to reconcile previous statements with subsequent ones, and my ignorance, I have, repeated (in my explanations) textual words. There is a possibility of wrong words and expressions, that may be illogical, being used (in my work). Hence, should a scholar (come across anything unworthy) while perusing this commentary, he might pardon me.[2] This commentary has not been undertaken (by me) as a means of showing off my scholarship, but only to impart knowledge to mypupil who is not sufficiently intelligent." It is true that there are a few grammatical errors[3] which do not at all detract from its countless merits that have rightly made the work very famous and instructive.

I should like to point out here some examples of his clever arguments and deductions: Under I-7 while interpreting the first half which is a single compound composed of eight members, the author of the *D.A.* says on the basis of Govinda's explanation: "Synonyms of the first eight signs are grouped

1. His deep knowledge of *Yoga Śāstra, Advaita* philosophy, *Śrī Śaṁkara's* works, *Bhatṛhari's Vākyapadīya* etc. is discernible in his commentary under I-1.

2. He is not at all poor in the knowledge of grammar and prosody, because he quotes grammatical rules in defence of the expression, *Naikakiraṇaḥ*, one for *Dvandva* compounds being optionally singular. He also names all the metres employed in the text.

3. *Nyastavyaṁ, Pitātmakatvāt, Rājasikaḥ, Nyāyavirodhaśca Sambhavaḥ, Pracchakaḥ.*

together, while those of the rest are mentioned separately. This suggests that among the first four Houses beginning with the Body, the latter, i.e. I, depends on *Dharma* (*Pūrva-Puṇya* or Religious Merit); II, i.e. Wealth, on Profession (Action); III, i.e. Prowess, on Gain of Wealth; IV, i.e. Happiness, on Finance; V, i.e. begetting children, on *Dharma*; VI, i.e. Eradication of Enemies, on Action; VII, i.e. Conjugal Happiness, on Gain of Wealth; and VIII, i.e. Death (disease, scandal etc.), on Sin, Destruction of Wealth." Next he interprets 1-9 thus: Here the six *Vargas* viz. *Decanate*, *Horā*, *Navāṁśa*, *Triṁśāṁśa*, *Dvādaśāṁśa*, and *Kṣetra* or *Rāśi*, suggest in order *Kālapuruṣa's* six *Ādhāras* or *Mystic Centres* or Circles viz. (1) *Mūlādhāra* with the Sun as its ruler and Significator for Father; (2) *Svādhiṣṭhāna* with the Moon-Mother; (3) *Maṇipūra* with Mars—Brother; (4) *Anahata* with Mercury—Speech; (5) *Viśuddhi* with Jupiter—Offspring as well as with Saturn—Demise; (6) *Ājñā*—with Venus—Spouse.

Regarding the planets signifying father and mother for diurnal and nocturnal births (IV-5) this author states that though this verse introduces special kinships of the luminaries, and Saturn and Moon for day and night births, still the significations of the Sun and Moon for father and mother respectively are not completely obliterated. Another example of his ingenious method of interpretation is found under VI-8:

"*Rāśyanatage iti-Rāśiṣu Mṛtyubhāgāḥ...Taṣu sthitaḥ Candraḥ Bhāgasaṃkhyeṣu abdeṣu Mṛtyudo bhavati.*"

The idea is that the Moon posited in the fatal degrees of the different signs would bring about the native's end in the year corresponding to the degree. Elsewhere he says that the Sun cooks the fruits of the *Daśās*, and the Moon serves the cooked food. He states under VIII-22. "When a King is proceeding against his enemy to wage war, the astrologer should ask the king in private, 'what is the attitude of your mind about this expedition'? If his answer be to the effect that his mind is full of enthusiasm and joy, it would be a decisive indication of victory irrespective of auspicious or inauspicious auguries." On the basis of the *Saṃgrāmavijaya* he allots the four political expedients viz. *Sāma*, *Dāna*, *Bheda* and *Daṇḍa* to Jupiter and Venus; the Moon; Mercury and Saturn; and Mars and the Sun respectively. Elsewhere he poses a question: If all planets, when possessed of strength, confer good results, then where is the need to distinguish them as benefic and malefic? His answer is the following: When benefics be strong, natives would be very virtuous, brilliant, noble and so on, whereas malefics, being strong, would cause the birth of those that are greedy, selfish, intent on murdering people, dirty, ungrateful, tale-bearers and ugly. He concludes thus: "Strong benefics confer benefits that are of a high order; and strong malefics do some amount of good. Similarly those strong planets that preside over good houses, would yield excellent results, and those ruling untoward ones, if they be weak, would aggravate troubles."

We have already seen that there were many scholars having the name Mādhava, but one of them seems to have attained an eminent position in the sphere of horary astrology. It is he that is remembered gratefully by the authors of *P.M.* and *D.A.* along with Kṛṣṇācārya. It is also clear that this Mādhava is not the same as Vidyā-Mādhava, who is not reported to have written a work on horary science entitled *Praśna-Mādhavīyam.* That is why the author of the *D.A.* has clearly named both Mādhava and Vidyāmādhava. Hence this Mādhava, who was an expert in *Praśna-Śāstra*, must have preceded the author of the *Daśādhyāyī* by about a century. So he must have lived about 1449 A.D. or a little earlier.

My original intention was to give the Sanskrit verses of such works as were used by with their English translation, notes and comments as I had done in my edition of the *Bṛhat Saṁhitā*, but I had to give up that idea and provide only the English translation in order to be able to complete the work in the shortest possible period of time for want of sufficient spare time in my daily life, as well as energy which is fast ebbing away. However, I have stuck to my original desire of having an alternate Sanskrit title as well as invocatory verses in the beginning and at the end.

Now it is my pleasant duty to express my cense of gratitude and indebtedness to the galaxy of distinguished authors mentioned above. This monumental work, which, I am sure, the scholarly and friendly readers endorse, is a younger brother and a worthy companion to my edition of the *Bṛhat Saṁhitā* (in two volumes) of *Varāhamihira*, would not have been possible in my present state of health but for the spontaneous and loving help rendered by many sincere souls like Śrī. B.P. Nair (Asst. Director, C.S.R. and T.I., Berhampore, W.B.) who assisted me, when he was in the C.P.C.R.I., Vittal, by translating a short work entitled "*Naṣṭapraśnadīpikā*" in Malayālam into English and by assisting me in preparing some chapters in the beginning; Śrī. V.R. Parameśvaran Nair of Trivandrum, who in spite of his age and ailments has given me invaluable help, encouragement, precious suggestions, detailed information about the great authors and commentators of astrological works of Kerala such as the author of the *Praśna-Mārga*, the line of succession of his pupils, their dates etc., and loving and fraternal help by resolving some knotty problems in the P.M., (which looked like a shower of nectar to a thirsty and tired traveller in a desert); Śrī, V.P.K. Nambūdiri (near Cannanore) who painstakingly prepared some useful charts like that of the *Ārūḍha Navāṁśas* and made some useful books available to me; Śrī. R.K. Rangan, Deputy Secretary, Govt. of India (Retd.) who has been a source of inspiration and encouragement in the matter of publication of my works as well as other matters ever since I landed in Delhi in 1956, and by going through the manuscript of this work and offering suggestions for improvement as well as for his good 'Foreword' for this work; and my own near and dear ones who have extended their loving help and cooperation in respect of my literary endeavours. To all these gentlemen and others, not mentioned here, who have helped me consciously or otherwise in making this work a reality. I express my deep debt of gratitude and pray to the Supreme Lord for showering grace on all of them. Finally I have to thank sincerely Messrs Motilal Banarsidass Publishers Pvt. Ltd., Delhi, for agreeing to publish this work, as they have done before my previous works, and bringing it out in an agreeable and attractive form without much delay.

Vittal

M. R. BHAT

CHAPTER I

INTRODUCTORY

मधुपुराधिपतिं विबुधार्चितं मृदुसुधाधिकपूपसुतर्पितम् ।
निधिमयो भजतां च समृद्धिदं स्वधिषणास्फुरणाय कविं श्रये ॥ १ ॥
ग्रहगणपतिमीडे सर्वलोकैकबन्धुं बुधजनहृदयाब्जोद्बोधकं बाधिताघम् ।
क्षपितगदमदे भव्रातपञ्चास्यमीशं सुरपरिवृढवन्द्यं सन्ततं वेदमूर्तिम् ॥ २ ॥
आलोड्य पूर्वशास्त्राणि सरसार्थपदोज्ज्वला ।
क्रियते शिष्यबोधाय सत्प्रश्नपदवी मुदा ॥ ३ ॥

IT IS ADMITTED that the origin of astrology-astronomy is to be traced to the *Vedas*, which represent the quintessence of all knowledge, secular and spiritual. This statement may be controverted by some progressive-minded modern scientists who condemn religion as a bundle of superstitious beliefs and practices, by asking men of religion whether the *Vedas* contain quantum mechanics. The answer to this is that they teach more fundamental truths or the Truth which is one in which all distinctions of mind, matter and universe cease to exist.[1] "In *Advaita Vedānta* alone, as expounded by Swami Vivekānanda, the dichotomy of man and God, good and bad, faith and reason finally disappears. A renowned Indian scientist avers that according to Swami Vivekānanda Vedāntic thought was not inconsistent with science. Western psychology has miserably failed to cope with the super-conscious aspects and laws of human nature. Where European Science has stopped short, Indian psychology comes in and explains, illustrates and teaches how to render the laws pertaining to higher states of existence..." The ancient sages have shown us the subtle and secret working of the human mind and the way to realize the One Existence.

It is the firm conviction of great thinkers of the world that the further modern science advances, the closer it comes to *Vedānta*. J.B.S. Haldane writes in his book, *Science and Indian Culture*:

1. Vide *Yuva Bharati*, August 1988 issue.

"Modern Science is converging to the Vedic view that the mind is the seat of memory." Another great scientist, Dr Paul Bonsfield says in his book, *The Omnipresent Self*: "The conscious mind is by far the smallest part as compared to the unconscious part of the mind which acts as the store-house of memories, ideas and emotions of the past." Typical among the scientists who have realized the potential of Yoga and meditation is Prof. Brian Josephson of Cambridge University, a Nobel Prize-winner in physics in 1973, who started to practise meditation which led him subsequently to the higher states of consciousness. As a result of meditation he was able to see that discoveries in physics were not as important as he had thought. When medical science failed to cure the distracted minds and unbalanced emotions, Yoga has successfully come out with a cure of self-culture and social balance. He adds that Yoga has been a very important evolutionary science and very soon *it is to be the culture of the world.*

If science can give two quite different results in determining the nature of light, how scientific is science itself? Heisenberg's principles of uncertainty showed that at the sub-atomic level there is no such thing as exact science. The Science of the Self is the only scientific Science in the realm of the great Vedic *Ṛṣis* who have declared that Truth which is self-effulgent is hidden in the *Guhā*—(Cave of the Heart)." "*Tat Tvam asi*," That thou art– is the Goal, the Ideal to be realized. Has not the world witnessed from time to time the mighty spiritual giants, especially those of the recent past like Śrī Rāmakṛṣṇa Paramahaṃsa, Bhagavān Ramaṇa Maharṣi, Swāmī Vivekānanda and Yogānanda, to mention a few luminaries of rare spiritual effulgence, who have demonstrated through their ideal life, and wonderful acts, the voice of wisdom beneficial to all living beings? The supreme teachings of *Vedānta* were made lucid by the great masters to help the householders to lead an ideal life while still living in the world.

While speaking of Yoga, we are reminded of an invocatory verse which eulogizes sage Patañjali who has illumined the path of humanity by eradicating the unspiritual cravings of the mind (actually sub-conscious) through Yoga, in curing diseases of the body through *Āyurveda*—as propounded in his *Carakasaṃhitā*—

and in removing blemishes of speech through his famous *Mahābhāṣya* on Pāṇini's Aphorisms. Thus the sage Patañjali had in view man's perfection.

The Vedas manifested themselves in the beginning of creation through the sages of yore who were plunged in the bliss of the Self. This perennial wisdom of the Veda had to be made available to the people by means of Ancillary Sciences known as *Vedāṅgas*, Limbs of the supreme being, representing that Wisdom. They are six in number viz. *Śikṣā* (Phonology or Phonetics), *Vyākaraṇa* (Grammar), *Chandas* (Prosody), *Nirukta* (Etymology), *Jyotiṣa* (Astronomy-Astrology), and *Kalpa* (Procedure Code for Vedic Rituals). *Phonetics* stands for the *Nose* of the Being; *Grammar* for His *Face* or *Mouth*; *Prosody* for His *Feet*; *Etymology* for His *Ears*; Astronomy-Astrology for his *Eyes*; and *Procedure Code for Vedic Rituals* for His *Hands*. The sages declare that one who studies the Vedas with proper intonation and pronunciation along with the six auxiliary sciences, attains *Brahmaloka* and enjoys great honour. In this connection it would be advantageous for astrologers to understand the rationale of the science of Astrology and its pre-eminent position in both secular or social and religious or spiritual systems. The *Siddhānta-śiromaṇi* asserts that the Vedas are meant primarily for the proper conducting of *Yajñas* or Sacrifices, which in their turn are controlled by Time which in turn is taught in all its ramifications through this science of Astronomy-Astrology, that is eulogized as the very Eye of the supreme Being. The reader should not be carried away by the impression that the Vedas are, after all, meant for the benefit of the priests who perform "some dry and meaningless rituals". This impression was created by ignorant translators who had an axe to grind. One must have a fund of knowledge of all the scriptures including the six *Aṅgas* (Ancillary Sciences), *Smṛtis*, the six *Darśanas* (Systems of Philosophy), *Purāṇas*, the two famous Epics viz. *Rāmāyaṇa* and *Mahābhārata*, *Āyurveda*, *Dhanurveda*, *Gāndharvaveda* (Music etc.) and *Arthaśāstra* (Economics-Politics). Last, but not the least, is Penance or *Deep Meditation*. This is what Swamī Vivekānanda resorted to when he wanted to get the correct import of difficult Sanskrit texts. In fact there is nothing in the world that cannot be achieved by Penance or Yoga. The great modern Yogin viz. Śrī

Aurobindo, who spent a major part of his ideal life in contemplation, meditation, penance and writing on spiritual topics for the regeneration of humanity, has said that the Indian religious and spiritual literature must be interpreted from three angles or levels viz. material, psychological and spiritual, according to the competence of the aspirants (*Adhikāra* of the *Sādhakas*).

Astrology is thus a very important discipline of life for those living in this mundane sphere. Nobody can, therefore, question the desire of people to consult a good astrologer who, according to Varāhamihira, must be one well-versed in astronomical calculations in arriving at proper conclusion after weighing its pros and cons, expert in mathematics, truthful, humble, devoted to gods and Brāhmaṇas, virtuous, engaged in performing meritorious acts etc. Even today every professional man or householder in this modern society looks at the calendar to find out the date, week, day etc. lest he should miss an engagement and suffer its consequences. Similarly every person, whether a householder, student, teacher, employer, employee or lawyer or litigant, would be much benefited in his or her career on a particular day, should he or she be careful enough to acquaint himself or herself with the elements of the Almanac, so that much trouble and worries could be avoided, by avoiding bad company and cantankerous meetings, and also by having recourse to special prayers to one's *Iṣṭadevatā* or deity of choice with sincere faith and devotion. In fact devout prayers to God are a sure bridge between this world and the other. In fine, astrology teaches the faithful as to how they could make even the worst situation in life tolerably good by practising Yoga and observing certain rules of life such as non-injury, self-control, earning money by fair means, and living an austere life, with contentment. As the *Upaniṣad* proclaims, this science is one of the avenues that lead mankind from untruth (unreality) to the *Truth*, from darkness to light, and from death, i.e. being immersed in the enjoyment of worldly pleasures, to immortality or eternal bliss, otherwise known as self-realization.

This science of *Jyotiṣa* is primarily divided under three heads viz. *Gaṇita*, *Jātaka* and *Saṃhitā*. Of these the first division, i.e. *Gaṇita*, is of two types viz. *Gola* meaning *Astronomy*, and *Gaṇita*, i.e. *Mathematics*. The second branch is otherwise known as *Horāśāstra* or *Horoscopy*. The third branch is otherwise known as *Śākhā* which treats elaborately many wonderful subjects such as astronomy, trade and commerce, water-divination, architecture, progress and decay of countries, earthquakes, physiognomy, erotics, auguries etc. In fact it is encyclopaedic in nature and highly instructive and exhilarating. The *Gaṇita* branch supplies the *Pramāṇa*, authority or proof for the other two branches. There is another classification of Astrology[1] into (1) Predictive Astrology, (2) Horary Science, and (3) Electional Astrology. Some include also Mundane Astrology as a separate branch. Great masters of yore have distinguished six limbs or branches of Astrology-Astronomy as (1) Horoscopy; (2) *Gola* or Astronomy; (3) *Nimitta* or Auguries; (4) *Praśna* or Horary Science; (5) *Muhūrta* or Electional Astrology, and (6) *Gaṇita* or Mathematics.

Horā or Horoscopy has been treated extensively by many eminent sages and scholars like Parāśara, Garga, Mṛkaṇḍu, Prajāpati, Sūrya, Skanda, Vasiṣṭha, Śaunaka, Kauśika, Māṇḍavya, Yavana, Varāhamihira and others. Among the historical authorities on the Horā, Varāhamihira, the illustrious author of the *Bṛhajjātaka*, *Pañcasiddhāntikā*, *Bṛhadyātrā*, *Bṛhatsaṃhitā*, etc. along with their abridged versions, stands out far above the others of his class, as an undisputed authority on all the branches of Astrology-Astronomy. Among the large number of commentaries on the *Horā* the commentary of Bhaṭṭotpala is of very great importance and utility. Another wonderful commentary is known as the *Daśādhyāyī* (or *Naukā*).

The unknown author of this commentary, probably a Kerala Brāhmaṇa, finds in the very first verse of the *Horā* clues about the essence of all *Śāstras* including Yoga, as well as rules for working out 'Lost Horoscopes'. He explains the word *Ravi* on the basis of the root *R* 'to sound' and concludes like Bhartṛhari that it stands for *Śabda-Brahma* or the Supreme Being in the form of the Primordial Sound Oṃ. It is also suggested that the Moon left to herself has no light, but her light is only '*borrowed light*' belonging to the Sun. Similarly Mars, Mercury, Jupiter, Venus, Saturn and the Ascendant are, we are told, suggested in

1. Vide the *Bṛhat Saṃhitā* edited with translation and comments by this author.

the invocatory stanza. The words meaning 'Path of those who do not get rebirth' suggest the Fiery Mars who is the significator for *Sattva*—Valour. The term '*Ātmavidāmātmā*'—Soul of the knowers of the Self—indicates Mercury. *Kratuśca Yajatām*—Sacrifice of the Sacrificers—points to Jupiter, bestower of fruits of religious rites. *Bhartā* etc. suggests Venus, who stands mainly for enjoyment of pleasures. The word '*Pralaya*', dissolution, indicates Saturn. The sentence beginning with *Śrutau* etc. points to the Zodiacal signs and the Ascendant, thereby showing that these eight elements, which are made use of in the systems of longevity, *Aṣṭakavarga* and *Yogas* are intended to be understood by the readers. So are the twenty-seven constellations in the Zodiacal belt, by the same number of words constituting the first verse. The word *Trailokyadīpa*, light of the Three Worlds, speaks of the past, present and future existence of the Soul, which are lighted, revealed, by the Divine Sun. In short, this benedictory verse, which is the *Gāyatrī Mantra* for all astrologers, suggests the whole gamut of this science which is the subject-matter of the *Horā*, that forms the basis for the several branches of astrology, as visualized by the author of this unique commentary. In this connection he speaks of *Karma* to be of three kinds viz. *Dṛḍha Karma* (Stable action of previous life), *Adṛḍha Karma* (unstable action) and *Dṛḍhādṛḍha Karma* (Action both stable and unstable). What is earned by means of *Dṛḍha Karma* is termed *Sat*; the result of *Adṛḍha Karma*, *Asat*; and that of *Dṛḍhādṛḍha Karma*, *Sadasat* (both good and bad actions mixed). How are we to know the modus operandi for distinguishing these actions and their effects? The *Sārāvalī* explains that the progression of planetary *Daśās* would show the fructification of Stable Actions, while the *Aṣṭaka-varga* charts and transitions of planets delineate the effects of unstable *Karma*. Those of the mixed ones should be read from the Yogas or special planetary configurations found in the natal chart. Sage Vasiṣṭha declares in this connection that after understanding thoroughly the science of predictive astrology as well as logic, in respect of the relative strength of planets and *Bhāvas*, one ought to apply appropriately all the principles and rules of natal astrology to queries or horary chart. In spite of this assertion the Horary Science is considered as a specialized branch of *Horā-śāstra.* In the light of the foregoing discussion it boils down to the principle that both the systems, general and special, are based upon Time-factor that is the *Supreme Ruler*.

Bhaṭṭotpala is of the opinion that a true astrologer should be conversant with the ten sub-divisions of astronomy and then predict the results, good and bad, of a nativity or query. He can then hope for unerring predictions coming out of his mouth. The ten types of astronomical calculations are the following:

1. Calculation of *Ahargaṇa*, i.e. the sum of Solar days elapsed from the beginning of the *Kali Age* up to the required day;
2. Computing the mean positions of planets;
3. Calculating the true position of planets;
4. Calculations regarding solar eclipse;
5. Calculating lunar eclipse;
6. Finding out correctly the phenomenon called *Graha-yuddha* or planetary war;
7. Calculating conjunction of planets;
8. Computing the eclipse of planets;
9. Calculating the emergence of planets after their disappearance;
10. Finding out planetary conjunction with the asterism during the movement of planets along the belt of stars.

Praśna-śāstra, or Horary Science is an important branch of astrology. This and two other *Śāstras*, viz. *Mantra-śāstra*—that which deals with the method of employing various incantations or spells for securing benefits or removing obstacles and enemies —and the third *Āyurveda* or ancient system of medicine, are very popular in Kerala. They speak of two kinds of Charts or *Cakras* viz. *Sthira*—Immovable and *Cara*—Movable, the first being fixed on the Earth, and the other moving in the Heavens. The chart that is drawn on the ground or a plank is called *Sthira-cakra,* while the *Heavenly* Circle is always moving. Hence the latter is termed *Cara-cakra*.

For the purpose of queries both the *cakras* are utilized. For, out of the two *Lagnas* viz. *Ārūḍha* and the *Udaya-lagna*—the Sign that is rising at the time of the query—the stronger of the two should be made use of for delineating the purpose of the query. According to the commentator of the *Kṛṣṇīyam* this science is otherwise known as *Cintajnanam*—Rules for finding out what is in the querist's mind. In other words it is "*Thought-reading*". This work of Kṛṣṇācārya who flourished about 1200 A.D. or a little earlier, is otherwise known as *Cintājñāna*. This work must have inspired the famous work entitled *Praśnamārga*, which holds undisputed sway over Kerala state and the West Coast, and which is supposed to have been composed in the middle of the 17th century by a Nambūdiri Brāhmaṇa (whose name is not clearly mentioned), worshipper of Śrīmahāviṣṇu of Edakkāṭṭu Village, and of Lord Śiva, Consort of the Divine Mother Pārvatī, of Peruñcellūr, and born of parents viz. Śrī Mahādeva Nambūdiri and Śrī Devī. This unique work bids fair to follow closely Varāhamihira's magnum opus the *Bṛhat Saṃhitā*, and to be called a Mini-Encyclopaedia. Just as the *Vārāhī Saṃhitā* quotes profusely ancient authorities, even so does this great work. The most outstanding contribution of this work is the *Aṣṭamaṅgala* System, in which there are eight kinds of auspicious objects as well as groups of eight cowries that are taken out from three heaps, left, central and right, and predictions for the past, present and future are made. The details of this system have been explained in chapter IV. A devout and austere astrologer draws a *Rāśi* Chart in front and after decorating it with flowers and other materials worships it according to the scriptural rules with prayers etc., having lit a holy lamp which represents the Goddess Lakṣmī. Then an innocent child or somebody who does not know anything about astrology is asked to touch with and place a piece of gold mixed with rice, flowers etc. in one of the signs of the chart. The particular sign thus touched or mounted by the gold piece is designated as *Ārūḍha*. Two other signs are also considered as the starting points that are (1) the sign rising at the time of query and (2) the lunar sign. The querist too, according to the *Praśnajñāna*, should adore with devotion and humility the Circle of Signs with fruits, flowers, gems and gold, and put whatever question he has in his mind to the astrologer. The *Ārūḍha* may also be read from the sign corresponding to the place occupied by the querist or to the limb touched by him.

The purpose of human life is to experience the fruits of actions, good and bad, performed in a previous life. This is called *Adṛṣṭa* or *Prārabdha*, which is the *Karma* that has already started yielding fruit. The course of this *Prārabdha Karma*, it is said, cannot generally be altered. However, expiatory rites like sacrifice, charity and penance ought to be performed. For, the Lord has assured the world that none who acts nobly would ever come to grief. That is why great saints and sages like Samartha Râmadâsa, Guru of Chatrapati Śivâji Mahârâj, Śrī Rāmakṛṣṇa Paramahaṃsa and many other distinguished souls have shown us the way for all-round peace, prosperity, progress, contentment and above all self-realization which is the *Summum bonum* of human existence. There is another type of *Karma* called *Sañcita*—Accumulated—which has not yet begun to yield its results. They say that it is this type of *Karma* that is capable of being altered by means of proper worship, meditation, Guru's grace and such other acts of atonement. Contrition and constant remembrance of God and His Divine virtues constitute one of the easiest ways of expiatory procedures. There are also karmas as (1) *Prāktana* and (2) *Adyatana*—*Past* and *Present*. Human beings who perform many a meritorious deed on the earth go to Heaven after their death, and enjoy the delectable fruits of such noble deeds, and then come down to the earth, when their accumulated merits get almost exhausted—not completely—for reaping the fruits of the remaining collection of *puṇya* or merit as well as for working out further *karmas*, good, moderate and bad. The human soul has a lot of freedom of action in the sphere of the present karma. When the *Prārabdha* Karma is completely exhausted owing to the dawn of self-knowledge, the soul becomes one with the Universal Soul. Just as a seed when well-roasted cannot sprout under any circumstance, even so a soul whose actions are completely burnt out by the fire of self-knowledge cannot be reborn on earth or anywhere else.

The purpose of astrology is to find out the outcome of the actions, good and bad, done in a previous life and to guide people towards the path of virtue, devotion to God and elders as well as saintly persons and to bring harmony and love in society. This Vedic science teaches neither fatalism nor pessimism. For, our ancient scriptures like the *Gītā* enjoin that 'man ought to raise himself to a higher level of spiritual life by his own effort, and he should never have recourse to the path of self-destruction'.

There are some who question the rationale of this *Praśna-śāstra*. They say that this branch depends mostly on blind chance. We have already got *Horā-śāstra*, *Gaṇita-śāstra* and *Muhūrta-śāstra*. Where then is the scope and necessity for this *Praśna-śāstra*? This question may be answered by means of an example. First: A general practitioner of modern medicine generally treats all kinds of diseases. However, when a typical case of malady is brought to him, after proper examination of the patient, he sends the case to a specialist in the subject. The latter will be able to diagnose the disease and cure the patient, provided he is destined to survive. For, in Āyurvedic texts it has been declared: "*Na vaidyaḥ prabhur āyuṣaḥ*", the physician has no control over longevity. Similarly if you want to analyse minutely the cause of a person's disease such as the wrath of gods, ancestors, gurus and the beginning of the disease, relief from it and the propitiatory measures to be adopted and such other information, you must seek the help of an expert in *Praśna-śāstra* who would be able to create a wonderful, serene and awe-inspiring as well as convincing situation by his uncanny powers of argumentation and judgments. If you want to test the veracity of this statement, you should go to one of the well-known families of astrologers in Kerala.

Sometimes a person's horoscope shows good time in *Daśā*, *Bhukti*, and *Gocara* (transit); but his experience is quite the contrary. In such cases horary science comes to our rescue. The querist might feel that he might have committed some mistake somewhere, of which he is not aware and as a result of which he is suffering mentally and physically, loss in business etc. To probe this problem and find out the answer for it, he has to repair to a specialist, i.e. expert in horary science. One comes to an astrologer to find out his prospects in life, but he possesses neither his natal chart (*Jātaka*), nor the date of birth. Naturally the astrologer resorts to *Praśna-śāstra*. Somebody has lost his purse or an important document in a mysterious way. How would he get at the truth except through horary science? There is an old temple without any idol in a place far away from the village. Which particular deity had been worshipped in the temple and by whom was it patronized, and when was it first established? These and other allied questions have to be tackled not by the ordinary rules of astrology but by those pertaining to *Deva-praśna.* Will a particular king or country win the war being waged at present? Such questions may be posed in respect of cricket matches, litigations, business deals etc. and answered only through Horary Science. The distinction between the acts of previous life and the present life as well as their results could be made only through queries. In a way both the predictive system and the horary one of astrology are alike inasmuch as the birth of an individual in a particular place, time and circumstance and of particular parents appears to be accidental; even so is a query put to an astrologer, because he repairs to the place of the astrologer, being goaded by some unseen power to meet the consultant on a particular day, time and circumstances. When a person goes to an astrologer, the latter finds out both the *Ārūḍha* and the Ascendant at the time. He makes prediction about the querist's life and problems from the planetary positions, strength, aspects etc. with reference to the stronger of the two, i.e. *Ārūḍha* and Ascendant, in the absence of the person's natal horoscope—*Jātaka.* Another point to be borne in mind is that any undertaking done at a good time bears beneficial results, not only during the person's sojourn on earth, but in his future existence too, nay, even for his descendants. This rule applies to the results of action done at a bad time too.

Gola is spherical geometry which treats of Astronomy. This includes the five ancient systems of astronomy viz. *Pauliśa, Romaka, Vāsiṣṭha, Saura* and *Paitāmaha* or *Brāhma.* It includes all subdivisions of time such as yuga, year, solstice, season (*Ṛtu* of two months), month, fortnight, day and night, watch (a period of three hours), *Muhūrta* (one of 48 minutes), *Nāḍī* (equal to 24 minutes), *Prāṇa* (time required for a breath), *Truṭi* (a small unit of time equal to that of two winks) with its subdivisions and the ecliptic. These are explained in the *Brāhma sphuṭasiddhānta, Siddhāntaśiromaṇi* etc. *Gaṇita* is dealt with in the *Lilāvatī* by Bhāskara II written in a lyrical style, consisting of questions on various types of mathematical problems posed to his daughter, who had been widowed in the prime of her youth.

Nimitta in Sanskrit primarily means reason. But it is a technical term meaning *Omen* or *Augury* in astrology. Śāstraic works like *Āyurveda*, *Dharma-śāstra* as well as literary works like *Kāvyas*, both *Dṛśya* and *Śravya* (drama and poetry), where a character apprehends some danger befalling the person in the near future, when he or she experiences a bad omen (*Nimittaṃ sūcayitvā*) like the throbbing of an eye (left in the case of men and the right of women). Indian literature is replete with references to these omens, because belief in them is a basic feature of the Indian cultural ethos. Kālidāsa and Vālmīki who are two of the most precious jewels on the crown of Mother India, refer in their unique works to the auguries of the sacred fire in "*Pradakṣiṇārcirvyājena hasteneva jayam dadau*". At a sacrifice good omens of the fire are some colours, sounds and movements of the flame as explained by Varāhamihira in connection with the "Glory of Indra's Banner". Similarly in the Rāmāyaṇa *Sītā* experienced suddenly a good omen in the form of the throbbing of her left arm, while she was kept in the Aśoka-Vana. *Muhūrta-śāstra* or electional astrology too is an important branch of astrology. What is *Muhūrta*? Vidyāmādhava says that it is the time fit for the performance of auspicious deeds. Time, according to the sages, is of two kinds viz., *Sūkṣma* (subtle) and *Sthūla* (gross). They are otherwise known as invisible and visible. Only the latter could be discussed and understood by ordinary human beings. The former is atomic in nature and so could be comprehended only through religious merit of previous life, according to sage Nārada. *Truṭi* (2 winks = 1 *truṭi*) and its fractions are beyond human comprehension while *Prāṇa* (Breath = $\frac{1}{6}$ *Vighaṭī*) and multiples are visible and are capable of being comprehended. As good and bad results are hidden in the womb of time, sages have prescribed good week days, lunar mansions, *Yogas* etc. for different activities such as seeking a bride for one's son, uniting with one's spouse for procreation, commencement of education, agricultural work, business transactions, journey or pilgrimage etc. About sexual union the *Smṛtis* instruct householders: "Select during the fertile period—*Ṛtukāla*—even night at an auspicious hour, synchronizing with a male asterism." They add that the stars *Maghā* and *Mūla* ought to be rejected. Sage Bodhāyana recommends the winter Solstice (*Uttarāyaṇa*) when the moon is waxing and transiting a good asterism viz. *Rohiṇī*, *Mṛgaśirṣa*, *U. Phalgunī* or *Svāti* for marriage ceremonies. For other progressive works the following stars are said to be beneficial: *Punarvasu*, *Puṣya*, *Hasta*, *Śravaṇa* and *Revatī*. The time of birth cannot be bettered by astrologers. Still the second birth (*Upanayana*) can be improved by human efforts through the election of an excellent *Muhūrta*. so that the studies and career of the religious student may become very beneficial to a large extent by the Lord's grace and best wishes of elders, teachers, kinsmen and friends.

Blemishes: While electing *Muhūrtas* for any auspicious work, one should try to avoid the following destructive elements:

1. Forbidden lunar days termed *Chidra Tithis*.
2. Malefic asterisms—that are not recommended for auspicious works. So are the signs owned by malefics.
3. Weekdays owned by malefics. So are the *Kāla-Horās* owned by malefics.
4. *Viṣaghaṭis* pertaining to the lunar mansions.
5. *Bhūkampa* and other phenomena born of the Sun's transits.
6. Injurious daily Yogas as well as six other types of unions.
7. *Uḍukūpa*—Stellar Wells—and *Tithikūpa*—Lunar Day Wells.
8. *Kālarakṣa* and *Kālānta*; *Cakrapāta* or *Vaidhṛta*; *Cakrārdhapāta* or *Vyatipāta*.
9. Three types of *Sthūṇas*, viz. *Sthūṇa*, *Kaṇṭaka-sthūṇa* and *Raktasṭhūṇa*.
10. Three kinds of Mṛtyu viz. *Dina-mṛtyu*, *Tārāmṛtyu* and *Rāśimṛtyu*.
11. Three types of *Andhanakṣatra*—Blind Star.
12. *Uṣṇaśikhā*, *Kaṇṭaka-Star* and *Yama-Kaṇṭakāṃśa*.
13. The forbidden stars with respect to one's natal asterism. Similarly the signs that are injurious to his natal sign.
14. The vacant months, *Tithis*, signs, and stars.
15. The three stars designated as burnt, smoking and blazing.

16. The last parts of the four kinds of months and the ends of the three kinds of years.
17. Combustion of Jupiter and Venus as well as their mutual aspect.
18. The asterism termed *Graha-sūla* and the one that suffers from *Graha-vedha*.

In fine, as it is not possible to avoid all the blemishes, the astrologer should see that the time elected enjoys greater merits and strength than the blemishes.

CHAPTER II

ASTROLOGER AND QUERIST

I HAVE ALREADY mentioned in passing that the illustrious Ujjayinī-based astrologer-astronomer, Varāhamihira enumerates the virtues and characteristics expected of an ideal astrologer: He should hail from a noble family, be good-looking, of modest dress, truthful, free from jealousy, unbiased, with well-proportioned, strong limbs and joints, undeformed, with handsome hands, feet, nails etc., with a deep and sonorous voice.

He must also be eloquent, with a creative intellect, well-versed in the details of time and clime, free from vices, having attained expertise in the performance of rituals of both curative and progressive types, and engaged in the worship of gods. He must be thoroughly learned in astronomical calculations and the three branches—*Gaṇita*, *Jātaka* and *Saṃhitā*—of astrology. Such an astrologer is the greatest asset to a king. "Just as the night devoid of lights or lamps is utterly blind, and the sky without the Sun dark, even so will a king grope in the dark in life like a blind man on the way, if he is not guided by a good astrologer." He closes the relevant chapter with the assertion: "Even his own father, mother, kinsmen or friends would not be solicitous so much for the prosperity of the king and his army as is a friendly astrologer who works only for his untarnished fame". These ideas have been echoed by Viṣṇu, author of the *Caturasundarī*, a commentary on the *Kṛṣṇīya*, and by the author of the illustrious *Praśnamārga*.

Location: The astrologer should select an ideal location for conducting the horary session: It should be covered with the cool shade of trees, full of blossoms, laden with fruits, with glossy barks and leaves, free from ill-omened birds, bearing auspicious names (like Palāśa, Pippala and Aśvattha) that provide a pleasant and cool environment, or a garden with green grass. The place should not be near a graveyard, deserted shrine, at a junction of roads, or a market place, or a rugged, sandy place covered with debris, charcoal etc.

It should not be a place haunted by wandering ascetics and naked persons, near a barber's shop, butcher's shop, jail, gambling den, wine shop, police station, hospital etc.

The best directions for query are the East, North and North-East, while North-West, South, South-West, West and South-East are inauspicious for the querist.

The morning time is very beneficial to the querist, whereas night time, afternoon, dawn and dusk are harmful.

The astrologer should foretell both good and bad effects of the query after carefully observing the direction occupied by the querist, his movements, limbs touched by him, articles brought by him, his utterances, expression on his face and last but not the least, the time of the query.

The *Praśnamārga* adds that an astrologer should be a regular worshipper of the Planetary Deities too. He must have studied his branch of the Veda and be daily chanting some part of it. That is not all. He must have mastered *Mantra-śāstra* as well. He must get up at dawn, meditate on his *Iṣṭadevatā* after doing his daily religious duties viz. *Āhnika*. Thereafter he must read the Almanac and calculate the planetary positions for the day and be ready to meet his clients. As soon as he espies a person approaching him, he should concentrate his attention on his movements and take into consideration all the omens, good and bad, and utterances of the person concerned as well as others. Thereupon he should study the condition of his own breath. Then he should jot down all these details in a notebook and erect the chart for the moment.

In this connection the reader should remember the general rule meaning "One ought not to make predictions to a person who does not put his questions". The same rule applies to one who does not ask questions with proper decorum. An astrologer should be guarded against hypocrites also. For, predictions made under such conditions will not be correct. According to others, the astrologer should find out whether the querist, though silent, is a genuine person or otherwise. Should he find that the person is genuine, then he should begin to make predictions, although he might not have opened his mouth. He can do the job by observing the chart erected for the moment and the ascendant, angles, trines and planets. According to

Vasiṣṭha predictions should be made on the basis of the *Ārūḍha-Lagna* even if the querist does not express his intention. This chart is called *Sthira Cakra* or Stable Circle.

The *Ārūḍha* will represent a particular direction as shown hereunder: Aries and Taurus represent the East; Gemini—South-East; Cancer and Leo—South; Virgo—South-West; Libra and Scorpio—West; Sagittarius—North-West; Capricorn and Aquarius—North; and Pisces—North-East. In this manner he must be able to recognize the eight directions spread out before him on the stationary circle. The direction occupied by the querist will point to a sign in the stationary chart and should be taken as the *Ārūḍha-lagna* for the horary session.

A doubt may arise in the minds of readers regarding the *Lagna*, as the four cardinal directions have two signs each. If he sits in a place in the East, should the astrologer consider *Aries* or *Taurus* as the *Ārūḍha*? This difficulty is obviated by observing the querist as to which side he is leaning, left or right. If it is *left*, the direction is near the North. So you have to take Aries; and if it is right, he is sitting near the South. So take Taurus as the *Ārūḍha*. Should doubt still persist, the querist should be asked to touch one of the Zodiacal signs in the chart before him, and that will be the required ascendant.

Astrologer's Duties: The 15 items we have already seen are discussed below: (1) Time of query; (2) location; (3) condition of the astrologer's breath; (4) the psychosomatic condition of himself and the querist; (5) the sign indicated by the quarter occupied by the querist; (6) the articles touched by the querist; (7) direction; (8) the syllables and words uttered first by the querist; (9) his posture—sitting or standing, leaning, looking up or down and the like; (10) limbs touched by him and other movements or gesticulations; (11) his facial expression—joy, dejection etc; (12) the direction at which he looks; (13) condition and colour of his dress; (14) ornaments such as garland, chain, wrist watch , bangle, rings etc. worn by him; and (15) the sounds heard at the time such as of music, cries of animals, weeping of children etc.

(1) According to the *Praśnasindhu*, if at a query there should be heard the sound of conch, tabor lute, trumpeting of elephants, lowing of cows, neighing of horses etc., only auspicious results

would accrue to the querist. On the other hand, the cries of crows, braying of donkeys, buffaloes etc. would produce untoward results. According to Varāhamihira the sight of the dung of elephants, cows and dogs will destroy wealth.

We have already seen the two kinds of *Cakra*, viz. *Sthira* and *Cara*. The former is to be resorted to in the following cases: (1) One questioning in a crowd; (2) one standing in the house puts the question; (3) a person lying on bed does it; (4) a query put in the evening and at night. If a person were to ask a question while walking, the *Cara Cakra*, i.e. the *Udaya-lagna* (not the *Ārūḍha*) should be employed. In case the ascendant is occupied by many planets, then the *Ārūḍha* should be taken up for consideration. If a scholarly person puts a question, it is the *Cara Cakra* (i.e. *Udaya-lagna*) that should be used.

The following persons should not be entertained:

(1) One who asks in a casual manner.
(2) One who uses abusive language while asking.
(3) One who is a heretic or atheist.
(4) One who comes empty-handed.
(5) One who is proceeding on a journey.
(6) One who is answering calls of nature.
(7) One who asks questions at dusk.
(8) One who does it in a nonchalant manner.

Still the astrologer should not give up good manners and gentlemanly behaviour, but engage the so-called querist in a pleasant conversation and send him away quietly without answering his queries.

The *Catura-sundari* quotes a verse meaning that an astrologer must be very learned, and must have achieved success (*Siddhi*) in respect of a Great Mantra imparted by an eminent Master or *Guru*. He must be decently dressed and ornamented (with rosaries etc.) and truthful. Such an astrologer's pronouncements will never go wrong.

(1) He must first of all examine carefully which of the two ascendants, stationary or moving, is stronger. If both be found deficient in strength, he should then take the lunar sign as the ascendant.

(2) He must also select a clean, level ground for drawing the Zodiacal chart, wherein the twelve houses should be identified

properly and their significance, characteristics etc. well understood as shown hereunder:

The First House represents the querist's body; the Second House, wealth; the Third, brother; the Fourth, kinsmen, mother etc.: the Fifth, his son: the Sixth, enemy; the Seventh, his wife; the Eighth, demise; the Ninth, religious observances, virtuous conduct, or father; the Tenth, profession or livelihood; the Eleventh, gain or elder brother; and the Twelfth, loss or expenditure. Whichever house or *Bhāva* is occupied by its own lord, who is possessed of strength, the querist should be said to be thinking of the persons or things pertaining to that *Bhāva*.

(3) *Characteristics of Astrologer's Breath*: Even as the astrologer is required to read daily the almanac or *Pañcāṅga*, so should he examine daily his breath as soon as he gets up from bed. On Sunday, Tuesday and Saturday the flow should be predominant in the right nostril. If it be otherwise, the day would be not to his advantage. On the other hand, on Monday, Wednesday, Thursday and Friday it should be in the left nostril.

At the time of the query too the astrologer should examine the condition of his breath. Should the flow of breath be equal in both the nostrils, the result would be bad for the querist. The breath flowing through the left nostril is the one belonging to the *Iḍā Nāḍī*, and the one through the right nostril, to the *Piṅgalā Nāḍī*, and the one flowing equally through both the *Nāḍīs* (Tubes or Canals), to the *Suṣumnā Nāḍī*.[1] If the querist stands on the same side as the astrologer's breath, it will give good results in spite of the lord of the weekday pointing to the contrary. If the querist should sit in front or to the left of the astrologer or at a higher level, and if it be the bright fortnight and the flow of breath through the left nostril, then all the wishes of the querist would be fulfilled. If the conditions be reversed in the dark fortnight, then too the results would be beneficial.

1. In Yoga the aspirant tries to raise the Serpent Power or *Kuṇḍalinī Śakti*, lying coiled up in the *Mūlādhāra* or sacral plexus through the Central Canal called *Suṣumnā*, passing through the other five mystic centres known as *Cakras* viz. *Svādhiṣṭhāna*, *Maṇipūra*, *Anāhata*, *Viśuddhi* and *Ājñā*, and culminating in the highest mystic centre located in the crown of the head called *Sahasrāra* or *Sahasradala Padma*.

If thieves, enemies, kings, hypocrites, traders, and such other persons are seen standing in the direction of the breathless nostril, neither the querist nor the consultant would have any trouble from such fellows. The flow of breath through the right nostril would prove beneficial at a query pertaining to disputation, gambling, fighting (or sports), bathing, eating, sexual union, trade and profession, fear or disgrace. Similarly the breath in the left nostril would be beneficial in the case of journey, making charity, marriage ceremony, solemn declaration, planning, starting on a mission and at the time of house-warming function.

(4) *Mood*: The mood of the astrologer as well as of the querist should be examined for the results. Similarly their physical condition will also affect the prediction. If one of them is in a morose condition or a jubilant one, the result will vary accordingly. If the astrologer should find that the querist has got a feeling of fright, as a result of his looking side-ways, the former should declare that the person is apprehending danger from thieves or enemies. On the other hand, if the querist looks jubilant, success should be predicted in respect of his proposed undertaking. This will include his physical movements such as gesticulations. Similarly, whatever experiences the astrologer has during the day with regard to his bath, food, sleep and other activities, he should declare similar results to the querist's problem.

(5) *Articles Touched*: Results are declared on the basis of the limb or article touched by the querist. If he touches some auspicious article like betel leaves or a mirror, while putting his question, the result would be success in his undertaking. The same result would follow, if he were to touch his chest. On the other hand, if he holds a knife or rope, ashes or flame, the result would be harmful. Should he touch his navel, nose, mouth, hair, nail, teeth, privities, back, breast, neck, stomach, ring finger or any of the nine cavities, the result would be disastrous.

If the querist, standing in the East, touches his head while asking the astrologer, the result will be gain of wealth. If he, standing in the east, touches his mouth, he will have gain or profit through animals. If he touches the neck, he would gain a vehicle. Touching the chest would indicate gain of ornaments.

Similarly, if he touches the mouth while standing in the south, the result would be destruction of enemies. If the limb touched be the neck, the result would be gain of wealth. If he touches the chest, the result would be birth of good sons; and if it be the head, getting friends.

If he stands in the west and touches his neck, he will gain an ox; if it be the chest, gain of a vehicle; if the head, acquisition of knowledge; and if the face, gain of kinship.

If he stands in the north and touches his chest, there will be gain of an elephant; if the head be touched, gain of excellent ornaments; if the mouth, gain of good kinship or alliance; if the neck, gain of good progeny. Table I would make the reader understand the results mentioned above at a glance:

TABLE I

Showing the Directions, Limbs and Result

	Direction	Limb	Result
1	East (*Dhvaja*)	Head (Nose)	Gain of wealth
2	,,	Mouth (Face, eye, ear)	Gain through animals
3	,,	Neck	Gain of vehicle
4	,,	Chest	Gain of ornaments
5	South (*Siṃha*)	Mouth	Destruction of enemies
6	,,	Neck	Gain of wealth
7	,,	Chest	Birth of good sons
8	,,	Head	Getting friends
9	West (*Vṛṣa*)	Neck (Hand)	Gets an ox
10	,,	Chest	Gets a vehicle
11	,,	Head	Acquires knowledge
12	,,	Face	Gains kinship or alliance
13	North (*Gaja*)	Chest (Leg)	Gets an elephant
14	,,	Head	Gains good ornaments
15	,,	Mouth	Gets good alliance
16	,,	Neck	Begets good progeny

TABLE II

	Direction	Limb	Result
1	South-East (*Dhūma*)	Nose (Head)	Fear of death
2	,,	Eyes or Ears	Sad news
3	,,	Hands	Loss of one's principle
4	,,	Legs	Destructions of family
5	South-West	Face (Eyes, Ears)	Illness
6	(*Śunaka*)	Hand	Loss of progeny
7	,,	Legs	Danger
8	,,	Nose	Loss of wealth
9	North-West (*Khara*)	Hands (Neck)	Dispute
10	,,	Legs	Loss of animals
11	,,	Nose	Danger from weapons
12	,,	Ears, Eyes	Wife's illness
13	North-East (*Kāka*)	Legs (Chest)	Trouble from/to relations
14	,,	Nose	Loss of teeth
15	,	Eyes (Ears)	Death through menials
16	,,	Hands	Danger to children

(6) Relationship between directions and the zodiacal signs has already been explained. In case the querist occupies one of the cardinal points with regard to the diviner, the results would be good, provided the query relates to a man, while, if it relates to a woman, it would be *bad*. Similarly, the result would be beneficial in the case of women, provided the querist occupies one of the corners; otherwise, it would be harmful.

If the querist occupies or faces the south of the astrologer, the result will be extremely bad. It is all the more so, if the query is about longevity.

The ***Praśna-Bhairava*** lays down the rule that if the querist should occupy the East or West, his object would be fulfilled, whereas if he spoke from the South or the North, he would go on a long journey. If the direction be either South-West or North-East, the chances of success would be remote. Similarly if it be South-East or North-West, his object would soon come to grief.

(7) *Syllables and Words Used*: Whatever syllable or word the querist utters first, will indicate the type of result of his queries. To achieve success in predicting results from this angle, the astrologer should know thoroughly the elements signified by the syllables and their effects. Primarily the letters of the alphabet are divided into two main classes viz. vowels and consonants. Vowels are termed *Jivagaṇa* (living group), while consonants *Śarīra-gaṇa* (physical group). There are 16 vowels and 35 consonants in all. So in horary astrology 51 letters have been recognized. The consonants are divided into seven groups or classes of five letters each: gutterals, palatals, linguals, dentals, labials, yavarga (from *Ya* to *Śa*) and Ṣavarga (from *Ṣa* to *Kṣa*). Among the vowels the short ones and the *A* followed by the nasal and aspirate respectively (Aṁ and Aḥ) belong to one group; and the long vowels to the second group, diphthongs being omitted. The following Table explains the relationship between the Syllables and the Elements:

(1) Ka, Ca, Ṭa, Ta, Pa, Ya, Sa—*Air*
(2) Kha, Cha, Ṭha, Tha, Pha, Ra, Sa—*Fire*
(3) Ga, Ja, Ḍa, Da, Ba, La, Ha—*Indra*
(4) Gha, Jha, Ḍha, Dha, Bha, Va, La—*Water*
(5) Ṅa, Ña, Na, Ṇa, Ma, Śa, Kṣa—*Ether* or *Eunuch*

Short vowels are ruled by Indra, and long ones by Water. The effects of these are:

If the first syllable of the querist's word happens to be in the Ether group, the result would be very very bad. Similarly Air and Fire too are considered as dangerous, while those belonging to Indra yield moderate results, and those to Water, are highly beneficial. Short vowels ruled by Indra would confer moderate results, while long vowels ruled by Water are beneficial.

If the first word uttered by the querist possesses a *Ja-gaṇa* (U-U) in the beginning, presided over by the *Sun*, the effect would be prolonged ailment; if *Sa-gaṇa* (UU-), ruled by the Wind, going abroad; if *Bha-gaṇa*-(-UU), ruled by the *Moon*, exceptional fame; if *Ma-gaṇa* (- - -), by the Earth, acquisition of wealth; if *Ra-gaṇa* (-U-) by Fire, Death; if *Ta-gaṇa* (- -U), by Ether, fruitless effort; if *Ya-gaṇa* (U- -), by Water, great prosperity; if *na-gaṇa* (UUU) by Heaven, prolongation of life-span. The above results are tabulated for easy reference:

Gaṇas	Form	Deity	Effect
Jagaṇa	U-U	Sun	Long sickness
Sagaṇa	UU-	Wind	Going abroad
Bhagaṇa	-UU	Moon	Great fame
Magaṇa	– – –	Earth	Gain of wealth
Ragaṇa	-U-	Fire	Death
Tagaṇa	- -U	Ether	Void
Yagaṇa	U- -	Water	Great prosperity
Nagaṇa	UUU	Heaven	Long life

If the querist's question be pleasing to the ear and heart as well as couched in a dignified language, his wishes would be fulfilled. On the contrary, if the words be coarse and jarring as well as one having an aspirate (*Visarga*) at the end, the result would be utter disappointment.

The ascendant at a query should be found out through the first syllable of the word uttered by the querist. Then the diviner should examine the chart and declare the effects. The rule for fixing the *Lagna* is the following: For the purpose of horary astrology the alphabet is divided into seven groups ruled by the seven planets as shown below:

(1) *Avarga* or Vowels ruled by the Sun; (2) *Kavarga* or Gutturals, by Mars; (3) *Cavarga* or Palatals, by Venus; (4) *Ṭavarga* or Cerebrals, by Mercury; (5) *Tavarga* or Dentals, by Jupiter; (6) *Pavarga* or Labials, by Saturn; and (7) *Yavarga* or Semi-vowels and one Sibilant, by the Moon.

If the letter represents an odd number in its group explained above, we have to take the odd sign of the ruling planet, provided the planet rules over two signs, odd and even. So this rule would apply to all the planets except the luminaries.

Fixing the Ārūḍha Easily: If the *Ārūḍha* be found out, it would not be difficult for the astrologer to fix the relative positions of the planets with reference to the Ascendant. Suppose a querist asks: "Could I get the post I aspire for?" and the first syllable of the query be *Ka*, which is an odd number. Then the Ascendant would be Aries ruled by Mars. In case Mars be posited in his exaltation in the 10th house, then the result would be excellent and it would be within his reach by the succeeding Tuesday.

(8) *Querist's Stance or Posture*: While putting question if the querist puts his left foot forward, the result will be beneficial, whereas if it be the right foot, the result would be unfavourable. Similarly if he shook his foot or leg, the result would be harmful. If the person sits quiet without making any movements, it will be to his advantage. If he sits at ease, erect, on a raised seat, in front of the astrologer, the result will be advantageous.

In case he puts the question sitting and then gets up immediately or vice versa, only good results will follow. As many times he gets up and returns to his seat, in so many days his object will be fulfilled. Should a stranger pass between the querist and astrologer, it would indicate that the querist would not get help from the expected quarters.

(9) If the querist shakes off his hand, presses it and stands up with his face turned to a side and appears to have forgotten something, his object will not be fulfilled. If some object suddenly falls and hits his body or some other object, it is a sure indication of impending death. The same result will have to be declared even when there is a talk, thought, sight or news of destruction or destructive objects or persons. Similar is the sight of one who is naked, impure, weeping, cutting something, pressing his eyes with his hand or one that is with dishevelled hair. If at the time of query somebody (or querist or astrologer) should twist a thread, scratch the ground with his nails, prevent a person or animal from proceeding further, change his position, perspire profusely, put something into the fire, go for an oil-bath, hold bones, ashes, dirt or lead, be troubled by some kind of illness, or one is seen with his neck covered with a towel, or talking harshly, the result would be unfavourable. Similarly if one carries a knife, sword, grass, net, paddy husk, sandals, peacock's feathers, horn, skin, broom-stick, sacred grass, red flowers, winnowing basket, ropes, or pestle (mortar), the result would be most untoward. Some of these articles are also considered inauspicious omens at a journey.

(10) *Demeanour*: Sinister or angry looks (of the querist or astrologer), gloomy face, dejection, fatigue or moroseness would lead to unhappy results. If the messenger or querist is of attractive features, of a noble family, polite, free from illness and of pleasant manners, the querist will achieve success.

(11) If he looks steadfast at the auspicious objects brought or kept there with wide open eyes and without looking up and down, his desires will be fulfilled. On the contrary, the result will lead to sorrow.

(12) The type of clothes that the messenger or querist wears also is an indication of the effects, good or bad: If the clothes be wet or dripping with water, torn, dirty, of red or black colour, or are marked with red flowers, the concerned person will be stricken with sorrow. On the other hand, if the dress be white, perfumed, marked with white flowers and other decorations, he would surely be blessed with prosperity. If he goes to the session carrying auspicious materials, he will get good results. On the contrary, i.e. if he goes empty-handed or with inauspicious materials, the effect will be untoward.

(13) If the person wears auspicious ornaments such as gold rings, a nice wrist watch, gold chain, good ear-rings etc., the result will be excellent.

(14) The sounds heard at the time will also have their effect on the outcome of the query. Whatever words are uttered by the querist or whatever sounds are heard at the place, or whatever actions of others are beheld, the result would be commensurate with the auspiciousness or otherwise of those things. If the sounds heard and things seen are of a mixed nature, then the effect will depend on the preponderance of the good or bad indications. In queries of certain projects or journeys, success should be predicted, provided the omens are favourable. Suppose a person queries an astrologer whether his intention to go abroad would be fulfilled, and if somebody reads a newspaper report of high-jacking of a plane or threat of a bomb, he should be asked not to undertake the journey for some time to come. Similarly, if somebody gives the news of a new ship being launched, he will certainly go abroad for success. At a query of marriage if a pair of good articles be brought together, or two persons turn up unexpectedly, the alliance that is proposed will

materialize early for all-round success. Similarly, if someone is found inserting his finger into a bottle or a hole, the astrologer would say that the proposed girl's character is not above board. If someone asks, "From which direction I shall be getting a girl for marriage?" The consultant will observe minutely all the quarters for necessary leading auguries. Then if a person arrives from a particular direction, say East, then the astrologer should declare that he will get a bride from the East. If the person coming from the East utters some words like, "A fight broke out between two groups", the proposed marriage with the girl hailing from that quarter will end in disharmony or quarrel.

At a query relating to progeny if the following omens occur, good result will have to be predicted: books, children's ornaments like anklets, a pregnant woman and a child. On the other hand, if burning fire is sighted or someone clears the throat and spits, or clears the nose, or somebody goes away from that place, that would point to miscarriage.

At a query about fighting, litigation, test matches, boxing bouts etc. the following six good omens would indicate victory to the party concerned:

(1) A person standing keeping his right foot firmly;
(2) Moving or playing with a knife in his hand;
(3) Rubbing the right palm;
(4) Sight of blazing fire;
(5) Arrival of a popular person; and
(6) Sight of a smiling gentleman.

On the other hand, the following five auguries bespeak defeat:

(1) One standing with the left foot kept firmly;
(2) Tremulous utterances;
(3) Shedding tears;
(4) Sight of dirty things; and
(5) Putting the sword in its sheath.

If at a query of illness the querist is standing on a green branch of a tree, or if such a person is sighted nearby, or if a living animal comes to that place, the patient will certainly be cured soon and will live long. The following are inauspicious omens suggesting demise of the patient: Red flowers, sesamum, fire, new cloth, holy grass, curds etc. that are used in obsequial rites.

At a query about journey, the following acts would create obstacles and delay the journey: After putting the question if the person sits down or lies down, the journey would not materialize. The same result should be predicted, if he changes the leg on which he was standing, or if he folds his leg. The following are considered as inauspicious omens in almost all queries: Cries of distress like Alas! Alas!, sneezing, fall of flag-staff, breaking, tearing of clothes, umbrella, sandals, words meaning killing or blasting, unusual cries of predatory birds or beasts in all directions, sudden extinguishing of the lamp, full pots tumbling down etc.

The sight of a cat, snake, owl, alligator, and such other creatures and the chuckle of a lizard heard from the *left* are evil portents bringing destruction in their wake. Similarly sneezing heard from the right is of dire consequence at a query. In this connection we have to recognize two kinds of auguries, some being harmful only if they are seen while others' cries, not sight, are inauspicious in a particular direction. For example, the lizards' chuckle heard to one's right cannot be harmful. So too is the sound of sneezing heard to one's left.

At a query the mention of a boar, alligator, hare, serpent, the reddish poisonous lizard (*Araṇe* in Kannaḍa) etc. would be auspicious, but their sight and hearing their cries inauspicious. On the other hand, the sight of a monkey or bear as well as hearing their cries would be auspicious.

The cries or sight of the following animals viz. elephant, horse, bull etc. is said to be good.

The astrologer should be shrewd enough to probe the mind of the querist to find out if the latter is a sincere person or a hypocrite who has come to mock at the profession of astrology by trying to pull the diviner's legs. It is said that a person trying to test the scholarship of an astrologer asked him to cast the chart for some birth. The astrologer being an expert in his profession discovered from the chart erected for the given time that it was the birth of a quadruped-calf.

In horary parlance too all querists cannot be trusted, as some might intend to make fun of the astrologer. So he must find out if the visitor is a genuine querist. In this connection the *Praśna-tantra* gives us some guidelines: Look at the ascendant at first and its strength and then declare your findings. When the Moon is posited in the ascendant, Saturn in an angle and Mercury eclipsed, or if the Moon in the ascendant is aspected by Mercury and Mars, the visitor should be declared to be insincere. On the other hand, if the ascendant be occupied by a benefic, he would be honest. In case it is occupied by a malefic, he should be considered dishonest.

Likewise, if the ascendant or the 7th house be aspected by a benefic, or if the Moon be aspected by Jupiter, the querist must be sincere. Should Jupiter or Mercury aspect the lord of the 7th house, who is their enemy, then too the visitor would be insincere. Even in the above case, should the aspecting and aspected planets be themselves aspected by benefics, the querist would be sincere.

Querist's Duties: Just as the astrologer is expected to observe certain rules of conduct, even so an ideal querist should observe certain principles in order to obtain maximum benefits. He should be pure and clean both mentally and physically and approach the astrologer on an auspicious day in the forenoon, carrying gold, fruits, flowers, betel leaves, betel-nuts etc. He must select a good lunar day and lunar mansion as well as a benefic weekday.

The following are good for him: Sunday, Monday (when the Moon is possessed of strength), Wednesday. Thursday and Friday. Auspicious and beneficial lunar days are those except the *Chidra-Tithis* (4th, 6th, 8th, 9th. 12th and 14th) and the New Moon.

Favourable lunar mansions are those except *Bharaṇī*, *Kṛttikā*, *Ārdrā*, *Āśleṣā*, *Maghā*, *P. Phalgunī*, *Viśākhā*, *Jyeṣṭhā*, *Mūla*, *P. Āṣāḍhā* and *P. Bhādra* (which are recommended for child's first feeding), provided the star selected be in agreement with his natal asterism and the Moon's transit not adverse. He must avoid also the *Gaṇḍānta*, *Uṣṇa-doṣa*, *Viṣa Ghaṭī*, *Viṣṭi* and the fixed *Karaṇas*, junctures of lunar days, those of asterisms and those of the *Rāśis*, (as *Lagnas*) as well as of the *Navāṃśas*, rise of *Māndi*, *Lāta-Vaidhṛta* (generally *Maghā* and *Śatabhiṣak* in the months of Aries and Libra; *Śravaṇa* and *Puṣya* in those of

Taurus and Scorpio; *P. Āṣāḍhā* and *Ārdrā* in those of Gemini and Sagittarius; *Rohiṇī* and *Jyeṣṭha* in those of Cancer and Capricorn; Bharaṇī and *Svātī* in those of Leo and Aquarius; and *Revatī* and *Hasta* in those of Virgo and Pisces), the blemish caused by eclipses (three days after the event), *Sarpa-Śiras* (among the daily *Yogas* the latter half of *Vyatīpāta*), *Ekārgala*, Yogas such as *Mṛtyu* and *Dagdha*, malefics aspecting or occupying the Lagna, *Pradoṣa* (fortnightly), midnight, 16 *Ghaṭīs* before and after every *Saṅkrānti* and presence of the Moon in the ascendant and the 8th house. It is not possible to avoid all these mentioned in this long list, but the most important blemishes should be eschewed. The querist must start from home in a good *Muhūrta* when there is *Amṛta Ghaṭī*. He must approach the astrologer politely. In this connection the *Praśnabhūṣaṇa* of Jīvanātha prescribes the following virtues on the part of the querist: "He should be serene, discriminative, of a pure heart, and honour the astrologer with a loving heart. Before putting questions he must worship the Zodiacal chart, offering gold, gems, flowers and fruits. He should then express his desire with devotion and humility."

CHAPTER III

PLANETS AND SIGNS

UNLESS WE KNOW the characteristics such as qualities, nature, caste, directions, countries, articles etc., represented by the planets and signs, we cannot do justice to horary work as in the case of horoscopy. For this purpose the ancient authorities have given different names for the twelve *Bhāvas* (houses) and their significations. According to the *Bhuvana-Dīpaka* the Ascendant signifies the following things: Happiness, longevity, age, birth, caste or community, health, characteristic marks, virtues, sufferings, form, shape, complexion, fame, prosperity, success, sex—popularly known as the *Tanu Bhāva*. From this it would be clear to students of astrology that the First House or Ascendant holds the key to the entire mansion of the Zodiacal chart. In other words, it is the seed, out of which the whole tree of the native's life grows gradually yielding all the experiences of worldly existence.

The Second *Bhāva* or House represents the following: Pearls, ruby, gems, minerals, wealth, clothes, horses, business, path, science, and art, family, speech, right eye, various lores—*Dhana-Bhāva*.

The Third *Bhāva* signifies: Communication, younger brothers and sisters, servants, slaves, labourers, courage, valour, wicked intention, right ear, help—*Bhrātṛ-Bhāva*.

The Fourth *Bhāva* represents: Garden, threshing floor, fields, potent herbs, pleasures, entering holes and caves, mother, friends, maternal uncle, nephew, treasures, vehicle, cot, seat, cleverness, winsome manners, water, bed, progress, cattle, place of birth, education and happiness—*Sukha-Bhāva*.

The Fifth *Bhāva* signifies: Intelligence, resourcefulness, genius, discriminative faculty, merits of past life, *Mantra* (Mystic Word), ministers, children cheerful mind, pregnancy, spiritual practices, literary composition—*Putra-Bhāva*.

The Sixth *Bhāva* stands for: Thieves, enemies, obstacles, diseases, physical injury, serious illness amounting to death, unnatural death through water and weapons, fear, battle, donkey, camel, cruel deeds, maternal uncles, servants—*Śatru-Bhāva.*

The Seventh *Bhāva* signifies: Marriage, passion, partner, husband, wife, companionship, union of lovers, inward and outward movements, bed-chamber, ladies' apartments, lost articles, business, litigation, light, dispute—*Kalatra-Bhāva.*

The Eighth *Bhāva* signifies: Total destruction, disaster, scandals, cause of death, place of death, servants, hostel, annexe of a house, hermitage, educational institution, house, diseases, all kinds of obstruction, ford, difficulties on the way, fortress, suffering caused by enemies, corruption, fight, vulnerable points —*Āyur-Bhāva.*

The Ninth *Bhāva* signifies: Fortune, religion, merit, compassion, good luck, penance, father, grand-children, charity, worship of Gods, spiritual practices, Vedic hymns, noble conduct, preceptor, wells, lakes, water-sheds, temples, vows, pilgrimage, monastery, merits of previous life—*Bhāgya-Bhāva.*

The Tenth *Bhāva* signifies: Temples, cities, assembly, street, residence, servants, all manners of services, profession, command, support, refuge, kingship, royal seal, position, father, utility, sky and related items—*Karma-Bhāva.*

The Eleventh *Bhāva* signifies: Acquisition of desired objects, elder brother, one's own progeny, left ear, gain of wealth, elephant-riding, horse-riding, clothes, crops, gold, maidens, acquiring learning -*Lābha Bhāva.*

The Twelth *Bhāva* denotes: Loss, sinful deeds, fall, hell, left eye, loss of position, physical handicap, defective limbs, renunciation, expenditure through charity, luxurious living, disputes, litigation, sacrifices and agricultural operations—*Vyaya-Bhāva.*

Special Features of the *Bhāvas*: Crawling movements should be deduced from the *Ārūḍha* ascendant. Lying down, resting and sleeping may be considered from the 4th *Bhāva*. Sitting-down may be delineated from the 7th and standing from the 10th *Bhāva*. When water is to be probed one has to consider the 4th *Bhāva* and find out if there is water at the bottom of the well or tank. The 7th *Bhāva* denotes the nature of the river-flow. Rainfall should be tackled from the 10th *Bhāva*. However, all the above things could be read from the Ascendant too.

In the case of a query about the food consumed, and of a

king's administration, there is a special procedure to be adopted as explained below:

From the ascendant we should read the physical conditions of the eaters, their number etc.; from the 2nd house the cooking vessels, eating plates and dishes; from the 3rd house, dishes served—eatables, fruits etc.; from the 4th house, pudding, pancake etc.; from the 5th, the servers; from the 6th, vegetable curry served (for mastication); from the 7th, milk, curds, ghee and such other items; from the 8th, rice; from the 9th, about the diners and their specialities etc.; from the 10th, satisfaction of the eaters; from the eleventh, the talks they had during dinner; and from the 12th, the bed used for rest after food.

In the case of queries pertaining to royalty, the following are signified by the twelve houses:

The First House signifies the king's physical features.

The Second House	,,	wealth in his treasury.
The Third House	,,	his armed forces.
The Fourth House	,,	elephants, horses and other vehicles.
The Fifth House	,,	discussion of administrative matters.
The Sixth House	,,	enemy kings.
The Seventh House	,,	national highways or marching.
The Eighth House	,,	longevity.
The Ninth House	,,	mental condition.
The Tenth House	,,	undertaking a course of action.
The Eleventh House	,,	gain in business.
The Twelfth House	,,	commission of errors, loss and missing of vital secrets.

Effects of the Bhāvas When They Are Occupied by Malefics and Benefics

1. When there be a malefic in the query ascendant, the person concerned would suffer loss and disappointment in all undertakings, sickness or pain in the head (cerebral region), sorrows, infamy, loss of position and wealth, physical malady or pain all over the body and all kinds of disasters. On the other hand, should benefics be posited in the *Lagna*, there would be all-round happiness, health, success in works, increase of prosperity, high reputation and promotion of one's rank or professional status.

2. Should there be a malefic in the 2nd house, there would be the dwindling of wealth hoarded by one's elders and ancestors, disease of the mouth or face, sickness among one's dependents, trouble in the right eye, hearing insulting words or oneself using such expressions, destruction of vessels. furniture etc. On the other hand, if benefics be in the 2nd house, the wealth inherited from ancestors would grow splendidly, there would be acquisition of new vessels, curtains, furniture etc., great jubilation in the family, health and happiness of family members.

3. Should malefics be posited in the 3rd house, the querist would be deprived of all help, his brothers would be afflicted with maladies, he would suffer from ailment in the chest, neck, right ear, mental observation and loss of courage. A benefic in that house would confer health, happiness etc. on his brothers, sisters, and helpmates, intellectual brilliance, increase of new endeavours and courageous acts.

4. If there be a malefic in the 4th house, there would be trouble to his mother, maternal uncle, nephew and friends, and danger to the cattle, house, couch, seats (furniture), landed properties, vehicles, as well as illness and heart-trouble and pollution of the water in the wells, tanks and other water sources; whereas a benefic in the 4th house would confer good vehicles, cattle, bed and furniture and all-round happiness.

5. A malefic in the 5th house, who is eclipsed, debilitated or posited in an inimical house, would lead to disease or death of children, destruction of religious merits, mental depression, irritability and illness among advisers and ministers. A benefic in this house being strong, would lead to the birth of a son or son's progress, increase of creative work, religious merit and mental peace and happiness.

6. A malefic in the Sixth house would produce diseases in the limb prescribed for the 6th house such as ulcers. If the 6th house be Aries, headache or head injury; if Taurus, disease in the mouth or face; if Gemini, trouble in the neck or throat, or it may be stomach-disease, according to some; trouble from robbers and enemies, pain or ulcer in the navel or hips, obstruction to all undertakings and diseases ruled by the particular malefic (such as wind, phlegm and bile). A benefic in this house would lead to eradication of enemies and diseases etc.

7. A malefic in the 7th house would lead to the wife's sickness or death, or separation from her, obstacles to his projected journey and diseases of the urinary tract. On the other hand, a benefic posited therein would lead to a marriage being solemnized, ideal conjugal felicity, recovery of lost articles and arrival at home of a friend or kinsman from abroad. On the other hand, a benefic possessed of strength, posited in this house would lead to the construction of a new house for his wife. A malefic in the 7th house would cause a fire-accident to the wife's (or husband's) house.

8. A malefic in the 8th house would cause sickness to servants, obstacles to one's undertakings, venereal diseases, quarrels with the people, loss of wealth and property through enemies, thieves and rulers, loss of appetite and such other ailments and fear of death; while a benefic in this house would bestow good health, relief from ailments, happiness and prolongation of life.

9. A malefic in the 9th house would bring about the rise of scandals, destruction of the querist's house-annexe; whereas a benefic therein would lead to the extension and beautification of the annexe and such other good things.

A malefic would produce the following harmful effects also: Disease and distress to elders, teachers, parents, grand-children etc., destruction of fortune and merits, lack of God's grace, and loss of penance, and rise of cruel deeds. A benefic, on the other hand, would confer the pleasure and grace of elders, parents, and teachers, mental peace and happiness, good fortune, merits, penance, God's grace, increase of auspicious ceremonies at home, happiness and progress of grand-children and their service and one's kindly and generous actions.

10. A malefic in the 10th house would cause destruction of one's undertakings, obstacles at every step, disrepute, disobedience of one's orders, loss of servants and support, disease of the knees and leaving one's native land. A benefic there would enable the person to construct a temple, roads and platforms or shelters for wayfarers, success in all undertakings, one's orders being obeyed implicitly, getting servants and supporters, good name or reputation.

11. A malefic in the eleventh house is likely to cause illness to children, elder brothers etc., disease in the knees and left ear

and acquisition of the articles allotted to the planets (such as copper); while a benefic in this house would lead to the cessation of troubles and sorrows, accomplishment of one's objects, gain of wealth and other articles assigned to the particular planet.

12. When a malefic is posited in the 12th house, the querist would suffer loss of wealth due to wasteful expenditure, and position, as well as disease in the leg and left eye, fall, sinful thoughts and activities. When a benefic is posited in the house, the man would spend money on charity and other philanthropic activities, be absolved of sins and ailments.

So far we have discussed good and bad effects of benefics and malefics occupying the 12 houses in a general manner. However, Varāhamihira has described in detail the specific effects of each planet occupying the 12 houses beginning with the ascendant in his *Horā* (Chapter XX)[1]. While studying the *Ārūḍha* and other *Bhāvas* in the query chart the astrologer ought to take into consideration all the detailed results described by the great astronomer.

External and Internal Houses

The Zodiacal chart has two classes of houses as (1) External, and (2) Internal. The significations connected with the body, viz. physical existence, family, brothers, kinsmen, children, enemies and wife belong to the external group while spiritual wealth, valour, happiness, wisdom, disease and passions are the internal houses. Whenever the houses are associated with their lords, we have to consider that they pertain to the internal houses; otherwise they are to be treated as external.

It is well-known that the limbs of the body represented by the 12 houses are the following:

(1) *Ārūḍha*—Head; (2) Second House—Face; (3) Third House—Neck; (4) Fourth House—Shoulders; (5) Fifth House—Heart; (6) Sixth House—Stomach; (7) Seventh House—Abdomen; (8) Eighth House—Privities; (9) Ninth House—Thighs; (10) Tenth House—Knees; (11) Eleventh House—Shanks; and (12) Twelfth House—Feet.

It may be remembered that the 12 signs beginning with Aries

1. Vide *Fundamentals of Astrology*, pp. 95-102.

represent the 12 limbs, head and others, of time or *Kāla-puruṣa.* One has to deduce the length of the limbs from the *Ārūḍha* and other houses. We have to apply the characteristics of the particular *Rāśis* in order to determine the length of the limbs.

The personal affairs of the querist have to be read from the *Ārūḍha-Lagna.* His financial position is to be studied from the 2nd house. Similarly other matters have to be inferred from the respective *Bhāvas.* Whichever *Bhāva* or its lord has benefic connection, will prosper. On the other hand, any *Bhāva* having malefic connection will suffer.

Measures of Signs

Aries and other *Rāśis* have been allotted respectively 20, 24, 28, 32, 36, 43, 40, 36, 32, 28, 24 and 20 units of measure. Whichever *Bhāva* has benefics in the 2nd and 12th, 7th, 4th and 10th houses, will prosper well. Malefics in the above houses with reference to any house would spoil that house.

In case the lord of the 6th, 8th or 12th *Bhāva* counted from the *Ārūḍha* or Ascendant, is inimical to the lord of the *Bhāva* in question, the significations of that *Bhāva* will suffer, even if these planets happen to be benefics. Similarly if a particular *Bhāva*, its lord and its significator are devoid of strength, that *Bhāva* will suffer. The same effect will follow, if the *Bhāva* is hemmed in between malefics, aspected by or conjoined with malefics or inimical planets. If there be no association or aspect of benefics or friendly planets, or if the 4th, 5th, 8th, 9th and 12th houses be occupied by malefics, the concerned *Bhāva* would be destroyed or damaged.

The effect of these malefics would be more pronounced in case these conditions are satisfied in more than one instance.

Significations of Planets

The Sun signifies: Father, spiritual powers, gold, wool and medicine.

The Moon ,, : Mind, mother, agriculture, water-products, and things connected with women.

Mars ,, : Brothers, strength, hand, metallurgy, violent acts.

Mercury signifies	:	Speech, knowledge, writing, mathematics, poetry, danoo and arts.
Jupiter	,, :	Wisdom, spiritual knowledge, progeny, physical happiness, brahmins, deities, scholars, mines.
Venus	,, :	Spouse, enjoyment of pleasures, vehicles.
Saturn	,, :	Disease, grief, servants, slaves, death.

If the significators be strong, their significations would thrive; on the other hand, if they be weak, the significations would be harmed. However, this rule does not apply to Saturn: If Saturn be strong, diseases, sorrow etc. would be felt very slightly. On the other hand, a weak Saturn would create untold suffering.

SIGNIFICATIONS OF PLANETS (DETAILED)

The Sun: East, Kailāsa, eastern regions of the Narmadā, Campāraṇya, eastern regions of the Dravidian country (China, Orissa, Assam), Prāgjyotiṣa (Kāmarūpa), Kāmboja country, the Yavana country. Southern Bank of the Yamunā, regions of the Vindhya forest, Goan country, number 20, wooden house, a house that is not sufficiently strong, Lord Rudra, father, minerals, roads, gold, copper, road-side objects, power, rays, Soul (*Ātman*), enthusiasm, light, senses of action, clouds, rain, mountain regions, strong trees, blooming, flame, collection, activities of sense-organs, wheat, fire, nails, thieves, spiritual lore, *Cakravāka* bird (ruddy goose), self-respect, brilliance or effulgence, lion, wild beasts, skin, journey, hot things, gems, electricity or lightning, worship of Śrī Rudra, devotees of Lord Gaṇapati, Śaivite people, president, king, grass, government, physicians, *Arka* plant, impenetrable path, medicines, firewood, thoroughfares, blanket, articles made of reeds, a period of six months, winter solstice, Sunday, lotus, lamp, enemy, money, courage, ruby, cereals, cowherds, neem tree, poison, predatory beast, a particular class of śūdras, quadrupeds, husbandmen, dense forest, poisonous snake etc.

The Moon: The Kosala country, Strīrājya (a country ruled by women), oceanic places, Rome, Yavana country, Cutch area, desert, snow-covered area, places of tribals, islands, North-West, mind, mental aberrations, sea-water, sea-bath, ebb and flow in the sea, joy and happiness, lily, conch-shell, salt, cotton, oils, liquids, sleep, bliss, enthusiasm, poesy, agriculture, husbandmen, food, eatables, moon-light, milk, ladies, physical charm, washerman, cold, snow, fisherman, rain-bearing cloud, milky tree, cow, lunacy, Mother Durgā, mother, Palāśa tree, rice, Śakti-worshippers, sacrificers, heaven, new house, soft-wood, number 1, jaggery, sugar, ghee, cold-fever, pearls, female-spells, sweets, water, gems, interest in sexual dalliance, white flowers, fruits, paddy, barley, white horse, those who drink Soma juice at sacrifices, royal descendants, Brāhmaṇas, cloths, horned animals, night wanderers, army commanders, those that covet beautiful women not belonging to them, women who show their clandestine love for other men, growth of crops, spirituous drinks like Āsavas, Ariṣṭas etc.

Mars: People living on the western half of the banks of the Narmadā, Śoṇa (Sone) and Bhīmarathī, the countries watered by the rivers Vetravatī, Godāvarī, Śiprā, Mandākinī, Mahānadī, Sindhu, Mālatī and Pārā, forest areas of Northern Pāṇḍya country, both the sides of the Vindhyas, regions in the neighbourhood of the Malaya mountain such as Mahendra mountain, the Cholas, Drāviḍas, Videhas, Āndhras, people of Bhāsāpura, Konkan, Kuntala and Kerala, Mlecchas, those who use the waters of the Tapatī and Gomatī, the regions of the Daṇḍaka Forest, city-dwellers, agriculturists, Śūdras, fire-workers, cooks, black-smiths, priests who perform sacrifices or Havanas, armed personnel of the army, foresters, postmen, those that go on errands, those that live inside forts and slopes, as well as in small towns, murderers, vain-glorious persons, sychophants, those who sing poems, vassal kings, princes, elephants, hypocrites, rioters, cowherds, gems, red-flowers, pearls, commanders, jaggery, liquor, cruel men, treasury, sacrificial house, mines, place used by Buddhist Bhikṣus, beggars, robbers, those that harbour hatred for long, gluttons, the number 2, tall body, southern direction, earth, stone, eating, famine, anger, lava volcano, Śakti (deity), Lord Skanda, surgeon lethal weapon, all kinds of machinery, brothers, blood, kitchen, perpetration of black-magic, revolution, wounds, goat, sheep, cock, jackal knowers of *Śāstras*, *Āḍhaka*, (Tuvar), thorny tree, Khadira tree, red colour, monkey, owl, landlord, boyhood, Cāmuṇḍā (a deity), physicist, ailment etc.

Mercury: Goa, Magadha country, plains of the Himālayas, Gangetic valleys, the eastern part of Mathurā, the country watered by the Indus and Kauśikī, the kingdom around the Citrakūṭa mountain, bridges, water-ways, market-place, burrows, caves, mountaineers, wells, water-pumps or piquotas, musicology, calligraphy, alphabet, lustre of gems, preparation of perfumes, portrait-painting, artists, grammarians, mathematicians, decoration, diviners, architects, tourists, fraudulent persons, lads, poets, proclaimers, informants, practitioners of black-magic, ambassadors, couriers, eunuchs, jestors, sorcerers, magicians, police personnel, actors, drama-troupes, ghee, oils, oil-seeds, bitter and astringent articles, those who observe vows, chemistry professors, donkey-riders, north, Vaikuṇṭha, incarnations of Lord Viṣṇu, seasons, intellectual eminence, number 9, fruitless trees, artist's workshop, the element earth, portents, green colour, snake-groud-curry, poem, intellectuals, kinsmen, friendship, vehicle, domestic animals, newspapers, periodicals, books, post office, control, pregnancy, house, house with many artistic designs, village officer, accountant, lawyer, astrologer, maternal uncle, scholar, emerald, literature and co-operation.

Jupiter: Eastern part of the Indus, Western half of Mathurā, the country of Sauvīra, regions on the banks of the rivers Vipāśā (Beas) and Śatadru (Sutlej), the Sālva country, Paurava country, Sārasvata regions (of the river Sarasvatī), one-half of the Matsya country, priests, elephants, horses, king, minister, auspicious objects, those engaged in progressive activities, compassion, truth, cleanliness, observance of vows, imparting education, philanthropic work, citizens, wealthy persons, philologists, economists, scholars in Vedas and systems of philosophy, experts in black-magic, royal insignia, stones, Bitumen, Jatāmāṃsi, Tagara, Kaṅkuṣṭha, juicy substances, marine-products, creeper-produce sweet taste, honey, Viśvedevas, Viṣṇu, Brahmā, deities of different sects or faiths, the number 18, month, north-east, Veda, various mantras, kindly disposition, the world of Brahman, fruit-laden tree, the element ether, herbs, seeds, progeny, son, devotion, knowledge, eloquence, worship, Vedānta philosophy, great eclat, orthodox life, dispassion, rainfall, court of justice, judge, teachers, professors, brāhmaṇas, ministers, the Aśvattha tree, Bengal-gram, tranquillity, swan, dove, conduct, wealth, aeroplanes, work relating to space, radio, cereals, fruits, respect, fame, status quo, protection, telephone, production, a Vaiṣṇava ascetic, Purāṇas advice, sacrifice, yellow robes, gold, success in mantra, hatred of people of other sects, Puṣyarāga gem (Topas). Jagadgurus, temple-worshippers, benediction, blessing.

Venus: Takṣaśilā, Gāndhāra (Kandahar), the countries of Kaikaya, Śibi, and those watered by the rivers Vitastā, Vipāśā, Irāvatī, and Candrabhāgā, chariots, silver, elephants, horses, very powerful mantras, opulent persons, pleasure-seekers, fragrant flowers, sandal paste, and such other scented things, gems, diamonds, decorative objects, lotus, couch, a nice young man or women, erotic appurtenances, sumptuous food, sweet dishes, garden, water, libidinous persons, fame, happiness, generosity, excellent features, learned person, minister, trader, business transaction, potter, colourful objects, birds, nutmeg, myrobalan, triphala, silk-cloth, fine rugs, leaf, paper, wool, lodhra bark, clove, agaru (agallochum), roots of the fragrant grass, long pepper, south-eastern quarter, heaven, woman, peacock, all kinds of ornaments, rain-water, sexual union, conjugal life, secrets of love-lorn women, *Niṣpāva* (variety of beans), balance sports, privities, pleasure-garden, wife, edibles, marriage, seat, cot, cow, milk, technical education, musical instruments, weaver, fig tree, manager, vehicular traffic, dramatic performance, talkies, palanquin, the number 20, sorcery, a fortnight, a beautiful house, goddess Annapūrṇeśvarī, Lakṣmī, a yakṣī, one-eyed person, Śaiva saints, fine arts, worshippers of mother goddess.

Saturn: Western bank of the Sarasvatī river, Kurukṣetra, Prabhāsa (in Gujarat), Vidiśā (in M.P.), people on the banks of the Vetravatī, Saurāṣṭra country, wicked or criminal tribes, dirty persons, those anointed with oil, weaklings, eunuchs, incarceration, those who prophesy the future from omens, slums or dirty things, sailors, ugly persons, aged men, pigsty owners, hunters, those who observe no principles or vows, archers, indigent persons, bitter taste, astringent taste, widow, snake, thief, buffalo, donkey, elephant calf, young camel, forest grain

(Nīvāra), sesamum, rheumatic patients, wind, western quarter, city of Yama, workers, punishment, wages, longevity, diseases, servitude, false deposition, Śūdra classes, fright, portents, death, humiliation, debts, sleep, indolence, fraud, carrying loads, coarse arts, agricultural implements, ploughs, jealousy, art of gambling, black colour, darkness, soft wood, lead, accidents, naked person, despicable woman, renovated house, ascetics, groups of minor deities, enmity, Lord Śastāra, unworthy conduct, censure, number 50, Sapphire, Śamī tree, murderers, those that live by the sweat of their brows.

Rāhu: Summits of mountains, valleys, Dravidian country, south-western quarter, poison, serpent, anthill, far-off islands, grandfather, policy of sowing seeds of dissensions between a woman and her husband, falling into hell, grass called Dūrvā, black-gram, barbarians, burnt meat, Śūdra, thief, falsehood, pollution, handicapped man, one devoid of religious merit, blot to family, Arabs, practice of black-magic, curses, demon, animals that sleep too long, one without charity, truncated person, epilepsy, the gem called Gomedhika, hot-tempered person, one who rides a donkey, foetus, jackal, expert in single combat, one who suffers attacks by others, followers of other faiths, atheists, Lord Skanda etc.

Ketū: Dravidian country, hills and forests, pits, south-west, the deity called Kṣetrapāla, Lord Gaṇapati, headless body, horse-gram, sacred grass (*darbha*), white-skinned people, hell, black magic, Huns, Coḷas, Afghans, excessive greed, agriculture operations, emancipation, discarnate spirits, religious imposters, paramours, maternal grandfather, disputants, arrogance, jealous persons, groups of low-class deities, Caṇḍālas, smoke, flag, people of some parts of China, those who live in the frontiers, *lapis lazuli* etc.

Some more details about the divine planets are given hereunder for the benefit of readers:

The Sun: He was born at Kaliṅga Deśa in the gotra (family) of Sage Kaśyapa (gotra is inherited both by descendants and disciples). He is represented as one wearing a crown on his head. Among the group of planets the Sun's image is kept at the centre of a square platform, facing the east. He is represented by a circular diagram. His companions are Agni

(Fire) and Rudra. His consorts are (1) *Chāyā* and (2) *Saṃjñā*. He is worshipped in the above diagram over a heap of barley (wheat) with red flowers and coloured rice (*Akṣatas*).

The Moon: She was born on the banks of the Yamunā river, in the gotra of sage Atri. She is installed to the south-east of the Sun and worshipped in a square diagram over a heap of *Śyāmāka* (a variety of forest corn) or rice with white flowers and rice grains, accompanied by water and Gaurī.

Mars: He was born in the country of Avantī in the gotra of Sage Bharadvāja and installed to the south of the Sun. He is worshipped in a triangular diagram over a heap of *Āḍhaka* (a pulse called Tuvar in Hindi) along with Earth and Kṣetrapati (two deities) with red flowers and coloured rice.

Mercury: He was born in the Magadha-country in the gotra of Sage Atri. He is installed to the Sun's north-east: and is worshipped in an arrow-shaped diagram over a heap of green-gram along with *Viṣṇu*, with yellow flowers and coloured rice.

Jupiter: He was born in the Sindhu country in the gotra of Sage Aṅgiras and is installed to the north of the Sun and worshipped in a rectangular diagram over a heap of Bengal-gram along with Indra and Brahmā, with yellow flowers and coloured rice.

Venus: He was born in the Bhojakaṭa country in the gotra of Sage Bhṛgu and is installed to the east of the Sun and worshipped in a pentagonal diagram over a heap of Niṣpāva pulse (or rice) along with Indrānī and Indra with white flowers and rice.

Saturn: He was born in the gotra of sage Kaśyapa and in the Saurāṣṭra region of modern Gujarat and is installed to the Sun's west, and worshipped in a bow-shaped diagram over a heap of sesamum seeds, along with Prajāpati (creator) and Yama (god of death), with black flowers and rice grains.

Rāhu: He was born in the Siṃhala (or Virāṭa) country in the gotra of Sage Paiṭhīnasi and is installed to the Sun's south-west, and worshipped in a diagram shaped like a winnowing basket (Śūrpa), over a heap of black-gram along with Sūrpa and N irṛti, with black flowers and rice grains.

Ketu: He was born in the Antarvedī country in the gotra of Sage Jaimini, and is installed to the north-west of the Sun and worshipped in a diagram shaped like a flag, over a heap of horse gram along with Brahmā and Citragupta, with ash-coloured flowers and rice grains. According to some Ketu may be propitiated by means of the gift of jaggery or salt.

Benefics: The Moon in strength, unafflicted Mercury, Jupiter and Venus are natural benefics.

Malefics: Mars, Saturn, Rāhu, Ketu and the Sun are natural malefics. The Moon becomes malefic, when she is weak. For benefics the 3rd, 6th, 8th and 12th houses are not favourable, and the rest favourable. On the other hand, malefics are good in the 3rd, 6th and 11th houses. However, in the case of a query relating to disease, a malefic in the 6th house cannot but yield only untoward results. Hence in effect, malefics would yield only bad results in the 6th house. So we have to infer that benefics increase the prosperity of the *Bhāva* they occupy, whereas malefics destroy it. Benefics posited in the 6th remove troubles from enemies. Neither benefics nor malefics are good in the 8th and 12th houses. Though malefics are strong and beneficial in the 6th house and may produce good results in respect of their significations such as copper and gold, yet in the matter of queries about illness they cannot cure diseases; but will aggravate them.

The net result, therefore, is that malefics in the 6th house are not at all beneficial.

The good and bad effects of planetary *Daśās* that are mentioned with respect to natal horoscopes, are to be applied to the horary chart also. For example, Varāhamihira states (in VIII-12): "If the Sun is good, he will bestow in his major and minor periods *Daśā* and *Antardaśā*) wealth through perfumes, claws (of animals), tusks, skins, gold, cruel deeds, roads, kings, and battles. He will also make the native high-minded, brave, active and famous. If the Sun be untoward, one would have to apprehend dangers through his wife, sons, wealth, enemies, weapons, fire or king. He would renounce everything, do wicked deeds, quarrel with servants and suffer from diseases of the heart or stomach." When you consider any *Bhāva* (house) counted from the natal or horary ascendant, you have to find out if at a particular time the Lord of the 8th *Bhāva*, counted from the reference *Bhāva*, or Saturn arrives in transit at that

Bhāva, or if the *Daśā* or *Bhukti* of the lord of the 6th, 8th, or 12th *Bhāva* or of the planets posited in those *Bhāvas* (counted from the *Bhāva* under consideration) is operating at the time, it is pretty certain that that *Bhāva*, i.e. things signified by that *Bhāva*, will be destroyed. So also one ought to predict that the limb or part of the body signified by the *Bhāva* is diseased.

Characteristics of Planets

The Sun has reddish-brown eyes and a square-built body. He is of a bilious temperament and has a limited quantity of hair.

The Moon has a thin and round body, has wind and phlegm in her constitution. She is learned, soft in speech and of attractive eyes.

Mars has fierce looks, short stature, youthful appearance, and a generous disposition. He is bilious in nature and exceedingly fickle and has a slender waist.

Mercury is always fond of fun and uses punning words. He has all the three humours in his constitution. He is of medium height and dark in complexion. He has slightly reddish eyes.

Jupiter has a big body, and brown eyes and hair. He is exceedingly intelligent and wise. He is phlegmatic in nature.

Venus is ever fond of ease, possessed of a beautiful body and charming eyes. He has both wind and phlegm in his constitution, and has black curly hair.

Saturn is disposed to indolence, tall in stature, with eyes of a reddish-brown colour, large teeth and coarse hair. He is windy in constitution.

The seven planets from the Sun represent the following physical constitutents in order: (1) Bones; (2) Blood; (3) Marrow; (4) Skin; (5) Fate; (6) Semen; and (7) Muscles.

The Sun represents a brahmin. a king or a śūdra government; the Moon, a brahmin or a vaiśya; Mars, a brahmin as well as a śūdra; Mercury, a śūdra. or vaiśya; Jupiter a śūdra or one of the depressed class. In case the concerned planet is debilitated, in an inimical sign (or *Aṃśa*) or combust, it would always stand for one of the lower caste. On the other hand, should the Sun be possessed of the strength of exaltation. or own house, we have to infer a king. Similarly, if the Sun be posited in a brahmin sign, viz. Cancer, Scorpio or Pisces, or aspected by a brahmin planet a brahmin should be predicted. If he is posited in a friendly sign or *Aṃśa*, a Governor of śūdra caste would be indicated. If the Moon be very powerful, aspected by Jupiter and posited in a Jovian sign, then too a brahmin would be understood. Likewise, a strong Mars aspected by Jupiter would point to a brahmin. A strong Saturn represents a śūdra, while a weak one, a person of the depressed class. In this manner the distinction of castes has to be made on the basis of the sign posited by and strength of the planets concerned.

When the treat of queries regarding lost or missing articles, Jupiter, and Mercury are to be considered as residents of a village; the Moon and Venus, as those places near water; and the rest viz. the Sun, Mars and Saturn residents of forests.

The residential localities assigned to the zodiacal signs are the following: Virgo, Libra, and Sagittarius represent urban area; Aries, Taurus, Gemini and Aquarius, village; Leo and the first half of Capricorn, forest area; and lastly Cancer, Scorpio, 2nd half of Capricorn and Pisces, an area surrounded by water, or near a lake.

The area allotted to a planet that is termed *Coragraha* denotes the thief's place of birth; while the sign he occupies, his present residence. In this manner the birth place and present residence of the thief may be determined. In case the area of residence allotted to the planet and the Rāśi happen to be identical, then the thief must be adjudged as residing in the same place as his birth-place.

If the *Coragraha* happens to be the Moon, the thief should be moving from a village to the woods; while Venus would indicate that the fellow is moving from the forest to a village. Venus also suggests a thief moving across shallow waters (wading through a shallow stream). In the case of the Moon, the thief moves across the ocean (i.e. goes abroad). Rāhu would suggest one who moves amidst anthills, pits, caves (like the Chambal ravines), pools, marshy land etc. The Sun would point to the person's movement in a forest, while Saturn shows movements in a cremation ground, or a dense, impenetrable forest; and Mars' movement would be among bushes (or bowers of creepers) on the hills or mountains.

Parts of the Body and the Planets

The following information is strictly confined to the system of Horary Astrology prevalent in Kerala:

Mars represents the head, Venus—face, Mercury—neck, throat, Moon—chest, Sun—heart, Jupiter—thighs, Saturn—knees, Rāhu—shanks.

If these planets be strong, the particular limbs represented by them, would be handsome, well-formed and decorated with ornaments. On the other hand, should they be weak, the concerned limbs would become ill-formed, defective or diseased or be having scars.

How to Distinguish the Sides?

Find out the Decanate occupied by a planet and then see if it is posited in the first 5° portion or the second. If it be in the first half of the decanate, it should be said that the limb denoted is on the left side; otherwise, it would be the right side of it. According to another view, the decanate is to be divided into three equal parts of 3° 20′ each. If the planet should occupy the first part, i.e. *Navāṃśa*, then the upper part of the limb should be thought of. If it be the second part, its central part; and if it be the last part, its lower part. If the angles are occupied by planets, find out if any one of them occupies his own direction (allotted to the planet), and declare the results on that basis.

If any *Bhāva* denoting a particular limb be occupied by three malefics, one could definitely declare that the particular limb would be having some injury, defect, scar, dart or mole. In the same manner, if benefics be posited, that part of the body should be declared to be handsome, well-formed and decorated with jewels. We have already seen the shapes of the planets, and their habitats.

In the case of a query relating to an article held in the fist, the planet posited in the ascendant or the 7th house has to be examined. The object concerned would have its shape corresponding to that of the planet.

Habitats of Signs

Cancer, Scorpio and Pisces have forest infested with reptiles. Virgo, Libra and Sagittarius (2nd half) urban area.

Aries, Taurus, Gemini and Aquarius—rural area.

Leo and Capricorn (Ist half): forest area.

Animals represented by Planets: Saturn and Mercury—birds. Moon—reptile. Jupiter and Venus—Bipeds—human beings. Sun and Mars—quadrupeds (the former herbivorous animals and the latter carnivorous ones). Some more details of the animals are given hereunder:

Aries rules wild animals.

Animals Ruled by Planets

The Sun rules the group of powerful animals headed by the lion. The Moon rules quiet animals like the hare. Mars rules cruel ones like the tiger. Mercury owns the class headed by the boar. Jupiter presides over the group led by horses and elephants. Venus rules those headed by the deer. Saturn presides over the group of monkeys, donkeys and camels. Rāhu rules the group led by the alligator. Both the Sun and Saturn represent biped creatures; the Moon and Mercury, six-footed creatures; Mars and Jupiter, quadrupeds; and Venus and Rāhu, eight-footed creatures (e.g. the octopus).

The Signs: Aries, Taurus, Leo and Sagittarius rule quadrupeds. When some planets occupy certain signs, particular animals are to be understood as given below. If the Sun be in Sagittarius, one should think of the elephant; if the Sun be in Aries or Leo, you should think of the lion; if he be in Taurus, think of the deer.

The Moon in Sagittarius points to a horse.
,, ,, ,, Leo ,, ,, a lion.
,, ,, ,, Aries ,, ,, a goat.
,, ,, ,, Taurus ,, ,, a bull or cow.

Mars in Sagittarius points to a horse.
,, ,, Leo ,, ,, a tiger.
,, ,, Aries ,, ,, a goat.
,, ,, Taurus ,, ,, a bull.

Mercury in Sagittarius or Leo points to a porcupine, some wild animal or monkey. The same result has to be predicted for Mercury in Aries and Taurus also.

Jupiter in Sagittarius points to a horse.

Jupiter	in	Leo	points to a	camel.
,,	,,	Aries and Taurus	,, ,,	camel and donkey.
Venus	,,	Sagittarius	,, ,,	horse.
,,	,,	Leo and Aries	,, ,,	elephant and donkey.
,,	,,	Taurus	,, ,,	bison.
Saturn	,,	Sagittarius	,, ,,	elephant.
,,	,,	Leo	,, ,,	bear.
,,	,,	Aries	,, ,,	buffalo.
,,	,,	Taurus	,, ,,	she-buffalo.

(*Note*: According to the *Kṛṣṇīya* the first half and the latter half of Capricorn and Sagittarius respectively are termed Mṛga or quadruped.) In respect of queries of hunting and bagging beasts, the astrologer should declare the sight of such animals as are prescribed for the planets posited in the *Ārūḍha Lagna*, Kendras and *Trines* which planet is associated with or aspected by *Māndi*, the animal represented by that planet will be killed. Minerals, roots and living beings are signified by the planets and the Zodiacal signs as follows:

Planets		*Signs*	*Objects signified*
1. The Moon, Mars Rāhu and Saturn	:	Aries, Cancer, Libra and Capricorn	*dhātu* or metals
2. The Sun and Venus	:	Taurus, Leo, Scorpio and Aquarius	roots or mūla
3. Mercury and Jupiter	:	Gemini, Virgo, Sagittarius and Pisces	*Jīva* or living beings

There is another view about planetary significations:

Jupiter signifies living beings.
Mars and Rāhu —metallic objects.
The Sun —metallic objects
Saturn —roots or trees.

Planetary Relationship

No.	Planets	Friends	Enemies	Neutrals
1	Sun	Jupiter	Mercury and Rāhu	Moon, Mars, Venus, Saturn
2	Moon	Jupiter, Mercury	Mars	Sun, Venus, Saturn, Rāhu and Ketu
3	Mars	Mercury, Venus	Jupiter	Sun, Moon, Saturn, Rāhu, Ketu
4	Mercury	Nil	Sun	The Rest
5	Jupiter	Sun	Mars	The Rest
6	Venus	Nil	Sun and Moon	The Rest
7	Saturn	Mercury, Jupiter, Venus, Rāhu, Ketu	—	—
8	Rāhu	Mars, Mercury, Jupiter, Venus, Saturn	Sun and Moon	—
9	Ketu	Moon, Venus	The Rest	—

Mūla-Trikoṇas of Planets

Planets	Sun	Moon	Mars	Mercury	Jupiter	Venus	Saturn
Mūla-Trikona	Leo	Taurus	Aries	Virgo	Sagittarius	Libra	Aquarius

There is another kind of relationship called temporary friendship and temporary enmity. Temporary enemies are those planets that are posited in the 6th, 5th, 9th, 8th and 7th houses from a particular planet as well as those posited in the same place, whereas those posited in the 2nd, 3rd and 4th houses as well as in the 10th, 11th and 12th houses are temporary friends.

Both Mercury and Jupiter posited in the Ascendant attain

strength, while the Sun and Mars as well as quadruped signs do it when they occupy the 10th house. Venus and the Moon as well as watery signs attain strength in the 4th house. Lastly Saturn and Rāhu as well as the signs designated as Kīṭa *Rāśis* attain strength in the 7th house. Sign Cancer is strong both as the 4th house and the 7th house, because it is both a Kīṭa *Rāśi* and Watery Sign.

Jupiter	is strong	in the fore-noon	Day time
The Sun	,,	at noon	
Saturn	,,	in the afternoon	
Mercury	,,	both in the day and night	Night time
The Moon	,,	in the first half of the night	
Mars	,,	at midnight	
Venus	,,	in the latter half of the night	
All the Benefics	are strong	in the bright fortnight	
All the Malefics	,, ,,	,, ,, dark ,,	

The Sun is strong in the winter solstice (*Uttarāyaṇa*)
A planet becomes strong from the time it begins or stops its retrograde motion.

In a planetary war that planet becomes victorious or strong, which is full of bright rays, moves in a dextral manner around the other planet, as well as the one that moves to the north of the other. In a horoscopic chart the six houses beginning with the 10th and ending with the 3rd house, are considered strong, while the rest viz. from the 4th to the 9th house, weak. The ascendant becomes strong when it is aspected or occupied by Jupiter, Mercury or its own lord. The six signs beginning with Leo are strong by day, while those beginning with Aquarius are strong at night. The signs that happen to be the Ascendant are of utmost strength. Those *Rāśis* that become *Kendras* beyond the ascendant are of moderate strength, while those *Kendras* prior to the ascending sign are deficient in strength. The Ascendant conjoined with the waning Moon as well as a biped sign, is strong in day time, while others (i.e. Quadruped ones) become strong at night. Both signs and Planets termed Kīṭa are strong at twilight. Planetary strength is derived from four sources: (1) *Sthāna* or position, (2) *Āśraya* or resort, (3) Time and (4) *Ceṣṭā* or motion. The first is based on the positions of planets such as own house, exaltation, own decanate etc. The second is based on the signs that happen to be ascendant, *Kendra*, *Panaphara*, *Āpoklima* etc. The third is derived from the time, i.e. day, night or twilight. The last one is based on the motion of planets e.g. the Sun and the Moon get excellent *Ceṣṭābala* in their northern course, while others in their retrograde motion. They have yet another four-fold source of strength based upon (1) *Tātkālika* (temporary or transitory), (2) *Naisargika* (natural), (3) *Sāmpātika* (concurrent), and (4) Relations as friendly, inimical and neutral.

Temporary strength is spoken of when the ascendant gets strength owing to its conjunction with the Moon. The second viz. natural strength, is seen in the statement that among the planets Saturn, Mars, Mercury, Jupiter, Venus, the Moon and the Sun each succeeding planet is more powerful by nature than its predecessor. The third type of strength has already been referred to in connection with the concurrent or *Sāmpātika* source. The type of planetary friendship termed temporary also comes under the same category. These eight sources of strength of planets have to be carefully noted both in natal charts and horary ones. We have just seen their natural and relative types of strength. Literally construed it would mean that of all the planets the Sun is supremely strong. Actually, it means that comparison of planetary strength should be resorted to only when their strength is of equal degree. For example, if the Moon be very weak or the Sun debilitated and afflicted, we could not give credit to either of them in preference to Jupiter or Venus.

The exaltation signs of the seven planets beginning with the Sun and their highest exaltation degrees are given hereunder: (1) Aries—10°; (2) Taurus—3°; (3) Capricorn—28°; (4) Virgo—15°; (5) Cancer—5°; (6) Pisces—27° and (7) Libra—20°. The debilitation signs of the planets are the 7th *Rāśis* from their respective exaltation signs and the lowest degrees of debilitation are the same as for exaltation.

Should one, two, three or four planets be in their exaltation in a person's chart, the results would be in order (1) a very happy person; (2) one who achieves great tasks; (3) one equal to a king; and (4) a great king. If more planets be in exaltation, the native would be a veritable divine being.

Mode of Rising of Signs

The twelve signs of the Zodiac are divided into three categories as (1) *Pṛṣṭhodaya* (those that rise with their hind part first); (2) *Śīrṣodaya* (those that rise with their head foremost) and (3) *Ubhayodaya* (those that rise bothways): (1) The signs Aries, Taurus, Cancer, Sagittarius and Capricorn rise with their back foremost; (2) the rest except Pisces are termed *Śīrṣodaya* or those that rise with their head foremost. In other words Gemini, Leo, Virgo, Libra, Scorpio and Aquarius are *Śīrṣodaya* signs. (3) Pisces alone is termed *Ubhayodaya*, one that rises both ways. The purpose of this distinction is to enable the astrologer to predict different results for different types of *Rāśis* that rise differently. At a query relating to progressive works a sign that rises with 'head in front' would suggest success and prosperity, while a *Rāśi* that rises with its hind part first would denote success in matters of destructive, separative or disintegrating nature. If the rising sign be an *Ubhayodaya* one (rising both ways like Pisces) success would be partial or delayed. This rule about the mode of rising of *Rāśis* should be applied only when the particular sign is devoid of planets. On the other hand, if it be occupied by one or more planets, prediction should be made through the planets.

(1) Stature of zodiacal signs: The following signs are of moderate stature, i.e. they are neither too tall nor too short: Cancer, Capricorn, Gemini, and Sagittarius.

(2) The following are short: Aries, Taurus, Aquarius and Pisces.

(3) The following *Rāśis* are tall or long: Leo, Virgo, Libra and Scorpio.

(a) Measures of *Rāśis* that are of moderate stature: Cancer —32; Capricorn—28; and Sagittarius—32.

(b) Measures of short stature: Aries—20; Taurus—24; Aquarius—24; and Pisces—20.

(c) Measures of *Rāśis* of tall stature: Leo—36; Virgo—40; Libra—40; and Scorpio—36.

Similarly there are three kinds of signs viz. (1) those with upward-looks; (2) those with downward-looks; and (3) those with side-long looks. (a) The signs left behind by the Sun and its angles are called upward-looking signs; (b) the signs presently occupied by the Sun and its angles are called downward looking signs; and (c) the *Rāśis* to be tenanted by the Sun and its angles are known as signs with side-long looks.

When the Ascendant at a query is an upward-looking sign, the querist's wishes would be fulfilled. In the case of the other two varieties success would not be achieved. However, they too would be beneficial, if the ascendant be associated with or aspected by benefics. In a query of theft, should the Ascendant happen to be an upward-looking *Rāśi*, the stolen article must have been kept above. The thief must have entered the house by removing the tiles of the roof. If it be a downward-looking *Rāśi*, that object was buried underground. If it be a sideways-looking sign, the object was kept on the ground itself and the thief must have entered the house by breaking the door or making a hole in the wall. The stolen article must have been kept, in the three cases, above the ground, underground and on the ground respectively.

Planets with the above special looks: (1) The Sun and Mars have upward looks; Venus and Mercury, sidelong looks; Jupiter and the Moon, straight looks; Saturn and Rāhu, downward looks.

Elements and Planets: Mercury rules the earth; Venus—water; Mars—fire; Saturn—air; and Jupiter—ether. The signs owned by the different planets have the same elements as their lords.

The above discussion of the elements would help us in finding out lost articles or those hidden in the fist: An astrologer should be able to predict the type of stolen object and its place from the element belonging to the particular planet.

The place where the stolen article has been hidden is to be deduced from the sign representing the 7th house, and through the planet aspecting and occupying the 7th house.

If the ascendant at a query be a movable sign, with upward looks and one rising with its head foremost, the astrologer should think that the query about disease is located above the neck and in a part of the head. Should the *Lagna* happen to be a stable sign with sidelong looks, and one rising both ways, the illness should be declared to be located in the region between the neck and the waist. If the Ascendant be a *Rāśi* with downward looks and a *Pṛṣṭhodaya* sign, the ailment should be located below the waist.

There is a difference between natal and horary astrology with regard to the location of the afflicted or ailing limb: In nativity decanates are employed to locate the limb; whereas in queries the method explained above should be made use of. If the Sun be weak, and if the signs and *Aṃśas* be of different types (such as movable etc.), then the criteria based on the *Pṛṣṭhodaya* etc. should be adopted. The weak points of the Sun are the last decanate of Virgo, Ist decanate and Ist *Navāṃśa* of Libra.

Regarding the delineation of limbs the basis is the number of degrees that has elapsed in the ascendant and other houses. At a query, however, that part of the ascendant which has already risen above the horizon should be taken as the left side of the limb concerned, while in the 7th house this rule is reversed. Suppose the part that is to be declared is the head above the neck, then the degrees yet to be covered in the *Lagna* should represent the right side of the head. The second house would then represent the right ear; the third house, the right eye. In this manner the limbs are to be predicted and studied. The following table would make the idea clear:

I House, yet to be covered	right side of the head (above the neck).
House already covered	left side of the head (above the neck).
II House — —	light ear.
III ,, — —	light eye.
IV ,, — —	right nostril.
V House — —	right check.
VI ,, — —	right chin.
VII House, yet to be covered	left side of the mouth.
—Do— already covered	right side of the mouth.
VIII ,, — —	left side of the chin.
IX ,, — —	left side of the check.
X ,, — —	left nostril.
XI ,, — —	left eye.
XII ,, — —	left ear.

In the case of the central portion of the body the ascendant represents the neck. The covered part of the *Lagna* denotes left side of the neck, and the portion yet to be covered, its right side.

II and XII	Houses—right and left shoulders respectively.	
III and XI	Houses—right and left arms.	
IV and X	Houses—right and left sides of the body.	
V and IX	Houses—right and left sides of the heart.	
VI and VIII	Houses—right and left portions of the stomach.	
VII House (yet to be covered)		—left side of the hip.
VII House (already covered)		—right side of the hip.

In the case of the lower part of the body, the ascendant represents that part below the navel (abdomen).

I House	(yet to be covered)	—right side of the abdomen.
House	(alredy covered)	—left side of the abdomen.
II and XII Houses	,,	—right and left sides of the genital organ (including the anus).
III and XI	,,	—right and left testicles.
IV and X	,,	—right and left thighs.
V and IX	,,	—right and left knees.
VI and VIII	,,	—right and left shanks.
VII House (already covered)		—left foot (sole).
House (yet to be covered)		—right foot (sole).

At a query of illness the physician is represented by the ascendant; ailment by the 7th house; the patient by the 10th house; medicine by the 4th house. If there be friendship between the patient and the physician, or between illness and medicine, there would be recovery of the patient. On the other hand, if they be enemies, the ailment would be aggravated.

COLOURS OF PLANETS

The sun and other planets possess the following colours in order: Sun—saffron; Moon—white; Mars—red; Mercury—green; Jupiter—golden yellow; Venus—colourful; and Saturn—black.

When a planet is in his own house, exaltation or in strength, it retains its natural qualities including its colour. If it be weak, it would absorb the qualities of the *Rāśi* it tenants. If the *Rāśi* is strong, then its colour becomes predominant.

Colours of Rāśis: The first four signs viz. Aries, Taurus,

Gemini and Cancer, have the colours of their respective lords, i.e. red, colourful, green and white. This rule applies to the trines of these signs also.

Other Qualities of Planets: The Sun, Mars and Saturn are dry in nature; Venus, and the Moon are wet in nature; and Mercury and Jupiter have the nature of the *Rāśi* they occupy, even if they are strong or weak.

Other Qualities of Rāśis: Taurus, Cancer, Libra, Scorpio, Capricorn, Aquarius and Pisces are wet in nature (Water). Aries, Gemini, Leo, Virgo and Sagittarius are dry in nature (Land).

The above-mentioned information would be useful in a query relating to the availability of water at a high or low level of the well to be sunk. If the *Ārūḍha* be a wet sign occupied by a dry planet, the result would be that the water would be found at some depth. On the other hand, should a wet planet be posited in a dry sign, there would be a superficial water-vein, but not at lower depths. If both the planet and *Rāśi* be wet in nature, there would be plenty of water in the well. If both be dry, there would be no trace of water. This rule may be applied to queries about rains. In this case we need the information about *Vīthī* and *Chatra Rāśi* also.

Vīthī and *Chatra*: When the Sun is in Taurus, Gemini, Cancer or Leo, Aries becomes the *Vīthī Rāśi* (Avenue sign). When the Sun is in Libra, Virgo, Pisces or Aries, Taurus becomes the *Vīthī*. When the Sun is in Scorpio, Sagittarius, Capricorn or Aquarius, Gemini becomes the *Vīthī*.

Chatra: Count the numer of signs from the *Ārūḍha* to the Ascendant *Rāśi*. Now count so many signs from the *Vīthī Rāśi*. The resulting *Rāśi* becomes the *Chatra Raśi* (umbrella sign). This method is adopted when the *Ārūḍha* is powerful.

In case the ascendant *Rāśi* be more powerful, the *Navāṃśa Lagna* becomes the *Chatra Rāśi*. This is the opinion of Kṛṣṇācārya.

Periods of Planets

Sun—6 months; Moon—a short while (*Kṣaṇa*); Mars—1 day; Mercury—2 months; Jupiter—1 month; Venus—15 days; Saturn—1 year.

How to use this? If the concerned planet to bestow the fruit of the query be the Sun, then find out the Sun's *Navāṃśa* sign. The accomplishment or otherwise would take place in so many 6 month-periods. For example, if the Sun be in the 5th *Navāṃśa*, the result would be realized in 30 months.

Another method of fixing the time of fruition is given below: When the concerned planet transits the *Lagna* or his own house or his exaltation, the result of the query would be realized.

The past experience of the querist will have to be stated through the *Rāśi* that has already risen. In the ascendant itself that portion which has already risen would give the immediate past good or bad results, depending upon the planet posited therein. Similarly the immediate future should be read from the portion of the *Lagna* that is yet to rise. Similarly, the past, present and future would be denoted by the planets that are posited (i) between the 10th house and 7th house, (ii) the 7th and 4th house, and (iii) the 4th and the Ascendant.

PLANETARY ASPECTS

Please note that in horary science the aspectarian pattern is slightly different: Planets do not aspect the following houses from the one occupied by them—2nd, 6th, 11th, 12th houses. The remaining houses they do aspect. In other words, they aspect only seven houses. For, no planet aspects the house occupied by it.

Regarding the aspect of planets, whatever effects are attributed to their aspects, only a half of those effects they are said to produce when they are posited in the trines, i.e. 5th and 9th houses. On the other hand, they produce full results when they are posited in the 7th house; 75 per cent results in the 4th houses; and only 1/4 of the result in the 10th house. This information would stand an astrologer in good stead in finding out what part of the lost or stolen article or money could be recovered.

At this juncture it would be very profitable for students of astrology to know the rays or *Raśmis* of the different planets: According to the *Kṛṣṇīya* the rays of the planets are as follows: Sun—25. Moon 91. Mars—25. Mercury—74. Jupiter—60. Venus—76. Saturn—25.

According to the *Naṣṭapraśnadīpikā* they are in order (1) 30; (2) 28; (3) 8; (4) 6; (5) 9; (6) 7; (7) 3; and (8) 2 (each).

Kṛṣṇācārya adds that a planet posited in his own house gets his rays doubled; in his exaltation, four-fold. One in retrograde motion also gets his rays four times the usual number. One in *Mūla-Trikoṇa* gets it trebled. A malefic posited in the 7th house loses $\frac{1}{6}$ of his rays; one (malefic) in the 8th house loses $\frac{1}{8}$ of his rays; one in the 9th house loses $\frac{1}{4}$ of his rays; one in the 10th loses $\frac{1}{3}$ of his rays; one in the 11th house loses $\frac{1}{2}$ of the rays.

According to another authority the rays are in order 5, 21, 7, 9, 10, 16 and 4. When Mars is posited in the *Lagna*, he aspects all his 7 rays. In the 3rd and 11th houses he aspects only a fourth of his rays, i.e. $\frac{7}{4} = 1\frac{3}{4}$ rays. When he is in trine (5th and 9th) he aspects $\frac{7}{2} + 3 = 6\frac{1}{2}$ rays. And when he is in the 4th house, he aspects $4\frac{1}{2}$ rays. Similarly Mars in the 7th house fully aspects all his rays. In the 10th house he aspects only two rays; and in the 9th house, half of his rays, i.e. $\frac{7}{2}$. This example of Mars is to be taken in the case of all planets, the only difference being their natural rays. These numbers of rays are to be made use of in queries regarding lost articles as explained below:

A planet posited in a friendly house would yield only $\frac{1}{4}$ effect; one in own house, $\frac{3}{4}$ effect; one in exaltation would yield results in full measure, and one in trines (5th and 9th), $\frac{1}{2}$ effect. The rays of debilitated planets are utterly null and void. Even so are those that are posited in inimical houses and those that are defeated in planetary war. In a query of loss the number of fruitless rays would give the number of stolen articles or fruits or crops. On the other hand, the querist would get back the number of articles indicated by the total number of rays aspected by benefics.

Ages of Planets

Mars is a sucking baby, i.e. aged about three years. Venus is 16 years in age. Mercury is 8 years. Jupiter is 30 years; the Moon is 70 years old and the Sun 50 years. Saturn and *Rāhu*, 100 years (or 120 years, according to some). The age of the ruling planet is to be assigned to a person. Now what are the ages of the *Rāśis*? Their ages are identical with those of their lords. It is to be calculated thus: Find out the degrees of the sign covered by the concerned planet. Add that number to the number of its natural years.

If Mars be the planet concerned with a query, when he has covered, say 3° in a particular *Rāśi*, the result would be 3+3=6 years. Others put it as follows: Mars is a child; Mercury a boy; Venus a youth; Jupiter a middle-aged person; the Moon one who is past the middle age. The Sun a grey-haired one; and Saturn a very aged man. Others would say Venus is 32 years; the Moon 71 years; the Sun 50 years; Jupiter 20 years; Mercury 30 years; Mars 20 years. This would help the consultant in guaging the thiefs' age.

Relatives and Planets

The Sun represents father; the Moon, mother; Mercury, brother; Venus, consort; Jupiter, intimate friend; Mars, son; and Saturn and Rāhu, enemies.

If a planet signifying a particular kinsman be situated in an inimical house, or be debilitated or combust, and is posited in a trine or angle and if, in addition, be aspected by or conjoined with a malefic, then that kinsman should be declared to be dead. If the concerned planet does not aspect the *Lagna*, it should be said that the querist does not have such a kinsman in existence, i.e. is not alive.

If the planet be posited in one of the first six signs, the kinsman would be dead in his own house. If the planet be in the latter half of the Zodiac, he would be dead in a foreign country. Such a planet, if posited in the 2nd, 11th, 4th, 7th, or 10th house, would produce good results for the relative. Should the planet be in the 6th, 8th or 12th house, the concerned relative would behave in an inimical manner.

Paternal relations are denoted by Mars and Saturn; Mars represents paternal cousin; while Saturn, paternal uncle. Maternal relations are signified by Mercury, Jupiter and Venus.

Mercury—Maternal uncle's son (if posited in a masculine sign or *Aṃśa*).
—If in a feminine sign or *Aṃśa*, denotes maternal cousin (mother's sister's daughter)

Jupiter —Maternal uncle.

Venus —Mother's sister.

PLANETS AND SENSE ORGANS

Saturn—Sense of touch.

Mercury—Sense of touch and taste (skin and tongue).

Mars—Sense of touch, taste and smell (skin, tongue and nose).

Venus—All senses except that of sound (ear), including that of sight (eye).

Jupiter—All the five senses viz. that of touch, taste, smell, sight and sound.

TIME AND SIGNS

If the Ascendant is a fixed sign, movable one and dual one, they denote in order time in years, days and months. Find out the *Navāṃśas* covered by the lord of the *Lagna* from the rising degree. Multiply this number by the number of degrees that have risen in the ascendant. Then divide the product by 108. The remainder would give the time of fructification of the result, according to the nature (fixed, movable and dual) of the sign representing the *Lagna*.

STATES OF PLANETS

Planets have two kinds of *Avasthās* or states viz. positional (*Sthāna*) and temporal (*Kāla*). The purpose of this *Avasthā* is to find out the present condition of the querist. The positional condition of a planet is of seven types based on the nature of signs occupied by it: (1) Place or sign belonging to a neutral; (2) To a friend; (3) One's own *Rāśi*; (4) One's *Mūlatrikoṇa*; (5) One's exaltation; (6) One's inimical house; and (7) One's debilitation. These are also called the seven stages of life of the planets in order: (i) Very young stage; (ii) Childhood; (iii) Boyhood; (iv) Youth; (v) Kingly status; (vi) Aged; and (vii) Dead.

The temporal states too are *seven* in number: (1) When a planet just emerges after eclipse, it is called a young baby (*Atibāla*); (2) Thereafter for 7 days it is called *Bāla* or Child; (3) Up to the time its movement slacks down, it is known as *Kumāra* or boy under teens; (4) When it begins its retrograde motion, it is called youthful or *Yuvā*; (5) During its retrograde motion, it is called king; (6) Seven-days prior to its eclipse to the day of eclipse, it is *Vṛddha* or aged; and (7) During eclipse, it is called dead or *Mṛta*. Now a question arises as to which planet's condition you are required to take into consideration. The answer is the following: There are three important and basic signs viz. the *Ārūḍha*, *Udaya-lagna* (Ascendant) and the *Chatra Rāśi*. The strongest of the lords of these three signs would reveal the querist's condition or status. All these elements have already been explained in detail.

Importance of Cara-cakra

When a query is considered through a *Cara-cakra* the sign that ascends or rises above the horizon alone is considered. In that case the *Chatra Rāśi* is nothing but the sign that is represented by the *Navāṃśa* of the ascendant.

Weekday and Query: If the lord of the day of query is exalted either in sign or *Navāṁśa*, the querist must be having much wealth and would live long.

Sometimes the querist might ask the astrologer: "What is my natal star, and what is my lunar sign?" The astrologer should, at the outset, locate the *Ārūḍha Lagna* from the position taken by the querist. Then he should prepare a chart for the day and find out the strongest of the planets that aspect the *Ārūḍha*. The sign or signs owned by that planet should be the querists' natal sign. If no planet aspects the *Ārūḍha*, then take the sign possessed of strength, that happens to be a *kendra* for the *Ārūḍha*. Should Mars posited in an odd sign aspect the Ascendant, then the person's natal sign would be Aries. If Mars, posited in an even sign, aspects the *Lagna*, it is likely to be Scorpio. The *Ārūḍha* is likely to be the Natal Ascendant. When this is fixed, you have to proceed thus for fixing the Natal Asterism. Count the total number of persons assembled in this horary session. Multiply this number by 3 and divide the product by 27. The remainder would give the particular number of star counted from *Aśvinī*, *Maghā* or *Mūla*, according as the Ascendant happens to be a movable, immovable or dual sign.

Another Method: Find out the exact *Dvādaśāṃśa* (1/12 of a *Rāśi*) that rises in the ascendant. If the 1/12 portion is the second, the querist's *Lagna* should be the second from this *Ārūḍha*. Similarly the natal signs of other members of his family should be worked out from the above *Rāśi*. When the querist's natal sign is located, the 5th house therefrom would be his son's natal *Rāśi*.

According to Kṛṣṇāçārya it is to be worked out from the *Navāṃśas* that have risen in the Ascendant: In the case of the querist's son, start from the rising *Navāṃśa* and take the 5th *Rāśi* therefrom and multiply it by the number of rays possessed by the ruler of the particular *Rāśi*. Then divide the product by 27. The remainder will give the natal star of the querist's son. In the same manner the natal stars of his mother, wife, brother, father and enemy should be worked out. The lunar day is worked out thus: The eight lunar days beginning with the *Pratipat* (1st *Tithi*) are allotted to Mars and others in the order of (1) Mars, (2) Venus, (3) Mercury, (4) Moon, (5) Sun, (6) Jupiter, (7) Saturn, and (8) Rāhu. Rāhu presides over the New-Moon as well as over Aquarius. When the ascendant at query is Aries, the lunar month is to be taken as *Vaiśākha*. We have already seen the rays of the planets. We have to understand the rays of the signs also: They are in order: 7, 8, 12, 11, 12, 6, 9, 7, 13, 8, 7, and 27, according to the *Praśnamārga*. However, the Rays of Aries and other signs, according to *Kṛṣṇācārya*, are 90, 90, 110, 110, 110, 110, 117, 110, 90, 100, 100 and 100. This list of rays of signs would be very helpful to astrologers in finding out the number of stolen articles, amount of gain, time taken for a journey, distance, depth of wells etc.

Three-fold Classification of Signs

There are three kinds of signs viz. (1) *Dvāra-Rāśis* (door signs); (2) *Bāhya-Rāśis* (outside-external signs); and (3) or *Garbha-Rāśis* (*internal signs*).

(1) All movable signs are called *Dvāra-Rāśis*. (2) All immovable *Rāśis* are termed external ones. (3) All dual signs are known as *Garbha-Rāśis*.

The above distinction of signs would help a consultant in finding out the place where the stolen article had been kept: If the *Ārūḍha* at a query of theft be a *Garbha Rāśi*, the article was kept inside the house; if it be a *Dvāra-Rāśi*, it was kept in the vicinity of the house; and if it be an external sign, it was outside the house.

Māndi: Each planet has at least one *Upagraha* or satellite, but *Māndi*, an *Upagraha* of Saturn, is said to be the worst in the matter of dealing destruction. So let us try to know its characteristics and its effects in the different houses, etc. When *Māndi* is posited in the *Āruḍha-Lagna* or natal ascendant, the querist or native would always be sickly and afflicted with scabies. He is also likely to be having cleptomania, be cruel, immodest, without knowledge of scriptures, not stout, of deformed eyes, with poor intelligence, and few children. He would be a voracious eater, unhappy, licentious, not long-lived, not brave, and irascible.

In the second house he might make one speak harshly, quarrel with others, be devoid of wealth and corn, live away from home and have untidy dress.

In the third house he makes one live away from his people, have pride and arrogance, be hot-tempered, be possessed of prowess, fearless and hater of brothers.

In the fourth house *Māndi* makes one unhappy, afraid of his enemies, without relatives or friends, vehicles and wealth; of unsteady mind and short-lived.

In the fifth house, the person concerned would speak ill of his elders and teachers, be issueless and suffering from stomach diseases as well as hallucination.

In the sixth, he helps one to defeat his enemies, be brave, and blessed with good sons, will hate his kith and kin as well as servants.

In the seventh house, the person is likely to possess a black eye, and be the worst member of his family, very lustful, ungrateful and have many wives or harm his wives. He will also be timid.

In the eighth house, he will have deformed eyes and face and a short stature, be sickly and short-lived. He is likely to meet with a tragic end through fire, weapons, or poison.

In the ninth house, the person would be without father and issue as well as religious merit, penance and *Mantras*.

In the 10th house, one becomes famous, helping others, and engaged in other's affairs, but very miserly.

In the 11th house, he becomes heroic, possessed of all material comforts, very wealthy, with many servants, brilliance and children.

In the 12th house, he becomes devoid of sensual pleasures, wretched, poor, spendthrift, troubled always by bad dreams, possessed of dirty nails and short of a limb. If *Māndi* be conjoined with the significance of *Bhāva* the native would spoil those *Bhāvas*.

Fruition of Bhāva

Find out where the lord of the *Bhāva* in question is situated. Count the number from that house. Now multiply the period allotted to that planet by this number. This will give the time of fruition of the concerned *Bhāva*. For example, in a horoscope of Aquarius ascendant we are required to find out when the native would be married. Here the *Bhāva* to be tackled is the 7th, i.e. Leo. Its lord, the Sun, is posited, say, in Libra which is the 3rd from Leo. The Sun's period is six months. So multiply 6 by 3, which gives 18 months. The desired event is likely to take place between 12 and 18 months. In the particular month of the event you may predict that it may take place when the Moon in her transit comes to the place occupied by the *Bhāva*-lord. You can pin-point the exact time when the Moon transits the particular degree occupied by the *Bhāva*-lord. Another way of looking at it is to see if the lord of the concerned *Bhāva* is in the visible or invisible half of the zodiac. If he be in the former, the result would be realized without much delay. The starting of the invisible half is got by adding 6 *Rāśis* to the longitude of the ascendant. Among the *Bhāvas* the 11th is considered as '*All-Success*'-House.

Kinds of Karma

Both good and bad results ensue from stable and unstable deeds. Both these varieties of actions are performed in triple ways viz. verbally, mentally and physically. We have already seen the method of working out the *Chatra-Rāśi*. If benefics be posited in the untoward houses viz. 6th, 8th and 12th houses, counted from the *Chatra-Rāśi*, and malefics in 1, 4, 7, 10, 5 and 9, it should be stated that the person's misfortune has been aggravated by the wrath of particular deities. If this configuration of planets be found when the counting is done from the *Ārūḍha*, the cause of aggravation of troubles would be the curse of worthy Vedic scholars. If this position is found when considering the houses from the *lunar sign*, the trouble should be ascribed to sorcery perpetrated by enemies, If it be found with respect to the rising sign or *Udaya-lagna*, the trouble would be caused by the curses of the people. Should the planet signifying the *sin* be posited in the Moon's Horā etc. it (sin) is to be adjudged as brought about by stable karma. On the other hand, if the planet be in the *Varga* (Horā etc.) of the Sun, it should have been done through unstable karma. In this context, angles and trines are favourable houses for benefics, while 6, 8 and 12 are for malefics. Should there be a weak malefic in the 5th *Bhāva*, the *sin* should be considered as mental; should the malefic be posited in the 2nd house, it would be a verbal sin; if it be in the 10th house, the sin would be physical. The remedies for sins caused by divine wrath, are worship of gods; for those born of curses of *Brāhmaṇas*, worship and feeding of Vedic scholars; for those arising from black-magic or sorcery, service to the poor and distressed, devotion to gods etc.

If at a query there be two malefics in the 7th, 9th and 5th places from the Sun, and if those places be malefic *Rāśis*, the querist's father runs the risk of imprisonment as a result of some political crisis, provided the Sun is strong. If he be weak, the incarceration would be due to indebtedness. If the Sun be in a movable *Rāśi*, the person's father's arrest and imprisonment would be in a far-off place; if it be an immovable *Rāśi*, the place would be near.

In the same manner other significators too may be considered. Varāhamihira has explained in detail the conditions for imprisonment. If malefics occupy the 2nd, 12th, 5th and 9th *Bhāvas* from the natal ascendant, or if the Lagna-decanate be a serpent one, or fetters, or noose, and if malefics aspect it, there would be a chance for imprisonment, depending on the speciality of the ascendant *Rāśi*. If it be Aries, Taurus, Gemini and Cancer (or Leo), the captivity would be through ropes, chains, in a cave and forest respectively. According to Kṛṣṇācārya, if the *Lagna*-decanate be of Saturn or serpent or be aspected by Saturn and the Moon, there would be a chance for imprisonment. It is certain, if Saturn posited in a malefic house in 5, 9, 4, 7 or 8 and is aspected by malefics. If Saturn in such a situation be in a movable *Rāśi*, there would be quick release from captivity. If it be immovable, the captivity would be of long duration. The visible half of the zodiac is called *Ásthāna* (Kings' court, here it means a town) and the other half, lonely place. When the lord of the ascendant is in the visible half, the querist lives in a well-populated place such as a city. In this manner results have to be predicted for all the *Bhāvas* according as their lords are in one or the other half of the zodiac. If the lord of the 7th be in the invisible half, the querist's love-affairs would be carried on clandestinely.

METHOD OF FINDING THE SOURCE OF TROUBLES

When it is established that the querist's trouble is due to some divine cause, the cause must be probed and remedied. If the cause is traced to one of the *Bhāvas* beginning with the first house, the *Bādhās* (troubles) are in order (1) Divine wrath; (2) Trouble caused by the *Dharma Devatā*, i.e. Deity of the village worshipped from ancient times; (3) Trouble from serpents; (4) Wrath of ancestral spirits; (5) Preceptor's curse; (6) *Brāhmaṇas'* curse; (7) Harassment by discarnate spirits; (8) Trouble created by hordes of *Bhūtas* (evil spirits); (9) Trouble caused by black-eye; (10) Verbal sins; (11) Effect of consuming poisoned food or drink; and (12) Black magic practised by enemies. First of all the astrologer is expected to find out whether the querist has God's grace, which is seen from Jupiter's favourable position at query. If Jupiter be unfavourable, proper remedial measures should be recommended. For, when Jupiter is favourably disposed, all the gods are said to be pleased. In all the *Rāśis* the Sun represents Lord Śiva. However, there is some difference on the basis of the nature of the sign and its decanate. If the Sun be posited in the *First* decanate of any of the four signs, the diviner should think of Lord Subrahmaṇya. If the decanate be the middle one, he should name Lord Gaṇapati, and in all other signs, Lord Śiva and other deities connected with *Him*. Similarly when the Moon be strong, one should think of the higher incarnations of Mother Durgā (like Vanadurgā). When the weak Moon is posited in Aries or Scorpio, Goddess, Cāmuṇḍā should be predicted; or it might be Rakteśvarī, Bhairavī, Rakta-Cāmuṇḍā or Mahāmārikāmbā. In this connection the deities are divided into three classes of *Sattva* (purity), *Rajas* (activity or passion) and *Tamas* (darkness). Lord Subrahmaṇya is to be deduced from Mars, *Rāhu* and from the first decanates of movable and immovable signs occupied by the *Moon*. Some opine that Lord Gaṇeśa should be thought of through Venus occupying an odd sign, and from the second decanates, in both *Cara* (movable) and *Sthira* (immovable) signs, occupied by the *Moon*.

When Mercury is posited in a movable or dual sign, one ought to think of Śrī Rāma and other incarnations of Śrī Mahāviṣṇu. If the planet be posited in the first or second decanate of an immovable sign, Lord Gopālakṛṣṇa should be inferred. However, as Jupiter happens to be the significator for all the gods, appropriate deity is to be adjudged through Jupiter's position, conjunction, aspect and strength. The deities are also divided into *four groups* as (1) Vaiṣṇava, (2) Śaiva, (3) Śākta and (4) Gāṇapata.

If Venus or a benefic be posited in his own house, think of Śrī Annapūrṇeśvarī or Goddess Lakṣmī. When he is in an odd sign and connected with a male planet, think of Gaṇeśa; through Saturn, think of Lord *Śāstāra* (Ayyappa), Bhūtanātha Śaiva groups etc. Rāhu points to serpents; and Ketu to Lord Gaṇeśa. Some refer lordship of *Bādhā-sthāna* to Rāhu. Some authorities are of opinion that Aquarius is Rāhu's *Mūla-Trikoṇa*; Gemini exaltation; and Kanyā, own house. The 7th *Rāśis* of these are the different positions of Ketu.

Now we must understand the *Bādhā-sthānas* or houses of affliction: When the *Ārūḍha Rāśi* is a movable sign, the place of affliction is the 11th *Bhāva*; for immovable signs it is the 9th house; and for dual signs it is the 7th house. The following Table gives the houses of affliction:

Signs	Aries	Taurus	Gemini	Cancer	Leo	Virgo
Bādhā-sthāna	Aquarius	Capricorn	Sagittarius	Taurus	Aries	Pisces

Libra	Scorpio	Sagittarius	Capricorn	Aquarius	Pisces
Leo	Cancer	Gemini	Scorpio	Libra	Virgo

According to another view; for one movable *Rāśi* all the other three movable signs are *Bādhakas*. Similarly for immovable and dual signs all other immovable and dual signs respectively are

Bādhakas. There is also a third method for locating this: sign Aquarius is the *Bādhaka* for all the movable signs; for Scorpio, Sagittarius, Leo and Virgo, it is Scorpio; for Taurus it is Capricorn; for Aquarius it is Cancer; for Gemini, it is Sagittarius; and for Pisces, it is Sagittarius. Among the three views the first is the best and most popular and the last is next best. How is this knowledge made use of?

When the lord of the sign called *Bādhā-sthāna* aspects the *Ārūḍha* or its lord (the aspect may be a quarter, half, three-fourths or full), it should be declared that the subject of query is suffering as a result of black-eye or *Dṛṣṭi-bādhā.* The same effect should be declared, when the lord of the 7th be posited in the *Bādhā-sthāna*, or if these two lords be together or fully aspect each other. When the planets, being lords of *Bādhā*-houses, are posited in inauspicious houses (6, 8 and 12), the trouble must be said to be caused by the deities represented by those planets. For example, if the *Bādhaka* planet, being posited in an untoward house, should lead you to surmise that there is God's wrath, see if there is a malefic posited in the 12th house from the *Bādhaka* planet. If this condition be fulfilled, you should declare that there is some damage in the God's image or in the temple buildings. In addition, should the *Bādhaka* planet be associated with *Māndi* or *Rāhu*, the idol must have been polluted by a rat or snake crawling on it. On the other hand, if the *Bādhaka* planet be associated with Mars, divine wrath must have been caused by the quarrels of temple workers.

The following *Yogas* lead to troubles arising from the displeasure or wrath of one's *dharma-daiva* (village deity): (1) Lord of *Bādhā*-place being posited in the 4th house; (2) the lord of the 4th house being posited in the *Bādhā*-place; (3) the lord of the *Bādhā-sthāna* occupying the sign ruled by the lord of the 4th house; and (4) the condition mentioned in (3) being reversed. The nature of the querist's *dharma-daiva* is to be read from the planet that rules over the 4th house.

How to Guess Serpent-Trouble (*Sarpa-Bādhā*)?

When Jupiter, being the lord of *bādhā-sthāna*, is posited in 6th, 8th or 12th house, and in *kendra* to *Rāhu*, the trouble is due to the wrath of high-class serpents, while if it is *Māndi* instead of

Rāhu, it is of low-class serpents. If *Rahu* be in the *bādhā*-place, 6th, 8th or 10th house, the remedy should take the form of *Āśleṣā-Bali*—an elaborate worship of a large number of divine serpents through sixteen varieties of offerings, i.e. food. lamps, *tarpaṇa*, *mantras* etc., at night.

The descriptions of the *Rāśis*, which we have already seen, would enable astrologers to fix the exact place of Bādhā or affliction of *spirits*.

It is well-known that bitter enemies resort to witchcraft, black-magic or necromancy with the intention of harming or killing their objects of hatred, through the incantations of low-class (*kṣudra*) deities, performed in a burial ground, on a new Moon night, under the asterism *Kṛttikā* or *Bharaṇi*, uttering the name of the victim, with *homa* or sacrifice done with buffalo-ghee, pepper and eight kinds of poisons as well as with faggots of stricknine (*kāraskara*). Through such dreadful rites the sorcerer sends a terrific spirit to the victim's place. If the lord of *bādhā-sthāna* be a benefic, the necromancy would be called *mahābhicāra*, while *kṣudrābhicāra* is that where darts, thorns, images of ghosts etc. surcharged with the powers of *mantras*, are planted near the victim's house. While undoing the harm done to the querist by his enemy, the caste of the necromancer is to be found out thus: Find out the caste of the sign that happens to be the 6th house or of its lord. This would give the caste of the querist's enemy. Similarly find out the caste of the *māntrika-priest*—thus: It is the same as that of the sign that happens to be the *bādhā-sthāna*; or it may be that of the lord of that place. It has been already explained that sign Pisces and its trines represent *Brāhmaṇas*; Aries, Leo and Sagittarius, *Kṣatriyas*; Taurus, Virgo and Capricorn, Vaiśyas; and Gemini, Libra and Aquarius, Śūdras. Planets too are divided among the various castes: Jupiter and Venus belong to the *first class*; the Sun and Mars, to the *second class*; the Moon, to the *third class*; Mercury, to the *fourth class*; and Saturn, to the *lowest class*. Mars is equal to a king but without the *sacred thread*; Mercury, a scholar without the sacred thread and serves in the temple. The cause of enmity between the querist and the other man must be metal, root or tree, or a living being based on the following planets and signs: (1) The sign representing the ascendant; (2) the planet posited in it; (3) lord of the 6th house; (4) the sign occupied by the lord of the 6th house; and (5) the sign occupied by the lord of the *bādhā-sthāna.*

I CONDITIONS FOR BLACK-MAGIC

(1) The *Ārūḍha-Lagna* should be a movable sign.

(2) It should be aspected by the lord of the 6th house.

(3) Mars should be posited in the 11th *Bhāva.*

II (i) The *Lagna* should be an immovable sign.

(ii) The *Ārūḍha* should be aspected by the 6th house.

III Mars should be posited in the 9th house.

(i) The *Ārūḍha* must be a dual sign.

(ii) It must be aspected by the 6th house.

(iii) Mars should be posited in the 7th house.

IV (i) Mars should be conjoined with the lord of the *Ārūḍha.*

(ii) Mars should occupy a *kendra.*

(iii) The *Lagna* should be occupied by the lord of the 6th house.

V (i) The lord of the 6th *Bhāva* should occupy the *Lagna*, the 7th house or the 10th house.

(ii) Mars should occupy or aspeet the *Lagna.*

VI *Ketu* being posited in the *Ārūḍha*, 4th or 10th house, Mars should occupy or aspect the *Lagna*, or *Māndi* be in a *kendra.*

VII (i) *Māndi* and Saturn jointly occupy *Ārūḍha*, *Udaya-Lagna* or lunar sign.

(ii) *Māndi* being aspected by Saturn should stay in 1, 4, 7 or 10.

Method for finding out the places where the materials or black-magic have been kept hidden: If *Māndi* be posited in the 4th from the *Ārūḍha*, ascendant or the Moon's sign or the *Aṃśaka* of the 4th house, the material of black magic should lie hidden inside the house itself. If the 4th house be a watery sign or watery *Navāṃśa*, it should have been put in the well or tank. If the sign or *Aṃśa* occupied by *Māndi* be of watery nature, the *Kṣudra* must be said to be in water. In addition, if *Māndi* be in *Vargottamāṃśa*, the *kṣudra* (material) must have been kept in two places. And if *Māndi*, in addition, be associated with *Rāhu* or if the ascendant, *Ārūḍha* or the Moon, be associated with Saturn and *Rāhu*, the *kṣudra* must be said to have been put in the vicinity of a *snake park* (*Nāga-vana*). If the Sun be in a *kendra* from Saturn and be associated with *Māndi*, the *kṣudra* (material) should be declared to be kept on a *tree*. Should Mars be in a *kendra*, it should have been kept in a field.

Should Jupiter be in such a position, in the house itself; should it be Venus, in the bed-chamber.

The description of the place where the *kṣudra* is kept may be determined from the nature of the sign such as downward-looking, upward-looking etc. and the direction would be that of the *Aṃśa* sign. If the *Aṃśa* be of the Sun, the place should be a store-house, where medicines, vessels etc. are kept. If it be the Moon's *Aṃśa*, the place must be water-vessels. If it be Mar's *Aṃśa*, it should be a place where weapons are kept. In the case of Mercury's *Aṃśa* it should be children's reading room. If it be Jupiter's *Aṃśa*, it should be in the niché of the worship room. If it be one of Venus, it is kept in the place where beds and *sāris* are stored. If it be Saturn's, the place is servant's quarters, dust bin etc. Similarly if the *Aṃśa* be of Taurus, the place must be the manager; if Libra, it is a place where cosmetics are kept. In this manner, the place has to be distinguished through the nature of the signs and planets.

If *Māndi* be posited in Scorpio, the *kṣudra* must be in the form of a talisman; if he be in a quadruped sign or *Aṃśa*, it would be in the form of bones. The number of the *kṣudra* (materials) is to be read from the number of Navāṃśas covered by *Māndi*. The direction of the *kṣudra* could be read from the sign or *Aṃśa* occupied by *Māndi*. In addition to *Māndi*, the significator for *kṣudrābhicāra* is the *bādhaka* planet, who is a malefic.

All the combinations mentioned above in this connection are to be applied to the *Bādhā-lord*.

If the *bādhā-lord* be in a watery sign which is an upward-looking sign, the *kṣudra* must have been buried on the sea-shore or river-bank. If the sign be a downward-looking sign, it must be underneath the water. The place denoted by the planet who becomes the *bādhā-lord* would be the place where the *kṣudra* has been hidden.

Removal of kṣudra: If the *bādhā-lord* be in a movable sign, the *kṣudra* could be removed without much effort. If he be in a dual *Rāśi*, with some effort. If it be a fixed sign, it could not be removed.

The materials used for the *kṣudrabhicāra* such as nails, bones, talisman, ashes, skull, bamboo cylinder, potsherd etc., should be removed and burnt. Thereafter the place should be purified through proper rituals. If the material cannot be taken out, then the exorcist should withdraw its power into some other object and destroy its power by proper rituals and the place be properly protected.

Method of Removing Mahābhicāra

Add the longitudes of the lords of the *Lagna* and the 6th house. If the sum is aspected by or conjoined with the Sun, then *Aghora-Rudra Bali* is to be performed. In case the above sum of longitudes receives the Moon's aspect or association, *kapāla homa* should be performed. If Mercury has the associations, *mahāsudarśana homa* is to be performed. For Jupiter's or Saturn's associations, *pratīkāra bali* is the remedy. For Mars' associations, *Bhūta-Māraṇa Bali* or *Khadga-Rāvaṇa Bali* or at least *Kṛttikā-Bali* should be done. For Venus' associations too *Bhūta-Māraṇa Bali* or *Pratīkāra Bali* is to be performed.

If the querist touches his chest, forehead, private parts or navel, we have to infer that the querist suffers from divine wrath. If he touches his sides, fingers or neck, wrath of serpents is indicated. Lastly if he touches the eye-lashes, ear or armpit, it is to be taken that the person is troubled by *piśāca* or ghost.

The particular deity that troubles the querist can be read from the planets posited in the *bādhā-sthāna*, its lord and their *Navāṃśas*: If the lord of the *bādhā*-sign be posited in Gemini or Virgo or their *Aṃśa*, the querist must be suffering on account of the deity worshipped daily in a high class *Brāhmaṇa* family. If the said lord be in a Jupiter's sign or *Aṃśa*, the trouble is from the deity worshipped in the temple. If it be a sign or *Aṃśa* of Saturn, the troubling deity is one which is worshipped by a low-class sect. Should the *bādhā*-lord be in his own *Aṃśa*, the trouble would be from the deity dwelling in a dreadful forest. If the *bādhā*-lord be Mars in conjunction with

Ketu, the deity would be *Cāmuṇḍā* (called *Cāmuṇḍi* by rustics) worshipped by untouchables. If there be a benefic in the 9th house from the *Ārūḍha* and the lord of that house (9th) being strong, be posited in a good house, and if the lord of the ascendant be aspected by or associated with the Sun, and if the *Ārūḍha-lord* be associated with Jupiter, all troubles arising from the wrath of deities could be warded off by worship of the deity, *japa*, chanting of the Vedas etc. On the other hand, should the *Ārūḍha-lord* be in the 9th house, being aspected by or conjoined with malefics, and the 9th lord too be in a similar position, the trouble could not be remedied.

Query on the Efficacy of Remedies: The astrologer should pray at first to the lord with sincere and staunch devotion, and shuffle the heap of cowries and take out a handful of them. The remainder obtained after deducting groups of 12, would give the *Ārūḍha-lagna*. Should this sign be one termed *Pṛṣṭhodaya* (rising with its hind part), or *movable* or *Adhomukha* (downward looking) and at the same time be a low-tide *Rāśi*, then it should be understood that the remedial measures would be effective in removing the *bādhā*. On the other hand, they would be ineffective, if the *Ārūḍha* be *Śīrṣodaya*, fixed, upward looking and a high-tide *Rāśi*. The idea is that for success, malefics should not be posited in 6, 4, 8 and 12 places; and benefics be in *kendras* (i.e. 1, 4 7 and 10).

Significators of Bādhā:

(1) The lord of the *bādhā-rāśi*.

(2) The planet posited in the *bādhā-sthāna*.

(3) The planets that aspect the *bādhā-sthāna*.

If such a planet be posited in Cancer or Leo, or in his own *Aṃśa*, the remedial rituals should be got performed through a *Brāhmaṇa*. If Sagittarius or Pisces be the sign or *Aṃśa*, the relief work must be caused to be performed through the temple singers (*Pāṭhakas*). If the *sign* or *Aṃśa* involved be Gemini or Virgo, the ritual should be done through a *Śūdra*. For Taurus and Libra signs and *Aṃśas*, it should be through *devil-dancers*. (This is very famous in the West Coast.) For Capricorn and Aquarius signs and *Aṃśas*, through members of the lowest-class.

If the *bādhā*-significator be a benefic and posited in a benefic house, the remedial rituals should be got done through Brāhmaṇas otherwise through low-class people.

In spite of all these remedial measures if relief be not forthcoming, the best method for achieving success is the worship of the tutelary deity (one's family deity or *Iṣṭadevatā*), performance of Yāga, Śrī Rudrābhiṣeka, Veda-Pārāyaṇa, *Mṛtyuñjaya-homa*, *japa* etc. If these be done with devotion and due attention to the rules of procedure, all troubles would cease and God's grace would descend on the querist and his family.

CHAPTER IV

AṢṬAMAṄGALA PRAŚNA

Aṣṭamaṅgala is one of the celebrated branches of horary astrology. This discipline is held in very high esteem especially in Kerala. This field has been nurtured and developed by many great scholars of this state. It is, of course no invention of the South. For, Praśna-Śāstra is a very hoary branch of the *Saṃhitā Skandha*. Varāhamihira, Bhaṭṭotpala, Pṛthuyaśas Kṛṣṇācārya, author of the *Daśādhyāyī*, Mādhava, author of the famous *Praśnamārga* of Edakkāti in Kerala have kept the lamp of knowledge of this science burning bright by feeding it constantly with the oil of meticulous and solemn query sessions held in holy surroundings. It is designated as *Aṣṭamaṅgala Praśna* on the basis of the eight auspicious articles used for the worship of the planetary deities in the chart of zodiacal signs. The following are the eight holy articles used: lamps, mirror, gold, milk, curds, fruits, book and white cloth. In the beginning a lamp must be lighted and some white rice be kept in a measure and betel leaves and arecanut as well as flowers kept separately.

The astrologer should draw the chart on a clean wooden plank, and offer *Arghya* (water) and worship to the preceptor and Lord Gaṇeśa through the holy lamp already installed. After the worship of Lord Gaṇapati, Lord Maheśvara is to be invoked in the four-petalled lotus (drawn in the centre of the chart). After completing the worship, the signs and planets should be worshipped as attendants of the Supreme Lord. In *Aṣṭamaṅgala* each *Rāśi* in the chart should be 6″×6″. In others it is 3″×3″. The astrologer must keep an account of the relevant items viz. the *Ārūḍha*, position of the gold coin, the eight auspicious materials brought, and time of commencement, year, month etc., the querist's natal star etc.

Then the eight auspicious articles kept in a vessel are to be worshipped as the embodiment of Goddess Sarasvati. Then the lamp should be worshipped as the embodiment of Goddess

Lakṣmī. Thereafter the gold coin to be used in this operation is washed and anointed with sandal paste and kept on a banana leaf mixed with flowers and coloured rice. The astrologer should then hold that banana leaf in his left hand, cover it with his right hand and repeat mentally the *Pañcākṣarī mantra* 108 times. The astrologer should sit in such a way that the chart drawn is to his right. Then he takes 108 cowries and sprinkles them with holy waters and decorates them with sandal paste, coloured rice etc. The cowries should be worshipped. He should invoke on the cowries the divine planets and his preceptors. He must then gently rotate his hand over the cowries while chanting *mantras* continuously. Then he should pray to the planets that by their grace all things, good and bad deeds of the querist and his family members, done in the past and present and those to be done in the future, may be clear to his mental eye.

An innocent child who has already bathed and is well dressed should be asked to bow before the lamp, pray to Lord Gaṇapati and the planetary deities. Then the astrologer keeps the gold coin mixed with flowers and coloured rice. The child should be asked to circumambulate the chart of zodiacal signs, thrice and stand facing the East and gazing at the chart with devotion holding the coin in his hand. Now the querist too should stand up in front of the chart and pray with folded hands, thinking of his object. Then the astrologer collects all the remaining cowries and moves his hand gently over them, repeating thrice the invocatory verse of Varāhamihira beginning with the word *Mūrtitve*. Then he should ask the child to place the gold coin along with flowers and coloured rice in any sign of the *Rāśi-Cakra* as he pleases, and thereafter sit somewhere nearby. All the while the astrologer should keenly observe the behaviour, acts, sounds, arrival, departure etc. of the people around including the querist and the child, while rotating the heap of 108 cowries. Then he takes out a handful of cowries from the heap and puts it on the left side of the plank; another handful similarly is taken out and kept in the middle, and all the remaining cowries kept on the right side. Thus three groups of cowries are spread before the astrologer. These three heaps represent past, present and future respectively. The astrologer also finds the effects of omens occurring at the time as well as of limbs touched by the querist or his relative. He also observes all the omens occurring from the time of his departure from his house until he arrives at the querist's house.

The following are considered inauspicious omens: cotton, medicine, black gram, salt, net, ashes, iron, charcoal, butter-milk, snake, stinking objects, night-soil, spittle, lunatic, dunce, deaf and dumb, eunuch, hermit, and all things that are unpleasant to the eye. Similarly the sight of snake, cat, alligator, mongoose, monkey (if they cross one's path), mustard, firewood, stone, grass (if these are carried in front of him). The following are considered as auspicious omens: raw meat, wine, alcoholic beverage, honey, ghee, white cloth, sandal paste, scent, precious stone, elephant, horse, king, great man, God's image, white chowry, cooked rice, milk porridge, dead body, two Brāhmaṇas, burning fire, birds and animals moving in a clockwise manner around a person, movement of dogs and jackals in an anti-clockwise manner, animals in odd numbers, peacock, cock, jackal, mongoose, tiger, cakora bird (if they move from left to right); and the movement of dog, crow, goat, deer and elephant (moving from right to left).

The following omens are said to be unfavourable: Those occurring in the quarters termed *Dīpta* (blazing), while favourable are those that occur in the quarters called *Śānta* (serene). What are these? (1) *Dīpta*: The three quarters (out of the eight) the one that has been abandoned, the one that is presently tenanted and the one that will be tenanted next by the Sun are called in order *Aṅgāra* (charcoal), *Dīpta* (blazing) and *Dhūminī* (smoking). They also stand for the past, present and future respectively. The fifth from each of these three *Rāśis* are called by the same names as the original ones. For example, if the east be blazing, then the west which is the 5th from the east, also becomes blazing. The direction of the omen at any time of the day or night is found out thus: The 60 *ghatīs* of a day are divided equally among the 8 quarters at the rate of 7½ *ghaṭīs* or 3 hours. From Sun-rise for 3 hours it is the East; for the next 3 hours it is the South-East; for the next 3 hour period it is the South; for the next period it is the South-West and so on. In this manner the last 3 hour period would belong to the

North-East. These eight directions have their own signals in order as (1) king, (2) prince, (3) commander, (4) messenger, (5) noble person, (6) spy, (7) twice-born, and (8) chief of the elephant corps. If a bird cries in a particular direction, the querist would meet with a person suggested by the quarter. Hearing Vedic recitation, mantras of *Puṇyāha* ceremony, sweet breeze, the wind moving in a clockwise manner, and lowing of cows and bulls are good auguries. On the other hand, if a vessel should fall down or break, it would denote danger to the patient in the querist's house. Similar is the indication if a lamp be extinguished without strong winds or if the fire in the fire-place were to go out in spite of firewood.

When a person going on a journey meets with an untoward augury, he should return home and after ablutions, repeat the holy Gāyatrī mantra eleven times along with *Prāṇāyāma* (breath-control). If he finds an inauspicious omen for the second time, he should repeat the purifying process by means of 16 Prāṇāyāmas and repetitions of the mantra. It still evil omens should persist he should drop the idea of the journey. The astrologer should remember all the good and bad omens he had seen on the way. He should then give the results of all the auguries one by one.

When the astrologer enters the querist's house for probing the causes (and their remedies) of ailments of an inmate of the house, if somebody goes out of the house, the effect would be death of the patient, whereas it would be recovery for the patient, in case someone enters it at that time. Should a woman in menses come out of the house, carrying fruits and roots, the house would be destroyed completely.

The lamp kept at the *Aṣṭamaṅgala* session will indicate future prosperity or adversity according as the lamp is clean or not, and the flame lustrous or otherwise. As soon as the lamp is installed, the astrologer observes keenly the direction in which the flame moves. If its movement is anti-clockwise, is pale, produces a crackling sound, suddenly goes out despite (sufficient quantity of oil, and good wicks, the tip of the flame being split, it suggests the presence of sins. Otherwise it would indicate happiness and prosperity. For, the lamp is considered as the representative of the Supreme Lord, the oil or ghee used stands for the querist's body, the wick for his *Ātman* (Soul), the flame for longevity, the can for his house, the breeze blowing pleasantly and mildly as well as roughly and violently, for a friend or enemy, as the case may be. If flies be lying dead in the oil, the querist must be suffering on account of worms trouble; if there be a green crust in the lamp, his blood must be polluted; if two wicks be inter-twined, he must be having breathing trouble; if the wicks be dirty, his mind must be dull; if there be many wicks in the lamp, there must be as many deities in the temple or as many branches of the family; if the wick be mixed with hair, there would be trouble from evil spirits; if the lamp be changed, the querist must have changed his residence from his family house; if the oil be dropping, there must be plenty of water nearby. If the flame be turned towards the south-east, there would be a fire-accident; if towards the south, death; if towards the south-west, loss of memory, epilepsy or lunacy.

The *Aṣṭamaṅgala* chart should be drawn with rice powder or white clay powder. Ashes are forbidden. In the central vacant square a four-petalled lotus must be drawn with its tips pointing to the east and other cardinal directions. If the lines are thin or cut in the middle the querist may experience grief or break in his happiness. If the line on the western side be drawn first, he might fall ill; if the southern side be the first, he might have danger to his life. If the following things are seen in the chart, viz. (1) straw, (2) drop of water; (3) piece of stone, (4) sand, and (5) mud, (1) there must be trees in the corresponding direction; (2) there must be a tank or well in that direction; (3) rock; (4) an elevated place or tall trees like the cocoanut trees; and (5) anthill. If a *Brāhmaṇa* arrives at the place, it should be said that there is an abode of *Brahma-Rākṣasa* in the place; if it is a wicked person, there is danger from thieves in that direction.

The sign in which the gold coin is placed is called *Ārūḍha Lagna.* Now refer to the three groups of cowries kept separately by the astrologer. Next he will remove from each heap groups of eight cowries and note the remainder in each heap. The remainder stands for the planets. If the remainder is 1, it is the Sun; if 2, Mars; if 3, Jupiter; if 4, Mercury; if 5, Venus; if 6, Saturn; if 7, the Moon; and if 8, Rāhu. The *Yonis* (sources) of these numbers are respectively (1) dhvaja (banner), (2) dhūma (smoke), (3) siṃha (lion), (4) śvā (dog), (5) vṛṣabha (bull), (6) khara (donkey), (7) gaja (elephant), and (8) Vāyasa (crow), Their corresponding animals are; (i) Tārkṣya (eagle), (ii) Mārjāra (cat), (iii) Siṃha (lion), (iv) Śvān (dog), (v) Sarpa (snake), (vi) *Ākhu* (rat), (vii) dvipa (elephant), and (viii) Śaśa (hare).

The five elements are related to the *Yonis* and animals thus:

(1)	Earth	(*Pṛthvi*)	=	Dhvaja and Siṃha.
(2)	Water	(*Jala*)	=	Dvipa and Vṛṣabha.
(3)	Fire	(*Tejas*)	=	Dhūma.
(4)	Air	(*Vāyu*)	=	Khara.
(5)	Ether	(*Ākāśa*)	=	Śvā and Kāka.

Thus we have four items here viz. *Planets*, *Yonis*, *Mṛgas* and *Bhūtas* or elements.

For ready reference the four items mentioned above are given in a chart below:

No.	*Planets*	*Sources/ Yonis*	*Animals/ Mṛgas*	*Elements/ Bhūtas*
1	Sun	Banner	Eagle	Earth
2	Mars	Smoke	Cat	Fire
3	Jupiter	Lion	Lion	Earth
4	Mercury	Dog	Dog	Ether
5	Venus	Bull	Serpent	Water
6	Saturn	Donkey	Rat	Air
7	Moon	Elephant	Elephant	Water
8	*Rāhu*	Crow	Hare	Ether

The effects of each of these four items will have to be read separately from the remainders of cowries in the three places. They will not be more than 8, 8 and 4, nor less than 1, 1 and 2.* The astrologer should take down these numbers in the three places of units, tens and hundreds.

He should also examine the betel leaves, brought to him by the querist, and declare the effects of all the 12 *Bhāvas*. In the

* In the *Aṣṭamaṅgala* scheme the sum of the three remainders cannot be less than 4, nor greater than 20. As per one of the 27 *Sūtras* of this scheme these sums viz. 4, 12 and 20, represent in order Jiva, Roga and Mṛti. About the total number of cowries employed in this query session it has been laid down that only 108 cowries should be used, neither more nor less.

forenoon the leaves are to be counted from the top keeping them with their face upwards. The first leaf represents the ascendant, the 2nd house of finance, and so on. The remaining leaves should be preserved. In the afternoon the leaves are to be counted by keeping them topsy turvy. Whichever leaf is found defective, the *Bhāva* denoted by it will suffer. While examining the leaves, one should see if any leaf is dirty, tiny, too big, torn, wet, good-looking or otherwise. If the 11th leaf be smaller than the 12th, it should be stated that the querist's expenditure is more than his income. Should there be a hole in a leaf, the concerned house would be affected on account of troubles from enemies. If there be water on a leaf, there would be plenty of water in the direction of the particular *Bhāva*. Any defect in the 6th leaf would point to trouble from enemies and ailments. Similarly some defect in the 7th would make his wife sickly. If it be a twin leaf, the person would have two wives. In a leaf the left and right sides stand for woman and man respectively. Should the fifth leaf be bent towards the left, the person would have more daughters; if towards the right, more sons.

Rise of planets from betel leaves: Count all the leaves, including those kept apart. Multiply that number by 10. Add 1 to the result and divide it by 7. The remainder would denote the seven planets beginning with the Sun. When there be no remainder, it would denote Saturn. Note the position of Saturn in the *Aṣṭamaṅgala* chart and take that house as the new ascendant and delineate all the *Bhāvas* therefrom. This method is called *grahodaya method*. If the rising planet in this method be the *Sun*, the effect would be suffering; if it be the *Moon*, *Happiness*; if *Mars*, *quarrel*; if Mercury or Jupiter, *gain of wealth*; if *Venus*, attainment of all desires; and if *Saturn*, *danger to life*.

Effects of Māndi Aspecting or Combining With Other Planets

Māndi and the Sun: Some person in the querist's house would be falling ill; the querist might incur the king's displeasure; or police-harassment without any reason.

Māndi and the Moon: There would ensue a quarrel between two women in his house, or quarrel in the family on account of a woman.

Māndi and Mars: A dead body would be carried in the neighbourhood, or someone be carrying meat nearby.

Māndi and Mercury: Somebody would bring in a new pot or a copper vessel; an important person's visit is expected, or a quarrel between a man and a woman might break out.

Māndi and Jupiter: A tree nearby might fall down. If Jupiter be in a movable sign, the tree might fall breaking into pieces; if he be in a fixed sign, then the tree might be uprooted. If it be a dual sign, the tree would fall breaking in the middle, and the direction of the tree would be north-east or north-west; or a demented *Brāhmaṇa* might arrive at the place; or somebody would bring fruits there; or some close relative would fall ill, or he might participate in obsequies.

Māndi and Venus: The querist's clothes are eaten by rats; or a vessel falls down and breaks; somebody brings milk or curds; or a cat brings a prey, a mouse or a chick; or a religious mendicant arrives.

Māndi and Saturn: A man observing vows comes and goes away in a rage; or a person of low caste dies near the querist's house; or there would be a quarrel among the people of that caste; or someone brings there iron, frying pan and the like.

Māndi and Rāhu: A fight takes place between a dog and a tiger; or a relation of the querist is bitten by a snake; or someone brings snakes or milk. (Ketu is similar to *Rāhu*.)

The name *Aṣṭamaṅgala* is given to this system for reasons: (1) eight auspicious articles are employed for the worship of the planetary deities; and (2) a heap of 108 cowries is divided at random into three groups, and from each group multiples of 8 cowries are removed and the remainder noted. Here the number 8 stands for the eight planets viz. the seven planets and the nodes counted as one. The figure finally obtained in the group on the right side denotes that part of the body below the hips; that of the central group, that part from the hips to the neck; and that of the left group, that part of the body above the neck. If the remainder happens to be an even number, the querist must be suffering from some ailment in the particular part of the body represented by the particular group. Similarly in the case of *deva-praśna* (query about temple deities) it should be declared that the particular part or limb of the idol is defective. The three figures may be taken as representing the external area, the central area and the sanctum sanctorum of the temple respectively.

Let us take an example: Let the remainder at the hundredth place be 2; at the tens place be 4; and at the units place be 6. Here number 2 denotes Mars; 4 Mercury; and 6 Saturn. In this manner we get these three planets in the three places of the *Aṣṭamaṅgala* scheme. Their corresponding *yonis*, *mṛgas* and elements are respectively (1) smoke, cat and fire; (2) dog, and ether; and (3) donkey, rat and air.

The effects of the planets are enumerated below:

1. *The Sun*: Accomplishment of desires, victory, fame, honour from the king, honour in an assembly, prominent position in a village or town.

2. *Mars*: Fear of thieves, kings, fire, weapons, troubles on account of Lord Subrahmaṇya and Bhavānī, quarrels, fever, vitiation of bile and blood, disease in the head, eyes etc.

3. *Jupiter*: Grace of preceptors and gods blessings of Brāhmaṇas, acquisition of auspicious materials, gain of garments, gold, elephant, and horses, birth of a son.

4. *Mercury*: Trouble from dogs, cattle, and such other animals, wrath of Lord Viṣṇu, scabies and other skin troubles, typhoid fever etc.

5. *Venus*: Acquisition of ornaments, fancy goods, fine clothes, beds, conjugal happiness, sumptuous food, agricultural produce, cattle, buffaloes etc.

6. *Saturn*: Rheumatic troubles, colic-ailments, trouble from thieves and wicked fellows, danger to one's life, trouble from evil spirits.

7. *The Moon*: Happy atmosphere in the family, mental happiness, association of kinsmen and friends, gain through cereals, corn etc., good food and drinks, conjugal felicity—all the good effects depend on the strength of the Moon. Even in the case of other planets their strength must be considered first for declaring good or bad effects.

8. *Rāhu-Ketu*: Leprosy, ulcer, scabies, affliction to the eyes and legs and feet, fear of poison, hostility or quarrel with low-class people.

Effects of Yonis: (1) *Dhvaja yoni*: Good health, profit, destruction of enemies, birth of sons etc.

(2) *Dhūma* (*smoke*): Mental trouble, dreadful disease, trouble from enemies, poverty, loss of position, quarrel etc.

(3) *Siṃha* (*lion*): Gain in health, birth of a child, mental satisfaction, increase of income, honour from kings and *Brāhmaṇas*.

(4) *Śunaka* (dog): Going away from home, fright, loss of wealth, trouble from diseases, unnatural death, quarrel.

(5) *Vṛṣabha* (bull): Marriage, birth of a child, gain of wealth, health, and happiness at home, prosperity.

(6) *Khara* (donkey): Attack by enemies, diseases, loss of position, and wealth, destruction of undertaking, grief etc.

(7) *Gaja* (*elephant*): Conjugal happiness, acquisition of wealth and corn, association with friends, honour from kings, gain of gems.

(8) *Vāyasa* (*crow*): Fall from position, loss of friends and house, great fear, danger to life from enemies.

It is noticed that some creatures cross over the *Aṣṭamaṅgala Rāśis* while the session is in progress.

So it is necessary for us to know the details of their evil consequences.

If the central heap of cowries denoting present affairs should be crossed by a snake, rat, elephant and hare, and the right heap by an eagle, cat, lion and dog respectively, the querist runs the risk of losing life, as these are mutual enemies. The same result has to be predicted, if in front of the querist a cat is found catching a rat or a dog is found carrying a piece of hare's flesh in its mouth. If a crow throws its droppings on the querist's person, he will have trouble from ailments. Among the elements only the first two viz. earth and water, are said to be harbingers of prosperity. If the middle heap shows cat, the querist's path will be crossed by a cat—its effect being illness. If it be dog—there will be trouble from dog or tiger. If it be *dhūma-yoni*—danger from fire. If the central planet is the enemy of the right-hand planet, or if both are malefics, the effects will be bad. If both the places have malefics but friendly to each other, the result will be good.

Among the three heaps of cowries, if the central one shows the fire (element) and the right one, water, the consequence would be either disease or death to the querist. Lunar days, lunar mansions, weekdays, zodiacal signs and elements—all derived from the *Aṣṭamaṅgala* heaps of cowries, also are utilized for predicting the querist's future as explained below: Take the remainders in the three places together as a number of three digits and divide it by 30. The remainder would give the lunar day (*tithi*). Let us take that there are 32 cowries in the units place; 51 in that of tens; and 25 in that of hundreds. When we divide each by 8 what remains is 8 3 and 1 in the three places. So the number comes to 138. If this is divided by 30, we get a remainder of 18 which stands for the 3rd *tithi* in the dark fortnight. Again if the number 138 be divided by 27, the remainder 3 gives the asterism that is the third from *Aśvinī*, i.e. *Kṛttikā*. Likewise by dividing the above number by 7, we get a remainder 5, which gives us Thursday. When the above number be divided by 12, we would get a remainder of 6, which gives sign Virgo. After that by dividing the number by 9 the remainder 3 would give the planet Mars among the nine planets. Lastly when it is divided by 5, the remainder 3 gives the element of fire* The above results got by dividing the number severally by 30 and others, are called in order *Aṣṭamaṅgala Tithi*, *Vāra*, *Nakṣatra*, *Rāśi*, *Graha* and *Bhūta*. The effects of these are to be read with reference to the querists' natal sign or ascendant. In case the *Aṣṭamaṅgala* star happens to be the third (*Vipat*), fifth (*Pratyak*), or Seventh (*Vadha*) from the querists' natal star, there will be trouble for him.

If the above *Aṣṭamaṅgala* items (*Tithi* and others) produce good and bad effects by combination, prediction should be made judiciously: If all the three groups in this scheme denote even numbers, the querist will meet with great danger. Similarly, the left and central places also, having even numbers, indicate serious illness. If the central number be multiplied by 45 and divided by 8, leaving no remainder, the effect would be extremely harmful. Should the remainder be an odd number, the querist would enjoy happiness.

Now look at the remainders of cowries in the three places viz.

*When the number 138 is divided several times, there is no zero remainder, but the divisor itself is taken.

left, middle and right. Multiply the first by 2, the middle by 3; and the right by 4. Then add all the three products. Let this sum be A. If the query is made in the light half, then odd 336 to the sum called A. If it be the dark half, add 648 to A. Then divide the new sum by 84. Take the remainder alone and divide it by 12. The remainder would show the zodiacal sign from Aries. When Jupiter arrives at that sign in his transit, the querist may quit the world.

Let us work this out: The three numbers are: 1, 3, 8. Multiplying these we get = $1\times2+3\times3+8\times4 = 2+9+32 = 43$. Let the fortnight of query be the bright one. So add 336 to 43 = 379. Divide this by 84, you get a remainder of 43, which being divided by 12, leaves a remainder of 7 which is Libra.

There is another method: The balance obtained after dividing the result by 84 should be multiplied by 12 and divided by 84. The quotient will give the *Rāśi*. When the balance is multiplied by 30 and divided by 84, it yields degrees. The balance multiplied by 60 and divided by 84, with give minutes. This figure in signs, degrees and minutes is called Saturn's *Sphuṭa*. So when Saturn transits this *Sphuṭa*, the querist may quit this world. By the second method we get Saturn's *Sphuṭa* as 6^s-4°-17′. Though the texts declare the result to be death, still the astrologer ought not to blurt out what he thinks is the correct prediction, but he should warn the querist that there is serious danger in store for him or somebody in his family. He should be advised to perform proper remedial rituals such as japa, dāna and homa.

Variety of query: There are many sessions of query in addition to the *Aṣṭamaṅgala* session. They are *Devapraśna* (The same as the previous one with special reference to gods and temples, *Ārūḍha-Praśna*, general query (generally known as *Tatkāla-Guṇadoṣa-Praśna*), *Naṣṭa-Praśna* (about lost articles) etc. In all these query-sessions the following six *Rāśis* are considered as very important: (1) The *Ārūḍha lagna* or the sign in which the *gold coin* mixed with flowers, rice, sandal paste etc. is placed; (2) the sign of the zodiac that rises above the horizon at the time of query; (3) the *Navāṃśa* that rises at the time; (4) *Chatra Rāśi*; (5) the sign that corresponds to the part of the body touched by the querist; and (6) the lunar sign at the moment. All these six *Rāśis* should be thoroughly examined in respect of association and aspect of benefics and malefics. Any sign, whether *Ārūḍha*, ascendant, or the one standing for the limb touched, that is occupied or aspected by malefics, will be afflicted with some disease such as ulcers. The querist must be adjudged as one enjoying sound health, fine, cheerful spirits and prosperity, if the Sun, Moon and the lords of the *Ārūḍha* and the ascendant, as well as others in association with the above are strong in *Aṃśa*, exaltation etc. The planets have seven sources of strength called states (*avasthās*):

(1) If the planet is in the *Rāśi* of a neutral, he is said to be in the state of an infant (*atibāla*).
(2) If he be in the sign of a friend, he is a child (*bāla*).
(3) If in his own house, he is a boy (*kumāra*).
(4) If in his *Mūlatrikoṇa* sign, he is a youth (*yuvā*).
(5) If in his exaltation, he becomes, a king (*Rājā*).
(6) If in an enemy's house, he becomes aged (*vṛddha*).
(7) If in his depression he is called dead (*mṛta*).

The seven temporal states of planets have already been delineated in *III*-87-88 *Supra*. These two types of planetary states should be taken into consideration, while assessing the present condition of the querist. In case the lord of the weekday of query is in his exaltation in *Rāśi* or *Aṃśa*, or if the *Ārūḍha* happens to be exaltation sign of the lord of the weekday, he will live long and enjoy good health.

We have already seen that the *Ārūḍha-Rāśi* is that where the gold coin mixed with flowers etc. has been placed. The articles associated with the gold coin are generally (1) water, (2) sandal paste, (3) white flowers, (4) paddy and (5) rice. These five things represent in order the five elements viz. water, air, ether, earth and fire. The gold piece stands for the individual soul, while the five articles, for the body constituted by the five elements. If these articles be properly mixed with the gold piece, the indication is that the querist's longevity, health etc. would progress satisfactorily. If nothing be found on the gold, his life would be cut short. If it is slight, his body must be weak. In case there be some dirt, or a piece of straw, his body must be suffering from some disease. The astrologer should observe keenly the foreign body that is in touch with the gold. He should make predictions of the ailments on the basis of the elements whose subtle forms are sound, touch, form, taste and smell. These are seen in the operation of the senses, ear, skin, eye, tongue and nose respectively. The astrologer should declare which of the limbs of the querist are well or ill. Should the gold be found with its face upward on the flowers and coloured rice, the querists life and prosperity would be advanced. If, on the other hand, it be found lying on the ground with its face turned down, it would denote that his life which was very pleasant till then, has shown a downward trend. If the coin be turned towards the east, the effect would be long life; if towards the south, death; if towards the west, poverty, and if towards the north, much wealth; and if towards the corners, illness and other troubles.

In this connection one should know the following three things: *Prāṇa-Sphuṭa* (life-figure), Deha-Sphuṭa (body-figure) and Mṛtyu-Sphuṭa (death-figure), as these longitudes denoting life, body and death, betoken long life, sound health etc. under certain conditions: Keep the longitudes of the ascendant, the Moon and *Māndi* separately. Multiply each by 9. These figures represent in order the figures of life, body and death.

Let us take an example: Let the *ascendant* be 10^s 22° 12′ 36″. *Moon*—8^s 23° 26′ 25″. *Māndi*—8^s 25° 13′ 47″. When these are multiplied by 9 severally, the three results are:

1. 0^s—19°—53′—24″ ... *Prāṇa-Sphuṭa* or Life-figure.
2. 7—0—57—45 ... *Deha-Sphuṭa* or Body-figure.
3. 7—17—04—03 ... *Mṛtyu-Sphuṭa* or Death-figure.

The first gets the *Navāṃśa* of Virgo, which is a dual sign. The second has the *Navāṃśa* of Cancer which is a movable sign. The third has the *Navāṃśa* of Sagittarius, a dual sign. If these be in movable signs, the querist's life and priosperty would improve; if in immovable signs, he would be afflicted with a chronic disease; and if in dual signs or all the three in the same sign, the result would be death. Similarly if they be in trines, the effect would be a deadly disease. If the figures of body and life be in the same sign, in opposition or in trines, the querist would live long. On the other hand, if the body and death be in one of the above positions, it would result in increase of ailments. If life and death be in the above positions;

coma would be the result. Find out also if the weak Moon, Saturn, Mars or the Sun be posited in the *vargas* (*Rāsi*, *Horā* etc.) of the *Prāṇa-Sphuṭa*. Then there would be aggravation of disease, loss of wealth, and death. On the other hand, if they (*vargas*) largely belong to Mercury, there would be intellectual eminence, provided Mercury is not associated with malefics. If the *vargas* belong to the full Moon, Venus and Jupiter, good health, progeny, prosperity and all-round success would follow.

Viṣa Decanate: Certain decanates are termed poison. They are in order *I*, *II*, *II*, *I*, *I*, *I*, *II*, *III*, *I*, *I*, *II* and *II* in the 12 signs beginning with Aries. This means that the first decanates of Aries, Cancer, Leo, Virgo, Sagittarius and Capricorn; the second of Taurus, Gemini, Libra, Aquarius and Pisces; and the third of Scorpio are Poison. If the longitudes of the ascendant (not *Ārūḍha*) and its lord are associated with poison decantes or *Viṣa Ghaṭīs*, the querist runs the risk of being afflicted with poison. If they be under the blemish called *Ekārgala*, he and his kinsmen might be attacked by some disease, or may meet with accidental death; and if they be under *Uṣṇaśikhā*, the querist might be attacked by high fever or some other ailment, or troubled by a fire-accident in his house.

Find out the sign representing the *Navāṃśa* of the ascendant. If that sign be occupied by benefics, the querist's past was good; and if by malefics, it was unpleasant. If it is asked as to when it was good or bad, the answer is: It was, for so many months as there are *Navāṁśa* that have already risen. If the Moon be posited there, the result would be death; and if the Moon be posited in the *Navāṁśa* of *Māndi*, the same result would follow.

So far we have been studying the three *Sphuṭas* (*Prāṇa*, *Deha* and *Mṛtyu*) on the basis of their *Navāṃśas*. Now we shall see the same from the angle of their longitudes, as a whole. Here the figures for the ascendant, the Moon and *Māndi* are to be multiplied by 5, 8 and 7 respectively. Then add the figures of *Māndi* to each of the first two. Then we would get *Prāṇa-Sphuṭa* (life) and *Deha-Sphuṭa* (body). Then add the Sun's longitude to the third result in order to get *Mṛtyu-Sphuṭa* (death). Let us work out these three *sphuṭas*:

(1) *Ascendant* = $10^s\ 22°\ 12'\ 36'' \times 5 +$ *Māndi*. $8^s\ 25°\ 13'\ 4''$
= 2-16-16-47...(1)

(2) *Moon* = 8^s 23° 26′ 25″ × 8 + *Mandi* = 7-2-45-07...(2)
(3) *Māndi* = 8-25-13-47 × 7 + 6-10-44-53 = 8-7-21-22...(3)
(Sum)

If among these three *Sphuṭas* the body (*deha*) be the greatest, disease would be cured; if life (*Prāṇa*), the greatest disease would be aggravated; and if death (*Mṛtyu*), death would result. In the above example the third viz. *Mṛtyu-Sphuṭa*, is the greatest in value. If the star obtained from this *Sphuṭa* be *Āśleṣā*, *Jyeṣṭhā* or *Revaṭī* or the querist's natal asterism, there might be danger to his life. In case among these three *Sphuṭas* viz. death, life and body, each succeeding *Sphuṭa* be greater than the preceding one, the effect would be beneficial.

Now going back to the topic of *Navāṁśa*, if the *Navāṃśa* of the *Prāṇa-Sphuṭa* be the greatest, the result would be increase of illness; if that of the *deha* be the greatest, cure of ailments; and if that of *mṛtyu*, death. Should any two of these be in the same *Navāṃśa*, then compare their degrees. Should the Moon be posited in the sign of the *Prāṇa-Sphuṭa*, the result would be excellent. Should the *Prāṇa-Sphuṭa* come in between *Mṛtyu-Sphuṭa*, and *Kāla-Sphuṭa* or between the longitudes of malefics; or if there be malefic aspect or association, the result would be danger to the querist's life. The same result would follow, should the *Ārūḍha*, its lord, the ascendant, its lord, the *Navāṃśa* of the ascendant, its lord (lord of the *Navāṃśa*), the Moon and Moon's *Navāṃśa*, be joined with *Mṛtyu-Sphuṭa*, or *Kāla-Sphuṭa*.

Now the reader should be anxious to know about the new subject viz. *Kāla-Sphuṭa*. As this is based on *Mṛtyu-Sphuṭa*, according to one view, first of all we must find out the time in *Ghaṭīs* and *Vighaṭīs* that has elapsed from sunrise on the day of query. Multiply that by 36 and divide the product by the duration of day-time. The result gives signs, degrees etc. If it is Sunday, you have to add to it one sign or 30 degrees. The result is called *Mṛtyu-Sphuṭa*. If this be deducted from 1 sign, it would become *Kāla-Sphuṭa*. On other days, i.e. Monday, Tuesday, Wednesday, Thursday, Friday and Saturday, it is as shown below: *Prāṇa-Sphuṭa* (Called A) is got: Time elapsed in *Ghaṭīs* etc. × 36 and divided by the duration of daytime in *Ghaṭīs* etc.

Weekdays	*Prāṇa-Sphuṭa A*	*Mṛtyu-Sphuṭa Addition of signs*	*Kāla-Sphuṭa*
			Sign
Sunday	A	+1 sign	1—A
Monday	A	+10 signs	10—A
Tuesday	A	+2½ signs	2½—A
Wednesday	A	+5½ signs	5½—A
Thursday	A	+4 signs	4—A
Friday	A	+7 signs	7—A
Saturday	A	+8 signs	8—A

Let us work out an example for Wednesday at 10-30 A.M., sunrise and sunset on this particular day being 6-20 hours and 18-41 hours respectively. The total duration of daytime is 12 hours 21 minutes = 30 Gh. 52.5 Vigh. The time elapsed from sunrise is 4 hours 10 mts = 10 Gh. 25 Vig. By multiplying 10-25 × 36 and dividing product by—

$$30\text{Gh. } 52.5\text{Vig.} = \frac{10\text{-}25 \times 36}{30\text{-}52.5} = 12.145748.$$

∴ *Mṛtyu-sphuṭa* = 12.145748 + 5.5 signs = 17.645748
= 5.645 = 5^s 19° 21′

Therefore *Kāla-Sphuṭa* = 5^s 15° 0′ minus 12.14578.
(on Wednesday)
= 5^s 10° 38′

As we have already found a simpler method for *Mṛtyu-Sphuṭa*, the above method may be laid aside. Only for the sake of the *Kāla-Sphuṭa* which has some common features, the former is mentioned here.

In this scheme scholars insist on knowing the longitude or at best the *Navāṃśa* of the *Ārūḍha* in addition to those of the three others viz. the Sun, Moon, and rising sign, i.e. ascendant. There is a cumbersome method mentioned in the verse, '*Kalaśam adhaḥ*'...of the *Praśna-Mārga*, which is explained elsewhere. It is enough if we understand the simpler method for the present. We can easily work out the ascendant in detail. Look at the longitude given above. Now take the degrees, minutes and seconds only of the ascendant and superimpose them on the *Ārūḍha*. Let the *Ārūḍha* sign be Cancer. The degrees etc. in the ascendant taken by us are 22^s 12′ 36″. Now the *Ārūḍha-longitude* would be 3^s 22° 12′ 36″.

Past and Future

The six signs from the mid-point of the 10th house with respect to the *Ārūḍha* up to the mid-point of the 4th house are considered as representing the past provided the *Ārūḍha* is situated in one of the six signs from Aries to Virgo; and if benefics are posited in this half of the zodiac, it is to be declared that the querist's past was very prosperous, while malefics there lead to contrary results. Similarly if the *Ārūḍha* be situated in the latter half of the zodiac, and if benefics be posited in the six signs from the mid-point of the 4th house, to that of the 10th house, his future would be excellent.

CHAPTER V

DEVA-PRAŚNA

IT HAS BEEN laid down in scriptures that idols of gods worshipped in temples are considered as the incarnations of the chosen deities of the devotees. It is called the *Arcāvatāra* of God, i.e. the Lord manifests himself in the form of the idol, which is made fit for his residence by means of the elaborate rituals prescribed in the *Āgama Śāstras*. It is believed and experienced by the faithful that divine presence is fully secured in the sacred idol after the performance of solemn religious ceremonies carried on for several days at a stretch and then at regular intervals during the year. If this is carried out with solemnity, purity and punctiliousness, accompanied by Vedic and Śāstraic recitations, poor feeding and such other things, such as periodical festivals, then the deity fully manifested in the glorious idol would confer all blessings on the devotees. In case the collective prayers of devotees are found to be infructuous, then the scholars and leaders of society come to the conclusion that some pollution must have taken place in the temple, robbing the deity of its divine powers. After finding out the causes of such pollution that lead to divine displeasure, through the aid of horary science, the people concerned bestir themselves to make amends for the lapses and past sins with a view to replenishing the power of the deity and making it once more the dynamo of spiritual power. In this connection I should like to warn those who scoff at idol-worship in their ignorance, that this mode of worship is meant only for the ignorant masses and *Sādhakas* who have not yet reached the summit of spiritual perfection. Those who have realized *Brahman* however, need no idol or any other prop, as they see the one without a second in their own heart as well as outside.

First of all we must know the general causes that curtail or destroy the divine powers of the deity leading to divine displeasure. They are said to be the following:

(i) Birth or death taking place in the temple precincts.
(ii) Presence of night-soil or other human waste.

(iii) Entry of wicked, impure persons polluting the premises.
(iv) Entry of people who are polluted by birth or death.
(v) Entry into the sanctum sanctorum of owls, vultures, rats, snakes, crows, dogs, donkeys, pigs, jackals etc. All these pollute the sacred shrine and curtail its spiritual powers.
(vi) Growth of mushrooms, toad-stools, anthills, beehive and such other things.
(vii) Sweating and shaking of the idol, ornaments or weapons, or limbs of the idol, showing signs of breakage as well as fall of the idol.
(viii) Sudden outbreak of firecausing destruction of temple properties.
(ix) Sudden stoppage of daily rituals, worship etc.
(x) Unforeseen troubles or disasters.
(xi) Blackmagic perpetrated by wicked persons.
(xii) Worship of the deity, not according to the prescribed rules and *mantras*.
(xiii) Worshipping the deity with forbidden flowers (e.g. Tulasī is forbidden for Gaṇapati, Ketakī for Lord Śiva). Anointing the idol with chilli powder.

There is close connection between the temple and the sanctum sanctorum: The temple is the visible physical frame of the deity. The idol is its subtle body, and the sanctum sanctorum, the support, and the idol, the thing supported. If anyone of these be affected by some flaw, all the three would be affected badly. So it is not enough if a particular part that is affected is cured by means of expiation or propitiation. But all the parts, i.e. the entire body, ought to be purified and rejuvenated for the replenishment of all the spiritual energies for the peace, happiness and prosperity of the people.

There are seven ways of puification (*Sapta-Śuddhi*) that are resorted to in connection with the house-warming ceremony. They are scratching or digging, removal of dirt, burning, filling, presence of cattle (a cow and calf), remnants of food eaten by Brāhmaṇas and sprinkling the place with the sanctified *Pañcagavya*. In addition to these, the purification of the temple precincts, the ritual called *Vāstu-Rakṣā*, and finally the rituals ending with the final consecration called *Brahma Kalaśa* or *Kumbhābhiṣeka* must be undertaken with due regard to their sanctity and details. If these be completed properly, the divine power of the deity or *Sānnidhya* (presence) would be restored to its pristine purity and glory. The following rituals are supposed to maintain the purity and glory of the temple and deity: (1) Penance of the supervising priest or *tantrin*. (2) Regular recitation of the Vedas. (3) Performance of all the daily rituals with due regularity and faith. (4) Conduct of the periodical festivals without any lapse. (5) Regular feeding of people. Everyone of these items has great spiritual potency to raise the spiritual status of the temple and the deity which would ultimately devolve on the worshippers as blessings.

Deva-Praśna has to be resorted to only when the cause of pollution is not known, as a result of which the deity's spiritual power has dwindled. First of all the astrologer should scrutinize the twelve *Bhāvas* of the *Deva-Praśna* with a view to finding out what is pleasing to the deity and what is displeasing or inimical to it. Different deities are to be read from the planets and *Rāśis* as explained below:

If Leo be the *Ārūḍha* at a *Deva-Praśna*, with the Sun aspecting or occupying it or a Kendra, the principal deity should be declared to be Śiva. If the *Ārūḍha* be Cancer and the Moon has the above-named relationship with it, the principal deity would be Śrī Durgā. If Aries be the *Ārūḍha* and Mars be in the above position, it would be Lord Subrahmaṇya. If the *Ārūḍha* be Scorpio and Mars be in the above position, the deity should be Kālī. For Capricorn or Aquarius *Ārūḍha* with Saturn in the above position, the deity would be *Śrī Śāstā*. For Gemini or Virgo *Ārūḍha* with Mercury in such a position the deity should be Lord Viṣṇu. For Sagittarius or Pisces ascendant with Jupiter in the above position, it should be the seat of all the gods.

In case there are more planets in the above position the strongest planet would determine the principal deity. In all the signs the Sun is the significator of Lord Śiva. Should the Sun be in the first decanate of any dual sign, Lord Subrahmaṇya should be thought of. If it be the second decanate of a dual sign, the deity would be Lord Gaṇeśa.

If the Moon is strong at a query, it should be declared that the deity is one of the higher incarnations of Śrī-Durgā Devī.

If the Moon be weak, it should be Kālī, or Mahākālī or a deity of *Rajasa* type.

If the weak Moon be in Aries or Scorpio, it would be *Cāmuṇḍā*. The *Tāmasa* incarnations of Devī are *Rakteśvarī*, *Rakta-Cāmuṇḍā*, *Bhairavī*, *Mahā-Mārikāmbā* etc. This aspect is gathered from the Moon's *Navāṁśa* being Aries or Scorpio.

The signs of the Zodiac are classified into three groups viz. *Sāttvika* (pure), *Rājasa* (active) and *Tāmasa* (indolent):

(i)	Leo and	Sagittarius	are	*Sāttvika*,	odd signs.
	Cancer and	Pisces	are	*Sāttvika*,	even signs.
(ii)	Taurus and	Virgo	are	*Rājasa*,	even signs.
(iii)	Scorpio and	Capricorn	are	*Tāmasa*,	even signs.

If Mars be posited in a *Sāttvika*, odd sign viz. +
Leo or Sagittarius, Lord Kārtikeya should be understood. In other odd signs, *Bhairava* should be thought of. If Mars be in even signs, *Cāmuṇḍā*, *Bhadra-Kālī* and such other fierce deities should be named. According as the sign posited by Mars is of *Sattva*, *Rājas* or *Tāmas*, the corresponding deity would be of similar nature that is named.

Should Mercury be posited in a movable sign or in a dual one, one should declare an incarnation of Lord Viṣṇu such as Śrī Rāma. The deity has to be determined on the basis of Jupiter's sign and the planet or planets connected with him by aspect or conjunction; as well as through their strength. And one has to conclude that the deity is the *Supreme Being*, as Jupiter represents the Supreme Lord. Let us suppose that Jupiter is posited in Leo, both in *Rāśi* and *Aṁśa* in association with or aspect of the Sun. Then the conclusion would be that it is Lord Śiva. Similarly, the Moon would be the significator for Śrī-Durgā; and Mars, for Lord Skanda. Through Venus we have to think of Śrī Annapūrṇeśvarī or Goddess Lakṣmī. If Venus be in his own *Rāśi*, the deity would be the former: Venus in a malefic house, would lead to the determination of the type of deity on the basis of *Sattva*, *Rājas* and *Tāmas*. The distinction of the devīs has to be made on the basis of the nature of the planets and signs as benefic and malefic. *Sāttvika* signs will point to the Goddess Annapūrṇeśvarī; *Rājasa* ones, to *Lakṣmī*, and *Tāmasa* ones, *Yakṣī*. When Venus is posited in an *odd* sign and connected with a male planet, one has to think of Lord Gaṇapati.

Through *Rāhu* we have to think of serpents and their groups. If *Rāhu* be posited in a benefic sign or *aṁśa* and connected with a benefic planet, Lord Subrahmaṇya is to be thought of. However, some scholars have given the opinion that Rāhu stands for the lordship of bādhā-sthāna. It is held that Rāhu has his *Mūla-Trikoṇa*, exaltation and own house in Aquarius, Gemini and Virgo respectively. The 7th houses from these are the respective positions for Ketu.

The Twelve Houses at a Deva-Praśna

1. *Ārūḍha*: Condition of the *mūla-bimba* (original idol), merits and demerits, identity of the deity, spiritual power of the deity (*sānnidhya*), condition of the sanctum sanctorum, condition of the temple courts, and other buildings, the limbs of the original idol, power of the shrine (*kṣetra*), its living, presence (caitanya), conditions, beauty, damage etc. of the image. etc.

2. Temple funds, treasures, articles kept in the temple treasury, temple guards and other servants, temple officials, managers or trustees, materials of worship, boxes for money offerings, properties belonging to the deity, his protection, and God's aspects.

3. *Naivedya* or food-offerings made to the deity, cooks, servants in charge of the kitchen, other servants, subordinate priests, the vessels used for *naivedya*, the kitchen where the sacred offerings are cooked, the fire-place, rice used for *naivedya*, the source of those articles and the mode of their receipt, pipers and drummers (temple choir), florists, sweepers (purifiers), temple bard, rhapsodists, castes, sex etc. of the servants.

4. Merits and demerits of the temple, subsidiary shrines, the sanctum sanctorum, the maṇḍapa, kitchen, dining hall, the enclosures or walls, treasure-house, sacrificial hall, *balipīṭha* and the court, temple elephant, chariot, palanquin, the platform for the banner, vehicle of the particular deity, raised platform for the band of musicians, front gate, house of chariot, cattle-wealth, manger, tank, well, temple decorations, landed property, condition of the temple site.

5. Living presence of the deity or sānnidhya, power, idols,

their number, subsidiary idols, recitation of Vedic mantras, images of attendant deities, *Bali-Mūrtī*, *Bali-Stone*, deity of the banner, banner-staff, minor deities, religious merit, purity, powers of the kalās (they are 16 in all), *tattvas* (24+1), life-force, *mūla*-mantra, consideration of the materials or constituents of the idol (such as mud, stone or metal), consideration of its original installation, movable or immovable, special properties, history—all these are considered.

6. Pollution, trouble from enemies, thefts, acts of black-magic (*kṣudra*), rubbish, rivalry of other temples, internal dissensions, loss of spiritual power, etc.

7. Devotees in general, tourists, glory of the shrine, devotion of city-dwellers, state of villagers, Lord's ornaments, wealth, decorations, its methods, titles and citations of his glory, landed property, lamps, pedestal lamps, vessels used in the worship, bell, different *āratis* (used for waving lights before the Lord), flower-offerings with mantras, garden, songs, dance, rhapsodies of bards (or singing the glories), articles like silk cloths (that are offered to God), gems, front part of the temple, gate, mural paintings—all these things should be considered from the 7th house.

8. The great power of the original deity, sufficiency or deficiency of the *naivedya*, satisfaction, servants of other castes or communities, disasters, fire-accidents, death, detention, idols that had been added later, the *Aṣṭabandha-glue*, condition of the supporting base, all the merits and blemishes, curses and angry scenes, offerings made by devotees, condition of the idol etc.

9. Meritorious acts, progress, fortune, dharmic functions, sacrificial works, chanting of the Vedas, officers, concourse of devotees, fulfilment, ancient glory, president of temple, trustees, chief administrator, charities, feasts, blessings etc.

10. Daily worship, number of *Pūjās*, festivals, the chief worshipper, the sanctum sanctorum, other priests, the village, villagers, glory of the temple, temple cooks, temple bards, daily duties of the temple, monthly duties, and annual functions, votive offerings, divine services, crowds, roads or passages, divine pleasure, displeasure, reputation, the mode and procedure of divine service, drummers, pipers, local customs, the person who carries the decorated idol on the head in procession, all

those that depend on the temple-service, florists, sweepers, players of musical instruments, panegyrist, temple history, government grant, renovation work, various designs in construction etc.

11. Divine glory, increase of wealth, fulfilment of desires, offerings made by devotees, income, gain of wealth, religious merit, sumptuous feast, progress, satisfaction etc.

12. Expenses, spending money on divine projects, waste of money, *tantrins*, other chief priests, sins, curses, breakages, degeneration of outer structures and such other things. *Deva-praśna* should be conducted like the *Aṣṭamaṅgala* in the concerned temple itself.

If there be association or aspect of benefics in any of the houses mentioned above, there would be increase of divine powers, and prosperity of the concerned house; on the other hand, should any *Bhāva* be connected with malefics, it should be declared that there is loss of divine power, or the materials signified by that *Bhāva* are spoiled. If a benefic be posited in the 12th house, he would guard against mismanagement of funds and wasteful expenditure. On the other hand, malefics in the 12th house, would bring about wasteful expenditure. Among the *Bhāvas* the 1st, 5th and 8th represent the *idol*. If there be Mars in any of the three houses, the idol must be broken or one of its limbs is cut, or burnt. Should Saturn occupy any of these houses, the idol is to be declared to be very old, undergoing decay. If both Mars and Saturn be there, the astrologer should declare that both the temple and idol are in a deplorable condition, being very old, broken or dilapidated. If *Rāhu* or *Māndi* or both be posited in these houses, it should be said that some creatures like rats or rat-snakes must have spoiled the sanctity of the idol. If Ketu be there, divine powers must have been destroyed by means of black-magic or use of magical ashes. If benefics posited in these houses be strong, the benefits to the devotees would be maximum, while if they be weak, benefits would be meagre.

If Saturn be posited in the 4th house, one should know that the temple, *maṇḍapa* (roofed raised square platform outside the main shrine), other parts of the temple including the sanctum sanctorum are in a dilapidated condition. On the other hand, should the Sun or Mars be there, some parts of the temple must have been burnt. If Mars be in the 4th house in association with another malefic and situated in the *agni-bhūta* (element of fire), it should be considered that the sanctum sanctorum itself had caught fire. As Mars rules over the south, you may declare that the fire-havoc occurred in that direction. If *Māndi* be in the 4th house, pollution must have occurred there resulting in the loss of *sānnidhya*—divine presence. Should Rāhu or Ketu be posited in the 4th house, the above loss of *sānnidhya* must be due to the entry of wicked and impure persons or *Caṇḍālas*. In this manner the *Bhāva* pertaining to the idol, building etc. should be tackled.

If there be weak malefics in the 3rd or 8th houses—these houses stand for *naivedya*—the sacred food must be considered as defective. If it is Saturn, the food offered is too meagre to satisfy the deity, i.e. as it is not relished by the deity. If it be Mars the food is detested, as it was singed giving out burnt smell. The Sun in that place makes the food dry and parched; the Moon renders it watery like *conjee*; malefic Mercury would make the vessel unfit and food uninviting; a weak Jupiter would make it impure; Venus, it is without good smell, and not sanctified with ghee. It will also suggest that milk and ghee have not been used in the preparation of the food. If Saturn be there, its quantity has been reduced; if Rāhu, it would be polluted being touched by some creature; if Ketu, it would be filled with insects; and if *Māndi*, it is polluted by the touch of impure persons. If the planets occupying this house be strong benefics, no blame could be ascribed.

If there be malefics in the 9th *Bhāva*, the administrative officer of the temple is not free from blame. If there be many such officers, find out the asterism occupied by the malefic in the 9th house. That officer whose natal star is the same as that or its trine, must be having some blemish attached to him. This will apply to other officials and servants as well. In this manner the astrologer has to define the blemishes of *jantrins* through the malefics posited in the 12th house. The priests' merits and demerits are to be read from the planets posited in the 10th house. While delineating the good and bad points of a particular officer or employee, the *Bhāva* relating to him should be considered as the ascendant and the 12 *Bhāvas* taken with reference to that malefic in the 7th house would indicate that the lamps in the sanctum sanctorum do not provide proper illumination, or they do not burn for sufficient period. If the malefic be Saturn, the light would be too dim, because the oil and wick are in sufficient. If it be Mars, the pedestal lamp must be broken. If it be Rāhu or Ketu, it must be dirty. If it be *Māndi*, the oil in the lamp is full of dead insects. In addition to the above, if the weak Moon also be associated, the oil must be declared to be mixed with water. If the 7th house be associated with the lord of the 8th house or the 12th, the ornaments of the deity must be damaged. If it is associated with the lord of 6th house, some part of it must have been stolen. If it be connected with the lord of the 9th house, the thief must be the administrative officer. If it be connected with the 10th lord, the priest must have concealed it. If Mars be connected with it, necklaces are damaged. If Mars be the lord of the 2nd house, the decorative silver eyes of the idol must be broken or damaged. If Saturn be associated with the 7th house, the silver eyes must be very old. If Rāhu be associated with it, then the eyes must be old and dirty. If Ketu be the planet, the eyes must be filled with soot. If strong Jupiter or Venus be in the 7th house, all the ornaments must be in good condition and be studded with gems. If there be malefics in the 10th house, the performance of *pūjā* is not properly carried out, and the equipments of worship are inadequate. Should Saturn be there, they must be too old. If Mars be there, they are broken or damaged. Malefics in the 10th house would lead to the conclusion that the festivals are not conducted properly. If the malefic be the lord of the 4th house, the temple chariot must be in disrepair. This remark applies to the palanquin also. If weak Jupiter be posited in the 10th house, the priest must be declared to be indifferent to his duties. If the lord of the 4th house be the weak Moon, posited in the 10th house, the Boat-Festival was not properly conducted. The houses, forests, hillock, rivulet, other temples, roads etc. have to be inferred from the directions of the signs.

The subject of *Aṣṭabandha*—sacred glue made of 8 ingredients—has to be determined from the 1st, 5th or 8th house. If these signs be movable, the glue has become weak. If they be immovable, it must be in good condition; and if dual ones, it is just tolerable. According to some scholars, the 4th house also gives details of the ghee.

If the sign representing the idol be movable, then the idol should be said to be shaky; if it be a downward-looking sign, it is to be understood that the idol has fallen from its place. If that house be occupied by strong Moon or Venus, the idol must be attractive.

The following propitiatory rituals are advised for warding off the evils affecting the temple and for the rejuvenation of divine presence:

Gaṇa-Homa sacrifice to propitiate Lord Gaṇapati is the first and foremost duty for invoking His blessings and for warding off all obstacles, worship of the divine mother, recitation of Vedic hymns are to be done. To purify the temple precincts and the idol consequent on their pollution, first of all *Pañca-gavya* has to be sprinkled, the idol should be bathed with *Pancāmṛta*, as well as with sanctified water with Vedic hymns, and *Navaka-kalaśa* ritual should also be performed. If these rituals are performed properly, the pollution and other evil effects troubling the temple and the people, would be removed and the deity's divine power restored to its pristine glory.

Bādhā (trouble): If the planets owning the places of *bādhā* be posited in the inauspicious houses, the trouble should be declared to be due to the wrath of the deity pertaining to the concerned planet. In case there be a malefic in the 12th house from the planet indicating divine wrath on account of the inauspicious position of the planet ruling the *bādhā* place, it should be inferred that the divine wrath has been caused by the defects of the idol. If, in addition, the planet be associated with *Māndi* or Rāhu, it must be due to the contact of a rat-snake with the idol. If Saturn alone be associated, the idol and/or the temple has become very old and dilapidated, or it may be said that pollution has taken place. If the planet be associated with Mars, the wrath is due to lack of protection as a result of internal quarrels among the temple guardians.

Mitigation of divine wrath: If the planetary configuration should indicate a series of breakages of the idol etc., then it should be replaced by a new idol, after the performance of the

Brahma kalaśa rituals. Should the damage of the idol be of a minor nature, replacing it is not necessary. However, the sacred *Kalaśābhiṣeka* and other expiatory rites ought to be gone through. If pollution has occurred, *Śuddhi kalaśa* alone is to be done. If the significator planet of divine wrath be posited in the 4th house associated with a malefic, the temple precinct and other adjacent areas should be declared to be dilapidated, as a result of the divine displeasure. In that case divine presence has to be withdrawn from the idol and temple by means of Vedic rituals. The temple building should be renovated and a new idol installed according to the rules of *Āgama Śāstras*. When the idol is to be replaced by a new one, the old idol is kept in a temporary shelter called *bālālaya* and daily worship continued until the new idol is installed.

If the *bādhaka* planet indicating divine wrath be posited in the 7th house, and if that house be Aries, Scorpio or Leo, the expiation should consist of the following items: (i) Waving of ceremonial lights before the idol (Lord); (ii) Offering oil for the lamps; (iii) a permanent burning lamp; (iv) a special festival called *Raṅgapūjā* (with lights and food offerings in two rows); and (v) offering of a pedestal lamp and such other things. If the planet be in Cancer, Taurus or Libra, the expiation should consist of offering of milk, milk porridge (pāyasa) ghee, *Pañcāmṛta* (a sweet mixture of milk, ghee, curd, honey and sugar) etc. If it be Gemini or Virgo, it should consist of anointing the idol with sandal paste, or offering sandal pieces, bathing the idol with water mixed with sandal paste. If the sign be Sagittarius or Pisces, divine pleasure could be regained through the offering of garlands of fragrant flowers, worship after decorating the idol, *Puṣpāñjali* (worship of the Lord with flowers accompanied by *mantras* or Names 108, 300 or 1000 times). If the sign be Capricorn or Aquarius, one should offer ornaments, silk cloth, or ṣilver or gold pieces etc. If the concerned planet be posited in the 8th or 10th house, the remedial measures should consist of several kinds of worship: Worship thrice a day and food-offerings to all the minor deities, and such other services. If the planet be posited in the 12th house, the service should take the form of music (both vocal and instrumental), group singing of devotional songs, recitals of Purāṇas, religious discourses etc.

If the concerned planet denoting divine wrath be posited in the ascendant, it is to be removed by the offer of a human figure made of silver or gold to the Lord. If the planet be in the 2nd house, Vedic scholars should be employed to do *mantrajapa* (repetition of a particular mantra), Vedic and Purāṇic recitations etc. If it be in the 3rd house, various types of *Pūjās* are to be done to propitiate the deity or deities. In the 4th house, by helping in the construction of subsidiary buildings of the temple. In the 5th house, by feeding well all classes of people to their heart's content, and providing feasts and gifts to the deserving along with monetary offerings. In the 6th house, a *bali* (minor festival), to the temple deity should be arranged, or a sacrifice where oblations are made with Vedic hymns pertaining to the deity. If it is a Śiva temple the sacrifice takes the form of *Aghora Homa*, while in a Viṣṇu temple, of *Sudarśana Homa*; in a Durgā temple, it is of *Pañca-Durgā-mantra Homa* (a sacrifice to the divine mother who has taken five incarnations); and in the case of Lord Gaṇapati, it is *Bāla*-Gaṇapati homa. If it be in the 7th house, the propitiation is through dance performance. In the 8th house, through the festival of victory, offering *bali* or sanctified food to the minor deities. In the 9th house, through devout worship, meditation, worship with basic mantra, *japu*, recitals of the Purāṇas etc. In the 10th house, conducting a special festival wherein the temple car is drawn through the streets with a caparisoned elephant leading the procession, *Raṅga-Pūjā* etc. In the 11th house, offering *tarpaṇa* through water, milk etc. and *Abhiṣeka* (bathing the deity). And in the 12th house, there is no necessity for any propitiation.

Next we have to think of particular planets causing divine displeasure and the signs occupied by them, while determining propitiatory measures. If such a planet happens to be the Sun, or if he be posited in Leo, propitiation should be done by means of special worship, offerings of various articles etc. This is resorted to for removing illness of the querist or his family members.*

*The details given above would be interesting and instructive to the readers as they hold the mirror to our rich social and cultural traditions that wield tremendous influence on the minds of the people of various strata of education and civilization.

If it be the Moon or the planet be in Cancer, poor children should be fed well, the deity in the shrine be bathed with water or milk or *Pancāmṛta* or with the conch-shell. If it be Mars, or if the significator be in Aries or Scorpio, propitiation is through the offering of lamps, arranging the special lighting festival, or *Lakṣadīpa*, and sacrifice to the sacred fire through the mantra sacred to the particular deity. If the planet be Mercury, or if the planet (significator) be in Gemini or Virgo, it is to be achieved through the service of a divine dance programme. If it be Jupiter, or if the significator be in Sagittarius or Pisces, feeding of Brāhmaṇas, presentation of cloth, monetary, gifts, or offering of raiments and ornaments to the deity. If the planet be Venus, or if the significator be in Taurus or Libra, all persons without distinction should be fed in the presence of the Lord. If Saturn be the significator or the concerned planet be in Capricorn or Aquarius, a piece of land should be gifted away to the deity or a worthy recipient. By feeding the lowest of the untouchables to their heart's content the Lord, who is the in-dweller of all creatures, gets pleased and automatically the diseased person's ailments get cured. This is said in a query regarding illness in the querist's family. These remedies are not mandatory, but only advisory. For, how could a poor labourer afford a costly course of remedies? What the Lord wants is man's pure heart and not a heap of gold. These rituals, charities, rigorous observances are meant to teach men and women humility, non-attachment, dispassion and discrimination. Rich persons are generally ease-loving, haughty and miserly. If a poor man prays steadfastly to the Lord, He will immediately respond to his prayer and relieve the devotee of his sufferings as exemplified by the lives of many a saint and seer of all countries.

Sometimes querists ask the astrologer—"Would the Lord be pleased in case I performed the prescribed remedies?" At this the astrologer again handles and shuffles the heap of cowries before him repeating prayers to the Divine Sun and other deities. He then lifts a handful of cowries from the heap and keeps it aside. He counts these cowries in groups of twelve and ultimately the number of remaining cowries, which denotes the *Ārūḍha Lagna*. If the planet representing divine displeasure be in a desirable house counted from this *Ārūḍha Lagna*, and if Jupiter should occupy or aspect that house, the intended remedies, it is to be declared, would remove the trouble and the Lord would confer. His blessings on the querist and his family. This method of finding out God's pleasure is resorted to at the end of the remedial ceremonies. If there be a planet in the *Ārūḍha* in association with a benefic, it should be said that the Lord who is signified by that planet is favourably disposed towards the querist. On the other hand, if the lord of the 9th house be in the house of *Bādhā* (harm), it should be taken that divine wrath has been caused by the person's neglect of that deity that had been worshipped by him or his ancestors; and if he should resume the worship and continue it as before, the Lord would with pleasure shower His blessings on him.

Some people who manage the affairs of a rich temple, may be tempted to misappropriate God's funds. In course of time this sin of utilizing public wealth meant for public weal for one's own selfish ends, falls on him by God's wrath or displeasure. After all God has neither pain nor pleasure, neither loss, nor gain, neither friend nor foe. It is the agony or sufferings of the public, especially the poor, whose tears of sorrow are the direct outcome of man's sinful acts, which has affected his subtle body and brought about the illness and other calamities in his family. 'As you sow, so you reap' is a well known adage.

Now we should know if there are other methods of detecting this kind of divine wrath. If the lord of the *Bādhā-sthāna* or those of the bad houses (i.e. 6, 8 and 12) be posited in the 11th or 2nd house from the *Lagna*, it should be predicted that divine wrath has been brought about by the theft of temple funds.

Kṛṣṇācārya states that the Moon, Mars, Rāhu and Saturn represent *Dhātu* or mineral; the Sun and Venus, *Mūla* or root (or trees); and Mercury and Jupiter, *Jīva* or animal. Signs Aries and others, and stars *Aśvinī* and others stand for: *Dhātu*, *Mūla* and *Jīva* in succession. His commentator explains that the Moon, Saturn, Mars and *Rāhu* posited in *kendra* or *koṇa* determine *dhātu*; the Sun and Venus in such a position, *Mūla*; and Mercury and Jupiter, *Jīva*. Among the signs all movable ones stand for *dhātu*; all Immovable ones, *Mūla*; and all Dual ones, *Jīva* or living beings. Similarly *Aśvinī Bharaṇī* and *Kṛttikā* represent mineral, root and living being respectively. In this manner three of the 27 stars are repeated nine times. If a mineral-planet be posited in his own *Aṁśa,* decanate or sign or aspected by a similar planet, the astrologer should declare that the querist would gain some mineral object. Similar is the case with regard to *Mūla*-planet and *Jīva*-planet. Suppose a *Jīva*-planet is posited in another's *Aṁśa,* decanate or sign, then declare the animal or living being to be of another class. Decanates of malefic planets as well as those that are posited in malefic signs, as well as those that are associated with or aspected by malefics, would point to iron vessels. The *mūla*-signs, *Aṁśas* and decanates as well as the planets stationed in *mūla*-signs and decanates that are associated with or aspected by *mūla*-planets, lead to the inference of trees, plants, fruits or creepers. The animal-planet, *Aṁśa* and decanate, as well as those decanates that occupy the houses of animal-planets, or the signs and decanates that are occupied or aspected by animal-planets would make us think of living beings. The distinction of these three classes of objects has to be made on the basis of the strength of the *Rāśis, Aṁśas* planets and decanates. It is also very essential for the astrologer to come to the judgment on the basis of whatever is seen, heard and whatever is touched by the querist, and whatever omen is seen at the time of the query. The author further says: Each of these three categories (*yonis*) is sub-divided into three groups as (1) *Kevala-Dhātu*; (2) *Dhātu-Mūla*; (3) *Dhātu-Jīva*; (4) *Kevala-Mūla*; (5) *Mūla-Jīva*; (6) *Mūla-Dhātu*; (7) *Kevala-Jīva*; (8) *Jīva-Dhātu*; and (9) *Jīva-Mūla.* So if a *Dhātu*-planet is posited in a *Mūla-Rāśi,* one should infer the object to be a tree, fruit, flower or creeper, which is the result of a combination of *Dhātu* and *Mūla.* On the other hand, if a *Dhātu*-planet occupies a *Jīva*-sign, it would be an animal made of a metal. If a *Mūla*-planet occupies a *Mūla*-sign (e.g. Venus or the Sun in Taurus), the result would be pure root. On the other hand, if a *Mūla*-planet be in a *Dhātu*-sign (e.g. Cancer), it would point to a burnt-root or fruit, ashes, Camphor or asafoetida (which is a *Mūla-Dhātu*). If the lord of a *Mūla-Rāśi* be joined with a *Jīva*-planet, it would be an object brought about by the combination of both the elements like fruits, roots and crops. If a *Jīva*-planet (Mercury) be in a *Jīva-Rāśi* (Sagittarius, it would be a pure living being. On the other hand; if a *Jīva*-planet (Jupiter) be in a *Dhātu-Rāśi* (Libra), it would be the result of these two, e.g. the wax of the ear, rheum of the eye, urine, taecal matter, flesh, blood, hair and nails—all things born of the body. *Jīva-Mūla* is a living seed.

How are the *Navāṁśas* of the signs treated in respect of these three elements? According to the Kṛṣṇīya the *Nāvāṁśas* of odd *Rāśis* are assigned to *Dhātu*, *Mūla* and *Jīva*; *Mūla*, *Jīva* and *Dhātu*; and *Jīva*, *Dhātu* and *Mūla* respectively. In even *Rāśis* they are assigned to *Jīva*, *Dhātu* and *Mūla*; *Dhātu*, *Mūla*, and *Jīva*; and *Mūla*, *Jīva* and *Dhātu*. This is to be applied both to the ascendant and lunar sign. The particular *Dhātu* of a planet should be read from his *Nāvaṁśa*.

(1) To *Mars* are assigned the following six *Dhātus*: Copper, bricks, potsherds, corals, mud and dust. If Mars is in the first 5° portion of an odd sign, it is copper.

(2) To the *Moon* belong: Moon-stone, salt, conch-shell, crystal, bronze and tin.

(3) To *Jupiter* belong: Red gem (ruby?), gold, red arsenic, glass, and yellow orpiment.

(4) To *Mercury* belong: A gem called *Vaikṛta*, emerald, gold clay and glass.

(5) To *Venus* belong: Silver, crystal, pearl and lapis lazuli.

(6) To *Saturn* belong: Iron, collyrium, sapphire and lead.

(7) To the *Sun* belong: Sun-stone, brass, lapis lazuli and pure lead.

If a particular planet is aspected by a malefic, the *dhātu* is to be said to be malleable; on the other hand, if he is aspected by a benefic, it is non-malleable. Though both gold and ruby belong to the class of *dhātu*, yet gold is malleable, while ruby is not. Others assign *dhātus* as follows to the planets: Sun = copper; Moon = Moon-stone; Mars = gold; Mercury = shells; Jupiter = silver; Venus = pearls; and Saturn = iron. The class of *dhātus* as high, medium and worthless is to be distinguished on the basis of the planet's position in exaltation, own house, *Mūlatrikoṇa* etc. in respect of articles lost, held in the fist, thought of and gained, provided the planets are strong and posited intrines or angles. The sub-division of *dhātu* is done on the basis of decanate, *Navāṁśa* and planet. If Mars and the Sun should aspect the decanate of Mars coupled with the Sun's *Navāṁśa*, or if the two planets being strong be posited in *kendras*, the result would be that the *dhātu* refers to a metal or *dhāmya*.

Now reverting to divine wrath, if a movable sign be the ascendant, or if a mineral planet (the Moon, Mars, Saturn and *Rāhu* stand for minerals) be posited in the *Lagna*, the cause of divine wrath must be a (mineral) metallic object. On the other hand, if the *Lagna* be an immovable sign, or if it be occupied by a planet denoting root or tree (the Sun and Venus represent a tree or plant), a tree should be the cause of the divine wrath. Lastly if a dual sign be the ascendant, or if a planet representing living being (Mercury and Jupiter), the cause of *deva-kopa* must be an animal. By *dhātu* we mean silver, gold, copper etc., by *mūla*, earth, garden, tree, creeper, planet etc; by *Jīva*, man, quadruped, cow, bull, cock etc. Gemini and Virgo ascendants lead to the thought of human beings, Sagittarius, of quadrupeds, and Pisces, of aquatic animals. This method is employed in determining the class of lost or missing articles. Here the nature of the sign representing *Lagna* should be able to tell us whether the stolen article belongs to animal category, vegetable group or mineral class.

Now we should see as to how we could determine the cause of divine displeasure among these three groups. An astrologer who is thoroughly conversant with the beliefs, customs and traditions, both social and religious, alone could undertake the task of answering such questions as God's wrath and its cause.

If it is found that some living being is the cause of the wrath, the astrologer should conjecture that as the querist, who had previously taken a vow to the effect that he would offer a bull to the temple, if his wish is fulfilled, has not made good his promise. Hence the trouble. If a metal be the cause of God's wrath, the querist must have failed in his duty to offer the promised gold or silver. On the person might have taken away some gold ornament belonging to the deity for his personal benefit.

The wrath of one's *dharma-daiva* (village deity) is based on four planetary configurations:

(1) Lord of *bādhā-sthāna* is to be posited in the 4th house.

(2) Lord of the 4th house is to be posited in *bādhā-sthāna*.

(3) Lord of the *bādhā-place* being posited in a house belonging to the lord of the 4th house.

(4) Lord of the 4th house occupying a house of the lord of the *bādhā-sthāna*.

The querist's particular *dharma-daiva* should be read from the lord of the 4th house. When the 4th house and its lord are ill-placed, worship of the deity indicated by the planet should be undertaken seriously for warding off the harm arising from the neglect of the *dharma-daiva*. This deity should thereafter be worshipped year after year strictly according to ancient custom. If the shrine of the deity be in a dilapidated condition, all devotees should join together and renovate it with due ceremony. If Jupiter, happening to be the lord of *bādhā*-place be posited in one of the bad houses viz. 6, 8 and 12, and if he be in a *kendra* to *Rāhu*, the trouble would be due to a high-class serpent. If Jupiter be in a *kendra* to *Māndi* (in the above condition), the trouble must be due to the wrath of low-class serpents. Similarly, if *Rāhu* alone be posited in the *bādhā-sthāna*, then also the trouble must be due to *sarpa-doṣa* (curse of snakes). If *Rāhu* be aspected by or associated with the Sun, the serpent causing trouble should be of a high class. If it be the Moon, the serpent must be of a lower class. If both the Sun and Moon be associated with *Rāhu*, both kinds of serpents should be thought of in this connection.

If *Rāhu* is posited in 6th, 8th or 10th house, the remedy for serpent-trouble is the performance of *Āśleṣā-Bali* a special *pūjā* performed to pacify the serpents; or it may be done through *nāga pratiṣṭhā*, where a new stone-image of serpent is duly installed in a special place in the garden and worshipped regularly.

If *Rāhu* be posited in the *bādhā-sthāna* that is a movable sign, serpents, wrath should be inferred, as a result of destruction of its eggs. If the sign is dual, its young ones must have been killed. If it be a stable sign, the trees, creepers etc. of the *snake-park* (*nāga-vana*) must have been destroyed. If *Rāhu* be in the ascendant identical with Scorpio, both these must have been destroyed. In such cases a golden snake with eggs should be worshipped in a snake-park and gifted away to a worthy person. If Mars be posited in a *kendra* from *Rāhu*, *sarpa-śāpa* (curse of snake) may be inferred as a result of destruction of trees in the *nāga-vana*, or killing of young snakes while digging the earth. Or it might be damaging of anthills. Similarly the sanctity of the serpent-park gets spoiled by the entry of impure and forbidden persons or animals like buffaloes and elephants. Should *Māndi* alone be posited in a *kendra* of *Rāhu*, the wrath must have been caused by such acts as spitting in the park, urinating, having sexual union, cutting down trees etc. The remedy for all such troubles is planting trees and opening a sacred park, purifying it or constructing a platform of snake-idols.

If the Sun be posited in the *bādhā*-place, identical with Aries or Scorpio, or in Mars' *Navāṁśa*, the querist's troubles must be attributed to his father's curse. Think of the mother's curse, if the Moon be similarly situated. A malefic in Leo and Cancer would point to the curse of respective parents, provided the house occupied by the concerned luminary happens to be an untoward house. The remedy consists of devout services made to them and getting their satisfaction and blessings. If the house of *bādhā* be Sagittarius or Pisces with a malefic in it, or if Jupiter be in that house (*bādhā*) with a malefic, the trouble must be due to the curse of Brāhmaṇas. Similarly the Sun in the house of *bādhā* with a malefic in it, or Leo with a malefic be the *bādhā-sthāna*, would suggest curses of ancestors or preceptors. The remedy lies in worshipping Gods and Brahmins through feeding, gifts of clothes and money.

The lord of the 6th house in the 9th or the lord of the latter in the former house would lead to the same conclusion. The above rule may be applied to the Moon, lord of the 6th house, as well as the 4th house and its lord, in order to find out mother's curse.

Trouble From Discarnate Spirits

Scriptures state that if adequate obsequial rites are not performed according to rules, the discarnate spirits do not get peace and happiness, and consequently become *piśācas* and harass their kith and kin. How are we to know this? It is done through *Māndi*. If *Māndi* be posited in the *bādhā*-place or in a *dusthāna* (6, 8 or 12), it should be declared that there is trouble from spirits. The condition of a discarnate spirit called *pretatva* is to be found out as follows: If *Māndi* be posited in the *bādhā* or an untoward house, or be associated with or aspected by Mars, or in a sign or *Aṁśa* of Mars, the departed soul became a *preta* on account of its violent death by fire, weapon or suicide or through small pox. Should *Māndi* be posited in the *bādhā*-place which belongs to Saturn, or has association or aspect of Saturn, or his *Aṁśa*, the departed soul must have quit the world under great distress as a result of the person's loneliness at the last moment. Consequently funeral ceremonies could not be performed for it. Here the distinction between the malefics viz. *Māndi*, Mars and Saturn, is that *Māndi* in association with Mars leads to violent or tragic death, while with Saturn, death must have taken place in a lonely place without any relative or friend in the know of the event or place. If this *Māndi* should be associated with or aspected by *Rāhu*, the soul must have become a *preta* as a result of snake-bite. If that *Māndi* be posited in a watery sign in association with malefics, the soul must have been turned into a *preta* as a result of the person falling into a well, lake or river. If *Māndi* be associated with malefics, the death must have been unnatural. If *Māndi* be related to benefics, the death must have been natural. If the sign or *Aṁśa* occupied by *Māndi* be an odd one the *preta* must be a Male; if it be even, a female. The number of *pretas* should be read from the number of *Aṁśas* covered by *Māndi* in the sign occupied by it.

In this manner the *preta* of a brother or any other relative could be read from *Māndi* in association with the respective significator. The same result can also be arrived at by the *bhāva* position of *Māndi*. Similarly the nature of the house of *Māndi* as movable and stable would lead to the knowledge of the *preta* as old and new respectively. *Māndi's* association with the 4th house (or its lord) would point to the *preta*, being that of a close relative. Saturn's association also will point to the *preta* being one of a *servant*. Similarly the age of the *preta* should be read from the decanate occupied by *Māndi*.

As a result of the wrath of *preta*, loss of progeny, illness and other troubles take place in the family. To obviate that the *śāstras* have laid down that *śrāddha* ceremonies should be performed in holy places along with *Tila-Homa* (sacrifice with sesamum), feeding of *brāhmaṇas*, etc. If this is done with devotion, the *pretas* become established in the world of *pitṛs* (manes) and being happy they bless the family with wealth, progeny, health etc. There are some attendant spirits of Lord Śiva called *bhūta gaṇas* who attack some people on account their blasphemous behaviour towards the Lord. These *bhūtas* are of three categories viz. *Hantukāmas* (wishing to kill), *Rantukāmas* (wishing to play with), and *Bhoktukāmas* (wishing to eat). The last group gives troubles to people with the intention of getting worship, food and other honours from the victims. The following list gives the *bhūta-Gaṇas* allotted to the planets:

(i) The Sun = *Rudra Gaṇa*, *Ugrabhūta* and *Nāga*.
(ii) The Moon = *Kinnara*, *Yakṣa* and *Nāgas*.
(iii) Mars = *Ugra Graha*, *Rākṣasa*, *Bhūta*, *Agni-Bhairava*, *Kāla Bhairava*.
(iv) Mercury = Kinnara and *Aṭṭālaga*.
(v) Jupiter = *Deva Graha*, *Śubha Nāga*, Trinity.
(vi) Venus = *Yakṣi*, *Mātṛ-Gaṇa* and *Nāga*.
(vii) Saturn = *Aśubha Graha*, *Bhūta-Nāthas* headed by *Śāstā* and *Rudragaṇas*.
(viii) Rāhu = Serpents. *Ketu—Caṇḍāla-Bhūtas*.
(ix) Māndi = *Pretas*.

Remedy: To get rid of these troubles one should perform *Mṛtyuñjaya Homa*, *Sudarśana Homa* and *Tīrtha Snāna*.

CHAPTER VI

MATRIMONY

WHEN THE ALL-PERVADING self stays in its single-blessedness which is beyond description and perception of any kind, and which is described only by negating all descriptions as *Neti, Neti*, not this, not this, there is no talk of relativity or duality. But when the One begins to become many, the first stage of evolution, like that of a seed, is an entity consisting of two dissimilar properties like the magnetic poles. This stage of one and the same entity having these two opposite poles, positive and negative, is best represented by the *ardha-nārīśvara* aspect of Lord Śiva. This has been beautifully expressed in a figurative language by the Prince of poets viz. Kālidāsa, in his unique *Kāvya*, the *Raghuvaṁśa*, as sound and sense inextricably joined together. Scientists also confirm that in creation too the first stage, i.e. molecule, is distinguished by the combination of the positive and negative elements, proton and neutron. There cannot be any creativity if these two, positive and negative elements, do not combine. So it is a spiritual necessity that *prakṛti* (primordial matter) and *puruṣa* (primordial spirit) should join together and work in harmony for the grand play of creation, resulting in variety and multiplicity. Then the cycle starts moving backwards giving fillip to the process of involution. If the two elements viz. *prakṛti* and *puruṣa* (matter and spirit) do not co-operate and work unitedly and harmoniously, the purpose of creation would be affected. Matrimony or marriage of two souls, one in female form and the other in male form, is established mainly according to Vedic injunction, for the purpose of "*dharma-prajāsampatyartham*"—for the realization of *dharma*, progeny and prosperity, (or prosperity or plenitude of these two) i.e. for the progress and happiness of *dharma* and progeny.

This rebuts the statement of social reformers to the effect that marriage is only a social contract between two independent individuals. On the other hand, it is an inseparable divine, religious bond or contract entered into by the parties along with their parents, preceptors, elders and kinsmen in the presence of the Holy Fire representing the greatest Godhood, as well as of leaders of the society. Another factor which makes the marriage ceremony doubly sacred and inviolable is that the bride and bridegroom take an oath before the sacred fire to the effect that their hearts are united and they have become permanent companions in *dharma*, *artha* and *kāma* (virtue, wealth and joy) and would not deviate from the moral path under any circumstance.

The ritual of *Saptapadī*, Seven Steps---the mantras, looking at the *Dhruva* star or *Arundhatī* among the Great Bear—all these bear testimony to the great sanctity and inviolability of this sacred institution called *marriage.* A question may be asked at this juncture. "Why should people consult astrologers for fixing marital alliances, as they are made in Heaven?" True, it has been already fixed by destiny or God. Still man tries his best to find out God's will on the basis of the rules prescribed by ancient sages. Unless there is *Ṛṇānubandha*, bond of *karma* of previous life binding two souls in holy wedlock, there cannot be true marriage. On the other hand, if the *kārmik* bond between two persons (partners) is not sufficiently strong and lasting, it might break in the middle. To get over all such hurdles and troubles, parents of girls and boys seek the help of learned and devoted astrologers to know about the compatibility of the two horoscopes in respect of *Gaṇa*, *Dina*, and others, ten or twelve in all, as well as health, longevity, issue, financial position etc.

When the parents of a girl or boy approach an astrologer, the latter should assess the longevity of the boy and the girl and only then proceed with other factors, relating to marriage. It has already been mentioned that the objective of marriage is to beget worthy children for pleasing the ancestral spirits. Even after comparing the horoscopes of the bride and bride-groom. *Praśna* is essential for finding out the prospects of their conjugal life, according to the rule laid down by Bṛhaspati and Mādhavācārya. The parties should approach an astrologer on an auspicious day for fixing an auspicious *Muhūrta* for the marriage ceremony.

If the 7th house of the query chart be occupied by benefics, the wedlock would lead to prosperity and happiness. In this connection the girl's parents usually ask the astrologer if the groom would be worthy of their daughter and their married life be prosperous and happy.

In the query chart the ascendant represents the bride, and the 7th house, the bride-groom. The groom's physical conditions, character etc. are to be read from the 7th house, and the bride's from the ascendant, according to Sage Bṛhaspati. The other *bhāvas* viz. 2nd, 3rd etc. would indicate the corresponding significations of the bride as in the case of a natal chart.

If the Sun be posited in his debilitation or inimical house, without aspecting the ascendant or *Ārūḍha*, the astrologer should declare that the girl's father would be dead. Similar result can be read from the Moon in respect of the bride's mother. On the other hand, if the Sun being strong be posited in a good house, her father must be alive, though the *lagna* be not aspected by the Sun. However, there is one difference: Though the father is alive, the girl may not be benefited by him. Similarly other relations should be considered from the respective significators. If the Sun be posited in an inimical or depression house, or if the 7th house is not aspected by the Sun, the groom's father may not be alive. The mother's existence has to be inferred from the Moon under similar circumstances.

Impediments

The following planetary situations indicate obstacles to the marriage:

(i) If the Moon, posited in 3rd, 6th, 10th or 11th house either from the *Ārūḍha* or ascendant, be aspected by Mars, there would be some obstacles to the marriage on account of the girl's monthly course. On the other hand, if the Moon be posited in 2, 4, 5, 7, 9 or 12, and aspected by Jupiter, the marriage would take place without any hindrance.

(ii) According to Bṛhaspati, if the query be made in the dark fortnight and the Moon be posited in an even sign or in the 8th house, or be aspected by malefics, the alliance would not take place.

Success of the Alliance

If the lords of the *lagna* and the 7th house, or Venus and *lagna*-lord, be joined together or aspect each other, or if they be in their respective exaltations or friendly houses, or exchange positions, there will be no obstacle whatsoever to the marriage.

Stoppage of Marriage

(i) Malefic is in the 8th house at query.
(ii) The malefic is aspected by other malefics.
(iii) The above malefics be in debilitation. Any one of the above conditions is likely to stop the marriage.
(iv) If the 6th house is occupied and aspected by malefics, the stoppage must be due to illness of the bride or groom, provided the house is the planets' debilitation of inimical sign. It may be due to the machination of relatives.

Early Death of Couple

(1) If the Moon combined with malefics be posited in the 6th or 8th house, the couple would meet with their end in the 8th year of marriage. (2) If Mars be in the 6th or 8th house from the Moon, the husband would quit the world within 9 years without begetting any issue. (3) The husband's death is to be expected in the 7th month itself, if the Moon and Mars be conjoined in the *lagna* or the 7th house.

Omens: Success of marriage is indicated by the querist holding his hands joined together or touching his chest or head. If he touches his knees or feet, there would be hindrance to marriage. The same result is indicated by his touching his back or hips with his left hand. If birds, animals or snakes are seen mating in the neighbourhood, the girl's chastity would be in doubt. If a man comes to the place of query accompanied by two women, or one woman accompanied by two men, or a cow and a bull are seen in the vicinity, it indicates remarriage. The following omens augur hindrance to marriage:

1. Sight of red flower would lead to postponement owing to the girl being in menses.

2. Scratching one's body, sight of blood, elephant's trumpeting buffalo's cry, falling of a red flower from the tree.

3. Two persons coming together and then going in opposite directions; sight of a dead body; two persons engaged in quarrel.

The following omens indicate quick marriage: Arrival of a cloth-vendor; a person wearing new clothes and holding washed ones in the hand; arrival of a dear person; a vessel—vendor arriving; sight of mirror with handle; sight of the white flower *Lucas* aspera or Tumbe (in *Kannada*), silver articles, someone rubbing his eyes, two objects bound together.

Bad Omen: If in the vicinity of the session somebody is seen digging the earth, or the sound of a wooden piece being sawn is heard, it would suggest that the girl in question is of questionable character.

Yāma Śukra: A minor planet called Yāma-Śukra is mentioned in this connection. It is made use of in determining the conjugal prospects of a couple. It is quite similar to *Māndi* in its rising during day and night, the only difference being the rising periods on the weekdays from Sunday onwards. The Yāma-Śukra rises at *Ghaṭīs*, 22, 18, 14, 10, 6, 2 and 26 *Ghaṭīs* respectively on the 7 days from Sunday to Saturday. At night like *Māndi* it rises at the time meant for the 5th day.

If the *Yāma-Śukra* (Y.S.) or the lord of the 10th house from it be posited in the 6th, 8th or 12th house from the ascendant, the marriage would not take place as planned. If Venus be posited in an untoward house from the Y.S., the same result would follow. Now add up the longitudes of the Y.S., Venus and the *lagna-Lord*. If the resulting sign be occupied by *Rāhu*, *Ketu* or *Māndi*, or aspected by *Māndi*, the married life of the couple would not be happy.

Prospects of Married Life

If Venus and lord of the 7th house be posited in 3rd, 6th, 10th or 11th house, the couple's fortune would increase after marriage. In the same manner their fortune would improve after the birth of a child, should the significator of progeny viz. Jupiter, and the lord of the 5th house be posited in *Upacaya* houses.

Quick Marriage

1. If the Moon and Venus be posited in strength in even signs or *Aṁśas*, and aspecting the ascendant, the person would be married soon.

2. If the ascendant be in a female decanate or even *Aṁśa*, the Moon and Venus, aspecting the ascendant, there would be quick marriage.

A Beautiful Bride

Should there be benefics in trines or angles, and the 7th house owned and aspected by benefics, the querist would get a charming girl as bride. On the other hand, if the 7th house be owned and aspected by malefics, he would be married to an ugly girl.

The following *Yogas* indicate quick marriage:

(i) The Moon should be posited in one of the houses, 3, 6, 10, 11, and 7, and be aspected by benefics.

(ii) The ascendant should be Virgo, Libra, Gemini or Aquarius, and the Moon and Venus in the ascendant or the 7th house.

(iii) Mercury, Jupiter and Venus should be in angles, especially in the 7th house.

Couple's Prosperity

If 1st, 5th, 7th, 8th and 9th houses be occupied by their lords, and benefics occupy or aspect them, this *Yoga* would bestow prosperity and happiness on the couple, provided malefics have no connection whatsoever with them.

If both the ascendant and the Moon be posited in benefic *Aṁśas*, the result would be auspicious. On the other hand, if they be in malefic *Aṁśas*, it would end in calamity.

According to *Bṛhaspati* the following two *Yogas* lead to the couple's death:

(1) Malefics should occupy the ascendant, which must be their inimical or debilitation sign.

(2) Malefics should be in the 7th or 8th *Bhāva* which is like the above.

If the 5th house be occupied by a malefic in his debilitation and aspected by an inimical planet, the girl would go astray, or her children might not survive; or she might give to still-born children.

Should the lord of the 7th house be endowed with strength, the bride after marriage would become wealthy and happy. On the other hand, if he be in his debilitation or inimical house, she might be without beauty and virtue.

If the Moon or Venus, occupying a friendly house, aspects the ascendant, which is an old sign, the bride will love the groom intensely.

If Mars, the Sun or Jupiter, occupying a friendly house, should aspect the ascendant that is an even sign, the man would have exceptional love for the girl.

If a girl turns up suddenly at the query session, and begins to talk, or stands looking on, or if somebody be talking about a girl, then the person would get a girl similar in features to the one who has come. The direction from which the girl would hail should be determined through the *Ārūḍha* or the ascendant, whichever is stronger.

Time of Marriage

The event is likely to materialize when the Moon arrives in transit at one of the following signs: (1) The *Dvādaśāṁśa* (1)/(12) sign of the Moon at query or its trine; (2) the *Abhilāṣa*—longitude of the Moon or its trine; and (3) the *Nāvaṁśa* sign of the lord of the 7th house from the *Ārūḍha*. Moon's *Abhilāsa* longitude: Convert the Moon's longitude at query into minutes and divide the result by 800. The remainder should be multiplied by 3, and divided by 200. The quotient gives the number of signs. The remainder should be multiplied by 30 and the product divided by 200. The quotient would give degrees and when the remainder is multiplied by 60 and divided by 200, you will get minutes. This figure represents the *Abhilāṣa-Moon*.

Longitude of Candra-Vela

Take the first remainder mentioned above and multiply it by 9. Divide the product by 200. The quotient you get would represent signs. The remainder multiplied by 30 and divided by 200 would yield the quotient in degrees. Lastly the remainder, when multiplied by 60 and divided by 200 would give the quotient in minutes. This is known as *Candra-Velā*.

Type of Girl

If the 7th house belongs to a benefic, the man will get a bride of the class, characteristics, complexion etc. allotted to that planet; but if it belongs to a malefic, the girl will have features etc. assigned to that planet.

When the lord of the *lagna* or the Moon be posited in the 7th house, the querist would get a bride without his seeking.

BRIDE'S CHARACTER

At a query about this, if the *lagna* be an immovable sign, and both the Moon and *lagna*-lord be in immovable signs, she should be declared to be of unsullied character. If the above three entities be in movable signs, the girl though in maidenhood must be spoiled; but if the Moon be in a dual sign and the ascendant, a movable sign, her flaw must be negligible.

If the Moon and Mars be joined in a sign which is not immovable, the girl must have been enjoyed covertly by somebody; while if Saturn and the Moon be posited in the *lagna*, she must have been enjoyed overtly. Should Mars and Saturn be in *kendras* and Venus in Scorpio, in sign or decanate, and be aspected by the Moon, she must be unchaste.

When the lords of the ascendant and the 12th house, or of the 1st and 7th houses, exchange their positions, or when Venus and the Moon occupy their own or exaltation houses, the man will get a girl whom he loves most. If at a query the Moon be posited in the *lagna*, 6th or 8th house, and a malefic in the 7th house, the girl would be widowed within 8 years. If a debilitated malefic, aspected by his enemy, occupies the 5th house, she would become either unchaste or barren.

(1) The querist would have no marriage, should the Moon or Saturn occupying an even sign identical with the 6th or 8th, be aspected by malefics.

(2) The same effect would follow, if the Moon and Venus along with malefics occupy an even sign identicai with the 6th or 8th house. The person would lose his first wife, if the lord of the 7th house, conjoined with a malefic, be posited in the 1st, 6th, 9th or 12th house, or in depression.

If in a natal chart of a male the 7th house happens to be Aries and other sings, the following effects are declared:

Aries: The woman would be interested in visiting temples.
Taurus: She would be fond of feeding others.
Gemini: Keeps the household, utensils etc. neat and tidy.
Cancer: Interested in bathing etc.
Leo: Finds pleasure in performing rituals like *homa.*
Virgo: She would be interested in collecting perfumes, utensils etc., or costly articles.

Libra: She would be an eloquent speaker.

Scorpio: She would be an expert in culinary art.

Sagittarius: Interested in listening to recitations of Vedas and Purāṇas.

Capricorn: Would be interested in collecting good sheets etc.

Aquarius: She would be clever in storing grains.

Pisces: She would have pleasure in collecting bronze articles and curios. She would be a nice speaker.

Wife's Death: The following conditions relating to the 7th house indicate wife's death:

(i) The 7th house must be weak, having malefic association and aspect.

(ii) Absence of the aspect of the lord of the 7th, 1st or a benefic on the 7th house.

(iii) The lord of the 7th house and Venus, being in inimical house, or debilitation *Aṁśa*, or combustion, are aspected by malefics, without benefic connection.

(iv) These two planets should be posited in 6th, 8th or 12th house.

If two of the above conditions be fulfilled, the wife's death would be certain. Otherwise the man would not be married.

1. If Mars be posited in the 7th house, the native would be separated from or bereaved of his wife. The same effect would follow, if Saturn should occupy or aspect the 7th house without benefic connection.

2. If Capricorn be the 7th house with Jupiter in it, or if Scorpio be the 7th house with Venus in it, the wife would die. Similarly if Taurus be the 7th house with Mercury in it, the person's first wife would die.

3. If Pisces be the 7th house with Saturn in it, the result would be the same.

4. Virgo being the 7th house with Jupiter in it, and the 4th house with malefics would do the same job.

5. Lords of the 5th and 8th houses occupying the 7th house also do the same thing.

Deformity of Wife

The Sun and Venus posited in the 5th, 7th or 9th house would make the wife deformed.

1. If Venus be surrounded by malefics without benefic connection, the native would suffer on account of his wife, or be bereaved of her.

2. The same result would follow, if the 4th and 8th houses from Venus be posited by malefics without benefic connection.

3. If the Sun and *Rāhu* be in the 7th house, the wife would be separated from him. The man thereafter would lose everything.

4. Should Venus occupy a movable sign with the aspect or association of Saturn, and be surrounded by malefics, the wife would be unchaste and leaving him.

5. If Venus be posited in Mars' *Rāśi* or *Aṁśa* and connected with Mars, the native would get a cruel wife. If this Yoga occurs in Saturn's sign or *Aṁśa*, or if Venus be in his debilitation in *Rāśi* or *Aṁśa* he would be married to a mean or low-class girl.

Aṣṭaka-Varga Method: Should there be more malefic dots in the 7th house in Venus's *Aṣṭaka-Varga* chart, the native's spouse would certainly predecease, provided *Māndi* occupies a trine from the ascendant.

Wife's Death Through Fire

Should Venus be posited in Aries, Scorpio or Leo, and aspected by or combined with the lord there of, and at a time when the Fire element rises, the native's wife would die through fire.*

Wife's Death Through Snake-Bite

When Venus is associated with *Māndi*, and *Rahu* occupies a

*The rising of the *bhūtas* or elements is explained in the *Praśna-Mārga XVI*—31. According to that 1 *Navāṁśa*—15 *Ghaṭis*. 1 degree—41 *Ghaṭis*.

The *Praśna-mārga* is of opinion that a *Yāma* (watch) is of 11 hours' duration. (Elsewhere it is equal to 3 hours.) Thus a daytime of 12 hours is divided into 8 *Yāmas*. The 1st, 3rd, 5th and 7th *Yāmas* are the *odd* ones, while the rest *even*. In these *Yāmas* the five elements rise in the following order with their different durations. In the odd *Yāmas* the order of the bhūtas (elements) is earth, water, fire, air and ether while in the even *Yamas* the order is reversed. The durations of the elements, which do not change in the odd and eve *Yāmas* are: (1) *Earth*—Half an hour or 30 minutes; (2) *Water*—24 minutes; (3) *Fire*—18 minutes; (4) *Air*—12 minutes; and *Ether*—6 minutes. Thus in a day of 24 hours *Earth* rules 8 hours; *Water* 6 hours 24 minutes; *Fire* 4 hours 48 minutes; *Air* 3 hours 12 minutes; and *Ether* 1 hour 36 minutes.

kendra or *koṇa* with respect to Venus, the wife would die as a result of snake-bite.

Her Disastrous Death

The wife would meet with a disastrous end, in case there be malefics in the 8th house from Venus in association with Saturn.

Death due to animal-attack: If Venus in the above condition occupies a sign signifying quadrupeds, her death will be due to animal-attack; and if the decanate of Venus be vulture, death would be due to birds; if Venus be in a watery sign, her end would be due to drowning in a tank; and if Venus, combined with the Moon, be in a movable sign (or Cancer, Pisces or latter half of Capricorn?) under the above condition, death would be in the sea.

Venus in combination with other planets and *upagraphas* (minor planets) causes the following effects:

1. *With the Sun*: The wife would be very prominent in the family, but possessed by a spirit (*bhūta*).
2. *With the Moon*: She would be superior to her husband.
3. *With Mars*: She would be unchaste and troubled by demons.
4. *With Mercury*: She would be charming, endowed with good character and learning, but troubled by *vidyādharas* (a class of demi-gods).
5. *With Jupiter*: Be a paragon of virtues and blessed with sons, but troubled by *gandharvas* (another class of demi-gods).
6. *With Saturn*: Be of bad character, friendly with the wicked, a hypocrite and foul-tongued.

Note: The above effects could also be attributed to the native's wife, if Venus occupies the houses of these planets.

7. *With Rāhu or Ketu*: She is likely to be deformed or short of a limb, and in league with despicable fellows.
8. *With Māndi Yamakanṭaka* or *kāla*: The native's wife is likely to meet with an early death.
9. *With Ardhaprahara*: Her death would be gradual, or after protracted illness.

Wife's Caste and Physical Features

Should Jupiter or Venus occupy the 7th house in the male chart, his wife would be of the same class or community. On the other hand, other planets posited in the 7th house are likely to make her one of a slightly lower status. Her physical features should be ascertained from the stronger of the lords of the sign and *Aṃśa* occupied by the lord of the 7th house. The wife's character, colour, stature, caste, nature etc. are to be read from the strongest of the following three or more planets viz. Venus, lord of the 7th house and those that are posited in the 7th house.

(1) The wife would be blessed with good sons, fortune and religious disposition, if there be a benefic in the 9th house from Venus, provided its lord (of the 9th house from Venus) is strong.

(2) If the lord of the 7th be a benefic and aspected by or conjoined with a benefic.

(3) or if the 5th, 7th, 9th and 11th houses, counted from the one occupied by the 7th-lord, are posited by benefics or any strong planet, the same result should be declared.

(i) On the other hand, if the lord of the 7th house be a malefic and associated with or aspected by malefics;

(ii) or if the 5th, 7th, 9th and 11th houses counted from the lord of the 7th house, are occupied by malefics, the man is likely to get a wife who would be distressed, being barren or sickly.

Happy conjugal life is the result of the following *Yogas*:

1. The lord of the 7th house, being possessed of strength, or benefics should occupy or aspect that house (i.e. 7th).

2. Venus and the lord of the 7th house should be strong, occupy auspicious houses and be associated with or aspected by benefics.

Bride's Family

If the lord of the 7th house be possessed of strength, the native would get a beautiful bride from a rich family. On the other hand, if that planet be weak, the girl would be ugly and be hailing from a poor family.

Should the 7th lord be combined with or aspected by benefics, or hemmed in between benefics, the man would be blessed with a good wife and children. The same result would follow, if the lord of the 7th house be in the sign or *Aṁśa* of a benefic, or if Venus be similarly situated, and the lord of the 10th house be possessed of strength.

On the other hand, if either the Sun or lord of the 7th house, being posited in a sign or *Aṁśa* belonging to a malefic, or aspected by or conjoined with malefics, he would get an unchaste wife.

Should the 7th house be occupied by *Rāhu* or *Ketu* and aspected by or associated with malefics, the person's wife would be characterless (sinful).

If *Rāhu* or *Ketu* should attain the *Aṁśa* of a malefic, she would poison the husband and be always quarrelling with the husband and be the butt of ridicule to the people.

Effects of Planets in the 7th House

The Sun: He will have liaison with another's wife.

The Moon: He loves his wife most.

Mars: He will have sex-relations with many women.

Mercury: He loves his wife.

Jupiter: She will be very virtuous and loved by the husband.

Venus: He is very lustful.

Saturn: He will have liaison with low-class women.

Wife's Superiority: If the lord of the 7th house is stronger than the *lagna*-lord, and posited in a benefic *Aṁśa* and aspected by a benefic, attaining *Vaiśeṣikāṁśa** or its highest exaltation, his wife will be hailing from a superior family, and possessed of excellent character and features. If the conditions are contrary, he gets a wife from a poor family or low class.

Remarriage

(1) The ascendant is a dual sign, the Moon and lord of the 7th house are posited in dual signs or *Aṁśas*.

(2) Two planets should be in the 11th house, and Mercury and Saturn occupy the 7th house.

(3) If the Sun and Mars be in the 7th house or its *Aṁśa*, it would show that the man has more than one marriage, but lives only with one wife.

Three Marriages

If the three planets viz. Venus and lords of the 7th house, counted from the ascendant and the Moon, be endowed with strength and posited in good houses, there would be three marri-

*Vide pages 42-43 of the *Fundamentals of Astrology* by this author.

ages. If only two be strong, the chance is for two marriages; and if only one be strong, one marriage only. If either the 7th lord or Venus be in his highest exaltation and if at the same time there be two or more planets in the 7th house, three or more marriages would result. The number of marriages may also be found out from the *Navāṁśa* covered by the lord of the 7th house. Another view is the following: If there are two strong planets in the 7th house, there will be two marriages. The following are some more *Yogas* for remarriage:

1. The 7th house being strong, its lord and Venus must be posited in one of the following *Rāśis* viz. own house, own decanate, *Vargottamāṁśa* (*Rāśi* and *Navāṁśa* being the same sign), exaltation *Aṁśa*, and be retrograde.

2. The 2nd or the 7th house must have malefic aspect or presence and its lord be weak.

3. The 7th or 8th house from *lagna* be occupied by malefics, and the 12th house by Mars, provided the concerned house is not aspected by its own lord.

4. The lord of the *Navāṁśa* occupied by the lord of the 7th house be eclipsed, debilitated, posited in inimical or debilitation *Aṁśa* (decanate), or surrounded or aspected by malefics.

5. If the second or seventh house be occupied by many (more than two) malefics, and if its lord be aspected by malefics, three marriages are indicated.

6. If the ascendant, 2nd or 7th house be occupied by malefics, and if the 7th-lord be debilitated, eclipsed or posited in an inimical sign, three marriages should be declared.

7. Lord of 7th house, being posited in *kendra* or *koṇa*, is to be in his exaltation, friendly sign, *Vargottamāṁśa* and other *Vargas* that are his own, and associated with the lord of the 10th house, he will have many wives.

8. The same result would follow if the lords of 7th and 11th houses be strong and be posited in trines.

Ṛāṇnubandha

How could we know if the bride proposed and the man have this kind of relationship of previous life? To know this you have to follow the following procedure: (1) Note in the male chart the sign occupied by VII-lord; (2) his *Navāṁśa* sign; (3) his exaltation sign; (4) his debilitation sign; (5) the sign occupied by Venus; (6) the 7th house from Venus; (8) the Moon's *Dvādaśāṁśa* (1)/(12) sign; (9) its trines; and (10) in the Moon's *Aṣṭaka-Varga* (A.V.) chart* the sign that contains greatest number of benefic dots; (11) the sign that has the greatest number of benefic dots in her (Moon's) *Samudāyoāṣṭaka-Varga* chart; and (12) in the A.V. chart of Venus the sign to which the lord of the 7th house from Venus, has contributed his benefic dot. Should the bride's-natal sign happens to be the same as the one found out by two or three methods mentioned above, the astrologer could declare the existence of this relationship of previous life, and recommend their union in holy wedlock.

Bride's Star

(1) Find out the star from the sum of the longitudes of Venus and the lord of the ascendant; (2) the Star from the sum of the longitudes of lords of I and VII houses; and (3) the star from the sum of the longitudes of the planet that aspects VII house and the latter's lord. The bride's natal star is likely to be one of these three. If the star be found to be the same on two counts, it would be exceptionally good. Even a trine of the star is acceptable.

Bride's Direction

This is to be read from the following: (i) The direction allotted to VII-lord; (ii) that of the sign occupied by the VII-lord; (iii) that of the *Navāṁśa* sign of VII-lord; (iv) that of the sign occupied by Venus; (v) of Venus's *Aṁśa* sign; (vi) that of the 7th *Rāśi* from Venus; and (vii) those of the planets that occupy or aspect VII house from the *lagna* and the Moon. When compatibility of horoscopes is considered, the above rules regarding the bride's direction may stand one in good stead.

Distance of Bride's Place

Take the sign and *Navāṁśa* of the 7th-lord and of Venus. The distance is to be read from these four signs. If the majority

*The subject of *Aṣṭaka-Varga* has been dealt with in detail with illustrations in XXII of the *Fundamental of Astrology*.

of them be movable signs, the bride would be living in a far off place; if immovable, it should be nearby; and if dual, neither very near, nor very far.

When you are called upon to discuss the details of the would-be husband from a girl's horoscope, you should consider the 7th house, its lord, Venus etc. as in the case of male chart. This would help you in finding out what kind of husband she would get.

If in the female chart a malefic be posited in the 8th house, the husband's death could be surmised. However, should there be a benefic in the 2nd house at the same time, the wife herself would predecease her husband. Should Saturn be posited in the 7th house and aspected by other malefics, she might remain a *spinster* till the end. If both the 7th and 8th houses are occupied by malefics, she becomes a widow. However, if in this case there be benefics in the 9th house, widowhood would be averted.

This is an important point to be remembered while examining female horoscopes.

The following view is held by some authorities. Just as we consider the 7th house and the significator Venus for the bride in a male chart, even so in a female chart the 8th house and Saturn should be considered for the husband and the significator respectively.

Early Marriage

The following *Yogas* lead to early marriage:

(1) A strong benefic owning the 7th house is combined with the lord of the ascendant.

(2) A strong Venus is combined with the lord of the *lagna*.

(3) Both Venus and VII lord are posited in *Kendras* or *upacaya* houses. The special effect of the *upacaya* is that the girl would be blessed with prosperity after marriage. If the lord of the 7th house be away from the 7th house or from the lord of the ascendant by three or more *Rāśis*, she would be married late.

(4) A person would have early marriage, if the 7th lord be posited near the *lagna*, or if a benefic be posited near I, or the 7th house.

(5) If I, II or VII house be conjoined with benefics and be in benefic *vargas*, and if its lord be aspected by benefics, early marriage could be expected.

(6) The same result would follow, if IV-lord be in a *Vaiśeṣikāṁśa** II-lord strong, and lord of the first house in the *Mu Aṁśa*, i.e. 46th part of 1/60 parts.

Prosperity of Adversity

Should Venus and lord of VII or II house be in *Upacaya* houses, and *lagna*-lord in benefic aspect, the native would be blessed with prosperity after marriage. On the other hand, fortune would frown on him, if Venus and lords of 2nd, 7th and ascendant be posited in bad houses (6, 8, 12) along with malefics, in combustion, or in the *Aṁśa* or an enemy or of debilitation.

Time of Marriage

Note the following: (1) The planet occupying the 7th house; (2) the planet that aspects the 7th house; (3) One that owns the 7th house; (4) Lord of the sign occupied by the 7th-lord; (5) lord of the *Nāvāṁśa* occupied by VII lord; (6) Venus; (7) the Moon; and (8) Lord of the *Aṃśa* of *lagna*-lord. There would be chances for marriage during the *dośā* or *bhūtki* (subperiod) of the above mentioned planets. Some authorities claim that even *Rāhu's* periods (both major and minor) are favourable for marriage. The time could be pin-pointed by observing the transit of the concerned planets as explained hereunder: (1) When Venus, VII Lord, *lagna*-lord, or lord of the lunar sign transits the 7th house, the sign and *Aṁśa* occupied by its lord, as well as its 5th 7th or 9th house, marriage is likely to take place.

2. The same event may take place, when Jupiter transits the sign or *Aṃśa* (or its trine), occupied by the lord of the 7th house.

Compatibility of Horoscopes for Marriage

Generally people in India consult astrologers to know whether there is agreement or not between the horoscopes of a bride and a bride-groom. In some societies it is the parents of girls who seek horoscopes of eligible boys, while in others it is the other way about. Every parent wishes that the girl to be married to his son should be agreeable in every respect and able to bring for-

*These are called *Pārijāta*, *Uttama*, *Gopura*, *Simhāsana*, *Devaloka*, *Suraloka*, and *Airāvata*.

tune to his family. It is also necessary to enquire about family background, character, physical features, age, education, financial status, relatives and such other details before the proposal is accepted, and then only the horoscopes are taken to the family astrologer to find out their suitability for matching. The compatibility of horoscopes is based on the following twenty criteria: (1) Lunar signs of the two; (2) Lords of their signs; (3) Their stars; (4) *Yoni*; (5) *Vaśya*; (6) *Dina*; (7) *Māhendra*; (8) *Strīdīrgha*; (9) *Varṇa*; (10) *Sex-agreement*; (11) *Gaṇa*; (12) *Gotra-agreement*; (13) *Pakṣi-agreement*; (14) *Mṛga-agreement*, (15) *Vedha*; (16) *Bhūta*; (17) *Rajju*; (18) *Age-agreement*; (19) *Aṣṭakavarga-agreement*; and (20) Mental attraction.

I. Lunar Signs

Counting is always done with reference to the girl's lunar sign and asterism. So if the boy's lunar sign be the 2nd, 3rd, 4th, 5th or 6th from the girl's *Rāśi*, the proposal should not be accepted. On the other hand, if it be any of the remaining signs, it would be all right. In case both are born in the same *Rāśi*, what should be done? Generally it is not allowed, but if the constellations are different, there is no harm in recommending the alliance. If the girl's lunar sign be odd and the boy's be the 6th or 8th from hers, it would be tolerably good. On the other hand, if the girl's Rāśi be an even one, the boy whose natal sign is the 6th from hers, is to be rejected, while one whose sign is the 8th from her sign could be accepted.

The following are the effects of the relative positions of the two signs (of the bride and bride-groom) that are bad, according to Mādhavācārya:

(1) If the man's *Rāśi* be II from the brides—loss of wealth.
(2) ,, ,, V ,, ,, —loss of progeny.
(3) ,, ,, VI ,, ,, —sorrow, disease, troubles and sepration.
(4) ,, ,, III ,, ,, —grief.
(5) ,, ,, IV ,, ,, —enmity.
(6) ,, VI or VIII ,, ,, —break of marriage.

1. However, if the lord of the signs of the two be one and the

same, or if the two lords be mutual friends, it is not to be rejected.

2. Similarly, if there be agreement in respect of *Vaśya* and *Vedha*, the last flow could be ignored.

3. Exception to Dvidvādaśa (2nd and 12th) and trines: These two kinds of relationship between the natal signs of male and female are generally highly injurious in spite of the man's star being *Maitra* (8th) from that of the bride. According to *Bṛhaspati* a male born in the 7th sign from that of the bride (*Sama-Saptama*) is exceptionally good in spite of the lords of the two signs are mutually inimical.

II. Lords of Signs

If the lords of the two signs be in each other's house, i.e. the lords of the girl's *Rāśi* is in the boy's *Rāśi* and *vice versa*, the couple would have happiness, birth of children, prosperity and progress. If the man's natal star be *feminine*, and the girl's masculine, and if their *Rāśis* be Virgo, Scorpio, Taurus and Leo, and if the male be born in the 5th sign from the bride's their marriage will lead definitely to absence of progeny.

Should the lord of the natal sign of the bride happen to be posited in the 2nd, 4th, 5th, 8th, 9th or 12th house from the *Mūlatrikoṇa* or exaltation of the lord of that of the groom, the former would be considered as friendly.*

III. Agreement of Stars

The stars are divided into three groups viz. masculine, feminine and neutral. The following are male asterisms:

Aśvinī, Rohiṇī, Punarvasu, Puṣya, Hasta, Anurādhā Śravaṇa, P. Bhādra and *U. Bhādra*.

The following are female asterisms: *Bharaṇī, Kṛttikā, Ārdrā, Āśleṣā, Maghā, P. Phalgunī, U.P., Citrā, Svātī. Viśākhā, Jyeṣṭhā, P.* and *U. Āṣāḍhās, Dhaniṣṭhā* and *Revatī*.

Neutral Stars: Mṛgaśīrṣa, Mūla and Śatatārā

Same Star for Both: If the boy and girl should have the same natal star among the following 12 stars viz. *Jyeṣṭha, Mula, P.*

*For greater details refer to pages 16-17 of the *Fundamentals of Astrology*.

Āṣāḍhā, *Puṣya*, *Āśleṣā*, *Maghā*, *Hasta*, *Rohiṇī*, *Dhaniṣṭhā*, *Śatatārā*, *Ārdrā* and *Bharaṇī*, the result would be untoward. The rest are good.

If the girl's sign be the fag end of Cancer, Scorpio or Pisces, and the boy's sign, the very next *Rāśi*, the result would be utter penury.

IV. Yoni Agreement

The word *Yoni* means source or *birth-place*. Both the signs and stars have their distinctive *Yonis*. They are four in number as (1) Bird, (2) Reptile, (3) Animal, and (4) Human.

(1) Second half of Capricorn, and Pisces belong to bird Yoni.

(2) Cancer and Scorpio are of reptile Yoni.

(3) Aries, Taurus, Leo and first half of Capricorn are of Animal source.

(4) Gemini, Virgo, Libra, Sagittarius (first half) and Aquarius are of Human origin.

If the Yonis of the two are the same, it is very good. If one is animal and the other human, it is moderate. One of animal Yoni should not be joined with the other of reptile or bird Yoni. Similarly one of human origin should not be joined with reptile or bird Yoni.

A male whose natal sign happens to be in the visible half of the girl's natal sign (not the *lagna*), the alliance will be very good. In case the boy's lunar sign happens to be the 6th from the girl's lunar *Rāśi*, it is moderate. Even the 4th sign from the girl's *Rāśi* would be good for alliance, provided there is agreement in respect of *Vaśya*.

V. Vaśya (Docile) Agreement

To Aries—Leo and Scorpio are *Vaśya* or Docile.
To Taurus—Cancer and Libra ,, ,,
To Gemini—Virgo ,, ,,
To Cancer—Scorpio and Sagittarius *Vaśya* or Docile
To Leo—Libra ,, ,,
To Virgo—Gemini and Pisces ,, ,,
To Libra—Virgo and Capricorn ,, ,,
To Scorpio—Cancer ,, ,,
To Sagittarius—Pisces ,, ,,

To Capricorn—Aries and Aquarius *Vaśya* or Docile
To Aquarius—Aries ,, ,,
To Pisces—Capricorn ,, ,,

Should the Male's natal sign (Lunar) be *Vaśya* (docile) to the female's lunar sign, the alliance would lead to a happy conjugal life. In the list given above some *Rāśis* are mutually *Vaśya*, not all; e.g. Gemini are mutually docile, while Leo and Libra are not mutually so. Though Sagittarius and Pisces are owned by one and the same planet, yet there is no mutual *Vaśyatva* (docility) between the two signs. In judging compatibility of the two charts, you have to start also from the boy's *Rāśi*, *Nakṣatra* etc. From that point of view if the girl's *Rāśi* be *Vaśya* to the boy's sign, it should be considered as a point of agreement.

VI. Dina Agreement

The natal asterism is called *Janma-Nakṣatra*, the 10th is termed *Karma-Nakṣatra* and the 19th *Ādhāna*. A groom whose star is the 3rd (*vipat*), 5th (*pratyak*) or 7th (*Vadha*) from the bride's star, is not accepted for alliance. If it be the 3rd from the 10th, *Karma*, star of the bride, only its first quarter should be shunned, and not other quarters. Similarly in the case of the 5th star the 4th quarter alone is bad, and other quarters are all right. In the case of the *Vadha* (7th) star the 3rd quarter is bad, other quarters may be accepted. In the case of the girl's *Ādhāna* (19th) star, the 3rd, 5th or 7th star from it happening the boy's natal star, only the first, fourth and third quarters respectively are to be rejected, especially when the particular quarter or *Navāṁśa* belongs to a malefic. For example, in star *Aśvini*, the first quarter belongs to a malefic—a *Pāpāṁśa*—because it is owned by Mars. It is exceedingly bad to have a groom born in the 3rd or 7th star from the bride's. The 5th star, however, is not that bad. Should the groom's birth happen in the 88th *Aṁśa* from the birde's *Aṁśa* of natal star, it would be extremely harmful. Similar is one born in the 108th *Aṁśa*, i.e. the last quarter of the previous star. The good result of this agreement is long life.

VII. Mahendra

Count from the bride's star to the groom's asterism. If it be

4th, 7th or 10th in any round it would be beneficial to the groom. Generally the groom's star is expected to be distant from the bride's. On the other hand, if the bride's star be the 4th from the groom's star, it should be termed *Māhendra*. If it be the 7th from the boy's *Nakṣatra*, it would be called *Upendra*. The results of these two *Yoga* are in order (1) Increase of wealth and corn; and (2) birth of sons and daughters. The reader may note here that according to the *Dina*-type of agreement the 7th star is to be rejected, whereas according to the *Māhendra* it is acceptable. It should not, however, be construed that the authorities make contradictory statements. As the contexts are different, there is no contradiction. For, in the 2nd and 3rd rounds the 7th star becomes the 6th and 25th, which bring about what is called *Strīdīrgha* and so they reduce the flow more and more.

VIII. Strīdīrgha

This means that the boy's star is far removed from the bride's. The result would be very good, if the distance is more than 15 stars. This is according to the *Mādhavīya*.

IX. Varṇa Agreement

In addition to the well-known four classes viz. priests or Vedic scholars, warriors and administrators, traders and workers, there are two more classes known as *Anulomaja** (those born of higher-class fathers and lower class mothers) and *Pratilomaja* (children born of lower-class fathers and higher-class mothers). Both these classes of people give rise to innumerable mixed castes. However, we are concerned only with these six classes. Each class has been allotted to certain stars as shown below:

1. Brāhmaṇa class: *Aśvinī*, *Punarvasu*, *Hasta*, *Mūla*, and *P. Bhādra*.

2. *Kṣatriya* class: *Bharaṇī*, *Puṣya*, *Citrā*, *Pūrvāṣāḍhā* and *U. Bhādra*.

*Classification of marriages is done on the basis rituals and *Varṇa* (class). Here class distinction is based on the natal stars of the parties. The other classification is eight-fold according to Manu, as Brāhma, *Daiva*, *Ārṣa*, *Prājāpatya* etc.

3. *Vaiśya* class: *Kṛttikā, Āśleṣā, Svāti, U. Āṣāḍhā,* and *Revatī.*

4. *Śūdra* class: *Rohiṇī, Maghā, Viśākhā* and *Śravaṇa.*

5. *Anulomaja* class: *Mṛgaśīrṣa, P. Phalgunī, Anurādhā* and *Dhaniṣṭhā.*

6. *Pratilomaja* class: *Ārdrā, U. Phalgunī, Jyeṣṭhā* and *Śatabhiṣak.*

It would be excellent, if the stars of both be of the same class. So also is the marriage that is contracted between a groom born in a star of a higher-class and a bride born in an asterism of a lower-class. On the other hand, should the bride's star and groom's star belong to a higher and a lower class respectively, the result of such an alliance would be inauspicious. This condition of agreement is not absolute. Hence this star-based caste-distinction is not at all considered now a days by astrologers. On the other hand, classes or castes are allotted to the *Rāśis* in comparing horoscopes. They are given below:

Castes of signs: (1) *Brāhmaṇas*—Cancer, Scorpio and Pisces.

(2) *Kṣatriyas*: Aries, Leo and Sagittarius.

(3) *Vaiśyas*: Taurus, Virgo and Capricorn.

(4) *Śūdras*: Gemini, Libra and Aquarius.

Compatibility of horoscopes in respect of *Jāti* is considered on the basis of the lunar signs of the bride and groom. Rules that have been stated for the castes of lunar mansions (stars) should be applied to the *Rāśis.*

X. Sex Agreement

This is another kind of *Yoni* agreement. The stars are divided into two classes as Male and Female. Other's bring them under three heads including Eunuch. According to the first view the following are Male: 1, 2, 8, 9, 10, 12, 15, 16, 18, 19, 20, 21, 22 and the rest Female; while according to others the following are 25; Male: 1, 4, 7, 8, 13, 17, 22, 25 and 26. Eunuch: *Mṛgaśīrṣa, Mūla* and *Śatabhiṣak.* The rest are Female.

Effects of Sex

It would be very good for all-round progress and prosperity, should the star of the groom be Male and that of the bride Female. In case both the stars be Female, it would be moderate; if both be Male, the effect would be injurious. So is the exchange of sex, i.e. boy's Female and girl's Male. Alliance between Female star of the groom, and Female star of the bride is moderate. It is bad for a man born in Female star to marry a woman of Eunuch star. Similarly it is bad to unite a man of Eunuch star with a woman of Male or Eunuch star. For easy reference the following chart may be useful:

Groom's star	Bride's star	Effect
Male	Female	Very good
Male	Eunuch	Very good
Female	Female	Moderate
Male	Male	Harmful
Female	Male	Harmful
Female	Eunuch	Very bad
Eunuch	Male	Unacceptable
Eunuch	Female	Moderate
Eunuch	Eunuch	Very bad

XI. Gaṇa Agreement

The word *Gaṇa* means group. There are three groups of stars: Those belonging to gods', humans' and demons' group. The following 9 stars come under the group of gods: *Aśvini*, *Anurādhā*, *Śravaṇa*, *Svātī*, *Punarvasu*, *Mṛgāśiras*, *Hasta*, *Puṣya* and *Revatī*.

Human Group: *Bharaṇī*, *Rohiṇī*, *P. Phalgunī*, *U. Phalgunī*, *P. Āṣāḍhā*, *P. Bhādra*, *Ārdrā*, *U. Āṣāḍhā* and *U. Bhādra*.

Demoniac Group: *Kṛttikā, Āśleṣā, Maghā, Citrā, Viśākhā, Jyeṣṭhā, Mūla, Dhaniṣṭhā* and *Śatabhiṣak.*

It is very essential for the two partners to have their stars belonging to the same *Gaṇa* for securing best result.

If it be a combination of the divine and the demoniac, there would be constant quarrels between the two. Union of the human and demoniac would lead to death; while human and divine Union is moderate, but according to another view it may cause fear. The effect of this agreement is said to be beauty and mutual attraction.

Now look at the chart given below for better understanding:

Male	Female	Effect
Divine	Human	Beneficial
Demoniac	Human	Moderate
Human	Divine	Not Good
Human	Demoniac	Harmful

Exception to the last combination : (1) Multiply the longitude of the Moon by 9 in both cases separately. Find out the star of each product. If these stars are found to belong to the same *Gaṇa*, the alliance between the man, whose star is of the Human group, and the woman, whose natal star is demoniac, is not to be rejected. (2) Take the longitudes of the *lagnas* of the two persons. If the two stars of the *lagnas* belong to the same *Gaṇa*, it would be good.

(3) In case there be *Strīdīrgha* agreement, the above combination would not be bad. This shows that *Strīdīrgha* is more powerful than *Gaṇa* agreement.

XII. Gotra Agreement

Ancient sages who handed down the Vedic lore, are seven in

number viz. *Marīci*, *Atri*, *Vasiṣṭha*, *Aṅgiras*, *Pulastya*, *Pulaha* and *Kratu*. There are many lists of ancient sages who are called progenitors of *Gotras* like *Viśvāmitra*, *Kaśyapa*, *Gautama*, *Jamadagni* and *Bharadvāja*. This *lineage* (*gotra*) of horary sages is based on two factors viz. birth and learning, i.e. from father to son; and teacher to disciple. The 28 stars including *Abhijit* (which is placed in capricorn between *Uttarāṣāḍhā* and *Śravaṇa*) have been distributed among the above sages at the rate of four asterisms per sage as follows:

1. *Marici*: *Aśvinī*, *Puṣya*, *Svāti* and *Abhijit*.
2. *Vasiṣṭha*: *Bharaṇī*, *Āśleṣā*, *Viśākhā* and *Śravaṇa*.
3. *Aṅgiras*: *Kṛttikā*, *Maghā*, *Anurādhā* and *Dhaniṣṭhā*.
4. *Atri*: *Rohiṇī*, *P. Phalgunī*, *Jyeṣṭhā* and *Śatabhiṣak*.
5. *Pulastya*: *Mṛgaśiras*, *U. Phalgunī*, *Mūla*, *P. Bhādra*.
6. *Pulaha*: *Ārdrā*, *Hasta*, *P. Āṣāḍhā*, and *U. Bhādra*.
7. *Kratu*: *Punarvasu*, *Citrā*, *U. Aṣāḍhā*, and *Revatī*.

It is said that identical *gotra* of boy and girl would lead to calamity. If they belong to different *gotras*, their union will lead to happiness, prosperity and progeny. This subject can be looked into from another angle. If the stars obtained from the longitudes of their respective *lagnas* belong to the same *gotra* or different ones, their effects would be in order moderate or excellent.

Note: This factor of compatibility of horoscopes is not taken into consideration nowadays.

XIII. Pakṣi Agreement

In this scheme each star has a *Totem-bird*. If both the stars have the same bird, the matching will be excellent. If the birds are different, but friendly to each other, it would be moderate; while if they be inimical to each other, the result would be injurious. For the Five stars from *Āśvinī* to *Mṛgāśirṣa*, the presiding bird is *Bherunda*; for the next *six* stars from *Ārdrā* to *P. Phalgunī*, it is *Piṅgala*; for the next six from *U. Phalgunī* to *Anurādhā*, it is *Kāka* (crow); for the next five from *Jyeṣṭhā* to *Śravaṇa*, it is *Kukkuṭa* (cock); and lastly for the next five from *Dhaniṣṭhā* to *Revatī*, it is *Mayūra* (Peacock). (*Note*: This too is not compulsory.)

XIV. Mṛga Agreement

This is compatibility of the horoscopes in respect of the animals signified by the stars.

The following chart gives the animals and their enemies:

Animals	Their enemies	Number of stars from *Aśvinī*
Horse	Buffalo	1
Elephant	Lion	2
She Goat	Monkey	3
Serpent	Mongoose	4
F. Serpent	Mongoose	5
Dog	Deer	6
F. Cat	Rat	7
Goat	Monkey	8
Cat	Rat	9
Rat	Cat	10
F. Rat	Cat	11
Bull	Tiger	12
Buffalo	Horse	13
Tiger	Cow	14
Buffalo	Horse	15
Tiger	Cow	16
Deer	Dog	17

Animals	Their enemies	Number of stars from *Aśvinī*
F. Deer	Dog	18
Dog	Deer	19
Monkey	Goat	20
Mongoose	Serpent	21
Monkey	Goat	22
Lion	Elephant	23
Horse	Buffalo	24
Lion	Elephant	25
Cow	Tiger	26
Elephant	Lion	27

The above chart gives the animals and their enemies according to the tradition followed in my place. However, the *Praśna-Mārga* gives camel as the animal for the 12th star viz. *Uttara-phalgunī*; lion for the 14th star, i.e. *Citrā*; bull for the 21st, i.e. *U. Āṣāḍhā*; buffalo for the 23rd, and *Aṅganā* (Female) for the 25th, but it should be interpreted as Mare.

If the stars of the boy and girl have rat and serpent as their animals; dog and cat; buffalo and horse; there will be no agreement in respect of *Mṛga*. Should marriage be contracted between such men and women, there would be no psychological adjustment between husband and wife. As elephant and lion are well-known as natural (born) enemies, it is difficult to accept the view that lion would fit in with any animal as far as match-making is concerned. Similarly dog and tiger; cat and tiger; serpent and rat are considered as mutual enemies. So too tiger is inimical to the following: dog, cow (bull), buffalo, deer, goat and monkey. Dog is inimical to bull, goat, monkey and deer. The following are pairs of mutual enemies—(1) deer and elephant; (2) horse and bull; (3) cat and serpent.

The animals of the bride and groom would be acceptable, should they be identical or friendly, or not disposed inimically to each other. What is the benefit one would reap from this? The couple would enjoy ever-growing prosperity on account of this agreement.

XV. Vedha

Literally this word means piercing or hurting. A particular star is said to be *Viddha* or pierced by another star. Where there is such a *Vedha*-relationship between the two stars, alliance should not be recommended. There are five kinds of *Vedha* as (1) *Kaṇṭha-Vedha*, (2) *Kaṭi-(Uru)-Vedha*, (3) *Pāda-Vedha*, (4) *Śiro-Vedha* and (5) *Kukṣi-Vedha*. They are so called because they hurt or pierce the neck, hips or thighs, feet, head and stomach respectively. The 27 stars are grouped under the 5 heads as follows:

(1) *Kaṇṭha-Vedha*: *Rohiṇī*, *Ārdrā*, *Hasta*, *Svātī*, *Śravaṇa* and *Śatabhiṣak*.

(2) *Kaṭi*-(Uru) *Vedha*: *Bharaṇī*, *Puṣya*, *P. Phalgunī*, *Anurādhā*, *P. Āṣāḍhā* and *U. Bhādra*.

(3) *Pāda-Vedha*: *Aśvinī*, *Āśleṣā*, *Maghā*, *Jyeṣṭhā*, *Mūla* and *Revatī*.

(4) *Śiro-Vedha*: *Mṛgaśīrṣa*, *Chitrā* and *Dhaniṣṭhā*.

(5) *Kukṣi-Vedha*: *Kṛttikā*, *Punarvasu*, *U-Phalgunī*, *Viśakhā*, *U. Āṣāḍhā* and *Pūrābhādra*.

The reader may note the symmetry in the allotment of the stars from *Aśvinī* to the five limbs (*pancāṅga*) in an ascending order from the foot to the head. For description of deities—the stars represent different deities—is done from the foot to the head.

This *Vedha* scheme has been mentioned in *Electional Astrology* in connection with house construction. How to find out which star is hurt on a particular day? See if any plant is posited in any star of any of the five groups. It there be one, treat the whole group as *Viddha* (pierced), and so none of the stars can be elected for house construction or house warning. Similarly, if the stars of the groom and bride occur in the first group, there would be (neck-piercing) *Vedha* leading to death of either partner. If it be in the second group, it would be *Kaṭi-Vedha* (piercing of hips or thighs) whose effect is poverty. If in the 3rd group, *Pāda-Vedha* resulting in wandering from place to place, poverty or loss of position. In the 4th group it, is *Śiro-Vedha* resulting in husband's death. In the last group, *Kukṣi-Vedha* would bring about destruction of children. Hence the stars of the two ought not to belong to the same group. In the absence of this blemish alliance would be beneficial. This is one way of finding *Vedha*. There is another method which is more popular. The following chart gives the stars that are hurt with regard to *Āśvinī* and others in order:

Stars from *Aśvini*	1	2	3	4	5	6	7	8	9	10	11	12	13	14
Vedha-Stars	18	17	16	15	14 and 23	22	21	20	19	27	26	25	24	5 and 23

Stars from *Aśvini*	15	16	17	18	19	20	21	22	23	24	25	26	27
Vedha-Stars	4	3	2	1	9	8	7	6	5 and 14	13	12	11	10

This chart shows that *Jyeṣṭhā* is the *Viddha* (pierced) star for *Aśvinī*. So marriage should not be encouraged between a male and female having these natal stars in spite of their having a common lord viz. Mars. Another point to be noted here is that this blemish is most dreadful and to be discarded, if there be *Saṣṭhāṣṭama* or quincunx relationship between the two stars (it is present in many instances), in spite of there being other points of agreement such as *Vaśya*.

XVI. Bhūta (Element) Agreement

There are five elements as *Bhū* (*Earth*); *Āpaḥ* (Water); *Tejas* (Fire); *Vāyu* (Air); and *Ākāśa* (Ether). The first five stars beginning with *Aśvinī* constitute the earth element; the next six stars from *Ārdrā*, water element; the next five ones from *U. Phalgunī*, fire element; the next six stars from *Anurādhā*, air element, and lastly the five stars, *Ākāśa* element (ether). If both have the same element, it is very auspicious. Similarly the combination of fire and air elements is beneficial If one party has earth, it could be joined with any other element for beneficial results. However, water and fire are inimical and harmful. But the union of the rest is not forbidden.

Elements are assigned to the signs too: Gemini and Virgo constitute earth element; Taurus, Cancer and Libra, water; Aries, Leo and Scorpio, fire; Capricorn and Aquarius, air; and Sagittarius and Pisces, ether.

XVII. Rajju (Rope) Agreement

The 27 stars are to be arranged in three avenues, going three steps forward and three steps backward continuously as shown in the chart given below:

Star Number	Star Number	Star Number
1	2	3
6	5	4
7	8	9
12	11	10
13	14	15
18	17	16
19	20	21
24	23	22
25	26	27

Application of this chart to the stars of the bride and groom is considered very important. If the two stars be found in the same avenue, it would be the blemish called *Sama-Rajju.* So the alliance should not be recommended. If they be found in the central avenue, it would be called *Madhyama-Rajju,* and extremely harmful.

XVIII. Age Agreement

In good old days when child marriage was the order of the day (this became prevalent during the medieval period) the ideal marriage was one where the male's age was treble that of the female. If it is double, the effect is considered moderate. If the boy be younger than the girl, extinction of family would follow. In the Vedic period, however, the rules were quite scientific. For, the ancient lawgivers have ordained that a girl should wait for three years after she comes of age and then elect a worthy youth for her partner. *Caraka,* the doyen of Ayurvedic Masters, has asserted that a youth below 25 years and a girl below 16 years ought not to beget issue.

XIX. Aṣṭaka-Varga Agreement

The next point of agreement refers to *Aṣṭaka-Varga*: Prepare the A.V. Charts of the Moon of both the boy and girl. The sign that contains the highest number of benefic dots in the male's chart, should be the bride's lunar sign. If it is actually so, the marriage would be ideal. Similarly see the *Rāśi* that contains the highest number of benefic dots in the Moon's *Aṣṭaka-Varga* chart of the girl. If the boy's natal sign (Lunar) happens to be the same as the above, you may be sure that they are born to be husband and wife. This principle may be applied to the 7th house of the two charts as well.

XX. Mental Attraction

In matrimonial alliance the most important factor is the mutual attraction and a jubilant or buoyant mental attitude of the two persons. On the other hand, if a show of interest is put up under compulsion, their wedded life would not be very happy. It is said "*Mano hi janmāntara-saṅgatijnam*"—'The mind remembers associations of previous life.' Hence even in the absence of other points of agreement, this alone would confer ideal conjugal felicity. For, the sub-conscious mind tells one "This is your life-partner according to your past *karma*." *Karma* is inviolable. It is otherwise known as fate.

Gain and Loss

(1) Count the number of stars from that of the bride to the groom's star (both inclusive). Multiply that number by 5 and divide the product by 7. The remainder would indicate *loss*. In this process there is no zero balance, but it should be taken as 7. Now repeat this process starting from the groom's star and going up to the bride's star. Multiply and divide as before. The remainder would show their gain. If gain is greater than loss, the alliance would be good; otherwise it is not.

(2) Count the stars of the two separately from *Aśvinī*, add these two numbers and add 13 to the sum. Then subtract 32 from the result, and divide what remains by 5. If the remainder be 1, there would be increase of children; if 2, both would perish; if 3, increase of prosperity; if 4, terrible disease; and lastly if 5, increase of prosperity.

(3) In this, counting is to be done separately from the stars of the two parties up to to *Aśvinī*. Then add these two numbers and divide the sum by 5.

The remainders from 1 to 5 yield the following effects in order: (i) prosperity; (ii) progress; (iii) disaster, (iv) immense wealth; and (v) great misfortune or calamity.

Prosperity and Adversity

The asterisms are divided into three groups as follows:

(1) 6, 13, 20 and 26.

(2) 2, 4, 5, 10, 11, 12, 17, 18, 19, 23, 24 and 25.

(3) 1, 2, 7, 8, 9, 14, 15, 16, 21, 22 and 27.

(1) If both the bride and groom have their stars in the first group viz. *Ārdrā, Hasta, P. Āṣāḍhā* and *U. Bhādra*, the result would be great prosperity.

(2) If their stars belong to the second group, their financial position is likely to improve remarkably.

(3) In the third group, the result is excessive expenditure and

indebtedness. These are also considered as additional points of agreement of horoscopes.

I have mentioned above many points of agreement, but you should not think that all of them are important and compulsory. The following alone are to be specially considered for achieving success and prosperity: (1) *Rāśi* (lunar sign); (2) Lords of the lunar signs; (3) *Vaśya*; (4) *Māhendra*; (5) *Yoni* (animal); (6) *Gaṇa*; (7) *Dina* (benefic place of male's star from female's star); and (8) *Strīdīrgha*. Even among these, the first five points of agreement are most important, according to many. For psychological adaptability, however, *Gaṇa* assumes great significance. According to the *Praśna-Mārga* there are altogether 23 points of agreement as follows: 4 of *Rāśi*; 1 of *lords* of *Rāśis*; 1 of mutual attraction; 1 of age; and 16 of stars. However, the first five are accepted unanimously by all as most important.

Now-a-days popular *Pañcāṅgas* (almanacs) publish a ready-reckoner from which one could read the benefic points or marks given under the groom's star against the birde's. The total marks are said to be 36; and in a case of match-making if the marks are 18 or more, the proposal, they say, can be proceeded with. The total of 36 marks is made up as follows: (1) *Dina*—3 marks; (2) *Gaṇa*—6; (3) *Graha-maitrī*—5; (4) *Rāśi*—7; (5) *Rajju*—8; (6) *Yoni*—4; (7) *Jāti*—1; and (8) *Vaśya*—2. Let us take an example: Take the girl's star as *Pūrva-Phalgunī* and the boy's *Rohiṇī*. As the boy's star is the 3rd (*Vipat*) in the 3rd round, no credit could be given on this score. However, if the counting be done from the boy's star, it would be the 8th star, i.e. *maitra*, which is very good. So 50% credit should be given, i.e. 1½ marks on the score of *Dina*. Under *Gaṇa* both the stars come under human group. Hence on this count it gets full marks, i.e. 6. For *Maitrī*, friendship, between the lords of the two lunar signs, no credit can be given, as they are mutual enemies. For *Jāti* only ½ mark is given. For *Rāśi* full mark, i.e. 7, is awarded. For *Rajju* full mark, i.e. 8, is given. Thus the total comes to 23. Hence this pair can be united in holy wedlock.

In addition to the above-named items, blemishes caused by malefics viz. Mars, Saturn, Sun, *Rāhu*, *Ketu* and *Māṇdī*, are to be considered in both the charts. In some circles *Māndi* is ignored. The blemishes should be counted in the ascendant, 2nd, 4th, 7th,

8th and 12th houses with regard to the malefics posited in the six houses. If the blemishes in both the charts are almost equal, the union of the two could be recommended, provided the girl's chart does not possess many more blemishes than the boy's. As far as conjugal matter is concerned, Mars is the greatest malefic; next comes Saturn and then others. While totalling the marks for the blemishes, some assign 2 black marks to Mars, 1½ to Saturn and 1 to each of the rest. These blemishes are counted from the *lagna*, Moon and Venus. In this scheme malefic aspect is not considered.

Kuja-Doṣa and in Exceptions

(1) It is well-known that Mars is highly destructive to the native's partner, provided he be posited in 1st, 2nd, 4th, 7th, 8th and 12th houses. If Mars' blemish be the same in both the horoscopes, alliance could be entered into, provided Mars' strength is taken into due consideration.

(2) If Mars be in his own house, exaltation, *Vargottama Aṁśa or Upacaya* house, the blemish of Mars is said to be nullified.

(3) When Mars, posited in the 7th house, is aspected by strong Jupiter, the blemish is made infructuous.

(4) If in one chart Saturn be in the 8th, 1st, 4th, 7th or 12th house, the blemish of Mars in the other chart would be ineffective, provided Mars and Saturn in the two charts be in the same house.

(5) If strong Jupiter or Venus be posited in the *lagna* or 7th house, the harm apprehended from Mars would be nullified, provided the latter is debilitated, posited in an inimical house or eclipsed.

Lunar Mansions Prescribed for Marriage

It is to be understood that different asterisms are prescribed for different religious functions. Stars are generally divided into three categories as auspicious, forbidden or inauspicious, and indifferent. Among auspicious asterisms too there are some special ones prescribed for marriage alone. They are the following: *Rohiṇī, Mṛgaśīrṣa, Maghā*, the 3 *Uttaras, Hasta, Svāti, Anurādhā, Mūla* and *Revatī.*

According to some, even *Áśvini*, *Citrā*, *Śravaṇa* and *Dhaniṣṭhā* may be accepted in exceptional circumstances.

Star Elected for Marriage

The best stars are those except the 1st, 3rd, 5th and 7th in any round for both from their respective natal stars. However, in the case of the bride even her natal star or its trine is not to be rejected.

Planetary Transits

Most important of all planetary transits those of Jupiter and the Sun are the *sine qua non* for marriage. This is highly beneficial to both the bride and groom. Should Jupiter occupy the 3rd, 6th, 8th, 4th, 10th or 12th (even the 1st is considered bad for him) from the natal Moon of the bride or the groom at marriage, he would bestow prosperity, conjugal felicity and such other cherished things, on them, provided the house is his own or exaltation sign. Even otherwise Jupiter should be propitiated through appropriate *Japa*, *Homa*, feeding etc., in order to invoke his mercy and benevolence on the couple.

Triple Strength

According to some, of all benefits the groom should secure the Sun's transitory benefit, while the girl, Jupiter's, and both, the Moon's (*Candrabala*). If this is not got, there is likely to be obstacles. If the Sun is in the 8th, 4th, or 12th in transit in the groom's case, it is likely to result in tragedy. Effects of this strength are said to be (1) long life on account of Jupiter's good transit; (2) Wealth through the Moon's transit; and (3) power, through the Sun's transit. If Mars be in good transit, the benefit to the couple would be gain of lands or position.

Auspicious Ascendants

For marriage the best signs are (1) Gemini, Virgo and Libra as *lagnas*. (2) Moderate are Taurus, Cancer, Sagittarius and Pisces. Even the latter ones would be excellent, should they be occupied by a benefic. Some texts recommend even Capricorn and Aquarius with Venus in them.

Godhūli-Lagna

This means marriage is held at dusk when cattle return home from pastures, raising a good deal of dust by their hoofs. This dust, according to ancient sages, has the power of warding off all evil forces causing obstruction or harm to the marriage.

Abhijit-Muhūrta

There is another auspicious period highly praised by ancient authors. It is the 8th *Muhūrta* of the day, i.e. midday. Take the duration of the day in question and make 15 equal points of it. Multiply the duration of daytime for 1 part by 7. After that begins this *Muhūrta*, whose duration is roughly 48 minutes. If we take an example with 6-56 hours as sunrise and 18-18 as sunset, 1 *Muhūrta* gets 45.466 minutes. This when multiplies by 7 we get 318.262 minutes or 5 hrs. 18th mts. So it comes to 12H. 12m. Hence we should take the commencement of *Abhijit* at 12-15 noon and its end at 1 P.M. (correct to the minute). This *Muhūrta* is said to confer progeny and other benefits on the couple. This *Muhūrta*, it is said, should not be elected on Wednesday.

Lunar Days

All lunar days (*Tithis*) except 4, 6, 8, 9, 12, 14 and New Moon are good. Even the 8th *Tithi* may be accepted in emergencies, provided the Moon is aspected by benefics. The days of the dark fortnight are to be avoided beyond the *Pañcamī* (5th day).

Lunar Month

Vaiśākha, Jyeṣṭha, Māgha and *Phālguna* are the best months. Out of the remaining 8 months *Āṣāḍha, Śrāvaṇa, Bhādrapada* and *Pauṣa* are considered as most inauspicious. A woman married in the month of *Mārgaśīrṣa*, would be quarrelsome and intent on visiting other houses, but be blessed with wealth and happiness.

Solar Month

Among the Solar months the best are Aries, Taurus, Gemini, Capricorn and Aquarius. Cancer, Virgo and Sagittarius are shunned. Some do not approve of even Libra and Leo, especially when the latter is occupied by Jupiter. Among the *Yogas* 1, 6, 9,1 0, 13 and 15 are to be avoided. Among the *Karaṇas Viṣṭi* and the four immovable ones are dangerous and to be rejected.

Chapter VII

PROGENY

It is found in society that many a couple is found unhappy because of issuelessness even after the lapse of many years after marriage, more so is the female partner. Some women suffer from some kind of weakness or trouble of the reproductive organs, as a result of which they suffer silently but with a heart full of pent-up feelings. Sometimes they become prone to attacks of hysteria. After all, motherhood is a very important mile-stone in the life of a woman leading to her physical and psychological development in full. In the above circumstance, couples seek the advice of trusted and famous astrologers and ascertain if they have any chance of being blessed with children, the cause of the delay and what remedial measures are to be adopted for getting success, and when could they expect it, on the basis of their radical charts as well as *praśna* or query pertaining to the subject. Horary astrology becomes the only tool in the hands of the astrologer in the case of people who have no horoscope, nor a correct idea about their birth-data.

When a house-holder, accompanied by his wife, goes to a divine, the former puts a question like this: "Am I destined to beget a child by my wife?" The querist is then asked to mention his name. Though the question of issue concerns both husband and wife, yet all about the man should be read from the sign rising at the time, and other houses, and all about his wife (health, fertility etc.) from the *Ārūḍha lagna* (including the one indicated by the place occupied by her),

Kṣetra and Bīja (Soil and Seed)

The astrologer has to find out first if the woman's reproductive organs are in normal health and free from defects. Similarly he must do this with reference to the man also. How are we to know if the soil, i.e. the woman, is fertile or otherwise? Should the lords of the *Ārūḍha* and the 9th house therefrom be eclipsed, one should declare that the soil has lost its fertility and there is no possibility of the woman conceiving. In olden days in such cases remarriage for the man would be recommended. In modern times, however, it is forbidden by law. So a man could have remarriage only if he obtains divorce from his wife. But before thinking of divorce, one should exhaust all avenues of correcting the deficiencies such as medical treatment and religious acts and observances. On the other hand, if the lords of the *Udaya lagna* (rising sign) and the 5th house therefrom be combust, it should be said that the man's seed is dead, i.e. his power of procreation or fertilizing the ovum is defunct. If the defects be not serious, the objective could be achieved by means of medical treatment along with the worship of Gods and observing vows.

If the Moon be posited in one of the *Upacaya* houses (3, 6, 10, 11) counted from the *Ārūḍha*, and in a *non-Upacaya* house counted from the *Udaya-lagna*, and if the *Ārūḍha* and the *lagna* be even and odd signs respectively and if both these *lagnas* synchronize with the rise of the *Agni-bhūta* (fire element), and if both the *lagnas* be included in the list of signs viz. Taurus, Leo, Virgo, and Scorpio, and if at the time of query there be no fruits (or flowers) on the tree allotted to the star occupied by Jupiter, the couple would have little chance of getting issue.*

Explanation: Scholars divide the problems connected with issue into five categories as (1) Issuelessness; (2) Taking a boy in adoption; (3) Grief on account of children; (4) Having a single child, which is termed *Kāka-Vandhyatva*; (5) Having a large number of children.

(1) *Yoga for Lack of Issue*: When Jupiter and the lords of the ascendant, 5th and 7th houses are all devoid of strength, one may conclude that the person concerned will have no issue.

(2) When a malefic occupies the 5th house without benefic aspect its lord being debilitated, the same result could be expected.

(3) When the 5th houses counted from Jupiter, *lagna* and the Moon are occupied by malefics without benefic aspect, the result is the same.

Adoption: (i) Should the 5th house be owned by a *Eunuch* planet (Gemini, Virgo, Capricorn or Aquarius), and associated

*Vide charts attached at the end of this chapter.

with Saturn or *Māndi* by occupation or aspect, the native would have a son by adoption.

(ii) When the 5th house is tenanted by a strong benefic, but not aspected by its lord.*

Grief on account of issue: If Jupiter be in the 5th house, which is either Capricorn or Pisces, there might be grief on account of children.

Birth of many daughters: If sign Cancer happens to be the 5th house, occupied by Jupiter, a large number of daughters would be born to the person.

Loss of children: (1) If the lord of the 8th house be posited in the 5th house, the lord of the latter be in the 8th house, debilitated or in inimical house and not receiving benefic aspect, loss of children would take place.

(2) If weak Jupiter be hemmed in between malefics, lord of the 5th house without strength and without benefic aspect or association, the above result should be declared.

(3) If the lord of the 5th house be debilitated, eclipsed, in inimical house, or associated with the lord of the 8th or 12th house, and if both the 5th house and its lord, devoid of benefic aspect, loss of children would ensue.

Birth of good children: The following conditions ensure the birth good children: 1. The lord of the 5th house should be strong and joined with or aspected by the lord of the ascendant, and the 5th house, free from malefics.

2. Aries, Leo, Scorpio or Pisces being the 5th house should be occupied by Mars and aspected by or conjoined with Jupiter.

3. The 5th house should be surrounded by benefics, or aspected by them, or combined with or aspected by its own lord.

4. The 5th-lord should occupy any house other than 6th, 8th and 12th, be strong and aspected by benefics.

5. The strong 5th-lord should be in that house or ascendant or the 7th house without getting malefic aspect or conjunction.

(*Note*: Part of this condition viz. the lord of 5th house being in the 7th house, is contrary to *Varāhamihiras* rule. So I propose to have an amendment to the effect that the 5th-lord may be situated in the 9th house.)

*For greater details *Vide* page 173 of the *Fundamentals of Astrology*.

6. Put Jupiter instead of the 5th-lord and proceed.

7. The lord of the 5th house being strong, is to be surrounded or aspected by or conjoined with benefics.

Birth of many children: (i) The 5th-lord, Mercury, Jupiter, and Venus are to be strong and posited in or aspecting that house. The number of children is proportionate to the strength of the lord of 5th house. It should be read from the lord's *Navāṁśa*.

(ii) The 5th-lord should be in his highest exaltation point, and in a male *Navāṁśa* and aspected by a benefic, provided 5th house is neither aspected by nor conjoined with malefics.

(iii) The following planets should be posited in any houses, except the bad houses, which are odd signs and odd *Aṁśas*: Lord of 5th house, Jupiter, the Sun and Mars. One would beget worthy sons, if the lord of 5th house be strong.

Birth of daughters: A wise astrologer would predict birth of many daughters, should the Moon, Venus and lord of 5th house be posited in even *Rāśis* and *Aṁśas*.

Hurdles in the Way of Progeny

The following Yogas are said to be capable of obstructing chances for getting issue:

(1) The ascendant should be in the Moon's *Horā*; and the breath should flow through the left nostril; and both the ascendant at query and *Ārūḍha* be even signs.

(2) The ascendant should be in the Sun's *Horā*, breath flowing through the right nostril; and both the *lagna* and *Ārūḍha* be in odd signs.

(3) The ascendant is to be in the Lunar *Horā* and breath flowing through the left nostril; and the Moon, *Ārūḍha*, and *lagna* be in Taurus, Leo, Virgo and Scorpio.

(4) Along with the rule (2) substitute the following for the last clause: The Moon, *Ārūḍha* and *lagna* in the *Alpasuta* (difficult issue)* signs mentioned already.

All the above Yogas should also synchronize with the rising of *Agni-Bhūta* (Fire-Element). (*Note*: The *Ārūḍha* is called *Chādya*

*Here the word *Alpa-Suta* has not been translated literally.

(to be covered or enveloped); and the *lagna*, *Chādaka* (that which covers).

Giving Away a Son in Adoption

When one has more than two sons, the middle one is generally given away in adoption to one who is in need. The following Yogas lead to the above result:

1. The lord of *V* house should be in *I*, *V* or *VII* house.
2. Lords of *I* and *VII* be posited in *V* house.
3. Lord of *V* be conjoined with the lord of *I* or *VII* house.
4. Since Jupiter is the significator for progeny and so on a par with the lord of *V* house, we may substitute him for *V*-Lord.

Birth of a Son

(1) If the lords of *I* and *V* houses are conjoined, there is chance for the birth of a son.

(2) The two lords should aspect each other.

(3) They should be in mutual reception.

In this connection Mādhavācārya gives the following additional Yogas, which are given below for the benefit of students of astrology:

1. At a query about issue the Moon should be in a non-*Upacaya* house from the *Ārūḍha*.
2. She should be posited in an *Upacaya* house from the rising sign. This shows that you have to divine a female-birth from the *Ārūḍha*, while male-birth from the rising sign.

If the above Yogas be reversed, i.e. the Moon in an *Upacaya* house from *Ārūḍha*, or in a non-*Upacaya* house from the rising sign, there would be no chance of child-birth.

Garbhādhāna or Consummation of Marriage

In olden days when pre-puberty marriages were in vogue, girls used to come of age only after marriage. Then they got menses every month until pregnancy set in. Astrologically what is the cause of this feminine phenomenon? Ancient authors of Ayurvedic classics state "*māsi māsi rajaḥ Strīṇām*", i.e. women between certain ages get menstrual flow month after month. Varāhamihira refers to this phenomenon as being caused by the interaction of Mars and the Moon (bile and blood). But when the

Moon comes to an *Upacaya* house from the woman's natal ascendant, and is aspected by Jupiter, sexual union will be fruitful. It is, therefore, essential that the man's Moon too in transit should be in an *Upacaya* house from his natal ascendant, and be aspected by Jupiter. Besides that his Sun and Venus should be strong, in own houses or *Aṁśas* at the time, and the night of union even during the fertile period. For *Garbhādhāna* (Impregnation), an auspicious weekday, asterism, *Tithi*, and *Muhūrta* should be elected.

The following procedure is adopted in respect of *Santāna Praśna*, query about issue:

First of all work out the position of *Yamakaṇṭaka* for the day in question. The rising time of this satellite of Jupiter on Sunday on words is at the end of *Ghates* 18, 14, 10, 6, 2, 26 and 22 respectively. Now add the longitudes of the ascendant (not the *Ārūḍha*) and *Yamakaṇṭaka*. Thesum is called *Yoga-Sphuṭa* (Y.S.). In this new longitude (Y.S.) find out which of the two viz. *Rāśi* and *Aṁśa*, is stronger. That will be the "Reference Sign" (R.S.). Now find out if this R.S. is a *Pṛṣṭhodaya* (backward rising), *Adhomukha* (downward-looking) or an even sign, and if it be aspected or occupied by Eunuch planets or malefics, there will be no chance of progeny. Should the R.S. be a *Biped* one, the querist would be blessed with children. If this be, in addition, upward looking, rising with the head in front, odd and having association and aspect of benefics, there would be progeny in the near future.

The same result could be achieved under the above-named conditions with the exception of the longitude of the ascendant being added to that of the *Yamakaṇṭaka*. Here we can get the *Yoga-Sphuṭa* by taking the longitude of the lord of the *Ārūḍha*, all other conditions being the same.

No Prospect of Success

If the lord of *V* house, Jupiter, and *Yamakaṇṭaka* posited in even signs or *Aṁśas* that are inauspicious houses (*dusthānas*), be aspected by or conjoined with Eunuch planets (Mercury and Saturn), and *V* house, being in an odd sign and having association or aspect of Mercury and malefics and not of benefics, and the Lord of *V* house be in an odd *Aṁśa*, and the *Santāna-Tithi**

*For getting this vide page 186 of the *Fundamentals of Astrology*.

be one after the 8th lunar day of the dark fortnight, there would be hardly any chance of success in respect of issue. It is true that we cannot think of a case wherein all the above-noted conditions are fully satisfied. If they be present only in part, success might be possible by means of expiation in the form of *Japa*, worship of Gods, observance of vows, recitation of sacred texts, feeding and such other religious acts performed with due devotion and solemnity.

PŪRṆA SANTĀNA (FULL PROGENY)

This means to have sufficient number of good children, both male and female. This could be attained under the following conditions:

1. Jupiter, *Yamakaṇṭaka* and *V*-Lord should be posited in auspicious and benefic houses identical with their exaltation or own houses.

2. They should in addition be in odd signs and/or *Aṁśas*, aspected by benefics, and neither by malefics nor by Mercury.

3. The 5th house should also satisfy the conditions mentioned in 2.

SANTĀNA-KĀLA (TIME OF CHILD-BIRTH)

(1) Find out the sign that happens to be the *Dvādaśāṁśa* of the *lagna* (not *Ārūḍha*) at query. Take the 5th house therefrom (i.e. from the *Dvādaśāṁśa* sign). If its lord be in the *Ārūḍha*, there would certainly be child-birth within a year. If that planet be in the 2nd house from the *Ārūḍha*, it would be within two years; if it be the 3rd house, within three years and so on. If it be a house beyond the 6th, success might be obtained after much delay and through many expiatory rites. And if he be in 6th house, 8th or 13th, very stringent expiation would be necessary for success.

(2) Take the *Rāśi* as well as its *Aṁśa* of the *Yoga-sphuṭa*; when Jupiter transits the 5th, 7th, 9th or 11th house therefrom, there will appear signs of pregnancy. Whichever house among these four (5, 7, 9 and 11) has benefic aspect or association, will certainly indicate successful pregnancy when Jupiter transits that sign. The idea is that at the time of query one of the four houses, say the 9th, has benefic aspect. In that case when Jupiter comes

in transit to that house, i.e. 9th here, at that time signs of pregnancy, if sighted, will prove undoubtedly effective. On the other hand, when Jupiter transits one of these four houses, which has malefic aspect or association, both signs of pregnancy and abortion would be felt.

(3) Add up the longitudes of the ascendant, Moon, *Yamakaṇṭaka* and *Māndi*. This will be called *Catuṣphuṭa* (sum of four longitudes). If this resulting *Sphuṭa* be an odd sign or *Aṁśa* and if it be in trine or angle to Jupiter, there would indeed be child-birth, provided it is not in trine or angle to Mercury, Saturn, Rāhu or Ketu. In the absence of the above conditions such as the resulting sign or *Aṁśa* being even, and in trine or angle to Mercury and others, and not to Jupiter, success is impossible.

Proper Time for Garbhādhāna

In spiritual parlance the act of sexual union is a sacred sacrificial act which ought not to be misused, if one wishes for good progeny. Ordinary mortals steeped in ignorance, sunk in sins, care only for momentary sex-gratification, the result of which is the birth of savages and human brutes that prove a menace to human society. Those who hanker after a child or a son, take astrological advice before they resort to sexual union. This is well and good. (i) Now take the lord of the 5th house from the rising sign at query. Note in which house he is posited. If this sign or its *Aṁśa* be occupied by Jupiter, success is assured; (ii) Note the *Navāṁśa* of the *Ārūḍha*; note also where its lord is posited, and if this *Rāśi* or *Navāṁśa* is occupied by the Sun; or (iii) see if the Moon is posited in the sign or *Aṁśa* occupied by the lord of the rising sign. That is the proper time for *Garbhādhāna* (or *Niṣeka* = Impregnation) leading to singular success. (iv) (a) Add up the longitudes of the rising sign and the Moon at the query and note the *Dvādaśāṁśa* of the sum. When the Moon transits this sign, or (b) when the Sun transits the *Navāṁśa* of this sum; or (c) when Jupiter transits the *Rāśi* or *Aṁśa* of the sum total got by the addition of Jupiter's longitude and the first sum got above (i.e. of the longitudes of the *lagna* and Moon); or (d) find the sum of the longitudes of the *lagna*, Sun, Moon, and *Māndi*, and treat the resultant sign as the ascendant for impregnation; and when Jupiter arrives at this sign in his transit, treat that year, and when the Sun transits that sign, that solar month, and when the Moon transits that place, that star as the best time for success in this direction.

The methods enunciated in this section are very good for fixing the exact time for *Niṣeka* for success. As a precondition for success the querist must have implicit faith in his family deity, his chosen ideal, i.e. *Iṣṭa Devatā* and the astrologer.

Female for Progeny

If a man asks an astrologer as to a woman of which caste or community should he marry in order to beget a son, the following procedure should be adopted: See in which sign or *Aṁśa* the lord of 5th house is posited, and which planets occupy or aspect it. The caste would correspond to the planets—that aspect or occupy the *Rāśi* or *Aṁśa*—and to the concerned *Rāśis*. Pisces is Brāhmaṇa; Aries, Kṣatriya; Taurus, Vaiśya; and Gemini, Śūdra. Among planets Jupiter and Venus are Brāhmaṇas; the Sun and Mars, Kṣatriya; the Moon and Mercury, Vaiśya; and Saturn, Śūdra.

(The commentator of the *Kṛṣṇīya* states thus in this connection: Should Saturn be in a Brāhmaṇa sign, the person concerned would be a Śūdra servant of a Brāhmaṇa. On the other hand, if a Kṣatriya planet be in a Brāhmaṇa sign, it would be one born of a Brāhmaṇa by a Kṣatriya woman. In the same manner the country or direction is to be deduced from the planet's *Aṁśa-Rāśi*.)

Two or More Marriages for Progeny

Add the longitudes of the ascendant and *Yamakaṇṭaka*. If the resultant *Rāśi* happens to be a dual sign, the man, not getting issue by the first wife, will have to take another wife or more for progeny. If the above *Rāśi* has malefic aspect or association, his wife is likely to quit the world, or be barren. On the other hand, should the resultant sign be aspected or occupied by benefics, he would have children by all the wives. Should Mercury and Saturn aspect it, none of the wives would be able to bear children. Consequently the man would be forced to have a son by adoption.

Adoption of Two

If the above resultant *Yoga-sphuṭa* sign be Virgo, aspected by Mercury and Saturn, he would have two adopted sons. Should Saturn and Mars occupy the above *Rāśi*; and both the Sun and Mercury aspect it, both the adopted sons would be quarrelling with each other constantly and be thrown out of the house. Should Jupiter and Venus aspect the Y.S. sign, the second adopted son would be well-behaved and obedient and inherit the lion's share of the property.

Welfare of Foetus, Parents etc.

At a query about the state of the foetus, the *Yoga-sphuṭa* (Y.S.) mentioned already should be treated as the ascendant. From this and the Moon all about the mother should be ascertained; through the 7th house counted from this *lagna* as well as the Sun, about the father; and from the sign occupied by Jupiter, about the child in the womb.

Parents' Demise

If the new ascendant, i.e. Y.S., its 7th house, the Moon, Sun, and Jupiter be all weak, or have malefic aspect or association and no benefic connection whatsoever, the parent would surely quit the world, and the child too be dead. If under the above conditions Jupiter alone be strong, and the rest afflicted, the child alone would survive.

Pregnant Woman's Death

If the above Y.S. Lagna, its lord and the Moon be weak and afflicted by malefic association and aspect, the pregnant woman would perish. Should Jupiter be strong, her death would take place after child-birth. Should the Sun, the 7th house and its lord be all weak and have malefic connections, the father would die before seeing the childs' face. If Jupiter be strong, the father would die after the child is born.

If the Sun and Mars be conjoined, the father would fall ill; if the Moon and Saturn be together, the mother would suffer from ailments. On the other hand, should the Moon be afflicted through association or aspect by only Mars, Saturn and Rāhu (or

Ketu) and not by benefics, the mother would die along with the foetus. This would be certain, if all the three malefics be involved in this condition. If the Sun be involved in the above Yoga, the father would die before the child is born. If these three malefics be connected with Jupiter by aspect or conjunction, the child would die in the womb, provided there is no benefic connection.

Another Yoga for Lack of Issue

Add the longitudes of Jupiter and the lord of the 12th house from the query ascendant. Treat the sum as the figure of the new *lagna*. If there be malefics, Mars and Saturn, in its 12th house, there would be no issue at all. If this result be confirmed by the natal charts of the couple, they would have no chance at all of having issue. The same result will have to be predicted, if the star of the sum (Y.S.) of the longitudes of *Māndi* and *Yāmakaṇṭaka*, happens to be the 3rd, 5th or 7th from the natal star of the husband or wife.

Curse of Serpents

Sometimes loss of children takes place on account of curse of serpents. If Rāhu be posited in the 5th *Bhāva*, or the lord thereof be conjoined with Rāhu without benefic aspect, the cause of issuelessness or loss of issue is to be said to be serpents' curse.

Curse of Ancestors

(1) If Saturn in association with *Māndi* be posited in the 5th or 9th house, receiving no benefic aspect, the person loses children owing to the curse of ancestors. (2) If the lord of 5th house be conjoined with Mars, or with the lord of 6th house, and be without benefic aspect, loss of children is due to some black magic done by enemies. (3) The same effect would follow, should 5th house be occupied by a malefic or the lord of the 6th house, and be without benefic aspect.

Curse of Gods

Should the 5th house, being tenanted by its lord, be aspected by malefics, but not by benefics, loss of issue would be caused by divine displeasure or curse.

Mother's Curse

Should the 4th house be occupied by malefics, lord of 5th house be conjoined with Saturn and 12th house afflicted by malefic presence, children would perish as a result of mother's curse.

Father's Curse

The following planetary configuration is likely to cause loss of children due to father's curse: Malefics in the 9th house, lord of 5th house together with Saturn, and *Māndi* be in the 5th or 9th house.

Curse of Gods, Brahmins etc.

When Jupiter and lord of the Lagna and 5th house are strong, and the lord of 9th house eclipsed, the loss is due to divine displeasure.

If in the above Yoga both Jupiter and Venus be afflicted, being conjoined with malefics, the cause of loss of issue is said to be Brahmins' curse. Similarly if the Sun and Moon, conjoined with malefics, occupy inimical, debilitation etc. houses, it is due to the curses of the father and mother.

Great Sin

The planetary *Yoga* in which lords of 1st and 5th houses, and Jupiter are weak, the lord of the 10th house posited in a bad or inauspicious house with malefic aspect or association, would indicate darkest sin born of some heinous crime committed by the couple in their previous life, which has visited on them by destroying their children.

(2) The lords of 1st and 5th and Jupiter being weak, Mars and lord of 6th house be strong or are jointly posited in the same house, or the lord of 6th and Mars be in 5th house—this *Yoga* bespeaks black magic practised by enemies resulting in the destruction of precious progeny.

Affliction of House

Although the lords of 1st and 5th houses and Jupiter be strong, yet there might be malefics in the 4th house, or its lord occupy the 6th, 8th or 12th house. In that case the disaster maybe due to the blemishes in the house-site. On the other hand, if the three planets viz. Jupiter, and lords of 1st and 5th houses, be strong, but the malefic in the 4th house be devoid of strength, then it is undoubtedly the inauspicious and afflicted state of the house-site that is responsible for the tragedy. If these three planets be associated with Rāhu, or Rāhu be in 5th house, serpents' curse must be the cause. If Mars be conjoined with Rāhu, serpents must have been deeply hurt by the destruction wrought on their tribe and developed much hatred for the perpetrators. This hatred coupled with their increasing grief is visited on the concerned couple in the form of this tragedy.

Posthumous Birth

If the three planets mentioned above are endowed with strength, the Sun conjoined with malefics, and 9th house, aspected by and conjoined with malefics, the father would breathe his last before the child sees the light of day in consequence of the former's sins. Under the above conditions if the Moon is afflicted being conjoined with malefics and the 4th house too afflicted by malefic association and aspect, the mother dies almost simultaneously with child-birth.

State of Issue Through Bhūtodaya

The subject of *Rise of Elements* has already been explained. The astrologer should find out by calculation which of the five elements is rising at the time of query. If it be the element of air, it would augur the 'curse of ancestors' as the cause of children's death; if it be the 'fire element', 'divine wrath'; and if 'ether element', it is a combination of the curses of both Gods and ancestors. On the other hand, 'the rise of earth' as well as 'water element' presages early child-birth. This shows that the first two elements viz. earth and water, are happy auguries.

Quick Success

The following six conditions are mentioned for quick success for those who hanker after issue:

1. The *lagna* be in the Sun's *Horā* and the breath flow through the left nostril.
2. The *lagna* be in the Moon's *Horā*, and breath through the right nostril.

3. The *Ārūḍha* be an even sign and ascendant an odd sign.

4. The lord of 5th Bhāva from the *Ārūḍha* and the lord of 5th house in the natal chart be one and the same planet.

5. Or, the above two lords (mentioned in 4) have mutual connection through conjunction, aspect, angular relationship etc. (*Note*: there are five kinds of connection.)

6. Note the star occupied by Jupiter at query. The tree ruled by that star be laden with fruits.

If one or more of these conditions are satisfied, the person will be blessed with a son ere long.

More Yogas of Early Success

(1) Add the longitudes of the luminaries and Jupiter. The sum should be taken as the new *Yoga-sphuṭa* (Y.S.). Look at the *Navāṁśa* of this *Sphuṭa*. Similarly, note the *Navāṁśa* of *Māndi*. Now see if there is connection between these two *Navāṁśa Rāśis*. If they be *Samasaptama* (nearly 180° apart), or in trine to each other, there would be child-birth ere long.

(2) Find the sum of the longitudes of the lords of 1st and 5th houses. If Jupiter be in trine to this *Yoga-sphuṭa*, i.e. either sign or its *Navāṁśa*, the same result could be expected.

(3) If *Māndi* be posited in trine to the *Rāśi* or *Aṁśa* occupied by Jupiter, early child-birth is indicated.

Possibility of Pregnancy

Should the *Ārūḍha* be aspected by Mars, you could take it as an indication that the woman's ovum is ready to welcome the male sperm for its fertilization. In case Mars' aspect be absent, there would be no pregnancy owing to excess of blood.

Time of Child-Birth

Have the querist's natal Sun's *Aṣṭaka-Varga* chart. Note also the sign occupied by *Māndi* in the query chart. Note also the 5th and 9th houses from *Māndi*. Now look at the Sun's A.V. chart (*Aṣṭaka-Varga*). Note in this chart the 5th and 9th houses from the *Rāśi* occupied by *Māndi* in the query chart. Whichever of these trines contains greater number of benefic dots, should be noted down. When the Sun transits that sign, that would be the month of child-birth.

To find out the possible natal sign of the child, take the person's Moon's A.V. chart and therein note the sign that has greater number of benefic dots in the trines from *Māndi*, as explained above. When the Moon transits that sign, the expectant woman would be delivered of her child. In the same manner we have to repeat this process in Jupiter's A.V. chart. The year of child-birth would be shown by Jupiter's transit through the sign that has greater number of benefic dots. Similarly, note the *Navāṁśa* sign of the ascendant. When Jupiter arrives at a trine to the *Navāṁśa* of the *Lagna*, success would be certain.

Detection of Pregnancy

(i) If a woman goes to an astrologer and expresses her wish to know if she is in the family way, the answer would be in the affirmative, should Rāhu be posited in one of the *Rāśis* viz. *Ārūḍha*, ascendant and *Chatra*.

(ii) If Jupiter occupy or aspect the 5th, 7th or 9th house, either from the ascendant or the Moon at query, she should be enceinte.

(iii) If the Moon occupying any *Rāśi* be conjoined with benefics, she must be pregnant. If the associating planet be Jupiter, the child would be male; if it be Venus, female.

(iv) If the lord of 5th house be in an odd sign or *Aṁśa*, and in square to *Māndi*, it should be an indication of pregnancy. In addition, if the lord of 5th house be in a sign that rises with its head foremost, it would definitely be an indication of pregnancy.

(v) Should the Moon or *Rāhu* aspect or occupy the *Navāṁśa* sign tenanted by the lord of 5th house, there would be no symptom of pregnancy so far.

(vi) If Mars be substituted for the Moon and Rahu in (5th), presence of pregnancy should be predicted; but if at the same time there be no Jupiter's aspect, it might lead to miscarriage.

(vii) If the *Aṁśa* occupied by the lord of 5th house, be a sign that is both immovable and downward-looking, and be occupied or aspected by Saturn, the concerned woman should be declared to be without any trace of pregnancy and monthly menstruation.

(viii) Should Venus occupy or aspect the *Ārūḍha*, or the rising sign at the time or the 5th house from either, indication of pregnancy should be predicted.

(ix) The following auguries too point to the same effect: Sighting a pregnant woman, a baby, hearing a thunder, sight of a pair of birds fighting with each other, the querist touching his or her arm, foot or nose, and somebody dragging some article.

The following nine Yogas too reveal pregnancy:

1. *Māndi* and the Moon be joined together in any house, especially in the 5th house.
2. The Moon and Mars be joined together.
3. The Moon being aspected by Mars.
4. Benefics occupying the 9th house.
5. Benefics in the 5th and 11th houses.
6. The lord of the 5th house be conjoined with *Māndi*.
7. The lord of the 5th house be aspected by *Māndi*.
8. *Aṁśas* of the Moon and *Māndi* being identical.
9. *Aṁśas* of the Moon and *Māndi* be in trine or *kendra*.

Her Longings

It is well-known that pregnant women entertain peculiar longings for certain food preparations or tastes, dress, ornaments, entertainments etc. This is seen in purāṇic characters too. For example, *Śrī Sītā* expressed a strong desire to see nature in her pristine purity and grandeur, when she was carrying in her womb the twin heroic sons of Śrī Rāmacandra viz. Kuśa and Lava. There are some who eat mud secretly. Find out the *Rāśi* corresponding to the place occupied by the concerned woman. If that *Rāśi* becomes the *Ārūḍha* she would be longing for the taste ascribed to the planet owning the *Ārūḍha*. If the planet be weak or afflicted, the woman would be afflicted by a disease caused by that taste. The region, precious stone, colour of garments, deity etc. signified by that planet she would be greatly interested in.

Indications of Abortion

The following five omens bespeak miscarriage:

(1) After the querist puts the question somebody goes away from the place.

(2) One who arrives there leaves the place almost immediately.

(3) Somebody is removing the wax from his or her ear, or doing a similar act.

(4) Among the betel leaves brought by the querist, the 5th being cut.

(5) A dead insect sticking to the betel leaf mentioned above.

(6) Mars and the Sun be in *kendras*, the 8th house being tenanted by some planet, and Jupiter in a non-kendra house.

(7) The Moon being in a kendra, Jupiter in a non-kendra, and some one in the 8th house.

(8) The Moon being in the ascendant and a malefic in the 19th decanate.

(9) Jupiter being in a *kendra*, Mars in the 8th house, and Saturn in the ascendant.

(10) A halo around the orb of the Sun being seen.

Sex of Child

(a) If the Moon be posited in an odd sign counted from the *lagna*, the child to be born would be male; while if in an even sign, female. (b) Add up the number of the weekday, lunar mansion, and the lunar sign. If the sum be odd or even, the child should be stated to be male or female, as the case may be. (c) If the Sun or Saturn be posited in the 3rd, 9th, 10th or 11th house, it would be male. (d) If all the planets be posited in odd signs, the child would be male. (e) If all the *vargas* of the *lagna* be strong and masculine, be aspected by strong male planets, the child would be male; if they be feminine, it would be female. If Mercury be in the *lagna*, it would be female. (f) If the ascendant, Jupiter, the Sun and Moon be all in odd signs, the result would be a male child. (g) If the luminaries, Jupiter and the ascendant be all in even signs, the result would be female. If this condition be mixed, the result should be declared on the strength of the planets. If Saturn be in an odd sign except the *lagna*, there would be a male birth. (h) If odd signs be occupied by strong Jupiter and the Sun, the result would be a male-birth; on the other hand, if Mars, Venus and the Moon be in even signs, it would be a female. (i) Saturn in an odd *Rāśi* from the *lagna*, leads to a male-birth; and in an even sign, female. (Saturn in an odd *Rāśi* at a query about marriage, leads to quick marriage, while in an even sign, spoils chances of marriage.) (j) The Sun, Mars, Saturn and Jupiter in the 7th house would lead to a male-birth; while other planets there betoken a female. Similarly, Saturn in the *lagna* leads to the birth of female. (k) Should the querist touch his or her limbs on the right side with the right hand, there will be a male; if the person touches the limbs on the left side with the left hand, it will be a female. If the condition are mixed, the result is miscarriage.

(*Note*: The head and neck belong to odd signs; while face and shoulder, to even signs.)

Birth of Twins

If the *Navāṁśas* of both the *lagna* and the *Ārūḍha* be even signs, there would be birth of female twins. For this result the condition must be reinforced by the aspect or conjunction of female planets on the *lagna*. In the above condition if odd signs and male planets be involved, the result would be male twins.

Note: With regard to query about pregnancy and birth, omens occurring at the time such as sight, sound, activities etc. too should be taken into consideration as additional and contributory causes for the result. Similarly, if the *Ārūḍha* be an odd sign, and male planets occupy or aspect it, the querist sitting or standing in a male direction, the number of articles brought there be odd in number, and on the right side etc.—all these factors would goad the astrologer to pronounce the result as male. If the conditions are contrariwise, it would be female. The cardinal directions are male; and the intermediate ones, female.

Sex of Child

(i) If the *Aṁśa* of the *lagna* be an odd *Rāśi*, or a diurnal one, or if the strong Mercury and Saturn be in the *lagna*, or in an odd sign, a boy would be born.

(ii) If the ascendant, Sun, Moon and Jupiter be strong and posited in odd signs and *Aṁśas*, it would be male, and if these be in even signs, female.

(iii) Should the Sun and Jupiter be in odd signs, male would be the result; while the Moon, Mars and Venus in even *Rāśis* cause female-birth. Should these planets have dual *Aṁśas* augmented by Mercury's aspect, twin-birth would result. To distinguish the sex of twins, follow the following rule: (1) The ascendant, Sun, Moon and Jupiter should be aspected by Mercury for the birth of male twins. On the other hand, Mercury's aspect on the Moon, Mars and Venus would lead to the birth of female twins.

Demise of Couple

If the querist should touch a limb on his left side with his right hand, the pregnant woman might breathe her last; while if it be the left hand and right side, the effect of that would be death of the husband.

Time of Delivery*

(1) Convert only the degrees and minutes of the *Lagna-sphuṭa* (Longitude of the query ascendant, leaving off the signs) into minutes and multiply it by 3, and divide the product by 50. The quotient would give the number of *Rāśis*. Now multiply the remainder by 30 and divide the product by 50. The quotient gives degrees, and the remainder multiplied by 60 and divided by 50, gives minutes. Now add the signs left off above to the result. If the signs are more than 12, deduct 12 from it. This would give the Sun's longitude at the time of child-birth. This gives the solar month, day and *Ghaṭis* of the birth.

(2) Or leave off the signs in the *lagna*-longitude and add the degrees and minutes to the Moon's longitude. Multiply the sum by 9. This too gives the Sun's longitude for child-birth. Among these three results whichever is nearest should be taken on the basis of the estimated time.

(3) Or multiply the Sun's longitude at query by 108. The product can be taken as the Sun's longitude at child-birth.

(4) Now we have to learn a new element called *Kakṣā* or Zone. A sign (*Rāśi*) is divided into 8 *Kakṣās*; and one *Kakṣā* is equal to 3°-45′. Without distinction all the days have the same *Kakṣā* at particular periods, as follows:

The first part everyday is presided over by Saturn; the second by Jupiter; the third by Mars; the fourth by the Sun; the fifth by Venus; the sixth by Mercury; the seventh by the Moon; and the eighth by the ascendant. Now find out from the longitude of the *lagna*, in whose zone it is situated. See also where its lord

*This may be read in continuation of the topic "Child-birth" on page 168 *supra*.

is situated and his *Dvādaśāṁśa* (1/12) *Rāśi*. When the Moon arrives at that sign, labour pains would start, and when the Moon transits the sign that is his *Navāṁśa*, delivery would take place. For the sake of clarity let us work out an example: Let the ascendant at query be 3^s-20°-38′-16″. See in whose zone this longitude lies. It is in the sixth zone owned by Mercury. His *Dvādaśāṁśa-Rāśi* is Pisces (Mercury's longitude being 1^s-26°-27′). The Moon transits Pisces 3 days later, and the *Navāṁśa* sign is Leo. The time interval between these two is about 14 days. This is only a dummy illustration. The ascendant of child-birth would be the sign ruled by the planet owning the *Triṁśaṁśa Rāśi* of the lord of the zone. In this example it is Mars who is posited in Pisces which is an even sign. So Mars' even sign viz. Scorpio, should be the ascendant at birth. The time of birth, whether day or night, could be found out from the *Horā* occupied by the lord of the zone. In our example, it is the Sun's *Horā*. So it should be daytime.

(5) Should the lord of the Moon's *Dvādaśāṁśa* be stronger than the Moon, take only the degrees and minutes of her longitude and multiply it by 12 and convert the product into signs, degrees and minutes. When the Moon in transit goes to that place, delivery is to be expected. If the above product be in the first decanate, and if the Moon be in the middle decanate, delivery would take place when the Moon transits the 5th *Rāśi* from the one tenanted by her at query. If the above product be in the third decanate, the event would take place, when the Moon transits the 9th house from her original position at query. On the other hand, if the Moon herself be stronger than the lord of her 1/12 *Aṁśa*, find out the number of the *Dvādasāṁśā*. The birth will synchronize with the Moon's transit through the *Rāśi* that is so many *Rāśis* away as the number of the *Dvādaśaṁśas*. The counting may also be done from Aries.

(6) Leave off the signs in the Moon's longitude and multiply the degrees and minutes by 108 and reduce the product to signs, degrees and minutes. If this sign or its trine be a downward-looking sign, then delivery would take place during the Moon's transit through that sign. If in addition, *Māndī* occupies or as-

pects it, one could be cocksure of the event taking place then. It may also take place when the Moon arrives at the sign which is got by adding the longitudes of the *lagna* and the Moon. If this *Yoga-sphuṭa* sign be a nocturnal *Rāśi*, subtract this Y.S. from 12 signs or 360°. The resulting sign should be noted for the Moon's transit.

(7) Add the longitudes of the *lagna* and the Moon; leaving off the *Rāśis*, multiply the degrees and minutes by 12 and note the star of the product or its 10th one; and when the Moon transits one of them, birth would surely take place.

ASCENDANT AT DELIVERY

It may be one of the following:

(i) The *Dvādaśāṁśa* sign of the ascendant at query; (ii) its *Navāṁśa* sign; (iii) a trine of the sign occupied by *Māndi*; (iv) that *Rāśi* wherein *Māndi* rises the same *night*, or its trine or one of its *Caturvarga*. (It is explained hereunder):

(*I*) The first *varga* is called *Navāṁśa*, which is obtained by multiplying the planet's longitude by 9.

(*II*) The second one is named *Nava-Navāṁśa*, which is got by multiplying the planet's longitude by 8.

(*III*) The third one is known as *Navāṁśa-Dvādaśāṁśa*, which is obtained by multiplying the first *varga* by12. While doing this, leave off the signs and multiply only the degrees and minutes. Then add the signs that have been left off. The result is *Navāṁśa-Dvādaśāṁśa*.

[*Note*: These and other numerous techniques employed in this system that are very popular in Kerala, which have been given here only for the benefit of scientific researchers. I doubt very much that an astrologer in his day-to-day practice would be able to do justice to all the methods mentioned above to find out the approximate time of delivery of the child.]

(*IV*) The fourth *varga* is known as *Dvādaśāṁśa*, which is got by multiplying the planet's longitude, without signs, by 12. Then add the *Rāśis* left off to this product. The result is called *Dvādaśāṁśa*.

(8) Find out the *Adhomukha* (downward looking) *Rāśi* between the 5th and 9th houses counted from the *Ārūḍha*. When the Moon transits that sign, the child would be delivered. This, they say, is the topmost secret of this question.

Expiation for Santāna-Doṣa

When planets are found to be in a frowning mood or unfavourable at a query session, owing to their ill-placement, proper ways of atonement are prescribed by competent astrologers, so that such planets and their presiding deities, being moved to pity by the utter helplessness of the faithful, do shower some amount of blessings:

1. When the Sun or Saturn combined with the Moon is posited in an untoward house (6th, 8th or 12th) which is an odd sign, propitiation of one's ancestors is very essential for success. If the Sun be in an even *Rāśi* under the above conditions, performance of *Kṣetra-Śrāddha* should be resorted to in a famous place of pilgrimage like Gayā in Bihar. Some other places are Kāśī, Rāmeśvaram, Nāsik, Haridvāra, Gokarṇa. Talakāverī etc., recitation of Vedas, Purāṇas, Rudrābhiṣeka etc. If Saturn be in an untoward house which is an even sign, a hearty feast should be given to all classes.

2. Expiation for the Luminaries

If the trouble for progeny be found due to the Moon, it should be attoned for by means of *Śrāddha* in a sacred shrine like Gayā or through the dances of *Bhūtas* in their shrines. If either the Sun or Moon be found afflicted by malefics, some ancestor must have become a wandering evil spirit (*Preta*) on account of unnatural or violent death. Hence for its salvation *Piṇḍa-Pradāna* or *Śrāddha*, wherein rice-balls are offered to the departed souls, should be done elaborately with faith and devotion.

3. Expiation for Mars and Mercury

If Mars be posited in an odd sign identical with an untoward house, the remedy is worship of the Lord Kārtikeya and feeding Brāhmaṇas with choice delicacies. If Mars be in an even sign, Goddess Durgā is to be worshipped like Lord Subrahmaṇya. If Mercury be ill-placed, worship of Lord Nārāyaṇa by means of *Abhiṣeka* (ritual bath) with *Pañcāmṛta* (a mixture of five sweet ingredients viz. cow's milk, ghee, curd, honey, sugar and banana pieces), offering of *Pāyasa* (milk-porridge), feeding of Brāhmaṇas, *Japa* and recitation of the *mantras* called *Saubhāgya Sūkta*.

4. Expiation for Afflicted Jupiter

When Jupiter is found to be the main cause of loss of children, because of his position in an untoward house that is an odd *Rāśi*, Ayurvedic medicines such as *Kalyāna Ghṛta* (a medicated ghee preparation), *Pañcagavya-Ghṛta*, *Sukumāra-Ghṛta* etc., consecrated by the *Japa* of *Puruṣa-Sūkta*, *Santāna-Gopāla* etc. should be given to the woman as medicine for eradicating the defects in her reproductive organs. Similarly *Gaṇa-Homa* too should be performed. If Jupiter, in addition, be in an even sign, both the Gods viz. Śaṅkara, and Nārāyaṇa should be propitiated, and a thousand Brāhmaṇas worshipped with a grand feast and *Dakṣiṇā* (monetary gift).

Atonement for Venus's Affliction

If Venus be found to be the cause of trouble to the cause of progeny on account of his stay in an odd and untoward house, the female deity viz. *Yakṣī* (or *Durgā*) should be propitiated by the offering of *Apūpa*, *Pāyasa*, fragrant articles like sandal paste, music etc. If Venus be in an even sign, the following remedial measures should be undertaken: Worship of *Dharma-Daiva*, *Havana*, libation of water (*tarpaṇa*), feeding of Brāhmaṇas sumptuously, taking consecrated medicinal ghee etc.

Expiation for Rāhus Trouble

If *Rāhu* posited in an odd sign be found to have caused trouble in respect of issue, the worship of serpents called *Āśleṣā-Bali* must needs be performed. If he be in an even sign, serpents should be propitiated through music, dance etc. If it be a dual sign, two images of serpents should be worshipped and given away to worthy recipients.

Santāna Candra-Sphuṭa

At a query about issue find out the time in *Ghaṭis* and *Vighaṭis* that has elapsed since sunrise. Convert that into *Vighaṭis* and divide the result by 50. What you get is in *Rāśis*. The balance is to be multiplied by 30 and divided by 50. The result gives degrees. If the remainder be multiplied by 60 and divided by 50, you would get minutes. If in the place of *Rāśis* there should be more than 12, deduct that from the larger number. The result is to be subtracted from 1 sign. If the latter is smaller than the former, add 12 *Rāśis* to it. Multiply the result by 5 and reduce it into signs, degrees and minutes, as shown above. This is termed the longitude of *Santāna-Ravi* (Sun). Now take the total number of *Vighaṭis* got from the time elapsed from sunrise in *Ghaṭis*. As before divide the *Vighaṭis* by 50 and reduce the result into signs, degrees and minutes; and add 8^s-15° to this, and multiply the sum by 5 and reduce the result into signs, degrees and minutes. This is called *Santāna-Candra*, i.e. longitude of the Moon pretaining to progeny. Another method of working out these two longitudes is given below: Take the Sun's longitude at query and multiply it by 5. The product represents *Santāna-Ravi*—longitude. Similarly, take the Moon's longitude at query and multiply it by 5. The product will give you the longitude of *Santāna-Candra*. The second method, no doubt, is simpler; but when should one utilize these methods? The *Praśnamārga* states that when the *Ārūḍha* is stronger, use the first method, whereas when the *lagna* is stronger, the second method.

Atonement for Affliction to Santāna-Tithi

First of all find out the *Santāna-Tithi*. For that subtract the longitude of the *Santāna*—Sun from that of the *Santāna*—Moon. The resultant longitude would give you the *Santāna-Tithi* at the rate of 12° per lunar day. If this *tithi* happens to be in the bright half, there would be issue. If it be in the dark fortnight, success would be attainable through expiation. Up to the 5th *tithi* in the dark half there would not be much difficulty in getting progeny. If it be the 6th *tithi* in the dark half, Lord Kārtikeya should be propitiated for issue. If it be the 7th, 8th, 9th or 10th lunar day, one would have issue by another wife. Even this would be possible only after performing worship of Lord Viṣṇu on a day ruling the star *Śravana*, and feeding Vedic scholars. If it be 11th or 12th *tithi*, even by performing the sacrifice called *Dvādaśi-Homa* it would be difficult to beget a living child. On the 13th and 14th *tithis*, adoption alone is the course open to the couple. If it be new Moon, even an adopted child would not live long. One of the chief causes for childlessness is the wrath of ancestors. To atone for that one ought to perform the *Śrāddhas* called *Aṣṭakā* and *Pārvaṇa* etc. and earn the goodwill and blessings of ancestors, which will pave the way to the realization of one's object. For the omission of obsequial rites and annual *Śrāddhas* attract their wrath. Even in the light half the *Riktā* lunar days (4th, 9th and 14th) are not favourable for issue. If it be one of the dark fortnight, the trouble would be due to black-magic practised in bygone days by the person's enemies. For the 4th *tithi*, the black-magic should be got exercised by an upper-class *Māntrika*; for the 9th *tithi*, it should be done by magicians of cruel deeds; and for the 14th lunar day, through low-class magicians. If the *Santāna-tithi* reveals *Viṣṭi* or *Bhadra Karaṇa*, curse of serpents should be the cause of trouble. If it be of the bright half of the month, the curse must be one of recent origin, while in the other half, it would be an old curse. If the *Santāna-tithi* is one in the light half, some issue is possible upto the 5th *tithi*; from the 6th to the 10th, a good number of children; and from the 11th to the full moon, more children would be born.

Adoption According to Tithi

If the *Santāna-Tithi* be the 7th, one's brother's son would be taken in adoption. If it be the 8th, it is one of his own *Gotra*; if the 9th *tithi*, two boys would be taken in adoption, and the second one would be of good character. If it be the 10th lunar day, one's sister's son would be adopted; and on the 11th day, it would be a boy of another *Gotra*. On the 12th day, no child could be adopted. Consequently the person's entire wealth would be snatched away by his kinsmen.

Remedies for Tithis

Though the *Riktā* lunar days and *Viṣṭi Karaṇa* of the light half are not helpful for issue, still for the 4th day *Gaṇa-Homa* is the remedy prescribed by sages of yore; for the 9th day, worship of Mother Durgā and for the 14th day, worship of Lord Rūdra. By following the above directions one could hope for success in respect of issue. Should the *santāna-tithi* be the full moon, one could hope to be blessed with children by worshipping Lord Viṣṇu in His shrine and doing *Japa* of *Puruṣa-Sūkta*, as well as by the chanting of the three Vedas, and feeding Brāhmaṇas on *Pūrṇimā* day, coupled with listening to the exposition of the ancient Purāṇas (epics) which were recited by *Sūta* for *Śaunaka* and other sages in the *Naimiṣa* forest in ancient days.

By these means one could hope to get success.

The following chart gives remedies to be undertaken for the different lunar days of the dark fortnight:

Tithis of Dark Half	Mode of Propitiation	Tithis	Mode of Propitiation	Tithis	Mode of Propitiation
1	Worship of Gopālakṛṣṇa by *Santāna-Gopāla Mantra*	3	Worship of Mother Durgā	5	Worship of one's *Iṣṭa-devatā*
2	Taking *Pañca-gavya Ghṛta* sanctified by *Gopāla Mantra*	4	Performing *Gaṇa-Homa* with *Aṣṭa-Dravya*	6	Worship of Lord Subrah-maṇya
7	Worship of Hari and Hara	10	Performance of *Gaṇa Havana*	13	Arranging Special Festi-vals in temples
8	Worship of serpents	11	*Kṣetra Śrāddha* or *Piṇḍa* offer-ings to the manes in a sacred place	14	*Kṣetra-Srāddha* and worshipping Brāhmaṇas
9	Feeding a thousand Brahmaṇas	12	Worship and feeding of 12 *Brahmaṇas* on *Śravaṇa* star	15	Performing *Aṣṭakā, Pār-vaṇa Srāddhas* and *Tila-Homa* etc.

SANTĀNA-JUPITER

As Jupiter plays a very important role in the sphere of issue, fortune, merit of previous life, his *Santāna-sphūṭa* is made use for discussing the topic of issue. Proceed thus for getting it: Add the longitude of *Yama-Kaṇṭaka* (Jupiter's satellite) to that of the ascendant at query. Multiply the sum by 5. This product is termed *Santāna-Jīva* (Jupiter). If this has all the following *doṣas* (afflictions), there will be some chance of getting issue with much difficulty, after performing propitiatory rites and observing strenuous vows:

(1) Venus aspecting the *Navāṁśa* sign of the *Santāna-Jīva.* (2) The *Aṁśa* sign belonging to Venus and being occupied by Venus. (3) The Lord of the *Navāṁśa* being posited in one of the stars ruled by Venus (according to *Viṁśottarī-daśā* system) viz. *Bharaṇī P. Phalgunī* and *P. Āṣāḍhā*. These Yogas or afflictions suggest remarriage for the concerned man. (4) Next find out the longitude of *Santāna-Śukra* by multiplying Venus's longitude by 5. (5) Now see if there is any connection between these two *Santāna-sphuṭas* (*Note*: *Sambandha* is of five kinds) in respect of their *Aṁśas* etc. If the answer be in the affirmative, the man would have as many marriages as the number of planets that are posited in the 7th house from the *Santāna-Śukra*. (6) In case the *Aṁśa*-sign is stronger than the one occupied by *Santāna*-Venus, the first wife would not bear him any issue; but the second one would be successful in bearing children. (7) On the other hand, if the *Santāna*- Venus sign be stronger than its *Aṁśa,* the man would, after marrying a second wife, beget children by the first wife herself. (8) If the *Aṁśa* of *Santāna-Śukra* belongs to a eunuch planet (Mercury or Saturn), and is occupied or aspected by a eunuch, one would beget children by the third wife.

1. SANTĀNA YOGA-SPHUṬA

Add the longitudes of *Yamakaṇṭaka* and the *Santāna-Jīva.* The result is known as *Santāna Yoga-Sphuṭa.* This is made use of in ascertaining the number of children. If this shows more than 5 degrees, there would be only one son; if it be more than 10°, two sons; if more than 15°, three sons; if more than 20°, four; if more than 25°, five; and if 30th degree, six children. If in this *Yoga-Sphuṭa* there be three *vargas* (Horā, decanate etc.) belonging to Jupiter, more than six children could be expected; and if the *vargas* of Jupiter be more, still more children could be expected.

(2) If the lord of the decanate of the *Santāna Yoga-Sphuṭa* be debilitated or in an inimical sign, and has just come within the 5th degree, and the *Yoga-Sphuṭa* too has advanced only so far, the first son is likely to perish; if the *Sphuṭa* has advanced within 10°, the second child is likely to die, if it be within 15°, the third son dies; for 20°, the fourth son, for 25°, the fifth son; and for thirty degrees, the sixth child may quit the world. In addition to this, the astrologer must need note if the *Yoga-sphuṭa* is in Taurus, Leo, Virgo or Scorpio. If that be so, there would be no issue at all.

(3) The three of the *vargas* (*Rāśi*, *Navaṁśa* and *Drekkāṇa*) of the above-named *Yoga-sphuṭa* be connected with eunuch planets, twins would be born, but their survival and death depend on the strength and weakness respectively of the planets concerned.

Datta-Sphuṭa Effects

Add the longitudes of Mercury, Saturn and the lord of 5th house, and multiply the sum by five. The product will represent *Datta-sphuṭa* or adoption longitude. If this be a diurnal sign, and its *Aṁśa*, a Nocturnal sign with malefic association or aspect, a son by adoption is indicated. On the contrary, i.e. the sign and *Aṁśa* be nocturnal and diurnal respectively, there would be no chance even for an adopted son. If this *Datta-Sphuṭa* suffers from all the afflictions mentioned above (see pp. 183-85), one could not hope for even an adopted son.

Yoga for Issue

If Jupiter and *Māndi* be posited in the first six signs from Aries, identical with trines to the longitude of *Santāna-Jīva*, they would promote chances of getting children. The same result would ensue, if they be in the six signs from Libra, identical with trines to the *Navāṁśa* of the above *Santāna-Jīva*. The sex of children should be read from the sum of the longitudes of *Yamakaṇṭaka* and *Māndī*. If this sum be an odd or even sign, it does not matter; but if its *Aṁśa* be odd, the child would be male; if even female.

Santāna Trisphuṭa

Here the lunar sign of the child to be born is explained. Add the figures of (1) *Santāna-Jīva*, (2) *Yamakaṇṭaka*, and (3) *Santāna-Māndī*. Multiply the sum by 81 and reduce the result into signs, degrees and minutes. Find out the star of this. When the Moon transits one of the three following signs, child-birth would take place: (1) The star of the final result; (2) a *Rāśi* trine to the *Trisphuṭa*, and (3) the *Rāśi* that happens to be the *Aṁśaka* of the star of this *Trisphuṭa*.

S. No.	Stars	Trees	Botanical Names	According to others	Botanical Names
1	*Aśvinī*	*Kāraskara*	Strychnos nuxvomica	Honge (Kan.) (Indian beech)	Pongamia glabra
2	*Bharaṇī*	Dhātrī	Emblica officinalis	—	—
3	*Kṛttikā*	Udumbara Indian fig.	Ficus racemosa	—	—
4	*Rohiṇī*	Jambū	Eugenia jambos	Nīrmāvu	—
5	*Mṛgaśiras*	Khadira	Acacia catechu	—	—

S. No.	Stars	Trees	Botanical Names	According to others	Botanical Names
6	*Ārdrā*	Pātalā	Stereo-spermum suaveo-lens	White Matti or Maruva	Terminalia tomentosa
7	*Punar-vasu*	Bamboo	Bambusa arundi-nacea	—	—
8	*Puṣya*	*Aśvattha*	Ficus reli-giosa	—	—
9	*Āśleṣā*	Nāga campaka	Mesua ferrea	—	—
10	*Maghā*	Nyag-rodha Banyan	Ficus bengal-ensis	Harītakī	—
11	*Pūrva-Phalgunī*	Palāśa	Butea monos perma	Flame of the forest	—
12	*U. Phalgu*	Guava Amrūd (Hindi)	Psidium guava	—	—
13	*Hasta*	Ambā	Spondi-as mangi fera	Bile tree	—
14	*Citrā*	Bilva	Aegle marmelas	Wood apple	—
15	*Svātī*	Challangai	Terminalia arjuna	Śleṣmātaka	Cordia-myxa

S. No.	Stars	Trees	Botanical Names	According to others	Botanical Names
16	*Viśākhā*	Aṅkola	Alangium Salvifolium	Vikankata	Gymnosporia spinosa
17	*Anurādhā*	Bakula	Mimusops elingi	—	—
18	*Jyeṣṭhā*	Sarala	Cedrus-deodara	Devadaru	—
19	*Mūla*	Candana	Santalum album	Sandal wood	—
20	*Pūrva Āṣādhā*	Jambū	Eugenia jambolama	Black plum	—
21	*U. Āṣāḍhā*	Panasa	Artocarpus integrifolia	Jack	Artocarpus heterophyllus
22	*Śravaṇa*	Arka	Calotropis gigantea	—	—
23	*Dhaniṣṭhā*	Śami	Prosopis spicigera	—	Acacia spicigera
24	*Śatabhiṣak*	Kadamba	Anthocephalus cadamba	—	Anthocephalus indicus
25	*Pūrvā Bhādra*	Cūta Mango	Mangifera indica	Nimba Neem	Azadirachta indica
26	*Uttarā Bhādra*	Nimba Neem	Azadirachta indica	Cūta Mango	Mangifera indica
27	*Revatī*	Madhūka Ippe (Kan)	Bassia latifolia	Indian butter tree	—

The following chart gives the Trees assigned to the twelve signs of the Zodiac beginning with Aries.

S. No.	Signs	Trees	Botanical Names	According to others	Botanical Names
1	Aries	Red Candana	(Red Sanders) Pterocarpus santalinus	—	—
2	Taurus	Udumbara	Ficus glomerata	Dūrvā	Cynodon dactylon
3	Gemini	Panasa Jack	Artocarpus integrifolia	Apāmārga	Achyranthes aspera
4	Cancer	Palāśa	Butea monosperma	—	—
5	Leo	Camphor Tree	Cinnamomum Camphora	—	—
6	Virgo	Mango	Mangifera indica	—	—
7	Libra	Bakula	Memusops elengi	White Nityapuṣpa	—
8	Scorpio	Khadira	Acacia Catechu	Red Nityapuṣpa	—
9	Sagittarius	Aśvattha	Ficus religiosa	—	—
10	Capricorn	Rose-wood	Dalbergia latifolia	—	—
11	Aquarius	Śamī	Prosopis spicigera	—	—
12	Pisces	Nāgakesara	Mesua ferrea	—	—

Chapter VIII

DISEASES

When a person falls ill, his relatives consult their family physician, who after a through examination of the patient treats him to the best of his ability. Sometimes the physician calls a specialist and takes his advice. If the patient does not show any sign of recovery, his family-members resort to their family astrologer for guidance in the matter of divine wrath and other extraordinary causes for the continuance of the ailment, and the means of removing those causes. While discussing this topic we have to remember and repeat the matter already delineated in previous chapter, especially the one on *Deva-praśna*. When planets are ill-placed in one's chart, natal or horary, the astrologer would declare the illness pertaining to such planets as well as the line of treatment for success. When some of the planets are favourably disposed, they would help the patient to recover fast after proper propitiation is done for the unfavourable planets.

Lack of Illness

Under the following planetary configurations at a query an astrologer would issue a 'No complaint' certificate to the patient:

1. Malefics should be posited in the 3rd and 11th houses from the ascendant at query.
2. Benefics should be in houses other than 3, 6, 8 and 12 houses.
3. *Māndi* too should be in any house other than the 8th a time and an angle.

In the absence of these conditions, i.e. malefics in houses other than 3rd and 11th houses, benefics in 3, 6, 8 and 12 places, and *Māndi* in 1, 4, 5, 7, 8, 9 and 10 houses, it should be said that the person-concerned has ailments all over the body.

Well-placed and Ill-placed Planets

For some it would be hard to distinguish between these two types of planets. Ill-placed are the following planets:

1. Week malefics being posited in 1, 4, 5, 6, 7, 8, 9 and 12 houses from the *Lagna*.

2. Benefics in 6, 8 and 12 places.

These ill-placed planets cause diseases and sometimes even death. Those that are deadly enemies of the lord of the ascendant are sure to cause serious illness and death. Even benefics, when they get the epithet, ill-placed do cause much suffering and demise.

Well-placed planets are those malefics pointed in 2, 3, 10 and 11 places; and benefics in houses other than 6, 8 and 12 houses. Any planet in conjunction with the Moon too becomes 'well-placed'. All such planets bestow good results according to the places they occupy.

The following planets cause diseases according to their office:

1. Those that are posited in the 6, 8 and 12 *Bhāvas*.
2. The planets that are conjorned with the lord of the ascendant.
3. Those that aspect the *lagna*-lord.
4. Those that occupy the *lagna*.
5. Those that aspect the *lagna*.

Among these planets find out one who is noted for causing trouble. He will create such ailments as are ascribed to him. If the ascendant be a movable sign and an upward-looking one, the ailment is above the neck. If it be an immovable and cross-wise looking sign, the disease is below the neck. Lastly if the *lagna* be a dual *Rāśi* and downward-looking one, the trouble is beneath the hips. If conditions are mixed, the disease too would be partly in one part and partly in another part of the body.

The ailment is located in particular limbs on the basis of planets in bad houses as follows: The Sun would point the place of disease around the navel; the Moon, in the heart; Mars, in the head; Mercury, in the chest; Jupiter, in the thighs, Venus, on the face; Saturn, on the knees; *Rāhu*, in the feet; and *Ketu*, also in the feet.

It is well known that the twelve houses stand for different limbs from head downward; so also do the planets owning the houses:

The ascendant and its lord signify	—Head
The second house and its lord ,,	—Face
The third ,, ,, ,, ,,	—Neck
The fourth ,, ,, ,, ,,	—Shoulders
The fifth ,, ,, ,, ,,	—Heart
The sixth ,, ,, ,, ,,	—Stomach
The seventh ,, ,, ,, ,,	—Beneath navel or Abdomen
The eighth ,, ,, ,, ,,	—Privities
The ninth ,, ,, ,, ,,	—Thighs
The tenth ,, ,, ,, ,,	—Knees
The eleventh ,, ,, ,, ,,	—Shanks
The twelfth ,, ,, ,, ,,	—Feet

The places of the body assigned to the planets and houses from the ascendant onwards are to be judiciously assessed as locations of ailments. Whichever house is occupied by malefics and whichever house-lord is conjoined with malefics, disease should be located in that limb allotted to that planet. In addition to this the location of disease is to be done on the basis of the *Rāśi* signifying the limb that is touched by the querist, the sign corresponding to the place occupied by him (*Ārūḍha*) and the one that rises at the time of query. According to the great Varāhamihira the *Tridoṣas* or humours *Vāta* (wind), *Pitta* (Bile) and *Kapha* (phlegm) are allotted to the planets thus: The Sun and Mars are of *Pitta* or Bile; Moon and Venus—*Vāta* (wind) and *Kapha* (phlegm); Saturn—*Vāta* (wind); Mercury—a mixture of all the three humours; and Jupiter—*Kapha* (phlegm). According to a later author the Sun produces bile and wind; the Moon-wind and phlegm; Mars—bile; Mercury—all the three; Jupiter—wind and phlegm; Venus—wind and phlegm and Saturn—wind and bile. In the case of weak Moon you have to think of the humour belonging to the lord of the sign tenanted by her. If the full moon be in a watery sign, it should be phlegm. This is not all: The planets are connected with the five elements or *Bhūtas*. So they are likely to generate diseases born of their elements. Hence the planets from the Sun onwards cause diseases in order:

(1) Heat-born diseases; (2) ailments borne by water; (3) those

caused by excessive heat like highfever; (4) those caused by the vitiation of all the three humours; (5) those born of the element ether such as deafness; (6) water-borne diseases like diarrhoea; and (7) rheumatic troubles. They cause the above-named ailments when they occupy bad houses (6, 8, 12). Similarly the planets create such diseases in the seasons (*Ṛtus*) as are appropriate to their seasons. The Sun rules over summer, the Moon over rainy season, Mars over summer; Mercury over autumn; Jupiter over dewy season; Venus over spring; and Saturn over winter. Some authorities declare that the afflicted planets generate such ailments as are due to their physical constituents (dhātus). In this connection three classes of planets are to be noted: (1) The planets that are ill-placed; (2) those whose *Nāvaṁśas* fall in the evil houses (6, 8, 12); and (3) those that preside over the Navāṁśas of ill-placed ones.

Natural and Accidental Diseases

Primarily diseases are of two kinds viz. natural and accidental. The first type has two varieties as physical and mental. The Accidental type too has two sub-divisions as those whose cause is known and those of unknown cause. Among natural diseases there are eight types: (1) caused by vitiation of wind; (2) of bile; (3) of phlegm; (4) of the combination of all the three; (5) of wind and bile; (6) of wind and phlegm; (7) of bile and phlegm; and (8) of admixture of all varieties.

The astrologer should tell the querist that the patient is suffering from the disease caused by the strongest planet among the four as shown here: (1) The lord of the 8th house, (2) the 8th house itself, (3) the planet that aspects the 8th house; and the one that occupies the 8th house.

Mental diseases: These are caused by mental imbalance born of very strong and uncontrollable feelings such as indignation, fright, grief, sexual passion etc. The astrological reason for this is the connection between the lords of the 5th and 8th houses. Please remember that connection or *sambandha* is of five kinds.

Among the accidental diseases those whose cause is known or knowable are those resulting from the curses of saintly persons and those that are caused by black-magic done by enemies. Accidental fall, wounds, fractures of bones etc. also come under this category. Diseases of this category should be delineated by means of the following: (1) The 6th *Bhāva*; (2) its lord; (3) the planet that aspects that *Bhāva*; (4) one that is posited in the 6th house; (5) one that is in association with the lord of the 6th Bhāva; and (6) the planet that aspects the 6th-lord. Should the lord of the 8th house be connected (in one of the five ways) with the 6th house, it could be conjectured easily that the disease is the result of strong curses or black-magic.

Regarding diseases whose cause is not known, the reader's attention is drawn to the chapter on *Deva-praśna*, varieties of *bādhās* (troubles) etc. Diseases born of the bādhās of *bhūtas* (evil spirits), *pretas* (wandering discarnate spirits) and such other invisible beings, are accidental.

Patients suffering from different ailments are advised to avoid certain foods, drinks and activities that are technically called *Apathyas* (unwholesome ones). If at a query session such things as are to be avoided by a patient are seen or talked about, the astrologer would at once declare the patient is suffering from the particular sickness. If water is seen there, the ailment is caused by cold; if fire be sighted, it would be a burning or bilious disease; if jaggery be brought, the ailment must be diabetes.

TASTES

The subjeet of taste (*rasa*) is relevant to the topic of disease. For, according to *Āyurveda*, *rasas* which are six in number, are found in food, by consuming which irregularly and wrongly people fall ill. The *rasas* are sweet, sour, salt, bitter, pungent and astringent. Among these the first three are possessed of curative properties for *vataic* (wind) diseases. The last three are good for phlegmetic (*kapha*) complaints. On the other hand, astringent, bitter and sweet tastes aggravate bile; and sweet, sour and salt accentuate phlegm. The planets who preside over particular *doṣas* (humours) generate diseases born of concerned humours when they are ill-placed or afflicted. In this connection the reader is referred to Varāhamihira's statement in the *Bṛhajjātaka* XXIII-7. Therein the astrological apostle mentions venereal disease. Intestinal disorders, white leprosy and paralysis—all born of sins committed in previous life.

Signs of Lunacy

The following eight *yogas* lead to lunacy:

1. The ascendant is to be occupied by Jupiter and the 7th house by Saturn.
2. Jupiter in the *lagna* and Mars in the 7th house.
3. Saturn in the ascendant and Mars in 5th, 7th or 9th house.
4. The Moon being in the *lagna* along with eclipsed Mercury.
5. Weak Moon in the 12th house along with Saturn.
6. Weak Moon along with malefics be in the ascendant, 5th, 8th or 9th house.
7. *Māndī* along with malefics being posited in the 7th house.
8. Mercury along with malefics be in the 3rd, 6th, 8th and 12th.

If one or more of the above conditions are found at a query, the querist or somebody in his house must be a mental patient.

Causes and Kinds of Lunacy

Excessive joy, longing, fear, grief etc. cause mental disease. So is eating unclean and forbidden food as well as wrath of *gurus* (spiritual masters), anger of Gods, curses of holy persons and the public. Lunacy is of five kinds viz. (1) born of *vāta* (wind), (2) born of *pitta* (bile), (3) born of *kapha* (phlegm), (4) born of *Sannipāta* (a mixture of all) and (5) *Āgantuka* (accidental).

Symptoms of Vātonmāda

Laughing without reason, shouting, striking hands against the ground, weeping, shreicking, singing, dancing, the body becoming tender and of coppery hue, emaciation of the body, making all sorts of gesticulations, talking incoherently—these are said to be the symptoms of lunacy caused by vitiation of wind.

Symptoms of Pittonmāda: Show of hatred intolerance, show of power, catching hold of another suddenly, using foul language against others, running towards shade, asking for cool drinks and food, getting angry, the body turning yellow owing to vitiation of bile, body temperature becoming always above normal—these indications point to the type of lunacy caused by bile.

Symptoms of Kaphonmāda: Wishing to have the company of

a member of the opposite sex, resorting to solitude, fondness for sleep, lack of appetite, talking very little, dropping saliva, vomitting, showing increase of energy after taking food; nails turning pale—these are indications of lunacy born of vitiation of *kapha* (*phlegm*).

Signs of sannipātonmāda: If there is an admixture of the signs of above varieties, it gets this nomenclature. This type of lunacy is said to be incurable.

Accidental lunacy is caused by the troubles of divine agencies, discarnate spirits, *piśācasa*, *bhūtas* etc. If it is born of *devagraha-bādhā* (affliction caused by divine spirits) the patient is said to be getting extraordinary strength, knowledge and scholarship as well as heroic acts. If the cause be affliction by demoniac spirits, the latter cast their evil eye on their victims and persecute them.

The following persons become their victims: one who is very avaricious, cruel, frightened, thirsty, a great rogue, one who nurtures old enmity, one who has lost heavily, who is lonely, defeated, dirty person, who is about to enter the jaws of death, sickly, in delirious laughter, one who is possessed of a handsome personality, who destroys hereditary wealth or treasures, timid person, well decorated person, who remains lonely at night—such persons become the target for the evil eye of the *bhūtas* or attendants of *Rudra* who catch and harass them sometime or the other. This must be due to the result of heinous sins committed in previous lives. The ancient authorities are of the view that a person experiences in this very life the fruits of both extraordinary good and bad deeds. A person loses his fortune as a result of *Rudras* wrath resulting from disrespect shown to gods and godly men. When the master is displeased, his attendants punish such sinners.

The seven planets and the modes when afflicted and ill-placed, suggest different *grahas* (catching agents). The Sun stands for *Rudra-Gaṇas*, terrific spirits and *nāgas* or serpents.

The Moon stands for: different classes of demigods called kinnaras, *yakṣas*, and *nāgagrahas*.

Mars stands for: ferocious *grahas* or beings, demons, *bhūtas*, *Agnibhairava*, *Kālabhairava* and such others.

Mercury stands for: Attālakas (A group of dreaded spirits) and *Kinnaras*.

Jupiter stands for: divine *grahas*, holy *Nāgas*, the holy Trinity.

Venus stands for: female *yakṣas* (called *yakṣiṇīs* in popular language), groups of *Mātṛkās* (Mother Goddesses) and *Nāgas* (serpents).

Saturn stands for: Inauspicious *grahas* or spirits, *Nisteja*, (Pale), *Bhasmaka* (Ash-smeared beings), *piśācas* (devils), *Kaśmala-grahas* (dirty spirits).

Rāhu stands for: *Nāgagraha*, *piśācagraha*, *sarpagraha* etc.

Ketu stands for: *Pretagrahas* (discarnate spirits) and *pitṛ-grahas* (ancestral spirits).

The Sun posited in *bādhā* house, points to diseases caused by the trouble created by lord Śiva's hosts and *Rudra's* groups of attendants.

The Moon in the *bādha-sthāna* suggests the wrath of Mother *Durgā* and of one's *Dharma-daiva* (village deity).

Mars in such a situation would cause troubles due to Lord Subrahmaṇya and *Bhairava* and such other deities.

Mercury points to diseases created by the troubles of *Gandharvas*, *Yakṣas*, *Ākāśa Gandharvas* and deities living in aerial chariots.

Jupiter suggests diseases resulting from the wrath of *iṣṭa devatā* and curses of Brāhmaṇas.

Venus points to troubles generated by female *yakṣas* and *Brahmarākṣasas*.

Saturn in *bādhā* place betokens troubles from *bhūtanāthas* like *Śāstā* and *Rudra's* hosts. If Rāhu be responsible for the trouble, ailments should have been caused by serpents' anger.

Ketu in that position suggest *Caṇḍāla bhūtas* or low-class spirits.

If *Māndī* be in the *bādhā* place, the ailment would be due to troubles of displeased ancestral spirits.

Remedies for the Above Mentioned Bādhās

Sacrifice to Lord *Mṛtyuñjaya* (Śiva who vanquishes death); or to *Kāla Mṛtyuñjaya*, worship through bali of the *Bhūtas*, Aghora Bali, *Sudarśana Homa*, *Rakṣābandhana*, both in sacred rivers or lakes, and such other votive rituals.

Causes of Lunacy: (1) If the Moon, Venus and lord of the

8th house be posited in bad houses, it would be due to wrong foods or fasting.

(2) If the above three planets be conjoined with *Māndi* or Rāhu or Ketu, it would be due to eating dirty and contaminated food.

(3) If malefics other than Mars be in the 5th house, it is due to fright and dispassion or detachment.

(4) If Mars be in the 5th house, it is due to wrath and hatred.

(5) Malefics in the 6th house denote lunacy caused by black-magic practised by enemies.

(6) If malefics be in the 9th house, the disease is due to divine wrath, curse of Guru or *Agnikopa* (displeasure of fire god).

The best remedy for the above type of lunacy is the performance of *Mṛtyuñjaya Homa* and use of *Kalyāna Ghṛta*, *Pañcagavya Ghṛta* etc. If medicines are given to the patient after the performance of remedial rites mentioned above, he will surely tide over the difficulties and live a normal life.

Epilepsy

1. If Saturn and Rāhu be posited in the 8th house and other strong malefics in the 5th and 9th house, one would be afflicted with epilepsy, provided both the Sun and Mars being in bad houses indicate disease.

2. Both Saturn and Rāhu be weak and in the 8th house and suggest disease, (without benefic aspect) point to the presence of epilepsy.

3. The same result will follow, if strong Mars and Sun and Ketu and Mercury with malefics be posited in 5th and 9th houses.

4. Both the Sun and Mars being weak, being owners of inauspicious houses, should occupy the 8th house bereft of benefic aspect and association.

In this connection the following opinion is worth nothing: The Sun alone posited in a bad house is capable of causing epilepsy. So is Mars in such a position.

Spread of this Disease: The person under the attack of epilepsy suddenly becomes very weak, trembles all over and becomes unconscious. He would be foaming at the mouth, producing a gurgling sound and lying quiet for long. His eyes would be rolling, with gnasling teeth, and face turning yellow; he will have interest in water and with his face turned wry. Some texts mention other symptoms of epilepsy. Generally they are distinguished by the names of twelve female messengers (*dutīs*) as follows:

(1) *Śvasanā*—One that breathes hard; (2) *Malinā*—one that makes the victim's body very dirty; (3) *Nidrā*—one that makes one fall asleep; (4) *Jṛmbhikā*—one that gives excessive yawning; (5) *Anaśanā*—one that detests food; (6) Trāsinā—frightening. (7) *Mohanī*—one that deprives the patient of consciousness; (8) *Rodanī*—making the person weep; (9) Krodhanī—one who makes the person very angry; (10) *Tapini*—one that raises the body temperature or causes a burning sensation; (11) *Śoṣiṇī*—one who makes the person dry; and (12) *Dhvaṁsinā*—one who destroys. The names of these messengers need no further explanation, as they are self-explanatory. These may attack their victims in different ways, sometimes singly and at other times in a group-according to the intensity of the sinful deeds committed by the persons concerned in their previous existences. The *prāyaścittas* or acts of atonement for this dreadful disease are the following: First a ritual named *Kuṣmāṇḍabali* should be performed and then *Tilahoma*—a sacrifice where oblations of sesamum seeds are made to the sacred fire with *Sudatśana* mantras. The *Tilahoma* is meant as expiation for *Ghorapasmāra*—dreadful epilepsy.

The following are some of the Ayurvedic medicines administered to patients of epilepsy:

1. A powder should be prepared with the following ingredients, and the patient should inhale it like snuff.

Ingredients: Rock salt, *Vṛścikatī*, *Kuṣtha* (*sauss lappa*) *pippal* and *Śriṅgī*.

2. A medicated ghee should be prepared with the following ingredients and taken regularly. It would remove this dangerous disease. A snuff too could be prepared with the same ingredients viz. *Brāhmi* (Centella asiatica) Śaṅkha-puṣpa and green *Dhātrī* (Emblica officinalis) fruits. Juice of these articles should be extracted and it should be mixed with a paste prepared from the powder of *Jyeṣtha Madhu* and *Kan Kuṣṭha* and then the whole

mixture cooked in ghee. This ghee is a good antidote for epilepsy.

3. Ghee should be prepared with bull's urine—Asafoedita and mustard and ghee. This too is said to be a good remedy.

4. *Pañcagavya ghṛta* is said to be very efficacious in treating epilepsy. These and other remedies are treated of in great detail in the famous work, "*Aṣṭāṅgahṛdaya*."

PRAMEHA-DIABETES

Under the following planetary conditions this disease crops up: (1) The ascendant at query should be aspected by malefics; (2) the 8th house aspected by Saturn; and (3) the lord of the 8th house weak.

II (1) Same as above (1); (2) lord of *lagna* be debilitated or in an inimical house; and (3) the 8th house aspected or occupied by Venus.

When planets are afflicted or ill-placed, they cause various ailments through their presiding deities. These are enumerated below: (The intensity of troubles is due to excessive affliction of the planets.)

The Sun: Bilious complaints, high fever, feverishness, fall, epileptic attack, heart-trouble, stomach disease, eye-disease, trouble from enemies, skin disease, bone tuberculosis, leprosy, danger from fire and weapons as well as poison, danger to wife, children etc., trouble from quadrupeds, thieves and rulers. The afflicting deities one: *Dharmadaiva*, serpents, Śiva's Hosts. Some of these troubles are expected when the sun is posited in a bad house counted from the sign rising at query (not *Āruḍha*, which has had its chance once).

The Moon: Excessive sleep, drowsiness, lethargy, increase of phlegm, diarrhoea, boils appearing on the body, fever caused by cold, trouble from horned animals and aquatic animals, indigestion, anaemia, worry on account of wife, jaundice, absence of mental peace, blood impurity, danger from water, trouble from *bālagrahas* (for children). The deities that are responsible for the troubles are Durgā, demi-gods like *kinnaras*, snakes and *yakṣas*.

Mars: Excessive thirst, blood-disease, fever born of vitiated bile, danger from fire, blood pressure, fear of poison, wounds caused by weapons, leprosy, eye-disease, tumours, epilepsy, injury to marrow, amputation, vomitting, trouble from rulers and thieves, war-mongering, misunderstanding among sons, brothers, kinsmen etc. The trouble makers are demons, *Brahma-Rākṣasas*, *gandharvas* and terrible *bhūtagrahas*. The area of disease is head and parts of body above the neck.

Mercury: Mental hallucination, uttering and hearing bad language, eye-trouble, ailments or pain in the neck or throat, nose pain, fever, diseases born of three humours, skin disease, white leprosy, nervous troubles, scabies, bad dreams, imprisonment and physical strain. The deities involved in these troubles are Viṣṇu, *gandharvas*, *kinnaras* that reside in big mansions.

Jupiter: When Jupiter is in a bad place, weak and highly afflicted, he is likely to create the following: disease resulting from tumours, intestinal disease, fever, grief, swoon, and ailments of ears, phlegmatic disease and diabetes; diseases and other troubles arising from attempting to take out buried treasures of a temple, curses of eminent Vedic scholars, afflictions caused by Śiva's wrath, *kinnara*, *Yakṣa*, gods, serpents, *Vidyādharas* etc.

Venus: Jaundice, phlegmatic disease, rheumatic pains, eye-disease (or loss of an eye), lethargy, exhaustion, venereal complaints, facial disease, urinary troubles, diseases caused by libidinous acts, loss of semen, loss of garments and ornaments, loss on the agricultural front, separation or loss of one's partner and physical lustre, and abscess—The deities responsible for such troubles are *yoginīs*, groups of Divine Mothers who cause loss of dear and close friends and kinsmen. Saturn indicates the following troubles and deities and evil spirits responsible for them: Different diseases born of vitiated wind and phlegm, pain or injury to legs, various calamities, lethargy, extreme fatigue, hallucination, stomach pain, burning sensation inside, loss of servants, death of cattle, danger to wife and children, amputation of a limb, heart-burning, wound caused by the fall of trees or stones. The deities that are behind these troubles are *kaśmala bhūta*, *piśācas* and such other groups of devils.

Rāhu, Ketu and Māndī: Among these Rāhu causes burning pain, leprosy, typhoid fever, danger from poison, black-magic and food-poisoning, pain or injury to the feet, troubles from snakes, devils etc., danger to wife and children, enmity with

Brāhmaṇas and Kṣatriyas, great suffering on account of necromancy committed by enemies. In addition to what has been ascribed to afflicted Rāhu, Ketu would create troubles on account of discarnate spirits. *Māndi* would give all these troubles and in addition danger from snakes, poison, poisoned food, pollution, contamination etc.,

Effect of Positions

If Saturn be in the 10th house, he would create troubles from devils. If *Māndi* occupying the *lagna* or the 8th house, be aspected by Rāhu, he would point to administering of poison on account of the evil effect of an evil person's looks or smelling. Malefics in the 6th house point to stomach disease; and Mars in the 7th or 8th house, to high fever; in the *lagna*, to indigestion; in the 7th house, to fever resulting from indigestion. The Moon in the 6th house, to troubles as a result of black-magic practised by enemies.

Note: The astrologer should carefully assess the strength of the planets, their afflictions, aspects, associations, the particular houses occupied by them, association and aspect of benefics, if any, the relative strength of malefic and benefic aspects etc. Simply because a planet is in a bad house, you should not pronounce these results.

Yoga for Querist's Illness

Should malefics occupy any house other than the 3rd and 11th, one could easily conclude that the querist is suffering from some disease resulting from the *bādhā* or troubles relating to the concerned malefics. Moreover, the location of the trouble or troubles should be made in the limbs of the body on the basis of the *Rāśis* representing the various limbs elaborated by Varāhamihira in his *Horā*.

Diseased Limbs

Should the query *lagna* be a movable sign, upward-looking one and one that rises with head first, the question pertains to an ailment in a limb above the neck. If the *lagna* be an immovable sign, one that is turned sideways, and one that rises both ways, the illness is to be looked for in a limb between the neck and waist; and if it be a sign which is looking downwards and one rising with its hind part foremost, it would be beneath the waist. In horoscopy the limbs of the body are distinguished on the basis of the lagna-decanate, while in horary works it should be done as explained above.

If both the query ascendant and its *Aṁśa* be one and the same, the limbs should be distinguished on the basis of the sign being immovable, movable and *dual.* While if one be movable and the other, one of the other two, the other method should be adopted, i.e. on the basis of *adhomukha*—(downward looking), *ūrdhva-mukha* (upward looking), and *Tiryaṅmukha* (looking sideways) nature of the signs. If the Sun is very weak, the distinction of limbs is to be done on the basis of the ascendant being a *Śīrṣo-daya*, *Pṛṣṭhodaya* or *Ubhayodaya*. When do you decide that the Sun is very weak? He is termed very weak when his decanate is the last of Virgo and the first of Libra and his *Aṁśa* is that of Libra itself.

Note: This proves conclusively that according to ancient scholars one is not justified in calling such positions as *Vargotta-maṁśa*. We have already expressed this view in our other works. *Kṛṣṇācārya's* method is given below for distinguishing the limbs.

This refers to the ascendant at query: The portion of the rising sign in degrees and minutes that has not yet risen is to be reckoned as the right side of the body, and that part that has already risen is the left side. This is reversed in the case of the 7th house. Now the body is divided into 3 parts as: I—Head above the neck; II—Middle of the body from the neck up to the hips; and II from the hips to the feet. If the first decanate be rising, the *lagna* itself would represent the Head and its right and left sides are represented by its unrisen and risen portions respectively. Similarly the first six signs point to the limbs on the right-side, while the six signs from the 7th onwards, on the left side. The 2nd and 12th houses represent right and left ears. The third and eleventh, eyes; the fourth and tenth the two sides of the nose; the fifth and ninth, cheeks; sixth and eighth, the two sides of *hanu* (space beneath the chin) and the seventh, the mouth or jaws (the commentator of the *Kṛṣṇīya* opines that it is *Adharād adhasthānam*, i.e. the part below the lower lip. Thus the twelve signs are disposed of, when rising decanate happens to be the first.

When the second decanate rises, the twelve *Rāśis* are distributed among the limbs in the middle part of the body. The ascendant should take the place of neck or throat; and the other *Rāśis*, that have already risen and those that have not yet risen should be given the left and right sides respectively of the respective limbs. The second and twelfth *Rāśis* represent the shoulders and arms; the third and eleventh, sides; the fourth and tenth, the back (two sides of it); the fifth and ninth, the heart; the sixth and eighth, stomach; the seventh, hips.

When the third decanate rises, treat the ascendant as the *navel* and repeat the process as before, i.e. the second and twelfth houses as abdomen; the third and eleventh as testicles; the fourth and tenth as thighs; the fifth and ninth as knees; the sixth and eighth, as shanks; the seventh, as feet.

In the manner described above, knowing diseases, their symptoms, causes and afflicting deities and *bhūtas*, proper religious measures including even the greatest spiritual remedy designated as *Karmavipāka prāyaścitta*, and proper medical treatment should be undertaken for the removal of the ailments.

When a querist goes to an astrologer to find out the details of the disease he or his ward is suffering from, the diviner would invariably convince the querist by telling him when, where and how it started and under what circumstances. First of all find out the star of the query-ascendant and the one occupied by the Moon. Now count the distance in stars between the *lagna*-star and the lunar mansion. Count so many stars from the latter star. When the Moon was in that star previously, disease must have begun that day. It can also be found out from the longitude of *Māndī* as explained: Find out *Māndī's Navāṁśa Sphūṭa* by multiplying *Māndī's* longitude by 9. Similarly, if you multiply *Māndīs* longitude by 12, you get his *Dvādaśāṁśa Sphūṭa*. When the Moon transits either of the two *sphūṭas*, the disease must have started. It may also be ascertained from the star indicated by the sum of the longitudes of *Māndī* and the Moon. Among these resulting stars, find out if anyone is the 3rd, 5th or 7th star from the querist's natal star or if the star be in the 8th *Rāśi* from his natal Moon. There is another method for this by finding out the *Rāśi* that is represented by the first letter of the sentence uttered by the querist or his messenger. If the luminaries, Jupiter and Saturn happen to be weak, afflicted and ill-placed, especially the one who suffers the greatest amount of affliction, when that planet transits the *Rāśi* signifying the *lagna* (shown by the first letter), illness must have begun its sojourn.

Direction Wherein Disease Commenced

(1) Find out the direction occupied or faced by the querist or his messenger. His trouble must have started in that direction.

(2) Similarly see in which direction commencing with the east with reference to the astrologer, the messenger is seated or standing. The ailment must have started so many *Yāmas* before (1 *Yāma* = 3 hours). Let us take the messenger is seated or facing the south-west direction. What is the number of this direction from the east? It is the 4th direction in the scheme of eight directions. Hence the trouble can be said to have begun its operation just four *Yāmas* or 12 hours before the arrival of the messenger.

Number of Persons Present at Commencement

Find out the number of persons at the session of query whose eyes are rivetted on the ground. So many persons must have been present near the patient at that time.

Past and Future of Illness

Find out between the lords of the 6th and 8th houses who is more capable of causing illness. See that planet's longitude and ascertain the portion of the sign that has already been covered by the planet as well as the portion yet to be covered. The former would give the number of days the ailment has been present. From this the starting point can easily be ascertained through the planet's motion. Similarly the end of the illness will have to be determined by the number of days the planet takes to reach the end of the sign. If the covered portion of the sign be short, sickness must have started quite recently and the cure would be-long-drawn. On the other hand, if the part to be covered be very short, illness must have started long back and its cure would be near at hand.

Night and Day--Beginning of Illness

If the lord of the 6th house or the planet posited in the 6th house, whoever is stronger, be a diurnal or nocturnal planet, the ailment must have started at daytime or nighttime, as the case may be. Increase, decrease and cure of the disease would have to be stated accordingly. The Moon, Mars and Saturn are nocturnal planets; while the Sun, Jupiter and Venus are diurnal ones. Mercury is both diurnal and nocturnal. Knowledge of this point will stand astrologers and students of astrology in good stand when they try to find the origin of illness at a query.

Count the number of *Rāśis* from the *Ārūḍha* to the house occupied by the lord of the 6th house. The illness must have originated so many months or days back, according to the transit of the Sun or the Moon, as the case may be. Another method is given by yet another author: Find out how many *navāṁśas* the lord of the 6th house has already covered; multiply the serial number of the star of the day of query by the *navāṁśa* number. The product should indicate the time in months, fortnights or days that have elasped after illness made its ingress into the querist's body.

Time of Cure

(1) Note both the *lagna* and the 6th house from it. When the Moon last transited the house occupied by the lord of the 6th house, illness must have cropped up, and it is likely to cease when the Moon transits next the *Rāśi* occupied by the lord of the 4th house (of happiness).

(2) Note the ascendant at query, the *Rāśi* occupied by the lord of the ascendant and the sign occupied by the Moon. Find out also when and which of these signs had malefic aspect or association. At that time illness must have made its presence felt. Similarly when all the three signs get benefic association and aspect, the person's ailments would be completely cured. If one or two signs have benefic connection, the disease would show signs of abatement.

(3) Multiply the longitude of the ascendant by 9. This is called

Navāṁśa Sphūṭa. If you multiply the *lagna*-longitude by 12, you would get the longitude of its *Dvādaśāṁśa*. When the Moon arrives in transit at any of these *Rāśis*, end of the disease could be predicted.

(4) When the Moon overtakes the sign tenanted by *Māndī*, illness would bid good-bye.

(5) If illness had started before the Moon arrived at the 8th house from the *lagna*, the ailments would come to an end as soon as the Moon goes beyond that house, i.e. 8th from *lagna*.

EXPIATION

(1) When planets are afflicted and ill-placed, troubles such as diseases crop up and when they go to benefic houses and are free from affliction, they cease. Perfect cure can be effected, if the person concerned performs with due devotion *Grahaśānti Homa*, worship of gods, *japa*, *dāna* (gifts of money as well as articles such as grains allotted to the nine planets) etc. in addition to taking medicines, tonics like *Cyavana-Prāśāvaleha*.

(2) Disease makes its presence felt when any one of the luminaries and Jupiter arrives at the house occupied by the most troublesome planet among the afflicted and ill-placed ones. The reason for the disease should be laid at the door of the ill-placed planet. For, he is the significator for the deity whose wrath leads to all kinds of afflictions in the form of diseases and other calamities. Troubles come to an end when remedial measures are undertaken and at the same time among the well-placed planets the *Rāśi* occupied by the most favourable one is tenanted in transit by the strongest of the three viz. the luminaries and Jupiter. The remedial religious acts include worship of the deities that are indicated by the ill-placed as well as very favourable planets. From the above discussion it is clear that the luminaries and Jupiter play an important role in determining the beginning and end of ailments, their types and severity or otherwise and duration in years, months and days (Jupiter, Sun and Moon indicate year, month and day). If the illness is minor like influenza, it will last for some days only; if it be whooping cough, jaundice etc. It may last for some months, and in very serious cases of lunacy or epilepsy and the like years may be required for cure.

Duration of Illness and Its Initial Star

The star in which a disease starts has the potential for controlling it after sometime. *Ācārya* Varāhamihira while detailing the number of stars constituting a constellation says that "a fever or some other ailment starting on a day ruled by a good star will come to an end in so many days as there are starlets constituting the group or constellation".* Should one's illness start on a day ruled by *Uttarāṣāḍhā* or *Mṛgaśiras*, he would be cured after a month; should it be *Dhaniṣṭhā*, *Hasta* or *Viśākhā*, after 15 days; if it be *Citrā*, *Śatabhiṣaj*, *Bharaṇī* or *Śravaṇa*, after 11 days; if it be *Maghā*, after 20 days; if it be *Puṣya*, *Uttaraphalgunī*, *Punarvasu*, *U. Bhādrā* or *Rohiṇī* after a week; if it be *Mūla Aśvinī* or *Kṛttikā*, after 9 days; and if it be *Anurādhā* or *Revatī*, recovery would be very difficult.

If illness starts on a day ruled by any of the remaining seven stars viz. *Jyeṣṭhā*, *Svātī*, *Āśleṣā*, *Ārdrā*, *P. Phalgunī*, *P. Āṣāḍha* and *P. Bhādra*, he may not recover. In addition, if the stars be joined with week days presided over by malefics and lunar days that are called *Riktā* (empty) and *Chidrā* (pierced) viz. 4, 6, 8, 9, 12 and 14 (including new moon), the result would be death. The same result could be expected, if the beginning of illness be on a Sunday, Tuesday or Saturday, synchronizing with one of the forbidden *tithis* viz. 8th, 4th, 9th, 14th, and New Moon, provided any of these stars be the patient's natal, 3rd, 5th or 7th star (in all the three rounds) and the lunar sign be 8th from his natal one.

Śūla Cakra

Similarly if illness starts on a day ruled by the star occupied by the Sun, or the 9th, 15th or 21st from it, the result would be tragic. On the other hand, if the beginning be under a star that is 2nd, 3rd, 4th, 8th, 10th, 14th, 16th, 20th, 22nd, 26th, 27th or 28th from the one occupied by the Sun, there would be no danger of death, even if the illness should look hopeless. (*Note*: Here 28 stars including *Abhijit* are taken into consideration.)

Children's Illness

In the case of a child under 12 years count the number of the

*Vide *Bṛ Saṁ XCVIII*-3.

star on the day of commencement of illness from the patient's natal star. Multiply that number by 3 and divide the product by 4. If the remainder be 1, death without delay would be the result; if 2, slow death; if 3, the disease could be cured after great efforts. If there be no remainder, no harm would come to the patient, i.e. he will be soon restored to normal health.

If the lord of the 6th house be moving slowly or be posited in an immovable sign, cure would take place very slowly. On the other hand, if the above planet be moving fast or be in a movable sign, his disease would be cured very shortly. If the planet's motion be moderate (neither slow, nor fast) and presence be in a dual sign, the cure too would be neither quick nor slow.

Prolonged Illness

The following conditions indicate prolonged disease: Malefics in the *lagna* of query, *lagna* being betwixt malefics, *lagna*-lord being weak, associated with malefics, and surrounded by malefics, the weak Moon be in the 6th, 8th, or 12th house, alongwith malefics or surrounded by them, and the three bad houses be tenanted by malefics; if any of these conditions be present, the patient's illness would be prolonged. If more be there, the result would be worse, i.e. he would be a permanent invalid. Though the astrological reading be not encouraging, still both medical treatment and spiritual propitiation through appropriate worship of gods and *japa* of mantra should be done on the authority of the ancient sages, and *Sāyaṇācārya*—for, nobody can be sure of man's birth and death. If a man clings to the Lord's lotus-feet in utter self-surrender and devotion, the Lord has the power to alter the fate of His creatures. After all the Lord is greater than the universe and its scriptures. Hence man's duty to live according to the injunctions of dharma-śāstras, doing good to others and living a good life. Then all the planets and deities would always help him.

Patient's Recovery

Under the following conditions even a healthy person would be found to be ill at the time of query: The Moon in an *Upacaya* (3, 6, 10 or 11) house, benefics in angles, trines and the 8th house, and the ascendant be aspected by malefics. On the other hand, even a person suffering from a serious malady would be cured completely under the following Yogas: (1) The full Moon should be posited in the ascendant and aspected by Jupiter. (2) Jupiter and Venus should occupy *kendras*.

Yogas for Patient's End

(1) If the lord of the 6th house who is a malefic occupies the ascendant at query and aspects the patient's natal Moon, the patient's survival is impossible.

(2) If the Moon be posited in the 4th or 8th house or be in between malefics, the patient cannot survive. On the other hand, if the strong Moon be aspected by benefics, he is likely to be cured after protracted treatment.

(3) If the Moon be in the *lagna* and the Sun in the 7th house, the patient would certainly perish.

Physician's Part

If the ascendant at query be occupied by malefics, the patient's illness would grow worse; and it is due to the physician's wrong treatment. On the other hand, should the ascendant be tenanted by a benefic, the physician's treatment is excellent. How are we to find out the details of patient, physician and medicine and their mutual relations?

Nīlakaṇṭha who is quoted in our work "*Praśna-Jñāna*" answers this question very ably. According to him, in a query chart the ascendant represents the physician; the 7th house the disease; the 10th house, the patient; and the 4th house, the medicine (or treatment). If there be friendship between the patient and physician, and between medicine and disease, there would be cure for the disease. On the other hand, should there be enmity between the two, it would be aggravated. The friendship of the signs is to be assessed through the *Vaśya* method of the *Rāśis*; and through the natural and temporary friendship of their lords.

The following *yogas* bring succour to the patient:

1. The *lagna*-lord should be strong and benefics in *kendras*, identical with their own or exaltation signs.
2. A strong benefic should be in the *lagna*.
3. Benefics should be in 3rd, 6th, 9th and 11th houses.

Tragic end: If there be a malefic in the 3rd, 6th, 9th or 12th house from the ascendant (and be further subjected to malefic aspect or association), the person is likely to die of diseases or drowning in water or of being attacked by weapons, as a result of an ancestral curse.

Divine Cause of Death

When the malefic mentioned above is in the twelve signs from Aries the cause of death is (1) Wrath of God; (2) Displeasure of the Manes; (3) Anger of atmospheric Goddess; (4) Trouble caused by the evil spirit called *Śākinī*; (5) Wrath of the local deity; (6) Curse of a noble lady; (7) Mother's curse; (8) Anger of serpents; (9) Wrath of the lord of *yakṣas*; (10) Dissatisfaction of water-deity; (11) Trouble caused by a female *yakṣa*; and (12) Anger of the family deity. The main cause for the ills of man is that he often swerves from the path of dharma or righteousness. This discussion would remind readers that the purpose of all Śāstras including astrology is to tell human beings that they should not forget dharma in the pursuit of earthly pleasures. "*For by* following dharma they could attain both *artha* (wealth) and *kāma* (worldly pleasures)."

Pacification of Deities

When the Moon be strong, posited in her own or exaltation house, in the query chart, the deities that are responsible for troubles like illness, can be easily appeased by means of *japa*, *homa* and *dāna*; if she be debilitated and shorn of *pakṣabala*, it is impossible to make them kind-hearted. They would, on the other hand, inflict the extreme punishment on the victim. The same result could be expected, should strong malefics occupy *kendras*.

Time of Death

When the Moon is posited in the 8th house from the *Ārūḍha* and aspected by malefics, the astrologer should predict the patient's death. It the third house be occupied by the Sun, and the 10th house by another malefic, the patient would quit the world in ten days. If Jupiter and Venus be in the 3rd house, the person would die in a week. Should malefics be posited in the *Ārūḍha*, 4th and 8th houses, death would overtake the person in

8 days. If malefics be in the 1st and 2nd houses, death would take place in a fortnight.

Recovery from Disease

Under the following conditions the patient whose condition is being discussed at the query, should be declared to be free from illness: The Moon should be in an *Upacaya* house, benefics in *kendras*, *koṇas* or 2nd or 8th house and/or the ascendant being aspected by benefics.

Cause of Disease

Sins committed in this life afflict human beings in the form of diseases in the next life. Recovery from such diseases can be obtained by means of sincere repentance, medicines, *japa*, *homa*, gifts and worship of gods as well as bathing in sacred rivers and performing *śrāddhas* in sacred places.

It has been already mentioned that diseases are caused by possession of the person concerned by *bhūtas* (devils), ill-placed planets and vitiation of humours. But the real cause of all ailments is the accumulated sins of previous lives whose time for ripening of their fruits has arrived.

Remedies

First of all, the patient should be given medicine prescribed by an expert physician. He must be made to observe strictly the rules regarding food, healthy environments, entertainments etc. Strict celibacy should be observed by the patient both physically and mentally. Sometimes violation of this rule ends in disaster. Hence it is advisable for a youthful patient to keep aloof from his spouse.

Some disease like consumption are the results of heinous crimes like *Brahmahatyā*, killing Brāhmaṇas, cows etc. The expiations for such diseases will be elaborated in a separate chapter. For the present we shall be content with giving a fore-taste of the same: The best remedy for disease is to perform *Mṛtyuñjaya Homa* with due solemnity along with feeding of Vedic scholars. For, this sacrifice is considered to be very efficacious in curing high fever, effects of black magic practised by enemies, removing troubles created by evil spirits, excessive fright caused by *bhūtas, pretas* etc., cure of lunacy, epilepsy etc.

Mṛta Sañjīvinī Homa

The best remedy that is recommended in the case of deadly diseases like leprosy, lunacy, epilepsy etc. is the *Sañjīvanī Homa* which is performed with seven materials viz. (1) the creeper known as *Amṛtavallī* (2) Banyan twigs; (3) *Pāyasa* or milk porridge; (4)*Tila* or sesamum seeds; (5) *Dūrvā* grass; (6) Milk and (7) Ghee. There should be 144 oblations (*Āhutis*) with each of the seven materials, the total number of oblations being 1008. The *Dūrvā* oblations should bedone after each oblation is first dipped in *Trimadhu*, i.e. a mixture of honey, ghee and sugar. As part of this grand sacrifice, it is incumbent on the performer or *Kartā* to have *Japa* (repetition of sacred mantras), *Tarpaṇa* (libations of water for the various deities), *homa* (oblations offered to the sacred fire with special mantras for the respective deities) and lastly worship of Brāhmaṇas with sumptuous food, garments, vessels and monetary gifts. According to some authorities these four items should be done at the rate of a tenth of the previous item.

According to others the number of Brāhmaṇas to be fed should be equal to the number of oblations. This is obligatory in cases of remedies and prosperity.

There are also three special vows called *kalpas* viz. (1) *Mahā-Mṛtyuñjaya kalpa*, (2) *Mṛta-Sañjivinī kalpa* and (3) *Mahā-Sudarśana kalpa*, all of which are recommended for better and quicker results.

In the following paragraphs some more information is given for the benefit of students as well as scholars: We have already seen the seven varieties of temporal states and an equal number of positional states of the planets, which indicate the current state of the querist's health.

Rāśis and Illness: (1) Should the *Ārūḍha* be Sagittarius or Pisces, mental aberration, ear-ache etc. would be suggested.

(2) Signs Taurus and Libra being the *Ārūḍha* would indicate urinary troubles or venereal complaints, loss of appetite, cold, dropsy, water-borne disease etc.

(3) Capricorn and Aquarius would point to psychic trouble,

fatigue of limbs, constipation, trouble in the legs and consequent incapacity for movements.

(4) Should the *Ārūḍha* have Rāhu's association or aspect, there would be scabies, itching on the body etc.

(5) If sign Leo be *Ārūḍha* the querist would be suffering from some stomach ailment, eye-disease, worries, lack of self-confidence, heat-borne complaints etc.

(6) In the case of Aries and Scorpio, headache, eye-trouble, fever, ulcers etc. could be predicted.

(7) If the *Ārūḍha* be Gemini or Virgo, pulmonary troubles, pain in the nose, skin affections etc. may be inferred.

The above results should necessarily be predicted in case the *Ārūḍha* be tenanted by malefics. This would be doubly sure in case the *Navāṁśa* of *Ārūḍha*, or rising sign, and the sign and *Navāṁśa* of *Māndī* be identical. On the other hand, should the *Ārūḍha* and the *lagna* be heavily afflicted, the result would be tragic.

A simple method of finding out the *Navāṁśas* of the *Ārūḍha* has been already explained, but hereunder is explained a more complicated method, so that curious readers and research-minded scholars may find some pleasure by appreciating the intellectual sharpness of its author. First of all draw a big Zodiacal chart where each sign is divided into 9 compartments by drawing 2 lines east-west and to others north-south as shown on p. 212.

This is used generally in cases of *Svarṇārūḍha Praśna.* The *Navāṁśa* of the *Ārūḍha* is found out from the number marked in the compartment in which the piece of gold is kept. There are four types of marking *Navāṁśas* in the twelve *Rāśis* as follows:

(1) In Aries, Gemini and Leo numbering is done from the north-eastern corner, ending in the opposite corner, as shown in the figure.

(2) In the second type which includes signs Cancer, Virgo and Scorpio the numbers start with South-East corner and end with north-west.

(3) In the third group containing Libra, Sagittarius, and Aquarius the numbers begin with the south-western corner and end with the opposite corner.

				I			II			III			
	7	8	9	1	6	7	7	8	9	1	6	7	
XII	6	5	4	2	5	8	6	5	4	2	5	8	
	1	2	3	3	4	9	1	2	3	3	4	9	
	9	4	3							3	2	1	IV
XI	8	5	2			Svarṇa *Ārūḍha Navāṁśa* Scheme				4	5	6	
	7	6	1							9	8	7	
	7	8	9							1	6	7	
X	6	5	4							2	5	8	V
	1	2	3							3	4	9	
	9	4	3	3	2	1	9	4	3	3	2	1	
IX	8	5	2	4	5	6	8	5	2	4	5	6	VI
	7	6	1	9	8	7	7	6	1	9	8	7	
					VIII			VII					

(4) In the fourth group of Taurus, Capricorn and Pisces numbers of *Navāṁśas* start with the north-western corner and end with the south-eastern corner.

Gaṇḍānta Aṁśa

Whether in the *Ārūḍha* or ascendant the Navāṁśa called *Gaṇḍānta*, being aspected by a malefic, would prove disastrous to the querist. The last *Navāṁśas* of Cancer, Scorpio and Pisces as well as the first ones of Leo, Sagittarius and Aries are termed *Gaṇḍānta*. The same result should be declared in case the *Aṁśa* falls on the 8th house.

Pisces as Ārūḍha

If afflicted Pisces be the *Ārūḍha*, the querist is likely to be lame. On the other hand, should Cancer or Scorpio be the *Ārūḍha* under affliction, the person concerned is likely to fall into a well or tank.

Discussion of Sūtras

What is a *Sūtra*? It is nothing but an *astrological methodology*; the most common one is that in which discussion is centred on the *Ārūḍha* and *ascendant*. This method is called *Sāmānya Sūtra*. Its extension is termed *Adhipa Sūtra*, which treats of the discussion from the standpoint of the lords of the *Ārūḍha* and *Udaya lagna*. The next *sūtra* is called *Aṁśa Sūtra*, in which the *Navāṁśas* of the ascendant as well as of the *Ārūḍha* are considered. Its next extension is known as *Nakṣatra Sūtra*, wherein the star of the query ascendant and the querist's natal star are subjected to scrutiny. There is a *Mahāsūtra* that treats of the *Ārūḍha* and the 10th house therefrom. We have now seen five *sūtras* in all. These five are called in order by the names of the elements viz. earth, water, fire, air and ether.

Sāmānya *Sūtra* becoming *Jīva Sūtra*: (1) In case both the *Ārūḍha* and the *Udaya lagna* happen to be movable signs; (2) if one of them is immovable and the other dual, it would be designated as *Jīva* (life) *Sūtra*.

Mṛti Sūtra: If both be immovable signs, or one movable and the other dual, it would be *Mṛti Sūtra* (death).

Roga Sūtra: If both happen to be dual signs; or one movable and the other immovable, it would be termed *Roga Sūtra*. Thus the *Sāmānya* (general) *Sūtra* becomes *Pṛthvī*, *Jīva*, *Mṛti* and *Roga Sūtra*.

(1) So if both are *movable* = *Jīva Sūtra* (life).
(2) If both are *immovable* = *Mṛti Sūtra* (death).
(3) If both *dual* = *Roga Sūtra* (illness).
(4) If one be *immovable* and the other *movable* = *Roga Sūtra*.
(5) If one be *immovable* and the other *dual* = *Jīva Sūtra*.
(6) If one be *movable* and the other *dual* = *Mṛti Sūtra*.

This can also be shown as follows:

(1) A movable sign with another movable, immovable and dual sign results respectively in *Jīva Sūtra*, *Roga Sūtra* and *Mṛti Sūtra*.

(2) An immovable sign with another dual movable and im-

movable produces respectively *Jīva Sūtra*, *Roga Sūtra* and *Mṛti Sūtra*.

(3) A dual sign with an immovable dual and movable sign produces respectively, *Jīva Sūtra*, *Roga Sūtra* and *Mṛti Sūtra*. If the lords of the *Ārūḍha* and ascendant be the same or are friendly to each other, it is called *Jīva Sūtra* and if they be neutral, it would be *Roga Sūtra*; and if they be mutual enemies, *Mṛti Sūtra*. This is the method of finding out the three types of *Sūtras* under *Adhipa Sūtra*.

Nakṣatra Sūtra

From the star of the *lagna* at query count the number of the querist's natal star. Divide the number by 3. If the remainder is 1, it is *Jīva Sūtra*; if 2, *Roga Sūtra* if no remainder, *Mṛti Sūtra*.

Mahāsūtra

If both the *Ārūḍha* and the 10th house therefrom fall in *Nocturnal* signs, it is called *Jīva Sūtra*, and if *diurnal* ones, *Mṛti Sūtra*. If one of the two be diurnal and, the other nocturnal, it would become *Roga Sūtra*.

Note: The following are diurnal signs: Leo, Virgo, Libra, Scorpio, Aquaries and Pisces.

Nocturnal Rāśis are—Aries, Taurus, Gemini, Cancer, Sagittarius and Capricorn.

The effects of these *Sūtras* would be clear from their names. *Jīva* denotes long life, quick recovery from illness, achievements of one's object etc. *Roga Sūtra* indicates prolonged illness, if it be a query about ill health, and failure in one's undertaking.

Mṛti Sūtra suggests somebody's death in the family of the querist or among his domestic animals, or sorrow, fear, destruction of his plan etc.

It has been already stated that these five *Sūtras* represent the five elements. When a *Roga* or *Mṛti Sūtra* is detected at a query, the astrologer should find out the corresponding element that is responsible for the querists' troubles. The following discussion explains the different constituents of the body that are presided over by the different elements.

(1) *Pṛthvī* or *Earth* presides over flesh, bones, skin, veins and hair, (2) *Toya* or water rules sweat, blood, urine, semen, phlegm

and saliva, (3) *Agni* or fire rules hunger, thirst, lethargy, sleep and complexion, (4) *Vāyu* or air rules movement of limbs, and physical activities, and (5) *Ākāśa* or ether rules love, hatred, passion, fight and infirmities of old age. Let us take an example: *Sāmānya Sūtra* is of the nature of Earth. Suppose this is *Jīva Sūtra*. Then you have to declare that the querist has well-developed muscles, strong bones, good skin and all the veins in his body functioning smoothly, and fine black hair. If it be *Roga Sūtra*, all these things should be declared to be vitiated. If it be *Mṛti Sūtra*, the patient should be said to be suffering from an incurable disease caused by complete vitiation of these constituents. Take another example: If the *Nakṣatra* or *Vāyu Sūtra* happens to be *Jīva Sūtra*, movements of limbs and physical activities would be excellent. On the other hand, if it be *Roga Sūtra*, there would be weakness in the limbs which may be shaky, and his physical activities much curtailed. If it be *Mṛti Sūtra*, there would be danger from epilepsy, rheumatic convulsions, etc.

Sūtras and Past, Present and Future

The *Sāmānya Sūtra* indicates past events; the *Nakṣatra* and *Adhipa Sūtras* denote present effects; and the *Aṁśa Sūtra* and *Mahā Sūtra* point to future events.

Planets in the Houses and past, present and future: The planets in the first four houses reveal present results; those in the second four houses future effects; and those in the last four, past events.

First of all find out the lord of the particular *Sūtra* and the *Bhāva* he occupies in the query chart. On the basis of this the results have to be delineated. It is known that Mercury is the lord of *Sāmānya Sūtra*, which is of the nature of earth element. Hence these three become equal.

The *Adhipa Sūtra* being significator for water element, has Venus as its lord. Similarly the significator for fire element is the *Aṁśa Sūtra* whose lord is Mars. *Nakṣatra Sūtra*, being the significator for air element, is ruled by Saturn.

The *Mahāsūtra* is the significator for the element ether. Hence its ruler is *Jupiter*. Similarly the Sun has been given the nature of the element of fire; and the Moon, the element of water. So the duty of the astrologer is to see in which house and in which of the three *Sūtras* viz *Jīva*, *Roga* and *Mṛti* the ruling planet is posited.

Some authorities speak of three other *Sūtras* in this connection. They are (1) *Ārūḍha*, (2) its *Navāṁśa* and (3) *Dvādaśāṁśa*.

Similarly (1) the *lagna*, (2) its *Navāṁśa* and (3) its *Dvādaśāṁśa*.

If all the three *Sūtras* come out as *Jīva Sūtra* and if the lords of the *Aṁśas* be friends, *Trisphuṭa* (sum of the longitudes of the *lagna*, Moon and *Māndī*) not in a dangerous junction, *dūta-lakṣaṇa* (omens at the arrival of the messenger) not auguring ill, the querist's planetary *Daśā* and *Bhukti* not harmful, and transitory effects not injurious, a patient, though in a serious condition, would escape death. On the other hand, if the above results turn out to be *Roga Sūtras* and conditions mixed, the patient could recover by performing poorer expiatory rituals such as *japa*, *homa* and worship of Gods. In case all the three *Sūtras* turn out to be *Mṛti* (death) *Sūtras*, and other conditions dangerous, the disease cannot be cured.

In case the sum of the longitudes of the three viz. *lagna*, Moon and *Māndī*, falls in Cancer, Scorpio or Pisces, the result would not be favourable. Among these three signs, seriousness of the trouble would be in the ascending order. Should the *Trisphuṭa* be in the last *Navāṁśa* of Cancer, Scorpio and Pisces, death would take place in order in a year, month and day.

The twelve signs are divided under three heads viz. creation, protection and destruction, each having the domain of four signs. These are also called by the names of *sṛṣṭi*, *sthiti* and *laya khaṇḍas*.

The signs are grouped in another way also: All the movable signs are called Creation *Rāśis*, all the immovable signs, protection signs, and all the dual ones, destruction *Rāśis*.

The 27 stars too are divided into 9 groups of 3 stars each. In each group of three stars, the three functions are held in regular order: *Aśvini*—Creation, *Bharaṇī*—Protection, *Kṛttikā*—Destruction. Similarly it is in the case of *Rohiṇī*, *Mṛgaśiras* and *Ārdrā*. If the *Trisphuṭa* falls in a *saṁhāra* (destruction) *khaṇḍa*, *Rāśi*, star, junction of signs or stars, *Gaṇḍānta*, 88th quarter from the querist's natal star-quarter or the 3rd, 5th or 7th star from his natal star, the result should be highly dangerous. If the *Trisphuṭa*-

Navāṁśa be Aries, Leo or Sagittarius, the patient would have long life.

Aṁśas of Trisphuṭa: Leaving off the signs in the *Trisphūṭa* multiply the degrees and minutes by 9. The resulting figure in signs, degrees etc. would give the *Trisphuṭa Navāṁśa.*

In the same manner, leaving off the signs multiply the *Trisphuṭa* by 12. The result in *Rāśi*, degrees etc. would give the *Trisphūṭa Dvādaśāṁśa.* In case these two results fall in the last *Navāṁśa* of the three signs viz. Cancer, Scorpio and Pisces, the result would be disastrous. In case the *Trisphuṭa* is associated with *Māndī* or any other malefic, the same bad result would follow. Suppose a child is born in the querist's house under the star of the *Trisphuṭa*, it would be affected by all kinds of ailments. Should the *Trisphuṭa* fall in creation *khaṇḍa, Rāśi, Nakṣatra* and *Navāṁśa*, with benefic association or aspect, the querist would have a long lease of life, or prosperity, promotion or victory, as the case may be.

Effects of Planets in Trisphuṭa Sign

The Sun being in that sign would create heat in the head, fever and burning sensation; the Moon, diarrhoea or dysentery; Mars, ulcers or wounds; Mercury, loss of vocal and mental alertness or power; Jupiter, eye-troubles; Venus, mental aberration, general debility and abscess; Saturn, pain in arms and legs; Rāhu, fall; and Ketu, ulcer, boils and abscess.

Beginning of Malady from Trisphuṭa

When the Sun and other planets are posited in the *Rāśi* or *Aṁśaka* of the *Trisphuṭa*, the ailments mentioned already would end in calamity. Now find out the *Navāṁśa Sphuṭa* of the *Trisphuṭa* by multiplying its longitude (leaving off the signs) by 9. The malady must have started on a day previously that ruled the star of this *Navāṁśa Sphuṭa*, and in the next round on the day of the same *Nakṣatra*, the patient would lose consciousness and have utter weakness and in the next round in the same star the patient would breathe his last. The astrologer should weigh all the pros and cons and if there be strong reasons for predicting death, then alone he should pass judgment.

Daśā System of Trisphuṭa

Just as we find out the balance of planetary *daśās* from Moon's longitude, even so *daśā* should be worked out for the star of the *Trisphuṭa*. In this system the *daśās* are in days as the Sun's= 6×3=18 days; Moon's=10×3=30 days; Mar's=7×3=21 days; Rāhu's=18×3=54 days; Jupiter's=16×3 = 48 days, Saturn's=19×3=57 days; Mercury's=17×3=51 days; Ketu's =7×3=21 days; and finally Venus's=20×3=60 days. Thus the total duration of all *daśās* put together is one year. There is yet another *daśā* system based on the *Nakṣatra* of *Māndī's* longitude. Here there is a single difference in respect of order of *daśās*: After Sun's *daśā* comes Venus's *daśā*, and then Ketu's, then Mercury's and so on in the reverse order. The effects of *daśās* are determined exactly as it is done in natal charts. There are some schools of astrologers that opt for the *daśā* system based on the Moon's longitude at query.

Deha-Prāṇa-Mṛtyu Sphuṭa

These three stand for body, life and death respectively. If you multiply Moon's longitude by 9, you get body-longitude; if the longitude of the ascendant be multiplied by 9, you get life-longitude; and *Māndī's* longitude multiplied by 9 yields death-longitude. One would have long life, if, among these three longitudes, the first two (body and life) have mutual connection such as combination and aspect as well as no connection whatsoever with *Mṛtya Sphuṭa*. On the other hand, if there be association or aspect between body and death, the result would be disease. If it be between life and death, swooning, similar troubles would arise.

Stars and Trisphuṭa

If *Trisphuṭa* falls in *Aśvinī* or its trine, there would be quarrel in the querist's house within three days. If this indication is perceived, the querist would meet with his end are long. If the star be *Bharaṇī* or its trine, a poor old *Bṛāhmaṇa* would arrive at the place of query. If it be *Kṛttikā* or its trine, there would be danger from fire. If it be *Rohiṇī* or its trine, vessels and furniture would be destroyed. If it be *Mṛgaśirṣa* or its trine, a sick or wounded person would present himself at the place. If it be *Ārdrā* or its trine, a snake would be seen there within three days. If it be *Punarvasu* or its trine, a great *Brāhmaṇa* of repute would come there. If it be *Puṣya* or its trine, there would be loss or death of cattle and fall of a servant. Lastly if it be *Āśleṣā* or its trine, there would be a death in the neighbouring house. The appearance of immediate symptoms mentioned above would make the prediction of death doubly sure.

CHAPTER IX

FRUCTIFICATION OF KARMA

THE WORK ENTITLED *Vīrasiṁhāvaloka* 'King *Vīrasiṁha's* View' is both interesting and instructive for more than one reason. For, he states in this work that he wrote it taking the essence of three Śāstras viz. *Āyurveda*, *Dharama-śāstra* and *Jyautiṣa*. In the beginning he discusses the diseases that crop up in the *daśās* of planets, especially when they are afflicted and ill-placed. He also cites the sins that are responsible for certain diseases and their treatment and *Prāyaścitta* (expiation).

In the *daśā* of debilitated Sun man suffers from eye-disease, fever, head-disease, imprisonment, exhausting journey and leprosy. A weak Moon too produces similar maladies. The remedy for weak Sun is bathing with *Manaśśilā* (red arsenic), *ela* (cardamom) etc. Wearing of coral is beneficial. When the Moon is weak, one should wear pearl and silver.

In Ketu *daśa*—Mercury's sub-period one can expect meeting with friends and kinsmen, but will have fighting for lands; fever and other ailments. Similar are the effects of *Rāhu Daśā Śani Bhuki*. For the propitiation of Mercury, his *japa* should be done and *homa* (sacrifice) done with twigs of *Apāmārga* plant. In *Rāhu-Śani* period one gets wounded by weapons, fever, dysentery. encounter with enemies, loss of wealth etc. Those who are cruel and tale-bearers, get continuous fever in the next life. One who neglects auspicious rituals becomes *Uṣṇajvarī* (afflicted with burning fever).* The remedy is performing *Rudrābhiṣeka*, bathing Lord Śiva, with the sacred hymns of *Rudrādhyāya* and worshipping Him. For fever caused by cold Lord Nārāyaṇa should be worshipped with *Abhiṣeka*.

Diseases of the anus, stomach and teeth, and lunacy are the result of taking away other's properties, killing a Brāhmaṇa, soiling one's preceptor's bed etc. One who puts out sacred fire or destroys a tank or well, suffers from dysentery in his next life.

*Scientific name of *Apāmārga* is Achyranthes aspera.

The author says that diarrhoea would be the effect of Mercury, posited in a house of Saturn, and aspected by (united with) the Sun or Mars. (*Note*: It is not possible for Mercury and the Sun to be 180° apart.)

If the Moon is posited in the 6th house, one will be lazy and cruel and will have many enemies, poor digestion and stomach complaints. One who discards without any reason one's own wife will suffer from sprue. For this the proper *Prāyaścitta* is to perform *Grahaṇī-Śānti*.

Piles: When the Sun stationed in Cancer, is aspected by Saturn, the person concerned becomes a tale-bearer, merciless and shameless, and is afflicted with piles (*durnāma*) and *leprosy*. He should wear a ring set with corals, and perform *Śāntis*. The Padma Purāṇa says that one kills cows suffers from piles dysentery, piles and sprue are symptoms of one another. If Jupiter be in 3rd house, one would be miserly, humiliated, have low appetite, be separated from his wife, and interested in bad activities. When he is in 6th house, one will destroy one's enemies and be very famous, but will be weak, lazy and of low fertility. One falls a prey to *Viṣūcī* (cholera) by eating the food offered by a *Śūdra*, money lender or one who does not observe vows.

Worms Troubles: If the weak Moon be in 8th house, one loses consciousness (or becomes giddy) and is consumed by worms trouble. He may be short of some limb.

If the Sun is situated in an enemy's house, his *daśā* might cause destruction of eye-sight, make one a hunch-back and cause worms trouble.

Jaundice: If Saturn with visible rings be posited in 8th house, one might be cruel and afflicted with many troubles like *jaundice* and consumption. One who had stolen properties of Gods (temples) and Brāhmaṇas is afflicted with *Pāndu-Roga*. Similar is the effect of cohabiting with a *Caṇḍāla* woman. In Venus's *daśā* and Moon's *Bhukti* (if they be ill-placed and afflicted) one gets trouble in the head like giddiness and mental aberrations, jaundice and hallucinations, caused by vitiated *Vāta*. Similarly, one who steals food, gets jaundice.

Acute gout: When Mars be in Cancer, or Mars and the Moon be together, one gets this disease. In the sub-period of Mars in the major period of the Moon, one is pestered by fire and thieves.

In Moon's *daśā*—Mercury's *Bhukti* one gets leprosy, itches, consumption, a fistula in the anus or pudendum (*bhagandara*), and danger from vehicles or elephants or horses. When Mercury is in Cancer, the person becomes consumptive from birth or suffers from leprosy. The same result is given for Moon-Mercury combine. Consumption is the result of *Brahmahatyā*—killing of a Brāhmaṇā—committed in previous life. According to the Padma Purāṇa one becomes consumptive by usurping another's *kṣetra* (wife or field). So also one who covets meat, other's articles and one who does not brook other's life of luxury and murders his own master (employer), gets the scourge of consumption.

Cough or Catarrh: When the Sun is posited at the end of Cancer along with Mercury, the patient is likely to lose his eye-sight as a result of vitiation of *vāta* and *kapha*. This is due to the sin of misappropriating other's funds, and perversity in thinking and acting. Similarly one who is ungrateful to a benefactor, but does harm instead, falls a prey to the disease catarrh in the next life. If an undeserving person receives gifts of salt, honey, antelope skin, etc. in sacred places like Kurukṣetra during eclipses, he will be afflicted with burning fever, *Vāta-pitta*, cough and catarrh.

Stammering: When the weak Moon is in Scorpio *Aṁśa*, one gets stammering as a result of having abused openly his preceptor.

Hiccough and Asthma: A Brāhmaṇa who does not perform *Sandhyopāsanā* (saying prayers during the three junctures) and *Agnihotra*, fire-worship, after bath, commits a sin and becomes liable to divine visitation in the form of these ailments.

Thirst and Fainting: The Moon in Leo causes stomach trouble, hatred towards women and excessive hunger and thirst. One who does not give water to a tired Brāhmaṇa or cow, gets swooning as a result of great thirst.

Burning Fever: When Mars is in the *lagna* and the Sun in the 8th house, one gets burning fever as a result of spitting at the fire during an eclipse known as *Kāpila-grahaṇa*. Such a person is attacked by a spirit named *Kāpila*. Results of this are fever, colic, yellowish eyes and burning all over the body.

Unmāda or Lunacy: Taking forbidden and polluted food and drink, and attacking Gods, preceptors and Brāhmaṇas invariably result in lunacy. When the mind is seriously affected as a result of troubles from thieves or robbers, king's officers, enemies and others, or by the loss of wealth and kinsmen or by sexual urge, mental aberrations set in.

Epilepsy: If Saturn, Mars and Sun be together in the 8th house, one gets this dreaded disease in consequence of the sin of murdering one's *Guru* or hating him. *Bodhāyana*, one of the ancient law-givers, states that one becomes epileptic as a result of suffocating a Brāhmaṇa.

Vātaic Diseases: The Sun in Cancer aspected by Saturn makes one suffer from rheumatic and allied diseases. The person becomes a tale-bearer and usurper of other's wealth. In the daśā of Saturn and *Bhukti* of Ketu, one suffers from ailments caused by vitiated wind and bile, quarrels with menials and goes abroad. When Saturn is aspected by Mars, *vātaic* diseases, wanderings, wicked deeds and despicable character would be prominent. One who rapes a virgin, or another's wife, is stricken with *Dhanurvāta* or Titanus. The remedy is the use of the *Mahānārāyaṇa Taila* (Oil). One gets acute gout as a result of Saturn aspecting Mars in the 10th house. This is the visitation of God on account of cohabitation with a woman of the same class, according to Bodhāyana.

Disability of Thighs and Rheumatism: Jupiter in the 8th house causes these troubles as a result of the sin of having put out the sacred fire. The treatment is through the recipe named *Yogarāja-guggulu*.

Colic or Spasmodic Pain: The Moon in Cancer aspected by Mars causes *Śūla*. This may be generated by Mars in Cancer (*Rāśi* or *Aṁśa*) aspecting the Moon in the 8th house. In the Sun's *daśā-Śukra Bhukti*, one is subjected to head-ache, throat-trouble, leprosy, sudden fever and colic. He may also leave the country. This, i.e. Colic in the stomach, is due to the sin of having promised a learned Brāhmaṇa all help and of disappointing him at the end (like *Droṇa* at the hands of king *Drupada*). Similarly one who hears about one's parents' sexual life, gets severe pain in the ear and becomes deaf.

Dropsy and Iliac Passion: If the Moon produces *Durudharā Yoga* on account of malefics, and if Saturn occupies the 7th house, one suffers from loss of breath, abscess, *Gulma-plīhā* (one of stomach diseases) etc. as a result of the sin of having destroyed brāhmaṇas, fields, tanks, wells, anthills etc. This is due to the trouble caused by a *graha*, evil spirit, called *Vāyasagraha*.

Heart diseases: When one commits the sin of having liaison with another's wife or hurting others' feelings, one is troubled by this disease. The planetary combination for this is the presence of the Sun and/or Saturn in the 4th house. Such a person is always sickly, full of nails and hair in childhood. *Mūtra-kṛcchra* or scantiness of urine results, when Saturn in the 7th house is aspected by Rāhu. One who is always jealous of his Guru (preceptor) and one who commits the sin of sexual intercourse in daytime, suffer from 'Retention of Urine'. The Vāyupurāṇa opines that a drunkard gets this ailment.

Calculi or Stone in the Bladder: If Saturn stationed in a house of Jupiter be aspected by the Sun, one becomes heroic and staid, but suffers from urinary disease.

Diabetes: There are 20 types of this disease, *Madhumeha*—diabetes mellitus—being one of them. One who rapes another's wife or cohabits with a virgin sister, or a revered woman, suffers from *Madhumeha*; one having illicit relations with one's brother's wife, gets *Udaka-Meha*; and one mating with an animal gets diabetes and colic. The Vāyupurāṇa gives the same result for one that steals a brāhmaṇa's gold.

Obesity: One having Venus in the 12th house, becomes stout, lazy, happy, a good eater, clever in sexual dalliance and defeated by women. The reason for this trouble is said to be *Dadhi-Caurya*, theft of curds.

Stomach Disease: The Moon in Leo being aspected by malefics makes one suffer from maladies relating to teeth and stomach, thirst and hunger. The person will have profuse hair and thick bones. The Moon in the 6th house makes one lethargic, and have poor digestion and stomach complaints. This is due to the sin of making distinction between Brahmā, Viṣṇu and Maheśvara. One is afflicted with dropsy, if one being appointed as a judge or minister fails in his duty or unnecessarily wastes money. The same trouble would dog one's footsteps; if one were to spoil one's teacher's spouse.

Oedima: In the *daśā* of debilitated Jupiter, one suffers from swelling in the body and diseases of the privy parts and ears. One who defecates or urinates on roads, sands, mountain-top, under a wood-apple tree or in water, is stricken with rheumatism, oedima and fainting. According to the elder Bodhāyana oedima is the punishment for obstructing others' meals.

Diseases of entrails, scrotum, testicles: The Sun (along with Rāhu?) in Cancer being aspected by Mars, causes severe diseases of the private parts. When the Sun in Pisces is aspected by an inimical planet (Saturn), the native will suffer from diseases such as enlargement of testicles, hydrocele and hernia. He will be very poor, full of ulcers, interested in murders and hater of an unfaithful wife. Similarly Venus in Scorpio makes one an artist or engineer who would be afflicted with diseases of the genital organ. One who has liaison with one's own daughter-in-law, gets enlargement of testicles.

Scrofula, tumour etc: In Venus-Sun *daśās* and *Bhuktis* one gets throat diseases, head-ailments, leprosy, fever and colic. The same is the case with *budha-daśā* and Mars' *Bhukti*. The reason is defrauding one's teacher and brāhmaṇas, as well as eating forbidden food.

Leprosy: In Āyurvedic texts 18 varieties of leprosy are mentioned. When Rāhu and the Sun are posited in the 8th house, this disease makes its appearance. There is a more virulent type of leprosy called *Mahākuṣṭha*, which is brought into existence, when Mars too joins the above combination. Similarly, a person becomes despicable on account of his vile character, and a leper, when Saturn, Venus and the Sun are joined together. The Sun in a house of Mars being aspected by Saturn produces the same result. Rāhu in Leo being aspected by Venus does the same thing. One who kills animals, or steals clothes becomes its victim. One who steals clothes gets white leprosy. One who murders a brāhmaṇa goes to hell and on return to the earth suffers from white leprosy. Generally it is seen in the Suns' *daśā-budha-bhukti*. One who covets or is jealous of other's pleasures gets this; and pus and blood would be flowing from his body. One who punishes others illegally gets a blackened face. So does one that kills little creatures.

Chicken-Pox: This is otherwise known as *Śīta-pitta*. When Saturn, Venus and the Sun are together this malady is seen.

Visarpa-erysipelas (herpes) is of 9 varieties. One who makes others eat ordure or spoils one's teacher's wife is attacked by this disease.

Minor diseases: When Saturn and the Sun are aspected by Mars, a disease called *Valmīkapāda* (an eruption on the foot looking like an anthill) breaks out. One who usurps the clothes and money donated to Gods gets *elephantiasis*. One that breaks others' vows gets knotty ulcers (*kīlaka vraṇa*). One who eats without purifying oneself after answering calls of nature, gets a disease whereby his anus would be dripping owing to ulcers.

Undiagnosed diseases: One who commits suicide by taking poison, hanging or shooting, gets, in subsequent births, such diseases.

Women's diseases: If at the time of marriage Mars be in the 8th house, the woman would be having menstrual flow for many days. One gets abortion as a result of killing a child in a previous life.

Procedure for protection of foetus: In the Ist month *bali* or worship, should be offered to Brahmā; in the 2nd, *bali* to the (divine physicians) *Āśvins*; in the 3rd, the *Rudras* are to be propitiated near a tank; in the 4th, the 12 *Ādityas* to be worshipped with red rice, flags, sandal paste, flowers, clothes, gold etc.; in the 5th, Lord Vināyaka should be worshipped in *gomaya* form under a mango tree, after covering the idol with a pair of clothes, ornaments etc. with *bali*; in the 6th, early morning *bali* should be offered to Lord Skanda on the bank of a river; in the 7th month, the eight Vasus to be worshipped on a river bank; in the 8th, *bali* to be offered to Śrī-Durgā or the *Mātṛkās* in the south; in the 9th, *bali* to be offered to Lord Govinda in the morning; and in the 10th, the lord is to be worshipped in a Viṣṇu temple and the *bali*, to be thrown under a tree.

Lack of milk in breasts: If Saturn be in the 4th house at marriage, the woman may not have milk for feeding her baby. She must have stolen milk in her previous life. She should worship brāhmaṇas by washing their feet and feed them with milk-porridge (*Kṣīrānna*). Cracking of breasts in a woman takes place, if she had insulted her husband and thought of another.

Karmavipāka means ripening of one's previous action which manifests itself in various forms of diseases, physical and mental. Ancient sages have prescribed certain *prāyaścittas* or expiation as well as medical treatment for alleviating the sufferings of the concerned people. So what we have already explained is *karmavipāka-prāyaścitta* according to one school of authors. We are now going to delve into another source of Vedic scholars who have delineated this subject at length.

Consumption: *Cause*: In the previous life the person concerned had troubled, harassed or killed brāhmaṇas, spoken ill of his preceptors or hated them, scandalised others or had indulged in sexual dalliance during eclipse or other holy occasions.

Expiation: Repetition of the thousand names of Lord Viṣṇu, Śiva etc., performance of *Rudra Homa*, sacrifice with the mantras of Indra and Agni with *Japa* and gifts of cloth etc. After these expiatory rites are completed medical treatment should be taken up, for getting success.

Wasting disease: One who steals another's food materials gets this malady. The *śānti* is performance of Lord Śiva's worship in a gold image, and at the end of the worship the image should be gifted away to the worthy preceptor.

Leprosy: Murdering brāhmaṇas, cohabitation with one's teacher's wife, knowingly giving wrong treatment to a trusting patient, poisoning a trusting person—these are the causes for contracting this loathsome disease.

Remedy: *Japa* of *Rudra-sūkta* and longevity hymns, worship of the divine Sun and cow in gold images and gifting them away after sufficient japa and performance of *Kūṣmāṇḍa homa*. White leprosy too has the same causes for its origin as are given for leprosy. Still the following is to be considered as most important: Stealing bronze vessels, cotton, salt and clothes. The remedy is the same as given above.

Herpes: *Cause*: Killing snakes, or others through a snake-charmer.

Expiation: Gift of a gold serpent after worship as prescribed in the *Smṛtis*.

Anaemia: *Cause*: Stealing temple properties, taking away brāhmaṇas' wealth, eating forbidden things.

Cure: *Kūṣmāṇḍa Homa* and gift of gold.

Diarrhoea: *Cause*: Destruction of water sources such as wells and tanks.

Expiation: *Japa* of *Rudra-sūkta* and *Ayus-sūkta* (Vedic hymns that confer long life).

(*Note*: According to *Āyurvedic* texts *Pāndu-roga* does not mean albiness, but it is a condition of bloodlessness which results in pallor of the body.)

Grahaṇī or *Diarrhoea*—due to liver disorder—*Cause*: Abduction of others' children and destruction of water sources.

Cure: Making gifts of a black cow, and an image of fire God in addition to the *japa* of *Rudra-sūkta* and *Āyus-sūkta*.

Diseases of the Mouth: *Cause*: Cutting off another's lip and tongue, breaking teeth, speaking ill of one's teacher, uttering falsehood and deposing falsely.

Expiation: Performance of *Kūṣmāṇḍa homa, japa* of the sacred Gāyatrī mantra, making gifts of a golden elephant, medicinal herbs, and corn.

(*Note*: 74 types of ailments of different parts of the mouth are explained in ancient texts.)

Arśas or Piles: *Cause*: Stealing God's and brāhmaṇa's wealth and food materials of others, indulging in sexual acts during eclipses and killing cows.

Cure: Giving away a gold cow.

Diseases of the Tongue: The cause is the same as for diseases of the mouth.

Cure: Giving away cereals, medicines, doing *Kūṣmāṇḍa homa*, *japa* of the planets, especially Rāhu and other *Śānti-sūktas*.

Diseases of the Eyes: *Cure*: Doing harm to one's benefactor, looking clandestinely at another's wife and destroying another's eyesight.

Expiation: Making gifts of *Mudgānna* (food prepared with green gram and rice), *Pāyasa* (milk-porridge), ghee, gold and an idol of *Garuḍa*, and doing *japa* and *homa* with the hymns of 'Protection of the Eyes'.

Night-blindness: *Cause*: Piercing cow's eyes.

Cure: Gift of a gold image of Śrī Gopālakṛṣṇa.

Diseases of Ear: *Cause*: Tale-bearing, cutting another's ear or spoiling another's undertaking.

Expiation: Giving away gold, cereals, a plot of land and blankets, as well as *japa* of the three Solar *hymns*.

Vātaic diseases: *Cause*: Speaking ill of respectable people, one's own parents and preceptors, and stealing food materials.

Expiation: Making gifts of a copper image of deer, clothes, gold, and sumptuous food as well as *japa* of the Vedic hymn named *Vāyusūkta* and its recitation.

Note: According to *Āyurveda* 80 varieties of this disease are known. Rheumatism is called *Āmavāta*.

Śūla-Roga—irritative pain: There are eight varieties of this disease. *Cause*: Sexual union with a virgin, animal, widow, or slave-woman, eating forbidden things, lack of decent conduct, tale-bearing habit, making a gift of unworthy articles, poisoning a friend or killing a person with a lance.

Remedy: Making gifts of sesamum-seeds, gold lotus and a trident made of gold, silver or iron, according to one's means.

(*Note*: This pain takes many forms such as colic, iliac passion etc.)

Diabetes: *Expiation*: Performing a sacrifice with the mantras meant for eradicating all diseases, recitation and *japa* of Lord Varuṇa and Varuṇa *Sūktas* as well as making *dāna* (gift) of gold, cow, food and water.

Dropsy (*Mahodara*): *Cause*: Desecrating teacher's bed and causing abortions of women.

Expiation: *Japa* of *Rudra Sūkta*, *Varuṇa Sukta*, as well as making gifts of water and a gold crocodile.

Urinary diseases: *Cause*: Cohabitation with virgins, animals, widows etc., harming and insulting brāhmaṇas.

Cure: Giving away sesamum-seeds and gold lotus.

Poor digestion (*Agnimāndya*): *Cause*: Feeding the sacred fire at a sacrifice with oblations when the fire does not burn well.

Cure: *Japa* and recitation of *Agni-mantra* and *Agni-sūktas*.

Fistula (*Bhagandara*): It is said to be of 8 types.

Cause: Disobeying directions of elders, benefactors, teachers etc., desecrating preceptor's bed.

Remedy: Making gifts of gems, silver, gold, gold elephant and *Japa* of the sacred Gāyatrī mantra and recitation of *Rudra-sūkta* and *Āditya-sūkta*.

Diseases of the Head: *Cause*: Contempt for the Sacred Vedas, Vedic scholars and such other holy personages.

Cure: Worship of brāhmaṇas with the *dāna* of the Sacred Thread (*Yajñopavīta*).

Menorrhagia (*Raktapradara*): This is one of the diseases of women.

Cause: Cutting wantonly sacred trees like the *Asvattha*; killing cows.

Remedy: Making a gift of a red cow to a worthy person.

Epilepsy (*Apasmāra*): *Cause*: Killing one's teacher, elder or employer.

Cure: *Japa* and recitation of Vedic hymns meant for good health, *dāna*, *homa* etc.

Insanity: *Cause*: Making fun of elders, teachers etc., hankering after sensual pleasures in the company of depraved women.

Cure: Giving *dāna* of a gold elephant.

Fevers: *Cause*: Killing snakes, speaking ill of one's teacher, having intimacy with his wife.

Cure: Performing a *homa* (sacrifice) for Mother Durgā.

(*Note*: Fevers are said to be 25 in number. Malarial fevers are five in number.)

Malarial fever etc.: *Cause*: Frightening all animals through dogs.

Remedy: *Japa* of Durgā mantra, recitation of *Rudra-sūkta*, *Ādityahṛdaya*. For Śīta (cold) fever the remedy is worship of Lord Viṣṇu with *Abhiṣeka* with *Pañcāmṛta*, for *Uṣṇa* (hot or burning) fever, *Abhiṣeka* of Lord Śiva.

Ulcer, *Boil*: *Cause*: Stealing vegetables, cutting short another's speech, man-slaughter, union with a forbidden woman.

Expiation: Making a gift of gems or gold to worthy brāhmaṇas.

Dumbness: *Cause*: *Plagiarism*. *Atonement*. A silver idol of goddess of Speech should be given away after due worship of gods.

Jaundice: *Cause*: Taking food without washing one's feet; cooking food in an uncleaned vessel.

Cure: *Dāna* of an image of *Garuḍa*.

Hernia: *Cause*: Destruction of a sacrifice undertaken by others.

Cure: Making *dāna* of an image of Lord Viṣṇu after worship.

Tumour: *Cause*: Hating one's preceptor, or forcing him to do something against his wish, harbouring jealousy against others, usurping other's food materials.

Cure: Performing a *homa* (sacrifice) with the hymns of *Indrāgni*, *Japa* of the sacred Gāyatrī, *Rudra-sūkta*, *Vāyu-sūkta*, *Aṣṭākṣarī*, *Pañcākṣarī* etc. and *dāna* of a gold image of Lord Gaṇapati. The best atonement for all ailments is a sincere effort to alleviate the sufferings of others through hospitals, giving food to ailing people and helping them to get good treatment. For, the *dāna* of good health is the best gift.

Loss or absence of issue: Sins responsible for it: Killing infants, eating eggs, hating one's teachers, elders or kinsmen, killing animals for food, hating one's own mother, killing young one's of animals during hunting, not performing Śrāddhas (ancestral worship).

Expiation: Performing *śrāddha* in a sacred place, worshipping one's tutelary deities and the divine planets as well as making gift of a gold cow.

CHAPTER X

SPAN OF LIFE

BEFORE DILATING on the auguries, limbs touched etc. at a query it is necessary for the astrologer to find out the querist's longevity. For, what is the use of good omens for a person who is going to quit the world of mortals in a short time? *Horā* or predictive astrology, explains the type of life, short, medium or long, the querist is destined to enjoy, through planetary configurations. The most important planet to discharge this function is Jupiter who in Sanskrit has the name, *jīva* (life), among others. Thus this science deals with the fruits of actions, good, bad or indifferent, done in a previous life. And its cause is given as the position, mood etc. of the various planets. Both life-span and vicissitudes of the journey of life on this earth are the utilities of this science of astrology. It is extremely difficult for an ordinary astrologer to correctly assess a person's span of life. Even great sages like Vasiṣṭha and Bṛhaspati find it hard to tackle this problem. In this connection, some scholars make a distinction in predictive astrology as *jīva* and *deha* (soul and body), the former being Jupiter himself who imparts life to the individual, while the latter delineates life's joys and sorrows, ups and downs, gains and losses etc.

Long life is to be declared when the lords of the ascendant and the 8th house are posited in the same house, or when they are stationed in their exaltation, own house or friendly house; or when the *lagna*-lord, Jupiter and Venus are in *kendras*, *koṇas* or 2nd house.

The following six conditions bespeak the querist's early demise, although at the time of query he is quite hale and hearty:

(1) *Māndī* at query is posited in the natal star or its trine, of the querist.

(2) *Māndī* be posited in the 8th house from the querist's natal sign.

(3) The lord of the sign occupied by *Māndi* at query, happens to be the same as the lord of the querist's natal star.*

(4) The querist or his messenger stands in the direction or place which stands for a sign that is 8th from the querist's natal sign.

(5) The *Ārūḍha* of the gold piece happens to be the 8th house from the querist's natal (lunar) sign.

(6) One of the following three planets be in the 8th house from the querist's natal sign: (a) Lord of querist's natal star; (b) lord of the star ruling the day of query; and (c) lord of the star occupied by *Māndi* at the time.

Tools for Working Out Longevity

The ascendant, its lord, the 8th house, its lord and the Moon—these five factors constitute the basis for the calculation of longevity. It depends on the strength or weakness, benefic or malefic conjunction and aspect.

The Ascendant: If it is hemmed in between malefics, aspected by or united with malefics, it suffers from blemishes leading to curtailment of longevity.

The 8th house: Same as for ascendant.

On the other hand, if these are between benefics, and aspected or joined by benefics, they attain merit leading to long life. Similarly, the aspect and union of their respective lords (of the *Lagna* and 8th house) conduce to great benefit.

Lagna-lord: His blemishes are: (1) Being surrounded by malefics, (2) being aspected by or (3) conjoined with them, (4) being eclipsed, (5) posited in debilitation, (6) in inimical house.

His merits: To be in exaltation, own house, friendly house, benefic association or aspect, to be surrounded by benefics and in retrograde motion.

Lord of 8th house: The merits and demerits of the lord of 8th house are practically the same as those of the *lagna*-lord with the exception that the presence of the lord of the 8th house in a *kendra* is definitely harmful, whereas it is highly beneficial for 1st lord.

*In this peculiar Kerala system of horary branch of astrology the planets that are *Daśā*-lords according to *Vimśottari*-system are taken as lords of asterisms.

The Moon: Her demerits are presence in the 6th, 8th or 12th house from the ascendant, being surrounded by malefics, association or aspect of malefics, weakness, presence in the *lagna* and in debilitation.

Her Merits are: Fullness, to be in between benefics, association and aspect of benefics. to be in a *kendra* to Jupiter or union with Jupiter especially in the *Lagna* and to be in exaltation.

Varāhamihira has extolled the Cancer ascendant which is occupied by both the Moon and Jupiter. Similarly he has praised the presence of malefics in the 3rd, 6th and 11th houses as conducive to longevity.

The following factors indicate long life:

1. The ascendant at query be a sign that rises with its head foremost, and is occupied or aspected by benefics or its own lord.

2. The 8th house is to be a sign that rises with its head in front, is occupied or aspected by benefics or its own lord.

3. Both the lords of the 1st and 8th houses are strong and intimate friends.

4. The *Ārūḍha* being an upward-looking sign and rising with head foremost and one indicative of high tide.

(High tide signs are said to be 1, 2, 3, 7, 8 and 9 signs from the Moon, and the remaining six signs, ebb tide ones. According to another view they are (1) 11, 12, 1, 6, 7 and 8 signs from the Moon and (2) the remaining ones. Upward-looking signs are the following: One that has been crossed by the Sun and its *kendras*.)

The following three conditions indicate death in the near future to the querist, even if he be healthy at the time:

(1) The rising decanate is *Gṛdhrāsya* (Vulture-faced), *Kolāsya* (Hog-faced) or *sarpa* (serpent).

(2) The above decanate being occupied by malefics.

(3) The Moon should be posited in the 8th house.

Death-dealing condition: The ascendant being a sign that rises with its hind part first (*pṛṣṭhodaya*) has the Moon in the 8th house.

A sick person would die soon, should malefics be in the 8th house or in *kendras*. (*Gṛdhrāsya* decanates are: III of Libra, and I of Leo and Aquarius. *Kolāsya* ones are III decanate of Scorpio, and I of Cancer and Capricorn. The sarpa decanates are: The first decanate of Scorpio and the last ones of Cancer and Pisces There is no unanimity in this matter. *Pṛṣṭhodayas* are the Rāśis 1, 2, 4, 9 and 10 and *Śīrṣodayas* are: 3, 5, 6, 7, 8 and 11. Some take Gemini as *Ubhayodaya* along with Pisces.)

The tools for determining the querist's longevity have already been explained. When these are free from blemishes and endowed with merits, the person concerned will live long with sound health, wealth and happiness. If demerits are more and stronger than merits, short life will have to be predicted. In this connection we have to think of the relationship between the body and soul (or life). From the ascendant you have to adjudge all things about the body, and from the 8th house the condition of life. If both are strong and their lords be associated with or aspected by each other, long life would be the result. If anyone of the three viz. lord of the ascendant, Jupiter and Venus, be posited in a *kendra* from the *Ārūḍha* long life would ensue; if two be in *kendras*, the result is undoubted, and if all the three be in such houses, does it need any mention? Should these three planets be in mutual angles (*kendras*), the same effect would follow.

If benefics be in the first, second, fourth, fifth, seventh, eighth, ninth, tenth, and eleventh houses, and malefics in the 3rd, 6th and 11th houses, long life should be predicted. These planets, good and bad, being posited in other houses lead to diseases and death. Please bear in mind that *Māndī* alone would cause early death, if he be posited in the 8th house. For, of all malefics he is most dreadful, more so, if he be in the *Varga*, aspect or association of Saturn.

The querist's natal horoscope too should be thoroughly examined in order to find out what type of longevity, long, medium or short, he is likely to have. If the results of query be supplemented by those of the current *daśā-Bhukti* and of planetary transits, the pronouncements on longevity would be more definite and authentic.

All beings take birth on this earth for the purpose of experiencing the fruits of *karmas* of their previous life or lives. Longevity, therefore, depends on the nature and strength of these *karmas*. Death would not visit a person until and unless the *karmas* are exhausted by experience. The results of *pūrva-karma*—previous actions—can be ascertained through certain Yogas in the horoscopes of individuals. What is the meaning of Yoga? This word is derived from the root *Yuj* to unite. In Yoga-Śāstra the same meaning is used for this word. For, ultimately the aim of Yoga is to unite or merge the individual soul with or in the Supreme Being. The first step of the science of Yoga however, is to quiet down the mind *Cittavṛtti-nirodha.* In astrological parlance it means addition, planetary combination that leads to eminence etc. In this context the word Yoga means one that unites a person with the fruits of his or her *karma* by means of planetary positions, strength, aspect and the like in a horoscope. "*Yojayanti iti Yogāḥ*" is its explanation. Ordinary people too use this term in the sense of luck or destiny. In short Yoga means the results of one's *prārabdha*, actions done in the previous life, that are revealed by the positions of planets at birth and their transits as well as through their *daśās*, *Bhuktis* etc.

Yogas are said to be of seven kinds: (1) That based on *sthāna* or positions; (2) on *bhāvas* or houses; (3) on planets; (4) on positions, houses and planets; (5) on positions and house; (6) on *bhāvas* and planets; and (7) on positions and planets.

(1) *Sthāna* or positional yoga is that which is derived from exaltation, *mūlatrikoṇa*; *vargottama* etc. (2) *Bhāva* based yogas are those that are concerned with the houses, *lagna* and others like *kendras.* (3) Those derived from the Sun and other planets, the strongest of whom builds up the yogas. (4) *Sthāna*, *bhāva* and planets. The examples are the *Mahāpuruṣa-Yogas* like *rucaka*, which need all the three viz. Exaltation etc. (position), *kendra* (*bhāva*) and the planets, Mars and other. (5) *Sthāna* and *bhāva*—example "*lagnam mūrdhodayam*". Here the first word stands for *bhāva* and the second for *sthāna* or *Rāśi*. (6) *Bhāva* and *graha*, example is *adhiyoga*, where both *bhāvas*, 6th, 7th and 8th and benefics (planets) are involved. (7) *Sthāna* and planets. In the chapter on *Āśrayayogas* malefic planets and odd signs as well as the first *horā* are mentioned as leading to a *yoga* that bestows fame, undertaking great projects, power, wealth and brilliance.

Longevity is of two types: (1) *Yogāyuḥ* and (2) *Daśāyūḥ*—i.e. one based on special Yogas and the other on the *daśās* of planets. *Yogāyuḥ* is of six varieties viz. (1) *Sadyoriṣṭa*—immediate calamity; (2) *Ariṣṭa*, (3) *Riṣṭa*, (4) Medium life; (5) Long life; and (6) Unlimited length of life. The first Yoga brings about death within a year; the second within 12 years; the third within 32 years; medium life is one that may go up to 70 years and long life is full hundred years. It is said that the first two varieties occur irrespective of ruling *daśās*. The others except the last variety stand in need of *daśā*-strength. Those who live more than 100 years come under the last Yoga termed *Amitāyuḥ*. Generally longevity is brought under three heads as (1) Short Life, (2) Medium Life, and (3) Long life. In the first instance see the relationship between the lords of the ascendant and the 8th house. Similarly, that between the lords of the natal sign (Lunar) and its 8th house, should be noted. In case these two lords, in each set be friendly, the native would have a long lease of life; if they be neutral, it would be medium; and if inimical, short life will be the result.

Likewise, consider the relationship between the following two planets: Lord of the *Navāṁśa* occupied by the Moon and the Lord of the 64th *Navāṁśa* from the Moon's *Navāṁśa*. Likewise note the relationship between the Sun and lord of the ascendant. If in each case the two are friendly, neutral or inimical, the span of life would be in order long, medium or short. Let us take an example: The *lagna* is Cancer, Lunar sign Taurus, the Sun in Aries. The lords of *lagna* and its 8th house viz. the Moon and Saturn, are neutral and inimical. Venus, lord of lunar sign and Jupiter, lord of the 8th house from the Moon, are similarly neutral and inimical. On the basis of these rules the result should be one between short and medium life. Next, the lord of the Moon's *Navāṁśa* viz. Leo, is the Sun, and the lord of the 64th *Navāṁśa* from that of the Moon is Mars, i.e. of the 8th *Navāṁśa* of *Dhanus*. These two, i.e. Sun and Mars are mutual friends. So on this score long life has to be pronounced. What about the Sun and the *lagna*-lord viz. Moon? They are also mutual friends. So on these two count friends. So on these two counts long life has to be declared.

Long Life

The following factors lead to long life:

(1) The ascendant should be strong.

(2) The Moon should be strong.

(3) The *lagna* is to be occupied by a benefic.

(4) The Moon should be conjoined with a benefic.

(5) The *lagna* should be aspected by benefics.

(6) The Moon is to be aspected by benefics.

(7) Benefics should be posited in *kendras*, *koṇas*, 2nd and 8th houses from the ascendant.

(8) Benefics should be in the above places, (as in 7) from the Moon.

(9) Malefics being in the 3rd, 6th and 11th houses from *lagna*.

(10) Malefics being in the 3rd, 6th and 11th houses from the Moon.

(11) Jupiter being in the ascendant.

(12) The Moon and Jupiter being together.

(13) The lord of the ascendant being posited in an angle from the *lagna*.

(14) The lord of the lunar sign being in an angle from the Moon.

(15) The Lord of the *lagna* being full of strength.

(16) The lord of the lunar sign being possessed of strength.

(17) The lord of the ascendant being in the 11th house.

(18) The lord of the Lunar sign being in the 18th house from the Moon.

(19) The Sun and Moon for day-birth and night-birth respectively to be in the 11th house from the *lagna*.

(20) Malefics and the lord of the 8th house being in *Āpoklima* houses (3, 6, 9 and 12).

(21) Jupiter and the Moon to be in the 4th house, lord of the ascendant in strength in the 11th house, and Mercury in the 10th house.

(22) The Sun, Mars and Saturn to be in Jupiter's *Navāṁśa* and in angular houses, Jupiter in the ascendant, and the rest in houses other than the 8th.

(23) Malefics to be in cruel houses, benefics in benefic houses and the lord of ascendant being strong.

(24) The Sun, Mars and Saturn being in movable *Navāṁśas*, Jupiter and Venus in fixed *Navāṁśas*, and the rest in dual *Aṁśas*.

(25) Benefics to be in odd *Aṁśas* and in the 4th and 9th houses, malefics in even *Aṁśas* and in the ascendant, and the Moon being strong in the *lagna*.

Take the following three pairs of *Rāśis*:

(1) Decanates of the *lagna* and the Moon.

(2) *Navāṁśa-Rāśis* of the *lagna*-lord and *Rāśi*-lord

(3) *Dvādaśāṁśa-Rāśis* of the lords of the *lagna* and the 8th house.

If in these pairs both are movable signs or one fixed and the other dual sign, long life is the result. If both be dual, or one movable and the other fixed, medium life can be predicted. And if both be fixed or one dual and the other movable, short life. Divide the 12 houses beginning with the ascendant into three groups. (1) 1, 2, 3 and 4, (2) 5, 6, 7 and 8, (3) 9, 10, 11 and 12. If there be four or more planets in the first group, second group and third group, the results would be (1) long life, (2) medium life, and (3) short life.

Count the rays contributed by all the planets. If the sum is greater than 25, the person's longevity should be stated to be long; if it be between 15 and 25 rays, medium life; and if less than 15, short life.

Now let us see how to calculate the *Raśmis* (rays) of the planets: The rays of the seven planets from the Sun are in order 10, 9, 5, 5, 7, 8 and 5, when they are in their highest exaltation. In the case of a retrograde planet as well as one that is in exaltation *Aṁśa*, the rays should be trebled. If a planet be in his own or a friendly *Aṁśa*, the rays are to be doubled. In the case of a debilitation and inimical *Aṁśa*, the rays suffer a reduction by 1/16th (here *Aṁśa* means *dvādaśāṁśa*). Eclipsed planets lose their rays completely except Venus and Saturn who lose only 50% of their rays.

In the *Sarvāṣṭakavarga* table of any nativity if the benefic dots in the ascendant or the lunar sign be greater than, equal to or less than those in the corresponding 8th house therefrom, the native would have long, medium or short life respectively.

In the case of a short life the person concerned meets with his end, when Saturn in transit comes in his first cycle to the particular point of the Zodiac signified by the sum-total of the longitudes at nativity of Saturn, Jupiter, the Sun and the Moon. If the native be found to be of medium life, death would take place in the second cycle. It would happen in the 3rd cycle in the case of one of long life.

The following are planetary configurations for short and medium life.

1. When the lord of the ascendant is conjoined with the Sun, and the lord of the lunar sign without strength, and all the malefics in *kendras*, the native may quit the world of mortals before his 20th year.

2. The same result could be expected, if the ascendant be a movable sign occupied by the Sun and Mars, Jupiter be in the 10th house, and the Moon in the 5th or 9th house.

3. Malefics in the 8th house from the Moon, the Moon in the 6th or 8th house from the ascendant, and benefics in the 3rd, 6th, 9th and 12th houses.

4. Jupiter should occupy Sagittarius ascendant, aspected by Saturn or conjoined with Rāhu, and the 8th house, i.e. Cancer, be tenanted by any planet—death in 22nd year. (It may be read as: A malefic be rising in the ascendant or a malefic sign be rising and Jupiter be aspected by Saturn or united with Rāhu.)

5. The *lagna* be occupied by Jupiter and Venus, the 5th by Mars and Saturn, and the Moon be weak—short life.

6. The waning Moon posited in the 8th house and in depression *Navaṁśa* and aspected by Mars and Saturn—the native lives for 25 years at the most.

7. The lord of the 8th house being in the ascendant, 5th or 9th house, and the lord of the *lagna*, aspected by a malefic, be posited in the 8th—the person lives for 26 years. If the above houses be aspected by benefics, he might tide over death. (Or does it (*Apamṛtyuḥ*) mean accidental death?)

8. Add the longitudes of the ascendant and the lunar sign. If the resulting figure indicates a *kendra* or the 8th house, and if a malefic be posited therein, death would occur to the person in his 27th year.

9. If the luminaries and Rāhu be in the *lagna* and Jupiter in the 12th house, death would be in the 28th year.

10. If the ascendant be hemmed in between malefics and Jupiter along with Rāhu in the 7th or 8th house, the maximum period of life would not exceed 30 years.

11. If the weak Moon be in her own house, the lord of the 8th house in a *kendra*, a malefic in the 8th house, and the lord of the ascendant weak, the result is the same.

12. The result would be the same, if the *lagna*-lord be in the

6th house, the Moon and Venus along with a malefic in the 5th house, and the 8th-lord in a *kendra*.

13. If both the *lagna*-lord and the Moon being weak and aspected by malefics, occupy, *Āpoklima* houses, one would live for 32 years.

14. One would live for 36 years, provided Jupiter and Venus at a twilight-birth be in *kendras*, and the *lagna*-lord, joined with a malefic, be in an *Āpoklima* house.

15. If there be a birth during *Māndi's* rise and the Moon and Mars be in the *lagna*, and benefics occupy houses other than *kendras* and the 8th, the person would live for 36 years.

16. If the lord of the 8th house, be in a *kendra*, that is a fixed sign, the native's longevity would be 40 years, provided there be no benefic in the 8th house.

17. If the lord of 8th house be in a *kendra*, Mars in the ascendant, and the Sun and Saturn in the 3rd and 6th, one would live for 44 years.

18. If the Moon in *Vargottamāṁśa* be in the *lagna* and be aspected by a malefic, and if the benefics be without strength, one would live for 48 years.

In conclusion, the following factors may be mentioned as responsible for short life:

1. The ascendant and the Moon being devoid of strength.
2. The above two having malefic association or aspect.
3. Combustion or weakness of the lords of the ascendant and lunar sign.
4. The above-named two lords being in the 6th, 8th or 12th house from their respective *lagnas*.
5. Birth at the time of occurrence of a misty circle around the luminaries, their eclipse, a twilight, or portents like earth-quake, fire in the quarters etc.
6. Birth in the fateful degrees (*Mṛtyubhāgas*) of the *Rāśis* or in the junctions of the signs.
7. The Moon being in fateful degree in a *kendra* or the 8th house along with malefics.
8. The Moon having the aspect of planets and occupying the 6th or 8th house.
9. Benefics in the 6th or 8th house being aspected by retrograde malefics.

10. Malefics' presence in the 8th house, angles or trines.

(*Note*: Each sign has a particular degree which is called fateful. They are from Aries onwards: (1) 1st degree; (2) 9th; (3) 22nd; (4) 22nd; (5) 25th; (6) 2nd; (7) 4th; (8) 23rd; (9) 18th; (10) 20th; (11) 24th; and (12) 10th degree. Similarly, the Moon has fateful degrees in the 12 signs: 26; 12; 13; 25; 24; 11; 26; 14; 13; 25; 5; and 12. For the *Mṛtyubhāgas* of other planets including *Māndi* refer to page 49, "*Fundamentals of Astrology*" by this author.)

If merits are in preponderance, life would be long; if demerits too many and very powerful, short life. Hence longevity has to be assessed on the basis of both the charts viz., at query and birth.

CHAPTER XI

DEMISE

THE QUESTION OF DEATH has to be tackled on the basis of both query and the native's horoscope. In this connection an astrologer is expected to divine the time, place, mode and cause of death. The time of death is to be inferred from the *Yogas, daśā, Bhukti* the place occupied by the luminaries, Jupiter, Saturn and the ascendant. When longevity is to be ascertained through *Yogāyuḥ*, that method should be employed, and death should be predicted to happen at the end of the year when the Yoga comes to an end. Along with this, longevity should be calculated through the death-dealing *dāśa* and *Bhukti.* If these two calculations tally, you can be sure of the event occurring at the expected time. In addition to the above use also the transits of planets appropriately.

Note the following in the native's horoscope:

1. The lords of the 8th house from the ascendant and the Moon.
2. Planets posited in the 8th house and those aspecting it.
3. Saturn, lord of a cruel decanate*, lord of the house occupied by *Māndī*, the lord of the *Rāśis* and *Aṁśas* occupied by these planets and Rāhu. Find out the weakest of the above planets at birth, posited in a bad house that is aspected by or conjoined with malefics. The major or minor period of that planet is most likely to bring about the exit of the person.

Death may be expected in the *daśā* and *Bhukti* of the following planets:

1. Both the lords of *daśā* and *Bhukti* being malefics.
2. Lords of the 3rd, 5th and 7th stars from one's natal star. If the end of a *daśā* synchronizes with those of other *daśās* mentioned below, or is found to be highly injurious from many stand-points, it should be adjudged as a definite clue of death.

*The cruel decanate may be the 22nd from the *lagna-decanate*. For *Krūra-drekkāṇas* see "*Fundamentals of Astrology*" page 234 also.

The dangerous nature of the *daśā* of the lord of the 8th house is common to all *daśā* systems. However, the reckoning of the *daśās* belonging to the lords of the three stars viz. *Vipat* or 3rd, *Pratyak* or 5th and *Nidhana* or 7th counted from one's natal star is peculiar to the *Uḍudaśā*-systems. For, this rule does not apply to the *Kālacakra-Daśā* (K.C. Daśā) system. Death is pretty certain during the major periods of planets that are debilitated (without cancellation of their debilitation effect) or eclipsed.

Kālacakra Daśā

There are many systems of *Āyurdāya* for reckoning one's longevity. They are (1) *Nisarga-daśā*, (2) *Aṁśa-daśā*, (3) *Piṇḍā-yurdaśā* (4) *Jīvaśarmāyuḥ*, (5) *Aṣṭakavargāyuḥ*, (6) *Viṁśottarī*, (7) *Aṣṭottarī*, (8-11) the four *daśās* beginning with *Niryāṇa-Daśā*, (12) *Kālacakra-daśā* etc. Each *daśā* is resorted to when the planet or planets are strong and well-placed. The first of these systems is based on the natural strength of the planets, as the name suggests. Number (2) system propounded by *Satyācārya* is adopted when the *lagna Navāṁśa* is strong. Number (3) is taken up when the *lagna* sign happens to be strong. According to (4) the maximum period of life contributed by all the planets is 120 years and 5 days.

Let me explain first the method of arriving at the four *daśās* named (1) *Niryāṇa-*, (2) *Ādhāna-*, (3) *Mahā-*, and (4) *Utpanna-*. Keep the Moon's longitude in four places separately. To the first add 3^s-3°-20′ or 7 asterisms; subtract from the second place 3^s-3°-20′; add to the third place 1^s-23°-20′ or 4 stars; and lastly add to the fourth place 1s-10°-0′ or 3 stars. Repeat this process with the longitude of the lord of the 8th house kept separately in four places. The results in each case indicate in order the four *daśās* mentioned above. The concluding periods of the several *daśās* evolved out of these four series portend death.

Kālacakra or Cycle of Time-system of longevity is based on the Moon's position in a Star-quarter or *Nakṣatra-Pāda*. In the context of this system the 27 stars from *Āśvinī* to *Revatī* are classified into nine groups of three stars each, counting them on the three fingers of the right and left hands alternately. So we get four groups of stars as (1) the right-hand stars, (2) left-hand stars, (3) right-hand central stars, and (4) left-hand central stars. While counting them in this manner we get the 10 stars, *Āśvinī*, *Kṛttikā*, *Punarvasu*, *Āśleṣā*, *Hasta*, *Svātī*, *Mūla*, *Uttarāṣāḍhā*, *Pūrvābhādrā*, and *Revatī* (leaving off the central ones) on the right-hand. And *Rohiṇī*, *Ārdrā*, *Maghā*, *U. Phalgunī*, *Viśākhā*, *Jyeṣṭhā*, *Śravaṇa* and *Śatabhiṣak* are the 8 stars that fall on the left-hand. *Bharaṇī*, *Puṣya*, *Citrā*, *Pūrvāṣāḍhā* and *U. Bhādrā* are the five central ones on the right-hand; and the four stars viz. *Mṛgaśiras*, *P. Phalgunī*, *Anurādhā* and *Dhaniṣṭhā*, are the left-hand central ones. This *K.C. Daśā* is calculated on the basis of the quarters of the asterisms. Among nine groups of three stars each, the five odd groups or triads are termed as *Savya* or *dakṣiṇa*, meaning right-hand; and the four even ones as *Apasavya* or left-hand. The peculiarity of the former (*Savya*) triad is that its 12 *Pādas* or quarters, are assigned to the 12 signs from Aries to Pisces without break, while in an *Apasavya* (Left-hand) triad, the 12 *pādas* belong to the 12 signs reckoned in the reverse order from sign Scorpio to Sagittarius. In the former triad the reckoning begins with *deha* or body, while in the latter, it stars with *Jīva* (life or soul).

The 12 quarter-stars, whether of the right-hand or left-hand triad can be brought under the four triangular signs according to the signs to which they are severally assigned. In accordance with this classification, four kinds of maximum life (*Paramāyuḥ*) would result. The total number of *daśās* in the *Kālacakra* scheme is nine presided over by nine signs and their lords. In the *Savya* cycle the *daśās* begin from Aries and progress towards Pisces where they end, and then they pass on to Scorpio and go in a reverse order upto Sagittarius and thence revert to Aries and end in Pisces. In this manner we have three cycles representing 36 *daśās* for the four quarters of the first asterism of a triad. The 4th cycle begins with Scorpio and passing on in the reverse order ends in Sagittarius. The 5th cycle runs from Aries to Pisces; the 6th from Scorpio backward to dhanus or Sagittarius. These three cycles give the *K.C. Daśās* to the four quarters of the star comprising the second star of a *Savya* triad. The 7th, 8th and 9th cycles are identical with the 1st, 2nd and 3rd cycles respectively. Thus it will be seen that the four quarters of the 3rd star of a *Savya* triad have the same *Mahādaśas* as those of the first.

(For details refer to charts on page 212)

These are nine cycles also corresponding to the twelve quarters of an Apasavya triad, but with this difference viz. the cycles in this *cakra* run in an order exactly opposite of what obtains in the *Savya* cycle. The first cycle begins with Dhanus and ends with *Vṛścika*. The second runs from *Mīna* to *Meṣa* in the reverse order. The third passes from Sagittarius to Scorpio identically with the first. These three cycles assign the *Mahā-daśās* to the first four *pādas* comprising the first star of an *Apasavya* star-triad. The 4th and 6th cycles are identical with the 2nd, i.e. from *Mīna* in a reverse order to *Meṣa*, while the 5th is with the 1st or the 3rd, i.e. from *Dhanus* to *Vṛścika*. These three enable us to find the *daśās* of the middle four quarters forming the second star of an *Apasavya* triad.

EXPLANATION

For those born in the first quarter of the asterisms *Āśvinī*, *Kṛttikā*, *Punarvasu* etc. the order of *daśās* is:

(1) *Meṣa-Kuja*, (2) *Vṛṣabha-Śukra*, (3) *Mithuna-Budha*, (4) *Karka-Moon*, (5) *Simha-Sun*, (6) *Kanyā-Budha*, (7) *Tulā-Śukra*, (8) *Vṛścika-Kuja* and (9) *Dhanur-Guru*.

For the second quarter of these asterisms the order of daśās is: (1) *Makara-Śani*, (2) *Kumbha-Śani*, (3) *Mīna-Guru*, (4) *Vṛścika-Kuja*, (5) *Tulā-Śukra*, (6) *Kanyā-Budha*, (7) *Karka Moon*, (8) *Simha-Sun*, and (9) *Mithuna-Budha*.

The order of *daśās* for the third quarter of these stars is: (1) *Vṛsabha-Śukra*, (2) *Meṣa-Kuja*, (3) *Mīna-Guru*, (4) *Kumbha-Śani*, (5) *Makara-Śani*, (6) *Dhanur-Guru*, (7) *Meṣa-Kuja*, (8) *Vṛṣabha-Śukra*, and (9) *Mithuna-Budha*.

For the fourth quarter the order is: (1) *Karka-Moon*, (2) *Simha-Sun*, (3) *Kanyā-Budha*, (4) *Tulā-Śukrā*, (5) *Vṛścika-Kuja*, (6) *Dhanur-Guru*, (7) *Makara-Śani*, (8) *Kumbha-Śani*, and (9) *Mīna-Guru*.

For the first quarter of the stars, *Bharanī*, *Puṣya*, *Çitrā*, *Pūrvāṣāḍhā*, and *Uttarābhādra*, the order of *daśās* is: (1) *Vṛścika-Kuja*, (2) *Tulā-Śukra*, (3) *Kanyā-Budha*, (4) *Karka-Moon* (5) *Simha-Sun*, (6) *Mithuna-Budha*, (7) *Vṛṣabha-Śukra*, (8) *Meṣa-Kuja*, and (9) *Mīna-Guru*.

For the second quarter of the said asterisms the order is: (1)

Kumbha-Śani, (2) *Makara-Śani*, (3) *Dhanur-Guru*, (4) *Meṣa-Kuja*, (5) *Vṛṣabha-Śukra*, (6) *Mithuna-Budha*, (7) *Karka-Moon*, (8) *Siṁha-Sun*; and (9) *Kanyā-Buddha*.

For the third quarter, the *daśā* periods are: (1) *Tula-Śukra*, (2) *Vṛścika-Kuja*, (3) *Dhanur-Guru*, (4) *Makara-Śani*, (5) *Kumbha-Śani*, (6) *Mīna-Guru*, (7) *Vṛścika-Kuja*, (8) *Tulā-Śukra* and (9) *Kanyā-Budha*.

For the fourth quarter of these asterisms the order is: (1) *Karka-Moon*, (2) *Siṁhā-Sun*, (3) *Mithuna-Budha*, (4) *Vṛṣabha-Śukra*, (5) *Meṣa-Kuja*, (6) *Mīna-Guru*, (7) *Kumbha-Śani*, (8) *Makara-Śani*, and (9) *Dhanur-Guru*.

The order of *dāśās* for the first quarter of the stars of the *Apasavya/cycle*, *Rohiṇī*, *Ārdrā*, *Maghā*, *Uttara-Phalgunī*, *Viśākhā*, *Jyeṣṭeā*, *Śravaṇa* and *Śatabhiṣak* is: (1) *Dhanur-Guru*, (2) *Makara-Śani*, (3) *Kumbha-Śani*, (4) *Mīna-Guru*, (5) *Meṣa-Kuja*, (6) *Vṛṣabha-Śukra*, (7) *Mithuna-Budha*, (8) *Siṁha-Sun*, and (9) *Karka-Moon*.

The order of *daśās* for the second quarter of these asterisms is: (1) *Kanyā-Budha*, (2) *Tulā-Śukra*, (3) *Vṛścika-Kuja*, (4) *Mīna-Guru*, (5) *Kumbha-Śani*, (6) *Makara-Śani*, (7) *Dhanur-Guru*, (8) *Vṛścika-Kuja*, and (9) *Tulā-Śukra*.

The order of *dāśās* for the third quarter of these stars is: (1) *Kanyā-Budha*, (2) *Siṁha-Sun*, (3) *Karka-Moon*, (4) *Mithuna-Budha*, (5) *Vṛṣabha-Śukra*, (5) *Meṣa-Kuja*, (7) *Dhanur-Guru*, (8) *Makara-Śani*, and (9) *Kumbha-Śani*.

The order of *daśās* for the fourth quarter of these stars is: (1) *Mīna-Guru*, (2) *Meṣa-Kuja*, (3) *Vṛṣabha-Śukra*, (4) *Mithuna-Budha* (5) *Siṁha-Sun*, (6) *Karka-Moon*, (7) *Kanyā-Budha*, (8) *Tulā-Śukra*, and (9) *Vṛścika-Kuja*.

For the first quarter of the Asterisms *Mṛgaśirṣa*, *Pūrvaphalgunī*, *Anurādhā*, and *Dhaniṣṭhā*, the order of *daśās* is: (1) *Mīna-Guru*, (2) *Kumbha-Śani*, (3) *Makara-Śani*, (4) *Dhanur-Guru*, (5) *Vṛścika-Kuja*, (6) *Tulā-Śukra*, (7) *Kanyā-Budha*, (8) *Siṁha-Sun*, and (9) *Karka-Moon*.

For the second quarter of these stars the order of *daśās* is: (1) *Mithuna-Budha*, (2) *Vṛṣabha-Śukra*, (3) *Meṣa-Kuja*, (4) *Dhanur-Guru*, (5) *Makara-Śani*, (6) *Kumbha-Śani*, (7) *Mīna-Guru*, (8) *Meṣa-Kuja*, and (9) *Vṛṣabha-Śukra*.

For the third quarter of these asterisms the order is: (1)

Mithuna-Budha, (2) *Siṁha-Sun*, (3) *Karka-Moon*, (4) *Kanyā-Budha*, (5) *Tulā-Śukra*, (6) *Vṛścika-Kuja*, (7) *Mīna-Guru*, (8) *Kumbha-Śani* and (9) *Makara-Śani*.

For the fourth quarter of these stars the order of *daśās* is as follows: (1) *Dhanur-Guru*, (2) *Vṛścika-Kuja*, (3) *Tulā-Śukra*, (4) *Kanyā-Budha*, (5) *Siṁha-Sun*, (6) *Karka-Moon*, (7) *Mithuna-Budha*, (8) *Vṛṣabha-Śukra*, and (9) *Meṣa-Kuja*.

In this *K.C. Daśā*-system the years allotted to the seven planets from the Sun onwards are (1) *5*, (2) *21*, (3) *7*, (4) *9*, (5) *10*, (6) *16*, and (7) *4*.

In the case of any nativity, the initial *Mahādaśā* belongs to the lord of the *Rāśi* owning the quarter of the natal star. The portion of this *Mahādasā* in terms of years, months etc. that remains at birth will correspond to the number of minutes that have yet to elapse in the star-quarter, divided by 200 minutes and multiplied by the years of the major period. Let us take an example; Let the Moon's longitude at a birth be 9s-14°-29′-39″. This is the 5th *Navāṁśa* of sign Capricorn, which is the second quarter of the star *Śravaṇa*.

According to the rule illustrated in the *Apasavya* chart the formula applying to this *pāda* is 6-7-8-12-11-10-9-8-7. The person was born after 69.65 minutes had passed. The total longevity for this series is 83 years. Hence $\frac{69.65}{200} \times 83$ or 28.90475 years had expired before birth. So 9 years of *Kanyā-Budha* and 16 years of *Tulā-Śukra* = 25 years have passed in these two sub-periods. Consequently we have to come next to the 7 years of *Vṛścika-Kuja*. This means 3.90475 years have already elapsed in this *Kuja-Daśā*, and only about 3 years of his *daśā* still remain to be passed at the time of birth. The major *daśā* that follows next is that of *Mīna-Guru*; then *Kumbha-Śanidaśā*, *Makara-Śani*; *Dhanur-guru-*; *Vṛścika-Kuja-*; *Tulā-Śukra-*; *Kanyā-Budha-*; *Tulā-Śukra-*; and *Vṛścika-Kuja*. The *Bhuktis* of each of these major periods belong to the above nine *Rāśis*.

These are in order (1) $\frac{10 \times 10}{83}$ years; (2) $\frac{4 \times 10}{83}$ years; (3) $\frac{4 \times 10}{83}$ years; (4) $\frac{10 \times 10}{83}$ years; (5) $\frac{7 \times 10}{83}$ years; (6) $\frac{16 \times 10}{83}$

years (7) $\frac{9 \times 10}{83}$ years; (8) $\frac{16 \times 10}{83}$ years; and (9) $\frac{7 \times 10}{83}$ years. (*Note*: Here the method of calculation according to the other school is not considered.)

In this *daśā*-system also we have *deha* or body and *Jīva* or life (or soul). In a *Savya* (Dextral) triad of stars the first *Rāśi* is called *deha* and the last *jīva*, while in the *Apasavya* (Sinistral) triad this order is reversed, i.e. the first sign is termed *jīva* and the last *deha*. When Rāhu or Ketu, Mars and the Sun be in conjunction with both *deha* and *jīva*, there would be death. If they happen to be only with *deha*, disease would be the result. When Mercury, Jupiter and Venus occupy *deha* or *jīva*, then everything conduces to happiness and prosperity as well as end of sorrow and sickness.

If the planets joining these two houses be both benefic and malefic, the effect would be of a mixed nature.

There are three types of progress or movement of *daśās* viz. *Maṇḍūka-Pluti* (Frog's Leap), *Aśvagati* (Horse's Movement) and *Siṁhāvalokana* (Lion's Backward Look). When the *daśā* changes from Virgo to Cancer or from Leo to Gemini, the movement is called 'Frog's Leap'; the change between Cancer and Leo is known as 'Horse's Movement'; and the transition between Pisces and Scorpio as well as between Sagittarius and Aries is termed 'Lion's Backward Look'. In all these cases the *daśā*-periods would cause great troubles and the subsequent *daśā* may also prove evil. The *daśās* of planets that are debilitated and eclipsed would generally prove extremely dangerous. (*Note*: The *Phaladīpika* states that the three types of movements of *daśās* take place at the end of (1) Cancer, (2) Scorpio, and (3) Pisces respectively.)

When there is a transition from Virgo to Cancer, the person concerned becomes great or very successful in life during the *dāśa* of the former *Rāśi*, and goes on a happy trip towards the north. On the other hand, if the change is from Leo to Gemini, the former part of the *daśā* should be avoided for undertaking any auspicious work; but a trip towards the southwest would be happy. If Jupiter be in the 3rd house, Mars in the 7th, Saturn in the natal sign, Rāhu in the 9th house, the Moon in the 8th house, the Sun in the 12th, Mercury in the 7th and Venus in an inimical house—all these places being termed *Mṛtyusthānas* or

'Places of Death' the person comes to grief, provided any planet in such a position is aspected or joined by a malefic, or stationed in an inimical or depression sign, or shorn of strength. (See Charts on pp. 267-83)

Podumana Somayāji, author of the famous work, *Jātakādeśa-mārga*, explains a different method of calculating the sub-periods of *K.C. Mahādaśās*. This rule applies only to a movable *Rāśi* with which the *daśā* begins. The procedure is the following: Multiply the *daśā*-years of the planet by the years of the planet whose sub-period is sought to be determined, and divide the result by the total number of years assigned to the particular quarter of star (*Nakṣatrapāda*). These years for the four *Rāśis Meṣa* and their trines are 100, 85, 83, and 86 respectively. There is a difference in this method: If the *dāśā* does not begin with that of movable sign, then take its trine that happens to be movable.

Saturn and Exit

(1) In the case of those that are born at night or in a nocturnal sign, death will occur when Saturn transits a *Rāśi* that is trine to *Māndī's Rāśi* or *Aṁśa* or the 7th from either. Similarly, in the case of those that are born at daytime or in a diurnal sign, it will take place when Saturn transits *Māndī's Aṁśa-Rāśi* or the 7th house therefrom or its trine.

(2) Note the following: (i) The sign and *Aṁśa* occupied by Saturn at birth. (ii) The sign and *Aṁśa* of the lord of the 8th house. (iii) The solar sign at birth and the 2nd and 12th houses from the natal Sun. When Saturn arrives at a sign that is in trine to any of the above-mentioned signs, the person's demise may take place.

(3) Find out the sign occupied by the lord of the 22nd decanate from the natal ascendant. When Saturn transits that sign or its trine, the event may take place.

Jupiter and Exit

(1) See in which sign the lord of the decanate of the natal ascendant is posited. When Jupiter in transit passes through that sign or its trine, the person may quit the world.

(2) Find out the *Rāśi* occupied by the lord of the *Kāla Horā*

(not the *lagna-Horā*) at birth. When Jupiter transits that sign or its trine, death is likely.

(3) Note the 2nd and 12th houses from Saturn at birth. When Jupiter transits anyone of these houses or their trines, the event is likely to occur.

(4) Add up the longitudes of the lords of the ascendant and 8th house. When Jupiter arrives at the *Rāśi* denoted by this sum, death may occur. Similarly, think of the same event to be likely, when the Sun, Mars, Saturn, Rāhu or Ketu passes through that sign.

(5) Keep the longitude of Saturn in four different places; to the first add 60° or 2 signs; to the second add 10 signs; to the third add 5 signs; and lastly to the fourth add 4 signs. In the case of the first sum take the 3rd sign from the sign denoted by this sum; of the second sum, take the 11th sign from the sign denoted by the sum, of the third sum, take the 6th sign; and of the 4th sum, take the 5th sign. See if among these *Rāśis* there is any one that does not receive Jupiter's aspect at all. When Jupiter transits that sign, death will overtake the native.

The Sun at Exit

(1) Note the sign occupied by the lord of the 8th house, as well as the natal star, and the star that rises in the ascendant at birth. When the Sun passes through these places, death may be expected.

(2) If the Sun at birth be in a movable sign, note his *Dvādaśāṁśa* (1/12) sign, and death is expected to take place when the Sun transits that sign or its trine.

(3) If the Sun be in an immovable sign, this event would take place when he passes through the sign (or its trine), occupied by the lord of the *Novāṁśa* of the lord of the 8th house.

(4) Should the Sun be in a dual sign, death may be expected to occur when he passes through the sign (or its trine) of the *Navāṁśa* of the lord of the ascendant.

The Moon at Exit

(1) Death is likely to take place when the Moon transits one of the following signs: (1) The sign occupied by the Sun at birth; (2) that *Rāśi* tenanted by the lord of the 8th house; (3) the stars

triangular to those occupied by the above two planets; and (4) the star occupied by the lord of the 8th house.

(2) It may happen when the Moon passes through the sign occupied by the lord of the 2nd house, or its 7th house or its trine.

(3) In case the person concerned falls ill on the day when the Moon passes through the sign occupied by *Māndī* at birth, death will take place when the Moon transits the sign that is 7th from the above sign.

LONGITUDE OF PRAMĀṆĀ-GULIKA

After arriving at this longitude, the time of death is read from the transits of Saturn, Jupiter, the Sun and the Moon. If the native is a day-born person, find out the rising of *Māndī* the previous night and add to its longitude 6 signs, which gives the figure for *Pramāṇa-Gulika.* If the birth be at night take the *Māndī-Sphūṭa* for that daytime. In this case no addition need be done. Find out the sign occupied by the lord of the sign of the *Pramāṇa-Gulika.* When Saturn transits that sign, or when Jupiter transits the *Rāśi* occupied by the lord of the *Navāṁśa* of the *P. Gulika*, or when the Moon passes through the sign occupied by the lord of the *Triṁśāṁśa* (1/30) of the *P.G.*, death may take place. It may also take place when the Sun transits the sign occupied by the Lord of the *Dvādaśāṁśa* (1/12) of this P.G.

It may also be inferred from the *Aṣṭakavarga* charts of Saturn, Jupiter, the Sun and the Moon. When the particular planet transits the sign having the lowest number of benefic dots in his own *Aṣṭakavarga* which coincides with one the vulnerable places mentioned above in this section, death may occur.

Another method: Death may take place when the Moon transits any of the following places:

(1) The sign that represents the sum of the longitudes of the Sun and Saturn, or its trine, or the one that is 7th from it.

(2) The *Navāṁśa* sign of the above-mentioned sign. When the Sun transits the following places. The sign that represents the sum of the longitudes of the Sun and the lord of the decanate occupied by Saturn, or its trine, or the one that is 7th from it or the latter's trine or its *Navāṁśa* sign.

When *Jupiter* transits the following signs:

The *Navāṁśa* sign of the sum of the longitudes of the lords of the *Navāṁśas* of the Sun and Saturn, or its trines, or the one that is 7th from it, or the latter's trine.

When Saturn passes through the following signs: The sign that represents the sum of the longitudes of the lords of the *Dvādaśāṁsas* of the Sun and Saturn or its trines. (*Note*: Here many alternatives are given with the object of bringing about synchronism of the passage of the above-named planets through their respective exit-points or *Niryāṇa* places.)

General Rule for Exit-Point

Here a general rule is given to find out the *Niryāṇa* point for everyone of the planets separately: First of all write in two place the longitude of the planet at birth whose exit-point is sought to be determined. In one, find out the number of *Navāṁśas* that have elapsed from Aries. leaving off the particular *Navāṁśa* that is occupied by the planet at birth. Then multiply the planet's longitude kept apart by this number of *Navāṁśas*; convert the result into minutes, (A). Now note the number of minutes elapsed in the particular *Navāṁśa* the planet is tenanting at birth (B). Then multiply the above result (A) by the number of minutes in (B); and divide the product by 200. Add the quotient to the result given above, i.e. (A). If the resulting figure is more than 12 signs, deduct it, i.e. 12 signs and if it be less than 12 signs, deduct the figure from 12 sings. When the planet concerned transits this point arrived at in this manner, death will take place. Let me make it clear by means of an example:

Let Saturn's longitude at birth be 10^s-29°-42′-09″. Leaving off the *Navāṁśa* (at the end) occupied by the planet we have 10^s-26°-40′, which is the 8th *Navāṁśas* of Aquarius. So the total number of *Navāṁśas* from Aries to this one is 98. Next multiply Saturn's longitude, leaving off the last *Navāṁśa* portion, and convert it into minutes: Thus 10^s-26°-40′ × 98 = 16,600′ × 98 = 1920800′ (A). The number of minutes passed by Saturn in the last *Navāṁśa* = 182′ (B) next multiply (A) by B, and divide by 200 = $\frac{1920800 \times 182}{200}$ = 1747928′. Adding this again to (A), We get = 366872′. This is equal to 2038.1822 signs or 2038^s-5°-28′. When multiples of 12 signs are deducted, we get a remainder of 10^s-5°-28′. This comes to the 4th quarter of *Dhaniṣṭhā*. When Saturn arrives at this critical point, death may be expected. Saturn would be transiting this point between May and July 1993.

Danger Period: For any planet see if in his *Aṣṭakavarga* chart there is any of the houses viz. 2nd, 5th, 9th and 12th from his position at birth, contains the least number of benefic dots, without having that planet's aspect. Then the person concerned is likely to meet with death or disaster when that planet arrives at that sign.

Ascendant at Death: The following places stand a good chance of becoming the *lagna* of Exit:

(1) The 8th house from the natal ascendant.

(2) The sign occupied by the lord of the 8th house.

(3) The sign that is 8th from the lord of the ascendant.

(4) The *Rāśi* that is 4th from the lord of the ascendant.

(5) The 8th house from the *Navāṁśa* sign of the lord of the *lagna*.

(6) The 4th *Rāśi* from the *Navāṁśa* sign of the *lagna*.

(7) The triangular signs of the above places save for those of (4) and (6).

You would see that many conditions, planetary behaviour and such other circumstances in the case of the planets have been enunciated above in order to pinpoint the time of a person's death. In the case of the major planets viz. Saturn and Jupiter, one could without much difficulty arrive at a 2½ year period and a one-year-period respectively, that come under the sphere of death. In respect of other planets consensus of various results would be a sure guide to determine the time of death.

Next the same topic will be discussed from a horary standpoint. Evidently, in case of queries about death the luminaries, Saturn, Jupiter and the houses, the ascendant and others, play an important role. The following *Rāśis* are supposed to be decisive for different planets as shown hereunder:

1. Death may catch hold of a mortal, when Saturn, passes through the sign (or its trine) that happens to be the *Navāṁśa* of *Māndī*;

2. When Jupiter transits the *Rāśi* or *Aṁśa* of the ascendant at query;

3. When the Sun arrives at the *Ārūḍha-lagna*;

4. When the Moon comes to the sign occupied by *Māndi*.

Ascertaining the Time of Death from the Querist's Words

Find out the *Rāśi* representing the last letter of the sentence uttered by the querist or his messenger. When Saturn, Jupiter, the Sun or the Moon, utterly devoid of strength, arrive at the sign, death is likely to overtake the person concerned, when the same sign rises.

(1) See if the *Navāṁśas* of both the Moon and *Māndi* are one and the same at query. If so, the patient will get into coma when the Moon arrives at that *Navāṁśa* sign. If the *Navāṁśas* of the Sun and *Māndi* be the same, death would take place, when the Moon transits that *Navāṁśa* sign.

(2) In the case of a sick person, his ailment will worsen when the Moon arrives at the sign representing the *Navāṁsa* of the ascendant. When the Moon transits her own Navāṁśa *Rāśi*, the person will fall into stupor; and when she transits the *Navāṁśa Rāśi* of *Māndi*, he will breathe his last.

(3) Calculate the *Trisphuṭa*-longitude of the ascendant, Moon and *Māndi* at query, and have the sum of all the three. Now add the longitude of *Yamakaṇṭaka* to this sum. When the Moon transits the asterism denoted by the resultant, it is the time of his exit.

(4) When the Sun transits the star occupied by *Māndi* or its trine, or when he passes through the sign that is occupied by the lord of the 8th house, the exit of the person takes place.

(5) Count the number of the stars *Āśleṣā*, *Jyeṣṭhā* or *Revatī*, whichever comes first, from the star of the *Trisphuṭa* in (3) above. Death will take place in so many years, months or days, according as the relationship between the lords of the ascendant and its *Navāṁśa* is friendly, neutral or inimical. If the two are bitter enemies, it will be in so many *Ghaṭīs*. Suppose these two lords happen to be one and the same; then there would be no death. If *Māndi* at query be in diurnal and nocturnal signs, the exit would be at night and day respectively.*

(6) Find out the stronger of the two viz. the ascendant and the Moon, and also the degrees yet to elapse in the *Navāṁśa* of the stronger of the two. Then the exit of the querist would take

*This applies only to natal charts.

place in as many days, months or years as the number of degrees remaining, according as the basic factors of the query are (1) very grave, (2) pretty bad and (3) slightly bad, as the case may be.

(7) The above number of days, months and years for exit of the person has to be declared on the basis of enmity, neutrality and friendship existing between the lords of the ascendant and its *Navāṁśa*, as the case may be.

(8) Find out the *Rāśi* posited by the planet that is most menacing among Rāhu, *Māndī*, *Trisphuṭa*, *Mṛtyu* etc. When Saturn, Jupiter, the Sun and the Moon transit that *Rāśi* or its trine, you may be sure of the person's death.

(9) First of all find out the stronger of the two planets, viz. lords of the ascendant and *Ārūḍha* at query; and count from the sign occupied by that planet up to the *Rāśi* of the *Trisphuṭa*, *Māndī*, *Kāla* etc., their decanate, *Navāṁśa*, and asterism—among them the most afflicted and dangerous—death would take place in so many days, months or years, as the case may be, provided there be an evil omen in the querist's house viz. death of a domestic animal, and fall of a tree.

Ascendant of Exit

The sign rising at the expected time of the querist's demise would be one of the following:

(1) The 8th house from the ascendant and *Ārūḍha* at the query.

(2) The sign occupied by the lord of the 8th house.

(3) That sign which contains the least number of benefic dots in the *Samudāyāṣṭakavarga* chart. (*Note*: The author of the *Praśnamārga* X 46 and 55 states that in these two cases the rule mentioned applies only to the natal chart.* But actually the context refers to the query alone. My humble suggestion is that the horary chart too admits of the *Aṣṭakavarga* delineation. For, the *Praśna* chart is on a par with the natal horoscope.)

Planetary Transit and Exit

(1) Saturn, Jupiter, Mars and the Sun transitting the 12th, 1st

*For the other case refer to footnote p. 257.

and the 8th house from the natal Moon cause loss of wealth and position as well as leaving one's country of birth, serious illness and even death.

(2) The following configuration of planets in transit undoubtedly lead, it is said, to death: The Moon in the 8th house, Mars and Mercury in the 7th place, the Sun in the 12th house, Venus in the 6th place, Jupiter in the 3rd house, and Saturn and Rāhu or Ketu in the 1st house.

(3) Malefics in the 1st, 4th, 7th, 8th and 12th houses act like blazing fire endangering life.

(4) The Moon in transit is invariably harmful in the 4th, 8th and 12th houses; though she is beneficial in the natal sign, yet the natal star is not good.

CAUSE OF DEATH

1. When the 8th house is occupied by the seven planets beginning with the Sun, the causes of death would severally be (1) fire, (2) water, (3) weapons, (4) fever, (5) undiagnosed disease, (6) excessive thirst due to diabetes, and (7) starvation.

2. If the several planets aspect the 8th house, the cause would be the ailment born of their respective physical constituents viz. (1) bone, (2) blood, (3) marrow, (4) skin, (5) fat, (6) semen and (7) sinews. Death may be caused by the vitiation of the humours assigned to the planets, such as *kapha* or phlegm. The significators for the three humours are: (1) the Sun for bile; (2) the Moon for wind and phlegm; (3) Mars for bile; (4) Mercury for all the three; (5) Jupiter for phlegm; (6) Venus for phlegm and wind; and (7) Saturn for wind.

Kinds of disease etc. (1) The disease which culminates in death originates in that part of the body that stands for the 8th house from the ascendant in the radical chart, or the one that is occupied by the planet that aspects the 8th house.

(2) In the absence of planets occupying or aspecting the 8th house, death should be inferred from the physical constituents and humours, being vitiated, of the lords of the 8th house, and the 22nd decanate.

(3) If Saturn be in conjunction with the Sun and other planets, in order, the disease responsible for demise would be born of bone and other constituents.

(4) If Saturn be aspected by the Sun or Mars, death would be due to vitiation of blood on the right side of the body; if by the Moon, due to diarrhoea; if by Mercury, due to a kind of paralysis whereby the person suffers from convulsions; if by Jupiter, due to swelling, dropsy and pain in the feet and the right side of the body; if by Venus, due to consumption and boils etc. if by Rāhu, due to rheumatism and pain in the joints; if by *Māndī*, due to insanity; if by *Yamakaṇṭaka*, due to epileptic fits leading to prolonged coma; if by *Ardhaprahara*, due to ulcers; and if by *kāla*, death takes place suddenly when the person is on the move, as a result of heart-failure. If none aspects Saturn, death would be caused by bronchitis, asthma etc.

TYPES OF DEATH

1. One would pass away peacefully, if there be benefics in the 7th house from the *Navāṁśa* sign occupied by *Māndī* at birth, whereas malefics there would cause unnatural death. If the malefic be the Sun, death would be caused by Government order; if it be the weak Moon, a watery grave; if it be Mars, death by fighting; if it be Saturn, death by treachery; and if it be Rāhu, by snake-poison or poisoned food. The above conditions apply equally to the radical and horary charts.

2. Different types of diseases causing death are attributed to the lords of decanates posited by Saturn. If Saturn be in the Leo decanate, death would be caused by continuous fever; if the decanate be Cancer, through some water-borne disease like dropsy; if it be Aries or Scorpio, through excessive heat like boils and ulcers; if it be Gemini or Virgo, through some *vātaic* ailment; if it be Sagittarius or Pisces, through tumour; if it be Taurus or Libra, through swelling on the body, abscess, diabetes, consumption etc., if Saturn occupies his own decanate, through cough, bronchitis and such other wind-diseases. In case the lord of Saturn's decanate be aspected by or conjoined with Rāhu, death would be due to poison.

3. If Saturn at birth be in a benefic sign, *Navāṁśa*, or in exaltation, *Mūlatrikoṇa* or own house, especially in Sagittarius or Pisces, the person would pass away in his own house and amidst his family-member and other kinsmen. On the other hand, if Saturn be in his depression, or inimical house, he would die in

great distress in a lonely place. One would die of snake-bite, if Saturn be in a serpent-decanate or be aspected by or conjoined with Rāhu and *Māndī*.

4. One is likely to die in fire in the following circumstances:

(i) Saturn should be in a sign owned by the Sun or Mars.

(ii) Saturn should be conjoined with either of the two.

(iii) The sign occupied by Saturn should be identical with the rising of the fire element.

(iv) The sign should also have the aspect or association of Rāhu and *Māndi*.

(v) In addition to the above conditions, if Saturn be conjoined with Venus or the Moon, the native would die as a result of boiling water being thrown on him or himself falling into boiling water.

Death in Water

If Saturn be in the water element, in a watery sign and in association with a watery planet, the person would die as a result of falling into water.

Death Through Several Agencies

(i) If Saturn be weak and posited in the Hog-faced decanate, and associated with Rāhu and *Māndi*, the native would die, being mauled by wild animals.

(ii) If Saturn be in the decanate called Vulture-faced, death will be due to birds.

(iii) If Saturn, in addition, be devoid of strength, having association or aspect of *Māndī*, and the weak Sun being the lord of the sign occupied by *Māndi*, be posited in an evil house, the person would have his death at the hands of his own father. In this manner you have to infer the relative from the respective significator, who will be responsible for the native's death. So substitute the Moon, Mars, Mercury, Jupiter and Venus for the Sun in the above statement, for mother, brother, kinsman, son and woman respectively.

(iv) Lastly, should the weak Saturn be the lord of the house occupied by *Māndi*, and posited in an untoward house, the native would commit suicide.

Death due to spirits: (1) If Saturn, being weak and posited in an evil house, be aspected by or conjoined with Mars, death must be due to the wrath of *Śakti*-deities such as *Cāmuṇḍā* (called *Cāmuṇḍī* in local tongue).

(2) If in the previous Yoga there be association of Mars and *Māndī* with Saturn, death may be caused by the unseen troubles created by enemies.

(3) If Saturn in the above Yoga be aspected by or conjoined with *Māndī* and the Sun, death may be due to fever caused by the wrath of Śiva's attendant hosts dwelling in the Abode of Lord Śiva.

Now we shall discuss the topic of death on the basis of horary chart. Generally the disease responsible for a person's death is found out from the planet that aspects the 8th house at query. In the absence of that it should be read from the planet that occupies the 8th house. If that condition too is absent, then take the lord of the 8th house whose particular ailment would cause death. This suggests that everyone of the planets has the natural capacity to produce certain maladies, and when they are afflicted or ill-placed, they bring about a person's demise through the diseases appropriate to them. Next we shall see those diseases that pertain to the planets in order.

1. The Sun produces excessive heat, pain all over the body and feverishness or continuous fever.

2. The Moon causes vomiting and nausea, if she be posited in an upward-looking sign; if in the sign termed *Tiryaṅmukha* (looking sideways), retention of urine; if in a sign called *Adhomukha* (downward-looking), diarrhoea, excessive thirst leading to heavy drinking of cold water, diabetes etc., and generally in all signs, swelling of the body.

3. Mars is capable of producing ulcers born of blood impurities, great heat and fever.

4. Mercury is responsible for mental aberration, typhoid and *Śīta-Jvara* (fever caused by cold).

5. Jupiter causes cerebral diseases and intellectual disturbances.

6. Venus creates abscess, indigestion, thirst and fainting.

7. Saturn gives rise to thirst, lack of appetite, and pain all over the body.

8. Rāhu is responsible for wind-diseases; *Māndī*, for hiccup, veiny ailment etc. (For Ketu the ailment is the same as for Rāhu).

The diseases mentioned in the context of the *Trisphuṭa* are to be declared in this connection, provided the planets are found to be occupying the *Trisphuṭa*, or they aspect it, or their *Rāśi* or *Navāṁśa* be found in the *Trisphuṭa*.

If the Moon be posited in the *Navāṁśa Rāśi* of the ascendant at query, and if the querist's ailment is increasing steadily at the time, it is sure to bring about his death. In order to confirm the results of planetary configurations, omens of various types are also to be taken into consideration in connection with the topic of death. For example, should the Sun be the lord of *Mṛtyusphuṭa* (which is explained on p. 264 *Infra*) powerful men would come to the place and begin to quarrel. This would be a sure portent for the impending death of the sick person. On the other hand, should the Moon be the lord of the *Mṛtyusphuṭa*, a woman would come to the house where the horary session is in progress; if the lord be Mars, somebody would bring milk and jaggery to the place; if the lord of the *Mṛtyusphuṭa* be Mercury, a learned person would arrive there; if it be Jupiter, a brāhmaṇa would come there; if it be Venus, there would befall some disaster to a brāhmaṇa, and a domestic animal at the querist's house; and if it be Saturn, a wicked and despicable fellow would visit the place. All these ill-omens portend immediate death. If Rāhu or Ketu be posited in the *Mṛtyusphuṭa*, the portent of death would be the arrival of beggars and a snake or a snake-charmer. If Ketu alone be there, death of the person concerned would be due to his fall. If the above *Sphuṭa* be conjoined with both Mars and the Moon, a vessel would fall down and break. This also is a sure portent of immediate death.

The *Navāṁśas* of *Trisphuṭa* and fatal disease: (1) If the *Navāṁśa* of this *Sphuṭa* be a sign of the Moon or Venus, the fatal diseases would be vomiting, swelling (dropsy) and dysentery, according as the *Navāṁśa* signs are upward-looking, sideways-looking and downward-looking respectively. If the *Navāṁśa* sign be Leo, Aries or Scorpio, it would be mounting heat or burning sensation and fever; if it be Gemini or Virgo, mental trouble or some ailment of the vocal chord; if it be a sign of Jupiter, Cerebral ailment and Speech-malady; and if it be a Sign of Saturn, obstruction to breathing and bronchial ailment. The above results may be declared also for the aspects of the respective planets on the *Navāṁśa* sign of the *Trisphuṭa*.

New Sphuṭas

1. *Prāṇa-Sphuṭa*: Multiply the ascendant by 9. The result is *Prāṇa-Sphuṭa*.

2. *Deha-Sphuṭa*: Multiply the Moon's longitude by 9. What you get as product is called *deha-Sphuṭa*.

3. *Mṛtyusphuṭa*: The product of *Māndī's* longitude and 9 is termed *mṛtyusphuṭa*.

4. *Kāla-Sphuṭa*: The product of *Trisphuṭa* and 9 is *Kāla-Sphuṭa*. (*Note*: These special *Sphuṭas* should be used only in this context and the reader is advised not to confuse these with those mentioned in a previous chapter.)

Place of Death

If the 8th house of the natal chart be movable, dual or immovable, the person's death would take place in a foreign country (or a far-off place), on the way or in one's own place, as the case may be. Should the 8th house be a rural sign, the person would breathe his last in a village; if it be a watery sign, near water such as river, lake and the sea; if it be a forest sign, in a jungle; if it be a benefic house, death would be in a clean, nice, place; if it be a malefic *Rāśi*, he will die in the region inhabited by uncultured people; if it be a downward looking sign, death would be in a low-lying place; if the sign be upward-looking, in an elevated place. The question of light, lamp, attendants etc. will have to be tackled exactly as in the case of the lying-in-chamber, the only difference being the *lagna* in the one, and the 8th house in the other case, as the starting point.

We have seen the place of death as far, near or half-way on the basis of the nature of the 8th house from the natal *lagna*. This question may also be tackled on the basis of the *Rāśis* occupied by the lords of the ascendant and its *Navāṁśa* at birth. Take the stronger of the two planets and consider the nature of the sign occupied by that planet. From that you can say the distance of the place of death as well as its nature as rural, hilly or sylvan. The type of the house in which the native dies should be inferred from the following planets:

(i) *Lagna*-lord, (ii) Lord of the *Navāṁśa* of the *lagna*; (iii) the planet that combines with or aspects the stronger of the above two planets. The places assigned to the seven planets from the Sun onwards are in order (1) a place of worship, (2) a marshy place or tank, (3) kitchen or blacksmith's workshop, (4) playground or pleasure-garden, (5) treasure room, (6) bed-chamber, and (7) a place where rubbish and discarded things are collected.

The type of house such as new, old, dilapidated or decorated, may be inferred from the strongest of the following:

1. The planet that occupies the ascendant.
2. One that is associated with the lord of the ascendant.
3. One that aspects the *lagna*.
4. One that aspects the lord of the *lagna*.

The houses represented by the seven planets from the Sun, onwards, when they are strong, are in order:

(1) An old house built of timber; (2) a new building; (3) a house which had once caught fire; (4) a house full of artistic decorations; (5) a strong house; (6) a lively new house possessing works of art; and (7) an old but renovated house.

Dreams Presaging Calamity

The subject of auguries and dreams has claimed unusual importance in the hands of authors of ancient Śāstras, Purāṇas (Epics), Kāvyas, Āyurveda, Astrology and other branches of literature, both religious and secular. In this connection the famous works of Caraka, Suśruta, Vālmīki and Vyāsa merit special mention. Even our folklore is replete with references to this topic—one such reference relates to the period prior to the game of dice between the Pāṇḍavas and Kauravas. One morning Draupadī goes to her mother-in-law, Kuntī, and narrates her dream experience. She says, "I saw in my dream a parrot dancing before me for a while and disappearing thereafter". Apprehending danger to her sons, Kuntī at once advises Draupadī to make proper expiation (*prāyaścitta*) for the evil forebodings of the dream. "Oh Draupadi make *Annadāna* (offering of food) to the hungry; give away gold (*honnu*) and, above all, clothes to the poor. For, that would ward off the evil effects of your dream."

Well-known is Trijaṭā's admonition to the demonesses in the Aśoka garden in Laṅkā, asking them not to harass Śrī Sītā Devī whose husband is going to be victorious in the impending war against Rāvaṇa by destroying the entire race of *rākṣasas*, as forewarned by her dream. Vālmīki tells us in the words of Śrī Sītā Devi that one could not hope for prosperity after seeing a monkey in dream.

Now look at the prophetic words of Patañjali in the *Caraka Saṁhitā*. Should vessels fall down with a thud and break to pieces in a sick person's house, he would not survive. One who, while dreaming, rides a dog, camel or donkey, and goes towards the south, would quit the world, being attacked by consumption. The following dream presages fatal fever: One drinks liquor in the company of discarnate spirits and then is dragged by a dog, is attacked by a dangerous fever before death. One who sees the sky like a piece of cloth dyed with red lac at close quarters, would fall a prey to *raktapitta* (haemorrhage, internal) and breathe his last. The same fate overtakes one who dreams that his body is all red, decorated with red garlands and clad in red garments, and is dragged by a woman, while he is laughing all the while. One becomes a victim of *Gulma-Roga* before death, if in dream grows a thorny creeper from his heart. One dies of leprosy, if he dreams that he is naked with his body fully smeared with ghee and is performing a sacrifice in a flameless fire, when lotuses grow on his breast. Before a person is attacked by fatal diabetes, there would be the symptom of flies or bees coveting his contact in spite of his having had his bath and anointing his body with sandal paste etc. Such a person drinks in dream several varieties of oils and ghee in the company of *caṇḍālas*.

Before one gets into fatal insanity, one exhibits the following symptoms: Being in reverie, utter exhaustion, tension or agitation, sudden stupor, utter weakness and indifference to everything. A patient of this disease who gets into fits of temper, who gets frightened very much, suddenly laughs heartily and is afflicted by fainting and excessive thirst passes away are long. What is the preliminary symptom of this fatal malady? Such a person dreams of himself as dancing with a group of demons or evil spirits and finally falling down into water.

Epilepsy as Fatal Disease

One who while being quite awake sees darkness around him in broad daylight and hears all kinds of sounds, although there is no sound at all in the air, would soon fall a prey to epilepsy and shuffle off his mortal coil. This disease is presaged by a dream wherein the victim, who dances in a drunken state, is caught by the neck and dragged by a discarnate spirit. Similarly, the following incidents seen in dreadful dreams by the person concerned or his friends or relatives forebode his early death:

(1) One gets shaved in dream; on his head grow bamboos, bushes, and creepers, wherein birds build nests.

(2) One gets surrounded by swarms of vultures, owls, dogs, crows and others as well as by evil spirits, *pretas*, female goblins, *Caṇḍālas* and other forest tribes.

(3) One falls down; gets lost and swoons in a thicket of bamboos, canes, creepers, grass and thorny trees.

(4) One enters a pit filled with ashes, dust and anthills in a burial ground, or dirty waters or silt, dark and deep well or is dragged away by the current of a river.

(5) Drinking oil or ghee, taking oil-bath, defeat and captivity, gain of gold, quarrels, vomiting, defecation, loss of footwear, peeling of the foot-skin.

(6) Rejoicing, threats from angry ancestors, fall of teeth, stars, the luminaries, deities, lamps and eyes; breaking of mountains or trees; sight of red flowers, forests, cremation, houses of prostitutes, going naked to the south in monkey-chariot.

(7) A patient who sees in dream persons clad in orange robes, those of sinister looks, those that are holding clubs, dark men with red eyes, as well as a dreadful, sinful woman—*Kālaniśā* with long hair, nails and bosoms, clad in red garments and wearing red garlands, would not survive. Even a healthy person seeing such persons or things in dream often meets with death.*

Now let us try to understand the physiological reasons for sleep and dream. According to Āyurvedic theory the senses, both sensory and active, are under the control of the mind. During the wakeful or *Jāgrat* state both the mind and senses discharge their respective functions without rest. At the end of the day all of them including the mind get exhausted and take

*For greater details vide *Suśruta-Sūtrasthāna XXIX*.

rest. This is called sound sleep or *Suṣupti*. But sometimes, even when the senses are enjoying rest, the notorious mind, which is compared to the wind or monkey on account of its fickleness, wanders away in the world of its own making. When this state is reached, the wise call it the dreaming state. These three states are natural to the *Ātman* in his *Sāṁsārika* stage. The *Caraka Saṁhitā* states: "A man who has not completely fallen asleep sees all kinds of dreams, both good and bad as well as ineffective, with his mind which is the master of the senses". Dreams are said to be of seven types: (1) Seen, (2) Heard, (3) Experienced, (4) Wished for, (5) Imagined, (6) Precursor, and (7) Born of vitiated humours. The first five types are said to be of no consequence. Similarly, all those dreams seen during the day and very short or long ones seen during the night have very little effect. "Man sees dreadful dreams, when his days are numbered, as a result of all the internal channels of life being completely filled (i.e. damaged) by all the three vitiated humours."

Query About Dreams

As the question of dreams has cropped up in connection with disease and death, it may be discussed here as a subject of query. Somebody approaches an astrologer and puts a question to him, "Please tell me as to what kind of dream I have had". This subject has received no insignificant attention of scholars as shown hereunder:

(1) If the Sun be posited in the ascendant and be aspected by the Moon; or if the sign Leo be the 7th house from the *lagna*, the astrologer should tell him that the latter had a dream. If the *lagna* be a movable sign, it would be a long dream; if immovable, a short one; and if dual, neither long, nor short. If the lord of the *lagna* be the Moon, duration of dream would be a *kṣaṇa* or *vighaṭī* (for practical purpose).

(2) Should the Sun be posited in the ascendant or *Ārūḍha*, the querist must have seen in dream blazing fire, red clothes, red garland etc.

(3) Should the Moon be in the *lagna* or aspect it, it must be a woman, white flower, white clothes and the like.

(4) If Mars be in the *lagna*, the articles seen would be gold, coral, bleeding, flesh soaked in blood etc.

(5) If it be Mercury, the querist must have floated in the air.

(6) If it be Jupiter, he must have seen his kith and kin.

(7) If it be Venus, it must be something connected with water such as swimming in water, crossing a stream etc.

(8) If Saturn be in the *lagna*, he must have experienced climbing tall trees or mountains, or occupying some position of administrative powers.

If the sign of the ascendant be inimical or indebilitation *Rāśi* to the planet occupying it, it should have been a broken bad dream. The same result should be declared for the planet that is defeated in planetary war; or it may be a theatrical performance that he saw in a dream.

According to *Nīlakaṇṭha* for a bad dream it is not necessary for the Sun to be in the *lagna*, but it is enough if he be in the *Navāṁśa* of the *lagna*. For the Moon, the articles seen would be a white horse, gems, flowers, diamonds and charming damsels. For Mercury, they are: snakes, ascending to heaven and news of meritorious acts. For Jupiter, sight of gods, sport, association with ascetics and listening to spiritual discourses. For Venus, crossing the seas, sport of divine beings and sexual union. For Saturn, Rāhu and Ketu, journey over mountains and forests and association with mean fellows. If the Moon, occupying the 3rd, 5th, 6th, 7th or 11th house, is aspected by Jupiter, the Sun and Venus, and if benefics be in the 9th or *kendras*, the querist must have had an enjoyable union with a charming noble woman, in dream.

Dreams and Signs

(1) If Aries be the *Ārūḍha*, the person sees in dream a temple, its parts like tower; (2) if it be Taurus, sight of images of gods; (3) if it be Gemini, of brāhmaṇas, hermits and their spiritual practices, (4) if it be Cancer, of crops, grass, water, fields, and bringing water to fields from a tank; (5) if it be Leo, of hunters or buffaloes; (6) if it be Virgo, of association with young damsels; (7) if it be Libra, of merchants, market place, merchandise, a king, his entourage, coronation, and gold ornaments; (8) if it be Scorpio, of bees, wasps, poisonous things, horse, horse-man, running race etc.; (9) if it be Sagittarius, of leather, leather products, flower-garden, heaps of fruits and flowers etc.; (10) if it be

Capricorn, of couples engaged in talking: (11) if it be Aquarius, of a big mirror and oneself seeing one's image in it; and (12) if it be Pisces, of the ocean, waves, bathing in the sea, gold, collecting gold ornaments etc. (*Note*: In respect of dream-queries the following factors have to be taken into consideration: ascendant, *Ārūḍha*, the *Chatra Rāśi* and the 4th house, as well as the planets therein.) When a person sees inauspicious dreams, he must try sincerely to atone for the sins by means of *dāna* (charity), *homa* (sacrifice), *japa* (repetition of holy mantras). If this is done, the troubles would be mitigated. If a person, after seeing a bad dream, dreams of something very auspicious, the bad effects of the previous dream would be nullified. On the other hand, if a bad dream is seen after a good one, the effect would be bad.

Auspicious dreams: Sight of gods, brāhmaṇas, cows, bulls, kings, living friends, sages or hermits, renounced persons, burning fire, lake with clear waters, young girls and boys, who are cheerful, those of fair complexion, those who are clad in white clothes, brilliant persons, *Rākṣasas* anointed with blood, and eating human flesh, mirror, umbrella, meat, vessel containing poison, white flowers, one smeared with dirt or ordure, fruits, hills, temple, trees laden with fruits, lion, elephant, man, mounting horse and bull, crossing lakes, rivers and seas, going towards the north-east, going to an impenetrable place, death, going away from one's place, being congratulated by gods and the manes, weeping, falling and getting up, and trouncing one's enemies. The effects are (1) recovery from illness and getting progress and prosperity; (2) gaining wealth and cure of disease; and (3) obtaining auspicious results and recovery from ailments. Suśruta adds the following among auspicious dreams: Crossing a turbulant river with dirty waters, being stung by a bee, or bitten by a snake or leech. Such dreams presage good health and prosperity.

The same authority advises people who see bad dreams to perform the following expiation: After getting up in the morning they should make gifts of blackgram, sesamum, iron piece and gold to brāhmaṇas and do *Japa* of holy Vedic mantras along with the sacred Gāyatrī. Should a bad dream occur in the first watch of the night, the person should do *Japa* of some sacred mantras and go to sleep again, but observing continence, with a pure heart. He should not divulge the contents of his bad dream to anybody. He should spend three nights in a temple, observing a vow and worship daily *vipras*. This will nullify the evil effects of bad dreams.

Kinds of Dreams

Divide the span of human life into three equal parts. The dreams that are experienced in the first part of life or childhood are called *Anūka*—those influenced by previous life—and those seen in the remaining two parts are named *Gatija*—those influenced by the actions of this life. In addition to these, there are those caused by (1) the three *doṣas*; (2) those caused by the transitory effects of planets; (3) those arising from planetary *daśās*; (4) those wished for by the mind; (5) those recollected ones; (6) those brought about by the magic practices of enemies; and (7) those created by evil spirits that cause sufferings to the person concerned. In the dreams named *Gatija* events of future life are also involved. Dreams caused by *vataic* complaints are marked by events like climbing of trees or mountains, springing up into the sky etc. In *pittaic* variety, gold, gem necklaces and the like, the sun, fire and such other brilliant, shining objects are seen. In phlegmatic type of dreams, the moon, stars, white flowers, lotus, river, swimming in water etc. are seen.

Seasons and Dreams

In the rainy season people dream in the last part of the night, as a result of vitiation of the humour called *vāta* or wind; in the autumnal season, in the middle part of the night owing to the vitiation of *pitta* or bile; and in the spring season in the initial part of the night owing to the vitiation of *kapha* or phlegm. However, in the typhoid fever in which all the three humours get vitiated, one dreams in all parts of the night, as the patient is found to be in delirium. The effects of the dreams that are caused by the power of the lords of *daśās* as well as in planetary transits, are no more than those of the *daśās* and transits. Similarly, those seen as a result of wishful thinking and those already seen, are no more significant than wakeful sights. However, those born of divine wrath or black magic done by enemies, are of dreadful consequences. In such cases proper propitiation and medical treatment should be undertaken.

There are some dreams that are so vivid and well-impressed on the mind that they are remembered well for a long time to come. Their effects are felt within prescribed time-limits. The effects of dreams seen in the four watches of the night will come to pass within a year, in six or eight months, in three months and one month or ten days respectively. If it is seen at the time of the cattle being released from the manger for grazing, it will bear fruit almost immediately.

I have already referred to the warning of Trijaṭā who saw in a dream *Rāvaṇa's* pitiable plight and destruction which was witnessed by both mortals and immortals. Now I shall narrate briefly Bharata's dream just before King Daśaratha's death. The prince beheld his father, in dream, wearing dirty clothes, with dishevelled hair, falling from the top of a mountain into a pit filled with cow-dung. At that time he beheld the seas dried up, the moon falling down on the earth, and the whole world enveloped in darkness. He saw also the king's elephant's tusk breaking into pieces, and a blazing fire suddenly being extinguished. The king was seated in great sorrow on an iron throne and being laughed at by damsels of black and red colour. The righteous king who was wearing red garlands and smeared with a red unguent, and driving in a chariot drawn by donkeys, was seen going hurriedly to the south. He also saw his father being dragged by a demoness with red garments and dreadful looks. The prince adds: "My throat gets parched very much; my mind is much agitated. I fear that one of us viz. Rāma, the King, Lakṣmaṇa or I, will die soon. I hope my father, King Daśaratha, is happy. I hope also that Rama, the great, and Lakṣmaṇa are free from trouble. So do I hope for the welfare of the beloved mothers Kauśalyā and Sumitrā, and my own mother who is ever self-willed and arrogant." All these dream events, no doubt, bespeak great calamity.

Auspicious Special Dreams

(1) Should a Brāhmaṇa dream that he is drinking blood or liquor, he would have excellent progress in the educational field; while others would come by much wealth. One who dreams

again of a king, elephant, horse, bullock, cow, gold or a sick person, would get whatever he has wished for. Should the dreaming person be a king, he would ere long establish sovereignty over a kingdom.

(2) Sight of chowries, sandal paste, conchshell, pearl, betel leaves, *Jāti* (jasmine) flowers, money and lily would bring in much profit.

(3) Should one dream that his blood is sucked by leeches or stung by bees, he would get wealth and be blessed with a son.

(4) Should a person dream of ascending a temple tower or a palace storey, he would be blessed with the kingship of a country, although he might be one of very low birth.

(5) If one dreams that he has eaten milk-porridge mixed with ghee on a soiled lotus-leaf, in the midst of a lake, he obtains singular proficiency in a respectable lore which is held in great esteem by one and all.

(6) Should one dream that his feet are tied with fetters or ropes by others, he would soon experience great joy, a permanent position of power and a son.

(7) A dream in which one sees his own body, house, vehicles, furniture etc. being consumed by fire, would get much opulence almost immediately.

(8) Should one wake up immediately after seeing in dream a *Krauñcī* (a female curlew), cock or crane, he would get a sweet-tongued woman or maiden for his spouse.

(9) The sight of the sun or moon in dream would restore a sick person to normal health and in the case of others it would be a harbinger of a windfall. The same effect would follow the sight of oblations at a sacrifice, fruits, flowers, mirror, gems, curds, pot, rice, milk etc.*

When we have discussed the topic of death, it behoves us to say something about the destination of the departed soul. It is now practically an established truth that the soul or *Jivātman* is eternal, having neither birth nor death. At death the soul discards its carnal sheath and at birth puts on a new coat, as explained beautifully by Lord Kṛṣṇa in the *Bhagavadgītā*.

According to its *karma*, the soul goes to heaven, hell or the

*Vide Appendix on *Sleep*.

mortal world. If a person puts a query to the astrologer about his destination after death, he proceeds thus: He prepares the chart for the moment with all the details including the ascendant and *Ārūḍha*. These details consist of the following 16 elements viz. (1) *Sthūṇa*, (2) *Kaṇṭakasthūṇa*, (3) *Rakta-Sthūṇa*, (4) *Viṣa-ghaṭī*, (5) *Viṣṭi* (or *Bhadra*), (6) *Gaṇḍānta*, (7) *Vaidhṛta*, (8) *Lāṭa*, (9) *Pariveṣa*, (10) *Vyatīpāta*, (11) *Dhūma*, (12) *Ekārgala*, (13) Rise of Saturn, (14) Rise of Rāhu, (15) Rise of Ketu, and (16) Rise of *Māndī*. Should many of these blemishes affect the ascendant at query, the Moon and/or the Sun, the querist would go to hell, there being two types of hell viz. one of this world and the other of yonder world. If it be of this world, the person is subjected to all kinds of ailments, degradations, poverty and sorrows. Should the Moon be subjected to the above blemishes, the hell would be of this world. (*Note*: *Lāṭa* and *Lattā* are the same.*)

There are four acute blemishes viz. (1) *Kaṇṭaka*; (2) *Sthūṇa*; (3) *Kaṇṭaka Sthūṇa*; and (4) *Rakta-Sthūṇa*. Count from the star occupied by the Sun at query to *Mūla*; then count so many stars from *Mūla*. The star thus got is called *Kaṇṭaka*; similarly count from the star occupied by Mars to the star *Mūla*. Then count so many stars from *Mūla*. The asterism thus arrived at is called *Sthūṇa*. Now count separately from the star occupied by the Sun as well as by Mars to the star *Mula*. Add these numbers. Then count the number representing the sum, from *Mūla*. The star thus got is called *Kaṇṭaka Sthūṇa*. Lastly, subtract Mars' longitude from 4^s-18°-0'. The star got from the remainder is termed *Rakta-Sthūṇa*. All these blemishes are considered to be extremely dangerous. Hence they are to be rejected in all auspicious functions. (This and many other matters connected with electional astrology are explained in the *Vidyā Mādhavīya*, Chapter II).

If the 16 blemishes mentioned above afflict the person's natal ascendant, he is sure to fall into hell proper. On the other hand, if the *Ārūḍha* and the Moon at query be overwhelmed by these blemishes, the hell the person is going to be confined to would be on this earth. If the Sun at nativity and query be assailed by

*Vide page 255 of the "Fundamentals of Astrology".

these *doṣas*, the person's soul would be subjected to the sufferings of the distant hell.

Life Expectation

In the *Kṛtayuga* men used to live for a thousand years; in *Tretāyuga* for 500 years; in *Dvāpara*, for 250 years; and in *Kaliyuga*, for a maximum period of 125 years. The twelve signs of the Zodiac are assigned to the four *Yugas* as (1) Aries, Leo and Sagittarius to *Kṛta*; (2) Taurus, Virgo and Capricorn to *Tretā*; (3) Gemini, Libra and Aquarius to *Dvāpara* and (4) Cancer, Scorpio and Pisces to *Kali*. A planet posited in a sign or *Aṁśa* belonging to the *Kṛta Yuga* is expected to yield its effects in full during its *daśā*; those planets in the *Rāśis* or *Aṁśas* of *Tretā Yuga*, only a half of its effects; those in the *Rāśis* or *Aṁśas* of *Dvāpara Yuga*, one-fourth of its full effects; and lastly in those of *Kali Yuga*, only $\frac{1}{8}$ part of its benefits. If a person be born in the *Rāśi* or *Aṁśa* of the golden age, he would get the necessities of life without asking, i.e. they would come to him automatically. In the second *Yuga*, the native will have to strive to some extent; in the third age, one would have to work very hard for earning his livelihood by trade and commerce, agriculture etc.; and in *Kali Age* one would be put to extreme difficulties to make the ends meet. What has been said about *Daśās* of planets should be applied to their *Bhuktis* as well.

Savya

Kāla-Cakra-Daśā

Stars	Pādas of Stars	Lord of Deha				
	I	Mars	Meṣa-Kuja 7	Vṛṣabha-Śukra 16	Mithuna-Budha 9	Karkata-Moon 21
1. *Aśvini* 7. *Punarvasu*	II	Saturn	Makara-Śani 4	Kumbha-Śani 4	Mina-Guru 10	Vṛścika-Kuja 7
13. *Hasta* 19. *Mūla*	III	Venus	Vṛṣabha-Śukra 16	Meṣa-Kuja 7	Mina-Guru 10	Kumbha-Śani 4
25. *Pūrvābhādra*	IV	Moon	Karka-Moon 21	Siṁha-Sun 5	Kanyā-Budha 9	Tulā-Śukra 16
2. *Bharaṇi*- 8. *Puṣya*	I	Mars	Vṛścika-Kuja 7	Tulā-Śukra 16	Kanyā-Budha	Karkata-Moon 21
14. *Citrā* 20. *P. Āṣāḍhā.*	II	Saturn	Kuṁbha-Śani 4	Makara-Sani 4	Dhanur-Guru 10	Meṣa-Kuja 7
26. *Uttarābhādra*	III	Śukra	Tulā-Śukra 16	Vṛścika-Kuja 7	Dhanur-Guru 10	Makara-Śani 4
	IV	Moon	Karka-Moon 21	Siṁha-Sun 5	Mithuna-Budha 9	Vṛścika-Śukra 16

Cycle					Max. Span of Life in Years	Lord of *Jiva*	*Aṁśas*
Siṁha-Sun 5	Kanyā-Budha 9	Tulā-Śukra 16	Vṛścika-Kuja 7	Dhanur-Guru 10	100	Guru	Aries
Tulā-Śukra 16	Kanyā-Budha 9	Karka-Moon 21	Siṁha-Sun 5	Mithuna-Budha 9	85	Budha	Taurus
Makara-Śani 4	Dhan-ur-Guru 10	Meṣa-Kuja 7	Vṛścika-Śukra 16	Mithuna-Budha 9	83	Budha	Gemini
Vṛścika-Kuja 7	Dhanur-Guru 10	Maka-ra-Śani 4	Kumbha-Śani- 4	Mīna-Guru 10	86	Guru	Cancer
Siṁha-Sun 5	Mithuna-Budha 9	Vṛści-ka-Śukra 16	Meṣa Kuja 7	Mīna-Guru 10	100	Guru	Leo
Vṛscika-Śukra 16	Mithu-na-Budha 9	Karka-ta-Moon 21	Siṁha-Sun 5	Kanyā-Budha 9	85	Budha	Virgo
Kuṁbha-Śani 4	Mīna-Guru 10	Vṛścika-Kuja 7	Tulā-Śukra 16	Kanyā-Budha 9	83	Budha	Libra
Meṣa-Kuja 7	Mīna-Guru 10	Kum-bha-Śani 4	Makara-Śani 4	Dhanur-Guru 10	86	Guru	Scorpio

Kala-Cakra-Daśā Savya

Star	Pādas of Stars	Lord of Deha				
3. *Kṛtti-kā*	I	Mars	Meṣa-Kuja	Vṛṣa-bha-Sukra	Mithuna-Budha	Karkata-Moon
			7	16	9	21
9. *Āśleṣā*	II	Saturn	Mak-ara-Śani	Kumbha-Śani	Mīna-Guru	Vṛścika-Kuja
15. *Svāti*			4	4	10	7
21. *U. Āṣāḍhā*	III	Śukra	Vṛṣa-bha-Śukra	Meṣa-Kuja	Mīna-Guru	Kumbha-Śani
			16	7	10	4
27. *Revati*	IV	Moon	Karka-Moon	Siṁha-Sun	Kanyā-Budha	Tulā-Śukra
			21	5	9	16

Cycle

					Max. Span of Life in Years	Lord of *Jiva*	*Aṁśas*.
Siṁha-Sun	Kanyā-Budha	Tulā-Śukra	Vṛścika-Kuja	Dhanur-Guru	100	Guru	Sagittarius
5	9	16	7	10			
Tulā-Sukra	Kanyā-Budha	Karka-Moon	Siṁha-Sun	Mithuna-Budha	85	Budha	Capricorn
16	9	21	5	9			
Makara-Śani	Dhanur-Guru	Meṣa-Kuja	Vṛṣabha-Śukra	Mithuna-Budha	83	Budha	Aquarius
4	—10	7	16	9			
Vṛścika-Kuja	Dhanur-Guru	Makara-Śani	Kuṁbha-Śani	Mina-Guru	86	Guru	Pisces
7	10	4	4	10			

Apasavya

Kālacakra-Daśā

Stars	Pādas of Stars	Lord of Jiva				
4. *Rohiṇi*	I	Guru	Dhanur-Guru 10	Makara Śani- 4	Kumbha Śani- 4	Mīna-Guru 10
10. *Maghā* 16. *Visakhā*	II	Budha	Kanyā Budha- 9	Tulā-Śukra 16	Vṛści-ka-Kuja- 7	Mīna Guru 10
22. *Śrāvaṇa*	III	Budha	Kanyā Budha 9	Siṁha Sun 5	Karka-Moon 21	Mithuna-Budha 9
	IV	Guru	Mīna Guru 10	Meśa-Kuja- 7	Vṛṣabha Śukra 16	Mithuna-Budha 9
5. *Mṛga-śiras*	I	Guru	Mīna-Guru- 10	Kumbha-Śani 4	Makara Śani 4	Dhanur-Guru 10
11. *Pūrva-Phal-gunī*	II	Budha	Mithuna-Budha 9	Vṛṣabha Śukra 16	Meṣa-Kuja 7	Dhanur-Guru 10
17. *Anurā-dhā*	III	Budha	Mithuna-Budha 9	Siṁha-Sun- 4	Karka-Moon- 21	Kanyā-Budha- 9
23. *Dhani-ṣṭhā*	IV	Guru	Dhanur-Guru- 10	Vṛścika-Kuja 7	Tulā Śukra 16	Kanyā Budha 9

Cycle					Max. Span of Life in Years	Lord of *Deha*	*Aṁśa*
Meṣa- Kuja 7	Vṛṣa- bha- Śukra- 16	Mithuna- Budha- 9	Siṁha Sun 5	Karka- Moon- 21	86	Moon	Vṛścika
Kumbha Śani 4	Makara Śani 4	Dhanur- Guru 10	Vṛścika Kuja- 7	Tulā- Śukra 16	83	Śukra	Tulā
Vṛṣabha Śukra 16	Meṣa- Kuja- 7	Dhanur- Guru 10	Makara Śani 4	Kumbha Śani 4	85	Śani	Kanyā
Siṁha Sun 5	Karkaṭa- Moon 21	Kanyā Budha 9	Tulā Śukra 16	Vṛścika Kuja- 7	100	Kuja	Siṁha
Vṛścika- Kuja 7	Tulā Śukra 16	Kanyā- Budha- 9	Siṁha- Sun- 5	Karkaṭa- Moon 21	86	Moon	Karka-
Makara- Śani 4	Kumbha Śani 4	Mīna Guru 10	Meṣa Kuja 7	Vṛṣabha Śukra 16	83	Śukra	Mithu- na
Tulā Śukra- 16	Vṛścika Kuja 7	Mīna- Guru- 10	Kumbha- Śani- 4	Makara Śani 4	85	Śani	Vṛṣabha
Siṁha- Sun 5	Karka- Moon- 21	Mithuna- Budha 9	Vṛṣabha- Śukra- 16	Meṣa- Kuja- 7	100	Kuja	Meṣa

Apasavya

Kālacakra-Daśā

Stars	Pādas of Stars	Lord of Jiva				
6. *Ārdrā*	I	Guru	Mīna-Guru-10	Kumbha Śani 4	Makara Śani 4	Dhanur-Guru-10
12. *Uttara-phal-guni*	II	Budha	Mithuna-Budha 9	Vṛṣabha-Śukra 16	Meṣa Kuja 7	Dhanur-Guru-10
18. *Jyeṣṭhā*	III	Budha	Mithuna-Budha 9	Siṁha-Sun-5	Karkata-Moon 21	Kanyā Budha 9
24. *Śata-bhisak*	IV	Guru	Dhanur Guru-10	Vṛścika Kuja-7	Tulā-Sukra 16	Kanyā-Budha 9

Cycle					Max. Span of Life in Years	Lord of *Deha*	*Aṁśa*
Vṛścika-Kuja- 7	Tulā-Śukra 16	Kanyā-Budha- 9	Siṁha-Sun- 5	Karka Moon 21	86	Moon	Mīna
Makara-Śani 4	Kumbha-Śani 4	Mīna-Guru 10	Meṣa Kuja 7	Vṛṣabha-Śukra 16	83	Śukra	Kumbha
Tulā-Śukra- 16	Vṛścika-Kuja- 7	Mīna Guru 10	Kumbha Śani- 4	Makara-Śani 4	85	Śani	Makara
Siṁha Sun- 5	Karkaṭa Moon 21	Mithuna-Budha 9	Vṛṣabha Śukra 16	Meṣa Kuja 7	100	Kuja	Dhanur

CHAPTER XII

TRAVEL

PEOPLE UNDERTAKE TRAVEL for pleasure and profit. It also helps people in acquiring knowledge, which they call power. One who travels widely with an observant eye gains a lot of benefits, both physical and psychological. Travel has acquired a religious aura in our ancient literature. In olden days *Tīrthāṭana*—Pilgrimage to holy places—was undertaken by students—*Brahmacārins*—and householders as well as by ascetics or *Parivrājakas* for amassing religious merit, for warding off impending calamities as well as for destroying sins. Religious students travelled widely and gained worldly knowledge before they settled down as householders. Rulers too travelled throughout their territory with a view to finding the people's welfare and to supervise the administration. They also set out on *Jaitra-Yātrā*, marching with their army to curb unruly elements in the administration and among the subjects. When a person starts on a pilgrimage to Kāśī, he is expected to elect an auspicious weakday and *Muhūrta* for the journey. He must also see that the lord of his natal sign is strong, the elected asterism both agreeable and auspicious, the ascendant, a movable sign that is *Mūrdhodaya* (rising with its head) and *Urdhvāsya* (upward-looking). There must be good and pleasant auguries. The signs Gemini and Pisces as ascendant are not recommended as they tend to create obstacles on the way. Gemini is specially condemned in spite of merits. Even immovable signs can be accepted if they are occupied by benefics and are possessed of the above-named merits; but *Aquarius* is just tolerable. If the ascendant be a *Śirṣodaya* sign, the journey would be crowned with success. The sign that rises at the time should be one allotted to the particular direction towards which the traveller intends to go. Otherwise his journey would be fruitless. Aries and its trines represent the east; Taurus and its trines, south; Gemini and its trines, west; and Cancer and its trines, north.

Diurnal and Nocturnal signs are good for starting on a journey at day time and night time respectively. A king may start on a military expedition against a foreign country in a movable *Rāśi* as ascendant, which is occupied by the luminaries. The best *lagnas* for a king's journey are (1) his natal ascendant, and (2) any of the following signs as ascendant: 2nd, 3rd, 6th and 11th from his natal sign.

A king should select an ascendant that happens to be the 8th house from the enemy's natal sign or ascendant, which is tenanted by malefics. This will ensure the enemy's destruction.

Should the Moon occupy the 4th house from the ascendant of travel, it would result in grief. The same effect would follow, should the lord of the 6th house be in the ascendant. In case the planet presiding over the direction of journey be weak and posited in an untoward house (6, 8, 12), the result would be loss of power, grief and death.

Calamity

In the following conditions a journey would end in disaster:

(1) The travel ascendant happens to be 1st, 6th or 8th from the traveller's natal sign or ascendant.

(2) The travel ascendant should be occupied by the lords of the 6th and 8th houses counted from his natal *Rāśi* and *lagna*.

(3) The lords of the natal sign and ascendant be weak.

(4) The planets mentioned in (3) are associated with malefics.

(5) The lord of the direction of travel be without strength.

(6) In addition to the condition mentioned in (5) there should be conjunction of weak benefics.

(7) The Moon in the 4th house of the travel ascendant may bestow some benefits on the traveller at first, but later will cause death.

(8) The lord of direction being weak or posited in the 6th or 8th house, would create great worries.

The untoward houses viz. 6th, 8th and 12th, are to be shunned in all undertakings. However, for shave, marriage and journey the 6th house is very good for the native.

Parigha-Daṇḍa: Obstructive Rod

The 28 stars (including Abhijit) are allotted the four cardinal directions along with their contiguous corners to the right at the rate of 7 stars starting with *Kṛttikā*. The diagonal drawn between south-east and north-west is called *Parigha-Daṇḍa*, which should not be crossed in journeys by men. This prohibition does not apply to women and cattle. In the 14 asterism from *Dhaniṣṭhā* to *Āśleṣā* the *Parigha-Daṇḍa* is situated in the north and east. Hence a journey towards the south and west is forbidden in those stars. Similarly in the 14 stars from *Maghā* to *Śrāvaṇa* the *Daṇḍa* is situated in the south and west. So journey to the east and north under these stars is forbidden. However, for short journeys, i.e. up to eight miles, this Rod would not stand in the way.

DIKŚŪLAS

Each of the 8 directions has one star as its *Śūla* or spike. Under these stars one ought not to undertake journeys towards the respective quarters for fear of getting into troubles. The star *Jyeṣṭhā* is the *Śūla* for the east; *Pūrvabhādra* for south-east; *Rohiṇī* for south; *Uttaraphalgunī* for south-west; *Puṣya* for west; *Hasta* for north-west; *Śrāvaṇa* for north; and *Aśvinī* for north-east. Should one start on a star that is *Śūla* for the particular direction of his journey, the journey would end in trouble and disappointment. However, according to Bṛhaspati the following stars are good for travel towards any direction: *Aśvinī*, *Mṛgaśiras*, *Puṣya*, *Hasta*, *Anurādhā*, *Śrāvaṇa*, *Dhaniṣṭhā* and *Revatī*. According to Varāhamihira *Aśvinī*, *Puṣya*, *Hasta* and *Anurādhā* are beneficial for all directions.

According to some authorities the following stars have the blemish called *Parigha* for the respective directions: *Uttarāṣāḍhā* and *Śrāvaṇa* for the east *Aśvinī* and *Uttarabhādra* for the south; *Rohiṇī* and *Puṣya* for the west; and *Uttaraphalgunī* and *Hasta* for the north. Hence these stars are to be avoided for journey towards the concerned directions.

For journey, it is said, the 25th and 27th stars from one's natal asterism are to be shunned. Others are of opinion that they are bad for all auspicious works.

For travel the star *Mūla* is beneficial for all quarters, while *Citrā* is rejected for all directions. Among the lunar days some recommend the *Pratipad* (the first), while others do not for journey.

The lunar days (*tithis*) called *Nandā* are good for journey towards the east; those called *Bhadrā*, towards the south: those called *Jayā*, towards the west; and those called *Pūrṇā*, towards the north. The *Rāśis* called downward-looking are not at all good for travel.

Weekdays for Journey

Tuesday is good for journey to the east; Monday and Saturday to the South; Wednesday and Thursday, to the west; and Friday and Sunday, to the north. The weekdays ruled by the Sun, Mars, Jupiter, Mercury, Venus, Saturn and the Moon are harmful for journey towards the east and other quarters in order. So for the four quarters from east onwards are bad the weekdays Sunday, Thursday, Friday and Monday respectively.

According to Bṛhaspati journey towards the east is forbidden on Thursday and Friday; towards the south on Tuesday; towards the west, on Monday and Saturday; and towards the north, on Wednesday and Thursday.

Weekdays

A journey undertaken on a Sunday would bring about calamity on the way; on Monday, loss of power or position and sustenance; on Tuesday, danger from fire and ailment of *Rakta-Pitta*; acquisition of new friends on Wednesday; on Thursday gain of victory and wealth; on Friday, increase of clothes, ornaments, wealth and conjugal felicity; and on Saturday, poverty, captivity, disease and death. The results of the weekdays are to be applied to the *kālahorās* of the respective planets. For the *kālahorā* of the Moon the effects are (1) help from a young damsel and gain of gems.

A journey would be profitable, if the lord of the direction towards which the person is going, be in a *kendra* and to the right of the asterism, and the sign of the planet, i.e. lord of the direction, be rising. Similarly the travel would be prosperous, if the lord of the weekday be in an *Upacaya* house from the *lagna*, or be to the right of the asterism. Now note an exception to this rule:

Although the weekday presided over by a planet is inauspicious, still a journey undertaken on such a day would be successful, provided the ruler of the day is posited in an *Upacaya* house from the journey *lagna*. Similarly a good weekday is likely to lead to evil results, if the lord of the day be posited in a non-*Upacaya* house from the *lagna* of travel.

Should malefics be conjoined with the Moon at the time of journey, the leader of the party would fall ill seriously. On the other hand, if she be associated with benefics, there would be quarrel in the party.

Venus in Travel

First find out the direction signified by the asterism occupied by Venus. If the traveller goes out keeping that direction to his left, he would not return alive. Besides that there would be calamities in the region such as drought, epidemics etc. However, should Venus be in his own house or exaltation, there would be no trouble for short journeys.

Good Direction

Find out the direction occupied by *Māndī*, Saturn and *Viṣṭi*. One ought not to go towards that direction, but he could select the opposite direction for success. The idea is that that quarter must be kept at the back. (Even the direction of Venus is highly injurious to travel. Kālidāsa says: "*Kāmaḥ Puraḥ Śukram Iva Prayāṇe*". The idea is that one who goes out in the direction of Venus, comes to grief.)

For Voyage

For long voyages the ascendant should be a watery sign except Capricorn, both sign and *Aṁśa*, and the asterism, movable, tender and quick for success.

Effects of Bhāvas of Journey

If the Moon in the light half be posited in 1, 6, or 8, and in the dark fortnight in 1, 4, 6, 7, 8 or 10 from the ascendant, the result would be unfavourable. So are Venus in 6, 7 and 11; Jupiter in 3, 6 and 8; malefics in all *Bhāvas* except 3, 6, 10 and 11, and Saturn and Rāhu in all houses except 3, 6 and 11. No planet is good in the 12th house. This is the considered opinion of Bṛhaspati.

EFFECTS OF THE SUN

(1) The Sun in the ascendant of travel creates pain, grief, illness and obstacles; (2) in the 2nd, loss of wealth, health, honour and military power; (3) in the 3rd, gain of gold, food, gems like corals and lands; (4) in the 4th, dispassion, quarrel with relatives, and worries; (5) trouble to children in the 5th house; (6) in the 6th, acquisition of wealth on the way, success in the desired work, destruction of enemies etc; (7) in the 7th, quarrel with one's wife and loss of money; (8) in the 8th house, ailment and danger to life; (9) in the 9th house, the Sun causes loss of religious merit and gain of wealth; (10) in the 10th house, success in one's work without effort; (11) in the 11th house, acquisition of plenty of gems; and (12) in the 12th house, loss of one's wealth, but gain through others.

MOON'S EFFECTS

If the Moon is not full, her presence in the 1st house would create quarrels and grief; in the 2nd she confers conjugal happiness, gems, friends and issue; in the 3rd, gain of gems, wealth, woman etc.; in the 4th, in the light half association of friends and kinsmen, and in the dark half separation from kith and kin; in the 5th, she gives wealth but grief on account of children; in the 6th, she makes friends turn inimical, and destroys happiness; in the 7th, she bestows, if strong, money, land and woman, but if weak, spoils them; in the 8th, causes grief and danger to life; in the 9th, she does not conduce to success quickly; if she be weak, she causes loss; if strong in the 10th, she brings about prosperity, and if weak, loss; in the 11th, she gives wealth, happiness and progress; and lastly in the 12th, she causes grief, loss of money, fear, debility etc.

MARS EFFECTS

Mars in the 1st house causes danger from poison and fire, bleeding, attack by weapons etc. In the 2nd, he causes destruction of enemies and gain of wealth. In the 3rd, one gets woman, wealth, gems, clothes etc. In the 4th, there will be loss of kinsmen, and fear of enemies. In the 5th, he causes trouble to one's children; in the 6th, destruction of enemies; in the 7th, loss of wealth, trouble from enemies and disease; in the 8th, he gives trouble to one's kinsmen, loss of wealth, illness and danger to life. In the 9th, Mars hinders progress of Dharma; in the 10th, he gives good results, according to others, he is bad in the 10th. In the 11th, there will be increase of wealth and income; and in the 12th, he causes all round loss.

MERCURY'S EFFECTS

In the 1st house, *Budha* will promote fame, happiness, gain of money and victory. In the 2nd, he gives wealth through efforts sometimes, and at others without efforts. In the 3rd, he fulfils one's wishes; in the 4th, gives good bed, food and drink, and wealth; in the 5th, birth of sons; in the 6th, destruction of enemies and troubles; in the 7th house, one gets a good spouse, clothes and money; in the 8th, he confers good things, but according to others, he causes troubles. In the 9th, Mercury promotes dharmic practices; in the 10th, success of undertakings; in the 11th, gain of knowledge and wealth without efforts; and lastly in the 12th, there would be great loss.

JUPITER'S EFFECTS

(1) Fame; (2) Acquisition of wealth; (3) Trouble from hunger and great exertion; (4) Devotion to dharma; (5) Quick success of one's work; (6) Enemies being curbed; (7) Gain of fame, wealth and woman; (8) Death, or long life (according to some); (9) Birth of a son and increase of religious merit; (10) Much income and fame; (11) Fulfilment of all ambitions; and (12) Trouble from various quarters.

VENUS EFFECTS

(1) Company of a courtesan, and gaining wealth, clothes, garlands, good feast and happiness; (2) Getting wealth; (3) *Status quo*, and fame; (4) Getting new friends; (5) Gaining position, honour and money; (6) Victory over enemies and grief on account of sexual union (according to others the opposite of what is stated); (7) Getting women and wealth and at the end destruction of one's country; (8) Success in one's undertaking;

(9) Quick success in one's desired work; (10) Plentiful income; (11) Victory, success and gain of wealth; and (12) Stubbornness and grief (others say, the effects are good).

Saturn's Effects

(1) Captivity and assassination; (2) Loss of wealth, grief; (3) Destruction of enemy's forces; (4) Murder of a kinsman through assassins; (5) Poverty and disappointment; (6) Conquest of enemies; (7) Eye-disease, loss of enthusiasm; (8) Murder of oneself through poison, fires and weapons; (9) Neither luck, nor happiness; (10) Lack of happiness and fruit of one's action; (11) Success and gain of money; and (12) Series of calamities.

It is a general rule that malefics are beneficial, when they are posited in 3, 6, 10 and 11. For Saturn even the 10th house from the travel *lagna* is not good. Benefics are good wherever they may be. Though Venus is good, yet he is not favourable to a marching monarch, in the 7th house. Even a benefic (Mercury) who is not helpful in the ascendant of birth, as he does not conduce to the development of prosperity and auspicious works, is harmful, if the travel *lagna* is the same as the one at his nativity. Even a malefic who is in his own or exaltation house, is beneficial, if he be in the ascendant at birth or journey.

A planet who is not strong at birth and is inimical to the current *daśā*-lord, and not favourable in transit too, will be harmful to the journey, if he be posited in the ascendant of the journey, even if he be a benefic.

In the same manner, even a malefic would be quite favourable to a journey, provided his *daśā* is found to be quite good, who is quite strong at birth, and is a close friend of the lord of the current *daśā*.

If the lord of the lunar sign at birth be debilitated or eclipsed and is now posited in the *lagna* or the 6th house of the journey chart, the tour would be crowned with success, they say.

Good Yogas According to the Mādhavīya etc.

It is said that the Yogas are common to the rich and poor alike; yet they specially apply to kings. Kings are to be guided in their journeys and expeditions by the special planetary configurations called *Siddhi-Yogas*; Brāhmaṇas by the strength of the asterism and lunar day concerned; thieves and such persons, by auspicious omens; and others by the *Muhūrtas*.

Kings' Journey

A king should step out with his right foot first and take 32 steps forward. Then he should mount his elephant, horse, chariot or palanquin. The rule about vehicles is that the elephant should be used for marching towards the east; Chariot towards the south; horse towards the west; and palanquin towards the north. One should not stop for rest while on tour unless he has travelled at least a distance of 1000 *Dhanus.* (One *Dhanus* is equal to four cubits). This minimum distance is reduced to 500 *Dhanus* and lastly to 100. A king on march ought not to rest for ten days at a stretch, while others should not stay for five days continuously. If this rule be violated, they should again make a fresh start on an auspicious day and *Muhūrta*.

Omens for Journey

(a) At the start sneezing is considered as an ill-omen, while the sneezing of a cow forebodes death. According to some a forced sneeze, one of aged persons, children and those that are suffering from nasal diseases are of no significance. Sneezing is considered as a happy augury on the following occasions: (1) While taking medicine, (2) mounting a chariot, (3) wearing dress, (4) going to bed, (5) eating, (6) commencement of education, and (7) sowing.

(b) Blazing fire, elephant, horse, a well-lit pedestal lamp, prostitute, goad, fine clay, rice, sugar-cane, fruits, chowries, eatables and weapons are auspicious omens.

(c) The following too are considered auspicious: Drum, tabor, conchshell, lute, sound of Vedic recitation, sweet religious music, young woman with child, cow and calf, and a washerman carrying washed clothes coming in front.

One ought not to start on a journey, when the person finds some persons quarrelling nearby, or weeping.

Query About Victory or Defeat

If a person puts a query as to whether he would come out victorious or otherwise in the battle he is going to fight, the procedure to be adopted is given here: Observe the star occupied by the Sun at the time of query. Take also the two stars, one prior to it and the other after it. If the querist's natal star be one of these three stars, there would be danger to him. Similarly, he will meet with death, great victory and victory depending upon the particular number from the star occupied by the Sun at query being occupied by his natal star. If his natal star happens to be one of the stars—1, 2, 11, 12, 13, 14, 15, 16, 17, 18, 19 and 28 counted from the one posited by the Sun, he will be killed; he will achieve brilliant victory in stars 3, 4, 20 and 21; and victory in stars 5, 6, 7, 8, 9, 10, 22, 23, 24, 25, 26 and 27. This rule can be applied to cricket and other tests. This method is called *Sūrya-Cakra* or Sun's cycle.

Sūryakālāgni Cakra

This is in continuation to the previous cycle. Here too the three stars viz. one behind the star occupied by the Sun and one after it and the 3rd being the one posited by the Sun, are bad for the querist, as they forebode danger (fear) to the person. These are stars 1, 28 and 2. The following six stars viz. 11, 13, 14, 16, 17 and 19 presage wounds and 12, 15 and 18 portend death; and lastly 3, 4, 5, 6, 7, 8, 9, 10, 20, 21, 22, 23, 24, 25, 26, and 27, victory.

Raviśūla Cakra

If a warrior's natal star be one of the following, counting from the star occupied by the Sun, he would lose his life: 1, 2, 9, 10, 11, 18, 19, 20 and 27, those born in the following stars would be defeated: 12, 13, 14, 15, 16 and 17; and those born in the following stars viz. 3, 4, 5, 6, 7, 8, 21, 22, 23, 24, 25 and 26 will be victorious. (See charts on pp. 295-97)

The Chart 12.1 given below is drawn for the time when the Sun is posited in Star Mṛgaśiras. In this Cakra and the following one the 22nd star is called Abhijit. So there are altogether 28 stars.

Bhūmi Bala—Strength of the Ground

Sometimes questions like the following are asked—"Which party of combatants fighting in different directions would get victory or defeat?" In such cases this method of *Bhūmi-Bala* is made use of: Take three fortnights for each quarter, starting from the beginning of *Caitra*. So the first 45 days are assigned to the east; the next 45 days belong to the north-west; the next·

Chart 12.1. *Sūrya Cakra*

S. No.	Natal Star (N.S.)	Effect	S. No.	N. Star	Effect
1	Aśvinī	Victory	15	Svātī	Ḍeath
2	Bharaṇi	Victory	16	Viśākhā	Death
3	Kṛttikā	Victory	17	Anurādhā	Death
4	Rohiṇī	Death	18	Jyeṣṭhā	Death
5	Mṛga-śiras	(1) Death	19	Mūla	Death
6	Ārdrā	Death	20	P. Āṣāḍha	Death
7	Punar-vasu	Great Victory	21	U. Āṣāḍha	Death
8	Puṣya	Great Victory	22	Abhijit	Death
9	Āśleṣā	Victory	23	Śravaṇa	Death
10	Maghā	Victory	24	Dhaniṣṭhā	Great Victory
11	P. Phāl-gunī	Victory	25	Śatabhi-ṣak	Great Victory
12	U. Phālgunī	Victory	26	P. Bhādra	Victory
13	Hasta	Victory	27	U. Bhādra	Victory
14	Citrā	Victory	28	Revatī	Victory

Chart 12.2. Sūrya-Kālāgni Cakra

Counting is done with reference to the star posited by the Sun

S. No.	Natal Star (N.S.)	Effect	S. No.	Natal Star (N.S.)	Effect
1	Aśvinī	Victory	15	Svātī	Wounds
2	Bharaṇī	Victory	16	Viśākhā	Death
3	Kṛttikā	Victory	17	Anurā	Wounds
4	Rohiṇī	Fear	18	Jyeṣṭhā	Wounds
5	Mṛga. (1)	Fear	19	Mūla	Death
6	Ārdrā	Fear	20	P. Āṣāḍhā	Wounds
7	Punar.	Victory	21	U. Āṣāḍhā	Wounds
8	Puṣya	Victory	22	Abhijit	Death
9	Āśleṣā	Victory	23	Śravaṇa	Wounds
10	Maghā	Victory	24	Dhani	Victory
11	P. Phalgu.	Victory	25	Śatabhi	Victory
12	U. Phalgu.	Victory	26	P. Bhād.	Victory
13	Hasta	Victory	27	U. Bhād.	Victory
14	Citrā	Victory	28	Revatī	Victory

Chart 12.3. *Sūrya-Śūla Cakra*

S. No.	N.S.	Effect	S. No.	N. S.	Effect
1	Aśvinī	Victory	15	Svātī	Death
2	Bharaṇī	Victory	16	Viśā.	Defeat
3	Kṛttikā.	Victory	17	Anurā.	Defeat
4	Rohiṇī	Death	18	Jyeṣṭhā	Defeat
5	Mṛga (1)	Death	19	Mūla	Defeat
6	Ārdrā	Death	20	P. Āṣā.	Defeat
7	Punar.	Victory	21	U. Āṣā.	Defeat
8	Puṣya	Victory	22	Śrava.	Death
9	Āśle.	Victory	23	Dhani.	Death
10	Maghā	Victory	24	Śata.	Death
11	P. Pha.	Victory	25	P. Bhā.	Victory
12	U. Pha.	Victory	26	U. Bhā.	Victory
13	Hasta	Death	27	Revatī	Victory
14	Citrā	Death	—	—	—

group of 45 days to the south; the next group to the north-east; the next group beginning with the month of *Āśvina* to the west; the group to the south-east; the next group to the north; and the last to the south-west. Thus 24 fortnights or half-months of the lunar calendar are distributed among the 8 quarters, not in order. In certain periods particular directions are considered strong. Here the order is east, N. W., south, N.E., west, S.E., north and S.W. A party that fights in a particular season of 45 days, having the direction assigned to that season either to its right or at the back, would be victorious. (*Notes*: This rule could be tested in sports and cricket and tennis matches.)

HUNTING

(1) If both Mars and Mercury are powerful at the time, the hunting will be very successful; otherwise not. When strong planets are posited in watery signs, the hunting relates to aquatic animals; and when they are dry signs, it takes place in a mountain or a forest.

(2) If the lords of the ascendant and 7th house are weak and posited in *kendras*, the hunting would involve in a good deal of suffering to the hunters. If they be strong, it would be very pleasant.

(3) At a query about hunting, if the 8th house from the *Ārūḍha* happens to be Aries or Scorpio or if the 8th house from the ascendant be posited by Mars, or Mars be in a *kendra*, a boar with its young one would be killed. If the Sun be in a *kendra* from the *lagna*, a tiger would be killed. If Mercury or Venus be in the *lagna*, a *kendra*, 8th house or the 11th house, no animal would be killed. On the other hand, if *Mars*, be in a *kendra* and Venus in 1, 8 or 11, the beast, though wounded, would run away.

(4) If Mars be in the ascendant which is a movable sign, *Māndī* be in the 8th and Saturn in the 4th, a boar would undoubtedly be caught.

(5) If the Sun, Saturn, Mars and Rāhu occupy in order the 4th, 7th, 1st and 10th, there will be great slaughter of beasts in the hunt.

(6) Should malefics be in movable signs and benefics in immovable *Rāśis* and *Māndī* in the 3rd house from the *lagna* at query, wild beasts like tiger would be killed.

(7) Should malefics be in the 1st, 4th, 7th, 10th, 5th and 9th from the *Ārūḍha* which is Capricorn, and *Māndī* be in the 3rd house, this is an excellent Yoga for success in the hunting expedition.

(8) If the Moon and Mars be in the 8th house, *Yamakaṇṭaka* in the 9th, and *Māndī* in the 3rd, pregnant animals would be killed. The class of animals that would be hunted should be gathered from the decanate of the *Ārūḍha*.

Place and Direction

The direction and type of terrain of hunting should be read from the directions allotted to the *Rāśis* and planets. So is the terrain. The number of animals will have to be calculated through the number of *Raśmis* (rays) that are assigned to signs and planets, taking into consideration the position of planets that are in inimical, or debilitation houses and eclipsed. (The topic of *raśmis* has been discussed in connection with thefts and wells.) Trapping of animals should be seen from the weakness such as debilitation of planets. Each sign and planet have their own direction and terrain.

Planets and Animals

Mighty beasts like lions are to be guessed from the Sun; gentle ones like hares from the Moon; cruel ones like tigers from Mars; boars and such other animals from Mercury; elephants and horses from Jupiter; groups of deer from Venus; monkeys, donkeys and camels from Saturn; alligators from Rāhu. The Sun and Saturn suggest biped beings; the Moon and Mercury, six-footed creatures; Mars and Jupiter, quadrupeds. Venus and Rāhu point to eight-footed creatures.

Signs and Animals

Signs Aries, Taurus, Leo and Sagittarius are quadruped ones. If the Sun is posited in Sagittarius, you should think of an elephant; if he be in Aries or Leo, of a lion; if he be in Taurus, of an antelope. If the Moon be in *Dhanus*, think of a horse; if she be in Leo, of a lion; if she be in Aries, of a goat; and if she be in Taurus, of a bull or cow. Mars in Dhanus suggests a horse; in *Siṁha*, a tiger; in Aries, a goat; and in Taurus, a bull.

Mercury in Leo and Sagittarius or in Aries and Taurus, porcupine, some cruel beast, and monkey group; Jupiter in *Dhanus* suggests a horse; in Leo, camel; and in Aries and Taurus, camel and donkey. Venus in *Dhanus* speaks of a horse, in Aries and Leo, of elephants and asses, and in Taurus, of wild bulls. Saturn in *Dhanus* shows elephants; in Leo, bears; in Aries, bisons (buffaloes) in Taurus, she-buffaloes. The first half of Capricorn and the latter half of Sagittarius are termed quadruped.

In a query about hunting judgment should be based on the planets posited in the *Ārūḍha*, *kendras*, and trines; and the animals should be those that are assigned to those planets. Those animals ruled by the planets that are associated with or aspected by *Māndī*, would be killed in the expedition.

ROYALTY

In a query about royalty the 12 houses from the ascendant represent: (1) king's physical condition; (2) his treasury; (3) the army and commander-in-chief; (4) vehicles, chariots, elephants, horses etc; (5) king's ministers and their decisions; (6) enemies, hurdles, espionage work etc.; (7) marching against an enemy; (8) longevity, health etc.; (9) mental disposition; (10) activities; (11) income, profit, replenishment of the treasury; and (12) expenditure, loss, defeat etc. The body of kingdom has seven limbs viz. (1) the king, (2) ministers, (3) allies, (4) treasury, (5) territory, (6) fortifications or defence measures, and (7) armed forces consisting of the four divisions of elephants, horses, chariots and infantry. In modern parlance we can have air force, navy, infantry and armoured corps.

Malefics would ruin the *Bhāvas* they occupy except the 3rd and 11th. Similarly the Sun and Mars spoil all the *Bhāvas* except the 3rd, 10th and 11th. On the other hand, benefics are good in all houses, as they convert even bad houses into beneficial ones. A benefic in the *lagna* conduces to the health and sound development of the body. A benefic in the 6th curtails the enemy's power. The Moon in the 8th, however, cannot improve the *Bhāva*. Similar is the case with Venus in the 7th house. All the effects, good, bad and indifferent, occurring to the king would affect the subjects directly.

A king's fortune depends on the state of the following eight elements: (1) His own self, (2) princes and princesses, (3) treasury, (4) vehicles, (5) capital, (6) harem or queens, (7) ministers and priests, and (8) subjects.

The king's kingship should be deemed to be very pleasant and enjoyable under the following conditions:

(1) The luminaries being strong are to be in 1, 4, 7 or 10.

(2) The *Ārūḍha* or *lagna* should be Cancer or Leo. On the other hand, if they (luminaries) be in the 3rd, 6th, 9th or 12th house,

the *lagna* or *Ārūḍha* being other than Cancer and Leo, the person would have no chance of having the powers of a ruling monarch. Before pronouncing judgment on the query chart, the consultant ought to consider the querist's own horoscope and Yogas as well as his *daśā* and transitory effects.

KING'S RETINUE

In the query chart Mercury represents the *Yuvarāja* (heir-apparent), Mars the commander of the army and Jupiter and Venus, ministers. If these planets be strong, posited in exaltation, auspicious houses, having benefic association and aspect, their *Bhāvas* would be strong, prosperous and popular. On the contrary, they would be in trouble, or the king would be in trouble on account of these officers of state.

KING'S PROGRESS

Under the following conditions a king's power and pelf increase considerably:

(1) The *Ārūḍha* should be an upward-looking *Rāśi*. (2) The lord of the *Ārūḍha* should be close to his exaltation. (3) And other planets should be strong and in their exaltation *Aṁśas*.

Benefics in the 7th and 10th houses would confer stability and prosperity on the king; and in the 1st, 2nd and 5th houses, both honour and wealth. In the context of king's query malefics are harmful in the 11th and 12th house. So is the Moon in the ascendant, but she is good in the 10th house.

A king would win victory in war and have territorial gain as well as much wealth, if strong benefics or Mercury aspect the ascendant or the Moon that has neither the aspect of nor conjunction with malefics.

If a king queries an astrologer whether he has any chance of getting an elephant, the latter should consider the following elements: The sign Virgo and Jupiter are considered as significators for the elephant. Should Jupiter be in 1, 5, 7 or 9 identical with Virgo, the querist would get an elephant. This would be qûite certain, in case the lord of the 11th house be the owner of a quadruped sign, and be posited in a *kendra* or *koṇa*. The gain of elephant would take place very quickly, if the lords of the 9th and 10th houses be in a *kendra*.

Offerings to Kings

Take the *Arūḍha* and see if strong planets are posited in auspicious houses, especially the 11th. Now note the articles such as metal, roots (wooden) or animal, belonging to them. Similarly, note their quarters. Then make prediction according to the articles and directions regarding the type of articles and the directions from which they would arrive.

Acquisition of Ships

Under the following conditions acquisition of ships could be predicted:

(1) Lords of the 2nd and 11th houses should be in good houses.

(2) The ascendant should be a watery sign.

(3) The planets mentioned in (1) should be posited in watery signs or *Aṁśas*.

Destruction of ship should be predicted if the *lagna* be Capricorn, the lords of the 2nd and 11th houses be in debilitation, combustion etc., having the aspect or association of malefics, and presence in watery signs and *Aṁśas*.

About the outcome of war, first of all see the directions signified by *Rāśis*, occupied by Saturn, Rāhu, Ketu, and *Māndī*. The army that fights from that direction, would be defeated. In the case of individual soldier's success and defeat, take their natal signs. Should the lord of one's natal sign be eclipsed at the time, that particular soldier would be defeated. The army that fights from an elevated place and direction signified by the *Rāśi* which is *Śirṣodaya* or *ūrdhvamukha*, would be victorious. If at question time the querist commander touches his head with his right hand, his army would win victory.

Death in battle: Soldiers who occupy and those who face the directions signified by the *Rāśis*, viz. the south, and south-east, as well as those who touch their knee at the time, or those who hold their weapons aloft, will perish in the battle.

Signs of Victory

(1) If the querists stands in a cardinal direction and his touch and sight are auspicious, he would snatch away the enemy's weapon and kill him. On the other hand, if the querist stands in

an intermediate direction or faces it, or occupies a lower place, or touches his left side, his weapon would be snatched away by the enemy and be killed by him. (2) Touching one's chest, head, or the weapon in his right hand, or striking, breaking or cutting something while asking the question would lead to victory.

Sometimes a king gets intelligence report that his enemy is busy preparing for an attack on his capital. So he wants to know if the enemy would actually attack him or go back. The question is to be answered thus: If the Moon be in an immovable sign, and the ascendant be a movable *Rāśi* and *Aṁśa*, the strong enemy would soon march against his city. On the contrary he will not come forward.

Should the Moon occupy a dual sign, and the *lagna* be an immovable sign, and Mercury, Jupiter and Venus be in the 6th house, the enemy, though strong, would beat a hasty retreat, being vanquished in battle.

If the Moon be in a movable sign and the ascendant a dual *Rāśi*, the enemy having come half-way, would go back. On the other hand, should the *lagna* be a movable sign and the Moon be in a dual sign, the enemy would attack from two sides. If the query ascendant be aspected by malefics, the enemy would be trounced. Similarly, if malefics occupy the 5th and 6th houses, the enemy would go back after going forward a little. Should malefics be in the 4th house, he would go back having suffered a humiliating defeat. If there be malefics in the following six houses viz. 1, 2, 3, 5, 6 and 12, the enemy-army would approach the city, whereas if all the malefics be in the 4th house, it would not. The enemy-army will not proceed forward, if the luminaries occupy the 4th house. When Mercury, Jupiter and Venus are in the 4th house, the enemy will come soon to fight.

Under the following condition the enemy will go back without fighting: The ascendant or the 4th house should be one of the four signs viz. Aries, Taurus, Leo and Sagittarius, and there be no planet in it. The enemy comes forward and fights, if the *lagna* be a movable *Rāśi* occupied by the Sun or Jupiter. On the other hand, if the *lagna* be an immovable sign occupied by Jupiter or Saturn, he will not come forward to fight.

The enemy would not arrive, if the lords of the *lagna*, 8th and 9th houses be in fixed *Rāśis*. The same prediction is to be made when the ascendant and planets are in fixed *Rāśis*. Should the lords of the *lagna* and 9th house be together or aspect each other, the enemy does not arrive. If the *lagna* which is a movable sign be occupied by anyone of the four planets viz. Saturn, Venus, Mercury and the Sun, the enemy would march forward. The result will be otherwise, if the ascendant is a fixed sign.

If there be a malefic in the *lagna* of query, the enemy would retrace his steps, and during his retreat would meet with his end owing to his ill luck. If the 4th house be Cancer, Scorpio, Aquarius or Pisces, aspected by benefics, the foe will be defeated. On the other hand, if Aries or Taurus happens to be the 4th house, conjoined with malefics, the foe would march forward. According to the *Ṣaṭpañcāśikā* the enemy would run away, should a quadruped sign be the 4th house.

Defenders and Attackers

The semi-circle beginning with the 9th house and ending with the 2nd, represents the marching foes (*Yāyins*) while the other half from the 3rd to the 8th defenders of the City (pauras). Whichever semi-circle contains benefics, wins victory, and the other suffers defeat.

Treaty

If benefics occupy the ascendant, 11th or 12th house which is a biped sign, there would be treaty between the contending kings. In case of malefics occupying it, there would be no treaty.

Enemy's Return

Count the number of the *Rāśi* occupied by the strongest planet from the *lagna*. In so many months the enemy (*Yāyin*) will return to his city.

The enemy's arrival will take place in so many days as are signified by the number of the *Rāśi* occupied by the Moon from the ascendant, provided there are no planets intervening between the two. Benefics posited in the 1st, 7th and 10th houses confer victory on the lord of the town that is attacked; and Mars and Saturn in the 9th house, cause a miserable defeat, whereas Mercury, Jupiter and Venus in the 9th bestow great victory on him. Similarly, malefics in 10, 11 and 12 cause sufferings to the defenders of the town, but prove advantageous to the besiegers. Malefics in the *lagna*, 12th and 11th houses which are dual *Rāśis* will lead to the prolongation of hostilities.

FORTRESS

If there be a malefic in the *lagna* at query, the fortress would not be broken, even if the planet be weak. Especially, when Mars or Rāhu be posited in the *lagna*, even Indra would not be able to break the fortress. If the 7th house be occupied by Rāhu, the fortress would be destroyed quickly. The rule is that a malefic in the *lagna* is favourable to the defenders, while malefic aspect on it is bad for them. The fortress would not collapse, if the *lagna* and the 7th house be devoid of planets, and the lord of the *lagna* be in the 2nd, 6th, 8th, or 12th house.

When all the four benefics or at least three of them endowed with strength are posited in the 8th house, the enemy will kill the defender of the town in the battle-field. On the other hand, should these benefics occupy the 4th or 10th house, there would, soon be treaty between the two parties. Benefics in the 5th house, and malefics in the 9th force the defender to flee the country as a result of the superiority of the attackers. Benefics in the 1st, 12th and 11th houses that are biped signs confer peace on the contestants. And this treaty would be brought about by the mediation of a person of the particular class signified by the planet situated between the lords of the *lagna* and the 7th house. If there be benefics between the two planets, it would be through the efforts of scholars and scientists. When all the three benefics viz. Jupiter, Venus and Mercury, endowed with strength, occupy together the ascendant, or at least two of them, or Jupiter or Venus occupies it, the lord of the town would kill the attacking king in battle. When all the five planets viz. the Sun, Moon, Mars, Saturn and Rāhu, or four or three at least occupy the *lagna*, the attacking king would soon kill the defender of the town; whereas when they be posited in the 7th house, the defending king would kill the attacker. If there be a malefic in the 7th house, and a benefic in the *lagna*, the defender would have to pay a ransom to the besieger. If it be otherwise, i.e. malefic in the 1st house and benefic in the 7th house, the attacking foe would dislodge the defender from his fortress, and then perhaps restore it to him.

Armed Conflict

The lord of the *lagna* who is retrograde, associated with malefics and posited in a *kendra*, brings about an armed conflict. The same result would follow, if a malefic or lord of the 6th house, be posited in the 7th house. If malefics occupy *kendras* at a query, there would be great slaughter inside the fortress. The same effect should be predicted, when the lord of the 8th house and Mars are conjoined. There would be no fear for the garrison, if Jupiter be in the 2nd, 5th or 11th house. When both Mars and Saturn are in *kendras* a large number of soldiers will be killed and several captured. There would be a sanguinary battle, should a malefic conjoin with or aspected by another malefic occupy the *lagna*, or if the *lagna* be surrounded by malefics. If two malefics occupying any houses fully aspect each other, both the fighters would be killed.

Time of Victory or Defeat

Multiply the number of *Navāṁśas* fully passed in the *lagna* by the time allotted to the lord of the *lagna*. The expected victory or defeat will take place in so many (*Ayana*) solstices etc. The time assigned to the 7 planets from the Sun onwards is (1) Six months, (2) a moment, (3) day, (4) two months, (5) a month, (6) a fortnight and (7) a year. This may be used to find out the time of the enemy's arrival or retreat.

Another Method

If the planet that suggests the time limit, is in a movable sign, there is no necessity for multiplying it further. On the other hand, if he be in an immovable sign, you should multiply the time by 3. If he be in a dual sign, it should be doubled.

Truce

If the querist sits or stands touching another person, or joins his hands, there would be truce or treaty. The same result will have to be stated, if a planet posited in own house or friendly one aspects the *lagna*. Similarly, Mercury in an *Āpoklima* house,

(3, 6, 9 or 12), a benefic in the ascendant or benefic-aspect on the *lagna* and the 9th house, would certainly conduce to truce.

If there be a strong malefic that is victorious in a planetary war in the 7th house, the querist king would get plenty of wealth without fighting. On the other hand, should a strong malefic be in the *lagna*, truce would be broken leading to *re-crudescence* of fighting. If the *lagna*, 11th and 12th houses, which are biped *Rāśis*, be occupied by benefics, there would be peace without much delay; whereas malefics in these houses that are dual signs, truce would not last long. If the *kendras* are occupied by benefics that are aspected by benefics, or if the ascendant is occupied by benefics, there would be mutual understanding between the parties. On the other hand, should malefics be there being aspected by malefics, hostilities would escalate.

Fighting

The following conditions lead to war:

(1) Malefics in the ascendant, Mercury in the 3rd house, and the Sun in the 4th house. In the war the defenders of the town would suffer defeat.

(2) Malefics aspected by malefics should occupy *kendras* in Mars' *varga* (*Rāśi, Decanate, Navāṁśa* etc.). If these malefics be inimical to the lord of the ascendant, war is quite certain.

(3) The minor planets, *Kāla*, *Māndī* and Rāhu, that aspect or occupy the *lagna*, would bring about a horrible holocaust.

(4) The Sun and Mars aspecting or occupying the ascendant.

Querist's Victory

At a query if Saturn, the Moon and Mars be in the 11th house Venus in the *lagna*, the Sun in the 3rd house, Mercury in the 4th house and Jupiter in the 5th, the querist king would vanquish his enemy.

Solar and Lunar Signs

Leo, Virgo, Libra, Scorpio, Aquarius and Pisces are termed the Sun's *Rāśis*; while the rest belong to the Moon.

Should both the luminaries occupy the solar signs, the *yāyin* (attacking) king becomes victorious, whereas if they be in the lunar signs, the defender wins.

If the Sun be in a lunar sign, the attacking king wins, while if the Moon be in a solar sign, the defending king wins. Should the luminaries occupy each other's *Rāśis*, both the contestants would be wounded. On the other hand, should the two occupy their respective *Rāśis*, the fighters would be unwilling to fight.

Fighter's Limbs

According to *Parāśara* the 27 stars are distributed as follows beginning with the natal star of the querist: The natal star is assigned to the face; the 2nd to the left eye; 3, 4 and 5 to the head; 6 to right eye; 7 to the right ear; 8, 9, 10 and 11 to the right hand; 12, 13, 14 to the right foot; 15 to 19 to the chest; 20 to the neck; 21 to 24 to the left hand and lastly 25, 26 and 27 to the left foot.

The querist would get wounds in those limbs signified by the stars occupied by strong malefics, that are posited in untoward houses.

Asterisms for King's Success

A king should acquire weapons in *Dhaniṣṭhā* star; collect wealth in *Uttarābhādra*; and pierce the enemy's defences in the same asterism for success in the war. He should start the war when both the Moon and Mars be in the *lagna* and in the same *Aṁśa* and in their respective *vargas*. If these conditions are fulfilled, the querist is sure to win victory.

He should select Tuesday when Mars is rising in the *lagna*, which synchronizes with *Viṣa Ghaṭī*, and discharge his arrow against the enemy-army after meditating on fire and water. He should stand in the direction of the rising of *Viṣṭi*. If this is followed, the army of the enemy king would run helter-skelter being routed in the war.

[*Viṣṭyudaya* is explained by *Vidyāmādhava* in Chapter II. In the *bright* fortnight on the 4th lunar day *Viṣṭi* rises in the first *Ghaṭī* of the fifth watch in the west; on the 8th lunar day it rises in the south-east in the 3rd *Ghaṭī* of the second watch; on the 11th lunar day in the north in the 5th *Ghaṭī* of the seventh watch; on full Moon day, in south-west in the last *Ghaṭī* of the fourth watch. In the dark fortnight on the 3rd lunar day it rises in the north-west in the 3rd *Ghaṭī* of the 6th watch; on the 7th day in the south in the 5th *Ghaṭī* of the 3rd watch; on the 10th day in the north-east in the last *Ghaṭī* of the 8th watch; and on the 14th day it rises in the east in the first *Ghaṭī* of the first watch.]

Bad Omens

(1) Should fire break out suddenly in a temple, palace, arch or banners, enemy-army would attack the kingdom within six months.

(2) Appearance of smoke without fire, excessive dust and pitch darkness—are dangerous portents.

(3) Disappearance of stars in the sky without clouds, and appearance of stars in the daytime.

(4) If suddenly branches of trees near the king's palace break, it forebodes preparation for war. Should the trees be uprooted, the king would flee the country. If there be sounds similar to crying emanating from the breaking trees, there would be an outbreak of epidemics.

(5) Unseasonal flowers point to destruction of the country. If creepers put forth flowers too early, it portends destruction of children. If the sap oozes from trees. there would be complete destruction of all produce and products.

(6) If a liquid resembling liquor oozes from trees, there will be destruction of military vehicles; if it is like blood, there will be war; if it is like honey, it portends pestilence, and if it is like oil or water, famine or great danger. The above portends bear fruit within ten months.

(7) If domestic birds wander in forests, or wild ones come to town; and if nocturnal animals are seen during daytime and diurnal ones at night, there would be great danger to the country.

(8) So are the following: Swarm of birds attacking houses, shrine, *Aśvattha* tree etc. in the capital, honeycombs appearing in these places, as well as sudden sight of jasmine, lotus or snakes there.

Bad Omens for House-Owner

(1) The owner of the house into which dogs enter or bring pieces of carcass or bones, would die soon.

(2) If there be smoke without fire in the forests in the morning and evening, the earth carving in without any cavity or earthquake, there would be danger ahead.

(3) A house which is full of cobwebs, where a sacred lamp is not lit morning and evening, where quarrels take place, which is not cleaned and managed by a woman, is not destined to prosper.

(4) The country ruled by a king who is a heretic, has no faith in God, whose conduct is reprehensible, who is cruel, jealous, irascible, and eager to fight, will be ruined.

(5) Should a group of carnivorous birds follow a marching army, it would suffer defeat.

The royal astrologer should observe good and bad omens and predict results. For, it is not easy to find out the strength and weakness of planets and *Rāśis* in all cases. Hence these auguries, which have been explained elaborately by *Ācārya* Varāhamihira, are found very useful. The omens also help the astrologer in comparing the results of the planetary positions, *daśās*, transits etc. with those of the omens as well as with those of the query, and confirm his judgments. If he finds that the results are discouraging, he should advise the king to perform proper expiatory rites. For, our ancient culture is not fatalistic. It gives full scope for the development of free-will. Accordingly says poet Māgha "A wise man does not entirely depend on fate, nor in his power or self-effort, but utilizes both to his advantage just as a good poet uses both sound and sense."

Time for War

A king wishing for victory should select a very convenient season (like autumn), asterism, lunar day and sign for starting on his *Jaitrayātrā*—victory march. He should start when the omens are good and transitory effects to his advantage, when the lord of his natal *Rāśi* is powerful, the planet presiding over his class is strong, under a permissible asterism and in a *lagna* which is a movable sign that rises with its head first and is called upward-looking. The star *Citrā* and *Chidra tithis* should be shunned for this. It has been already stated that Gemini ascendant is harmful to travel. It should also be in tune with the direction of the *Rāśi*.

(1) For day-marching a diurnal *Rāśi* is good; so is a nocturnal one for night-marching.

(2) If the Sun or the Moon be in the ascendant, which is a movable sign, a king may march against an alien enemy; if it be a fixed sign, he should go back to his capital; and if a dual sign, it would be all right for both marching out and returning home.

(3) The *lagna* should be so elected for marching out that it happens to be the 2nd, 3rd, 6th or 11th *Rāśi* from the marcher's natal ascendant or lunar sign.

(4) The king should find out secretly the enemy's natal ascendant and lunar sign, through spies. If he starts on a day when the ascendant and lunar sign are the 8th from the enemy's natal ascendant and lunar sign respectively, the enemy would undoubtedly be destroyed, provided the elected ascendant at least be conjoined with malefics.

Query About Journey

Sometimes people want to know if their proposed journey would materialize or not. Then the astrologer finds out the *Ārūḍha* etc. and proceeds to delineate the prospects:

(1) If a benefic be posited in the *lagna*, or the latter has attained the *Varga* (out of six) of a benefic, the astrologer would predict that the querist's proposed journey would materialize.

(2) The same result would follow, if the ascendant be a *Śīrṣodaya* sign occupied by a benefic.

(3) If benefics occupy *kendras* or trines and malefics the 3rd, 6th and 11th houses, the person would be successful.

(4) If the Moon be posited in the ascendant, which is a movable sign, or in a movable *Navāṁśa* of the *lagna*, or in the 4th house, the traveller would go out, complete his task and safely return home.

(5) When at least one of the planets viz. Venus, the Sun, Jupiter and Mercury, be in the 11th house, he would soon go on the journey. Should, however, one of them be in the 12th house, there would be no journey.

Return Journey

Find out the planet that is strongest among them. Count the number of *Rāśis* from the ascendant to the one occupied by the strongest planet. In so many months the traveller would return home. This is the rule regarding the time of return in months, if the above-named planet be posited in a movable *Aṁśa*; if it be an immovable *Aṁśa*, the number should be doubled; and if it be a dual *Aṁśa*, it should be trebled. According to some authors the time of return of the traveller would synchronize with the commencement of retrogression of the lord of the 7th house.

No Journey

(1) If there be a benefic in the 4th or 10th house, the person would not be able to go on the tour. However, should malefics be posited in these houses, the journey would materialize.

(2) Note the number of benefics posited in the 7th house from the *lagna* or its lord. The traveller would have advantages in so many places on the way.

(3) Similarly, he will have troubles in as many places on the way as the number of malefics occupying the 9th or 12th house from the ascendant or its lord.

(4) If Saturn conjoined with or aspected by malefics, and not connected with benefics, be posited in the 9th house, he would cause illness to the traveller, and if posited in the 8th house, death.

(5) Should the 7th house be surrounded by benefics, the traveller does not return owing to the compulsion of friends and masters; and if surrounded by malefics, his non-arrival is due to enemies, illness or thieves.

(6) If the luminaries be posited in the 8th house, aspected by Saturn, the traveller would run the risk of being hit by weapons. On the other hand, should Venus and Mercury be in the 8th house, he would be happy on the way.

(7) Should Mars or Saturn, aspected by or conjoined with a malefic, be in the 8th house, the person would be in danger during his journey.

(8) If weak benefics, aspected by malefics, occupy the three evil houses (6, 8 and 12), and the luminaries in conjunction with malefics in any house, the traveller would be dead.

(9) The above prediction of death due to illness will have to be made in the following conditions: The ascendant should be a *Pṛṣṭhodaya* sign having a malefic in it, and malefics devoid of benefic aspect be in *kendras*, trines, 6th and 8th houses, and the Sun be in the 9th house. (*Note*: The above predictions are to be made also in queries about the condition of a person who has gone on a tour.)

If a querist wants to know whether the person who has gone away from home is well or ill or dead, note the following planetary conditions for giving proper answers:

(1) If Jupiter and Venus be in the 2nd or 3rd house from the *Ārūḍha* or the ascendant, the traveller would surely return home very soon.

(2) The same result will follow, if Venus, Jupiter or the Moon be posited in the 4th house.

(3) A benefic being posited in the 6th or 7th house, Jupiter in a *kendra*, and Mercury or Venus in a trine, would make the tourist return home early.

(4) Death of the person on tour would result, should the ascendant be a *Pṛṣṭhodaya* sign, aspected by malefics and not by benefics, and the 6th house be occupied by malefics.

(5) When malefics be in the 3rd house, the traveller must have gone to another place from the country to which he had gone first. If they be in *kendras*, his belongings would be purloined by thieves.

(6) Should Saturn, aspected by a malefic, occupy the 4th, 5th, 8th or 9th house which is ruled by a malefic, the traveller would surely be in captivity.

(7) If the ascendant which is a fixed sign, be occupied by a benefic, the captivity alluded to in the previous condition, would be permanent; whereas if the *lagna* be a movable sign, it would be temporary. In the case of a dual sign with a benefic in it, imprisonment or release would have to be declared according to its proximity to the fixed or movable sign.

(8) When malefics, aspected by their enemies be in the 7th or trines, and the ascendant be a *Pṛṣṭhodaya* sign, the person concerned would be in difficulties.

(9) Should the Moon be in the 7th house, whose lord be in the latter half of the sign the, he is in traveller should be said to be on his way back.

Chapter XIII

RAINFALL

In India we have six seasons viz. spring, summer, monsoon, autumn, dewy and winter. No doubt, everyone of them is important in its own sphere. Still the rainy season has assumed special importance in that rain is an important source of water and so a significant factor in the production of food-grains and fodder. Hence we see in the Vedic *Sūkta* addressed to goddess Śrī a humble prayer—"May the clouds in the sky pour down rain on the earth, and all seeds sprout well". When rains are delayed or are excessive, inundating the earth and devastating fertile lands, agriculturists and rural people get naturally frightened and go to a good diviner to find out as to when they would get relief. In ancient times elders in society used to look up at the heavens for signs of clouds, storm etc. For, under *Pāṇini's Sūtra* (1-4-44) the Mahābhāṣya-kāra quotes the following *Vārtika* in verse, meaning, "A tawny streak of lightning presages strong winds; a deep red one, burning heat; a yellowish one, rain; and a white one, famine." The famous astrologer-cum-astronomer Varāhamihira treats of the subject of rain extensively in eight chapter in his unique work, *Bṛhat Saṁhitā*:

(1) There would be plentiful rain in the month, if at the time of the Sun's entry into Gemini the Moon be in a watery sign or *Aṁśa*, and Venus be in the 2nd or 12th place from the Sun.

(2) There would be heavy rain, should the Sun, Moon, Mars Saturn and Rāhu be posited in watery signs, and Mercury and Venus in earth signs.

(3) If both the Sun and Venus be posited in the same sign and *Aṁśa* along with Mercury, the earth would be inundated by heavy rains; it would be most certain, if these planets be in a watery sign or *Aṁśa*.

(4) If Venus and Mercury be in the same sign and *Aṁśa*, and be eclipsed, and if Mars be beneath Venus, there would be heavy rains.

(5) The same result would follow, if the Sun be in an earth-sign, the Moon, Mercury and Venus in watery *Vargas*, and a rainbow seen in the western sky.

(6) If a rainbow be sighted in the eastern sky, the Moon in a watery *Varga* and Saturn in an earth sign, the result would be the same.

If in the rainy season a rainbow appears in the eastern horizon, rainfall will not take place. On the other hand, if it appears in any other season, there will be rain. However, a rainbow appearing in the western sky would bring down rain irrespective of the season.

Mock-Sun

When the Sun's rays are covered by a bank of clouds, the rays appear to be in friction and show themselves as another Sun. This is termed *Prati-Sūrya* or Mock-Sun. If the Mock-Sun appears to the north of the Sun's disc, there would be rain; if to the south, storm, if on both sides, floods; if above it, danger to the king; and if beneath it, calamity to the people.

(1) If during the monsoon there be rainfall on the new-Moon day and the next day, i.e. the first day of the light half, there would be good rains in the fortnight. On the other hand, should there be rain on the full-Moon day and the next day too, there would be no rain in that dark fortnight.

(2) If there be rain in the first or last quarter of the *Pratipat* (1st lunar day) of both the fortnights, there would be good rains in the fortnight. Should the rainfall be scanty in that quarter of the lunar day, it would be poor during the fortnight, and if there be no rainfall at all, no rain in the fortnight.

Growth of Crops

(1) Should there be a north-easternly wind on the full-Moon day of *Āṣāḍha* at sunset. there would be excellent growth of crops.

(2) If there be rain on the fourth lunar day of the dark fortnight of the month of *Āṣāḍhu*, synchronizing with the asterism *Pūrvābhādrapada*, there would be good rains in the monsoon and consequently excellent crops.

(3) If the 5th lunar day of the bright fortnight in the month of *Āṣāḍha* happens to be Sunday and other days, the results would

be in order (1) scanty rains, (2) good rains, (3) torrential rains leading to much destruction, (4) cyclones, (5) good rains and excellent harvest, (6) deluge, and (7) drought and suffering.

(4) If the asterism *Rohiṇī* in the solar month of Kumbha should fall on the 6th lunar day, there would be very poor rainfall in the monsoon; if on the 7th lunar day, it would be slight; if on the 8th, pretty good rain, if on the 9th, heavy rain; and if on the 10th *tithi*, very heavy rain.

(5) When the Sun is transiting the very beginning of the asterism *Pūrvāṣāḍhā* in the sign Sagittarius, see if the sky is overcast and the Sun obstructed by a bank of clouds. If so, during the following rainy season, i.e. when the Sun transits the star *Ārdrā* in Gemini, there would be very good rainfall. Should there be no clouds at the time of observation, there would be no rain at all during the *Ārdrā* season. Similarly, when the Sun transits the 2nd division of 1/13 of the star, if there be clouds in the eastern horizon, there would be good rain during the period of the Sun's transiting the asterism *Puṇarvasu*. Similarly prediction about rainfall during the period of *Puṣya Mahānakṣatra* should be made on the results of observation of the sky when the Sun transits the 3rd division of 1/13 of the above star. The same rule applies to prediction about rainfall during *Āśleṣā Mahānakṣatra*, on the basis of the 4th division. In this manner rain is to be predicted in the 13 *Mahānakṣatras* beginning with *Ārdrā* and ending with Jyeṣṭhā corresponding to the 13 divisions of *Pūrvāṣāḍhā*, one division being 800/13.

Venus's Rise and Rain

The 27 stars of the Zodiac are grouped in 6 *Maṇḍalas* or Circles beginning with the star *Bharaṇī* as follows: (1) Four stars from *Bharaṇī*; (2) Four stars from *Ārdrā*; (3) Five stars from *Maghā*; (4) Three stars from *Svātī*; (5) Five stars from *Jyeṣṭhā*; and (6) Six stars from *Dhaniṣṭhā* to *Aśvinī*. Note in which star-circle Venus is posited when he emerges from combustion. If it be the 4th or the 6th circle, there would be very good rain and excellent harvest; if it be 1st or 2nd moderate rain; if it be the 3rd or 5th, scanty rain and poverty. Generally normal rainfall can be expected if Venus rises in any one of the 8 stars from *Bharaṇī* to *Āśleṣā*;

in *Citrā* to *Jyeṣṭhā*, scanty rain; and in the stars of the 4th and 6th circles, splendid rainfall and bumper crops.

If the Moon in the monsoon be posited in the 7th house from Venus and aspected by a benefic, there would be good rain. The same result would take place, if she be in the 5th, 7th or 9th from Saturn and receives benefic aspect.

I. Generally rain is expected in the following circumstances:

(1) Heliacal rising and setting of planets; (2) conjunction of the non-luminaries with the Moon; (3) their entering any of the six *Maṇḍalas* (and the Sun's passage into another sign); (4) end of a fortnight; (5) end of a solstice; and (6) the Sun's passage through the asterism *Ārdrā*.

II. When Mercury and Venus are together in a sign, there will be Copious rain. So is the case when Jupiter and Venus or Mercury and Jupiter come together. On the other hand, Mars and Saturn joining together without the aspect of and conjunction with benefics, would create danger from fire and storm.

III. Should the clouds be white like the Moon or Chunam at the edges and dark collyrium in the centre, glossy, have many layers, dropping particles of water, and are cut up like the steps of a staircase, and being formed in the east, sail westward or vice versa, they would drench the earth ere long with plentiful rains.

IV. If in the rainy season, the Sun, even while rising, cannot be looked at owing to its dazzling brilliance and appears like molten gold or possess the pure lustre of beryl, or if it burns with intense heat at the zenith of the sky, there would be rain the very same day.

Auguries of Rain

The following are symptoms of rain:

(1) Water becoming tasteless,

(2) The sky coloured like the cow's eyes (white and blue) or crow's eggs,

(3) The quarters being uncontaminated,

(4) Salt becoming moist,

(5) Wind being subdued,

(6) Fishes tumbling much ashore,

(7) The repeated croakings of frogs;

(8) If cats scratch the ground vehemently with their nails, rust

accumulates on iron or bronze vessels with the smell of raw meat or fish, and children construct bridges on the roads, there would be rain almost immediately.

(9) Mountains looking like heaps of collyrium, or their caves wrapped in vapour, and haloes round the Moon with colour of cock's eyes (deep red) are harbingers of rain.

(10) Ants shifting their eggs without any trouble, mating of snakes, climbing down the trees by snakes and cow's leaping are also auguries of rain.

(11) If chameleons perched on tree-tops fix their gaze on the firmament, and cows (or bulls) look up towards the Sun, there would be rain before long.

(12) Should the domestic animals like cows show their unwillingness to go out of the house and shake their ears and hoofs, or if dogs behave in the same manner, there would be rain soon.

(13) When dogs stand on house-tops, or bark continuously looking up towards the sky, or when lightning appears in the north-east at daytime, the earth would be submerged in water.

(14) When the Moon appears with the red hue of the eyes of a parrot or pigeon or of honey, and when a second Moon shines in the sky, there would be immediate rain.

(15) Should there be peals of thunder at night and blood-red streaks of lightning standing erect like rods at daytime, and if there be a cool breeze blowing from the east, there would soon be rain.

(16) If the sprouts of creepers are turned up towards the sky, birds bathe in water or dust, and reptiles or worms are seated on the tips of grass, there will be immediate rain.

(17) Should clouds at dawn or dusk possess the same colour as peacocks, parrots, blue-joys or *Cātaka* birds, or have the lustre of roses and red lotuses and resemble in shape waves, hills, crocodiles etc., and are piled up in many layers, rain would pour down before long.

(18) Should a rainbow, a cross bar of clouds, a mock Sun, a straight fragmentary rainbow, flashes of lightning and haloes round the Sun be sighted at sunrise or sunset, there would be copious rain in the near future.

(19) If the sky be variegated like the feathers of the *Tittiri* bird and groups of birds twitter merrily at sunrise or sunset, then the

clouds would pour down rain soon by day or night, as the case may be.

(20) When many planets are about to be eclipsed by the Sun in front or behind (slower planets in front and faster ones behind), they tend to turn the earth into an ocean, as it were.

(21) If there be glow-worms at night near the clouds, there would be rain ere long flooding all the fields. In spite of rains should jackals howl in the evening, there would not be a drop of rain, though the sky is overcast for a week at a stretch.

Query About Rain

If at a query about rain, the Moon be posited in the ascendant that happens to be a watery sign, or in the 4th, 7th or 10th house from the *lagna* in the bright fortnight, there would be copious rain in the monsoon, provided she is aspected by benefics.

If the querist touches any wet object or water or milk, or stands near water, or somebody utters that word at the time, there would be rain almost immediately. So is the sight of liquor, butter, a pregnant woman, elephant, Brāhmaṇa and buffalo.

(1) The following phenomena being glossy at a *Sandhyā* (juncture) indicate immediate rain: *Daṇḍa* (a rod-like formation caused by the combination of Sun-beams, clouds and wind), lightning, fish-like formations of clouds, a mock Sun, a halo, a rainbow, *Airāvata* (a long fragmentary rainbow) and the Sun's rays.

(2) *A cloud-tree*—a blue cloud with its top resembling curds, being situated at the Zenith of the sky, screening the Sun as well as those that are tinged yellow, having a dense bottom, would produce copious rains.

(3) A twilight which has the lustre of blue lily, beryl or lotus filaments, which is free from strong winds and which is brightened by the Sun's rays, brings down rain the same day.

(4) A twilight that possesses clouds of inauspicious forms (like those of an ass, camel, headless trunk, crow, cat etc.), an aerial city, fog, smoke and dust, produces drought in the rainy season.

(5) Should the Sun be screened on the right side by clouds that are white or white-fringed, there would be rain. The same result would ensue, if it be screened likewise by clouds which

resemble bushes of Andropogon grass, and which arise in an unblasted (not heated by the Sun) quarter.

(6) If there be mock Suns touching the Sun on both sides, there would be abundant rain. Should they, however, surround the Sun on all the four sides, not a drop of rain would fall.

Weekdays and Rain

Should the month of *Caitra* commence on a Sunday, there would be no rain in the initial part of the month. Even thereafter there would be no rain everywhere, but only scattered rain: if the commencement be on a Monday, there would be scanty and belated rain in the monsoon; if it be on Tuesday, the rain would occur mostly on mountains; if on Wednesday, rainfall would be copious; if on Thursday, very heavy downpour leading to much calamity; if on Friday, rainfall would be scanty but crops plenty; and if on Saturday, people would perish through diseases, and crops too be destroyed.

The Sun's Ingress into Capricorn and Aries

If the Sun's ingress into these two signs takes place under the asterism *Aśvinī*, there will be good rain at the appropriate time; under *Bharaṇī*, people will perish, but food-crops flourish; under *Kṛttikā*, trouble from kings (or to kings), scanty rainfall and outbreak of fire; under *Rohiṇī*, danger to Brāhmaṇas, but rain in the beginning; under Mṛgaśiras, rain scanty and destruction of cattle; under *Ārdrā*, good rain, and slight destruction of crops: under *Punarvasu*, rain in the beginning, diseases of men and cattle, as well as increase of wicked deeds; under *Puṣya*, copious rains but destruction of crops; under *Āśleṣā*, heavy rains, danger from dacoits, and serious fighting; under *Maghā*, much trouble from the rulers and loss of crops, but good rains; under *Pūrvaphālguṇī* and Uttara P., destruction of Brāhmaṇas and Śūdras, but abundance of food crops; under *Hasta*, health and happiness of the people and plenty of food; under *Citrā*, scanty rain and many disasters, but good health; under *Svātī*, copious rains, abundant food and progress and prosperity of Brāhmaṇas, but trouble to labourers; under *Viśākhā*, scattered rains, good crops, epidemics among the people and trouble to labourers; under *Anurādhā* and *Jyeṣṭhā*, good rains, and destruction of crops; under *Mūla*, heavy rain, diseases of men and cattle and obstruction to the acts of Brāhmaṇas; under *Purvāṣāḍhā*, abundant crops, and heavy rains which devastate the country towards the close of the season; under U. Āṣāḍhā, scanty rain; under *Śravaṇa*, good rainfall and bumper crops; under *Dhaniṣṭhā*, good rains in the beginning, but later no rain, and destruction of grains; under *Śatabhiṣak* and *Purvābhādra*, heavy rainfall and growth of base gains; under U. Bhādra, scarcity of rain and meritorious deeds, as well as poor stamina of the people; and under *Revatī*, splendid rains at the proper time and the earth being blessed with bounteous crops.

LUNAR DAY AND RAIN

Should the Sun's ingress into Aries take place on the first lunar day (*Pratipat*), there would be little rain; on the second as well as third *tithi*, good rainfall at the appropriate time, but growth of crops very poor; on the fourth day, a series of disasters and obstacles to men's undertakings; on the fifth day, abundant rainfall and bumper crops; on the sixth day, fierce battle, destruction of crops to some extent, and good rainfall; on the seventh day, good rains at the proper time, but trouble to the sovereign. (This rule should be applied to *Makara Saṅkrānti* too.)

If it takes place on the 8th lunar day, including the Sun's ingress into Capricorn as well as Cancer, there will be good rains and bumper crops; if on the 9th *tithi*, luxuriant growth of crops, but many disasters in the land; if on the 10th *tithi*, many troubles, good rain and sorrows; if on the 11th *tithi*, excessive rain, abundance of base grains and some trouble to the people; if on the 12th and 13th *tithis*, splendid rains in time, but trouble from violent robbers; if on the 14th *tithi*, there would be good rain in the beginning but not when needed; and on full and new Moon days, there would be fierce battles, excessive rain, and bountiful crops.

KARAṆAS AND RAIN

Should the *Bava* (Lion) *Karaṇa* synchronize with the Sun's entrance into sign Aries, there would be abundant rainfall, bumper crops and disasters owing to floods and diseases; if the

Bālava (Tiger) *Karaṇa*, good rains, but destruction of cattle and other domestic animals, and famine in some parts; if the *Kaulava* (Boar) *Karaṇa*, unpredictable rains accompanied by untold sufferings; if the *Taitila* (donkey) *Karaṇa*, growth of the cattle wealth, financial position and food crops, as well as bounteous rain for 12 days; if *Gaja* (elephant) *Karaṇa*, heavy rain in the beginning but not at the end; if the *Vaṇik* (Buffalo) *Karaṇa*, the previous effects are reversed; and all types of diseases; if the *Viṣṭi* (*Bhadra*-Horse), large-scale cattle disease, and other disasters, but luxuriant growth of crops and sufficient quantity of rain; if *Śakuni* (dog), the effects are the same as for *Viṣṭi*, but calamities would occur on a vaster scale; if *Catuspāt* (bull), excessive rain, destruction of crops and undertakings; if the *Nāga* (serpent) *Karaṇa*, unprecedented rains, and growth of crops; and if the *Kiṁstughna* (cock), partial destruction of crops in the beginning, but later at the time of harvest there would be a rich harvest and good rains.

Sun's Ingress Ascendant and Rains

If the *lagna* at the Sun's entry into Aries be Aries, Libra or Capricorn, there would be scattered rains for twelve days; if it be Scorpio, plenty of rain and crops; similar is the result for other *lagnas*, except Virgo, where rain would be scarce, and crops meagre.

Planets in Lagna and Rain

If the Sun be posited in the ascendant on the day of his entry into Aries, rains would be normal throughout the year; but they might be delayed a little; if the Moon be there, there would be abundant rains and bumper crops; if Mars be there, rains would be scanty, that too, in the middle; if Mercury be in the *lagna* which happens to be a watery sign, good rains could be expected, but elsewhere they would not be good; Jupiter be there, there would not be rain in the beginning, but later, and destruction of crops may also occur to some extent; if Venus be there, no rain would fall at the proper time, and serious fighting would break out leaving some kings in utter misery, and cattle disease also would be wide-spread, but crops luxuriant and life happy and contented; if Saturn be there, rain would be very scanty, and robberies and other great disasters, the order of the day; and if Rāhu or Ketu be there in a watery sign, good rains could be expected, while in others poor rainfall in the year.

(1) *Blemishes of the Saṁkrānti*: If at the time of the Sun's entry into sign Aries, there be any of the nine inauspicious daily Yogas viz. *Parigha*, *Vyatīpāta*, *Vajra*, *Vyāghāta*, *Vaidhṛti*, *Viṣkambha*, *Śūla*, *Gaṇḍa* and *Atigaṇḍa*, or of the *Upagrahas* (minor planets), like *Māndī*, there would be famine stalking through the land throughout the year.

(2) If the *Saṁkrānti lagna* be a watery sign occupied or aspected by a watery planet, there would be excellent rain in the year. On the other hand, if the concerned ascendant and the planets be fiery, no rain would fall that year.

(3) Generally predictions for the year are made from the Sun's ingress into Aries and those for the months from the *Saṁkrānti* of the particular month. If their *lagna* be possessed of benefic connection by contact and/or aspect, as well as high tide (*Jala-Vṛddhi*), there would be good rain and plenty of food crops in the year or month, as the case may be. On the other hand, should malefic aspect and/or occupation as well as ebb-tide be there (for the *lagna*), rainfall would be very meagre. So would be the food position. Morever, there would be threat of war.

(4) When the first day of the month of *Meṣa* occurs under the following asterisms viz. *Rohiṇī*, *Anurādhā*, *Abhijit*, *Jyeṣṭhā*, *Śravaṇa*, *U. Āṣāḍhā* and *Dhaniṣṭhā*, which constitute *Indra-Maṇḍala*, Indra's circle, there will be health, happiness and plenty of food grains in the land. On the other hand, if it takes place under the following stars viz. *Bharaṇī*, *Kṛttikā*, *Puṣya*, *Maghā*, *P. Phālguṇī*, *Viśākhā*, and *P. Bhādra*, which belong to the *Agni-Maṇḍala*, there will be drought, fires and famine, as well as destruction of crops, especially autumnal ones.

(5) Should the Sun's transit of Aries take place under the stars viz. *Aśvinī*, *Punarvasu*, *Mṛgaśiras*, *Hasta*, *U. Phalguṇī*, *Citrā* and *Svātī* which constitute the *Vāyu-Maṇḍala*, Wind-circle, there would be danger to (or from) the king, cyclone-havoc and drought.

(6) Should the Sun's transit of *Meṣa* take place under the following asterisms viz. *Ārdrā*, *Āśleṣā*, *Mūla*, *P. Āṣāḍhā*, *Śata-*

bhiṣak, *U. Bhādra* and *Revatī*, which form the *Varuṇa-Maṇḍala*, *Varuṇa's circle*, there would follow bountiful rains, health and prosperity in the country.

Saṁkrānti

When the Sun's transit of Aries occurs in the *Karaṇas* viz. *Kiṁstughna, Kaulava* and *Śakuni*, the *Saṁkrānti Puruṣa* is said to be standing, its effect being shooting up of prices of all articles. If it takes place in the *Nāga, Garaja, Taitila* and *Catuṣpāt*. He is said to be seated. Its effect is that prices of articles will be normal. When the above transit takes place under *Bālava, Viṣṭi, Bava* and *Vaṇik*, the Being is said to be lying-down, whose effect is great slump.

Watery Signs and Planets

(1) Pisces and Cancer; (2) Capricorn, (3) Aquarius, (4) Taurus, (5) Libra and (6) Scorpio—these six groups of signs are termed watery in a descending order. The remaining *Rāśis* are dry and called land signs.

The Moon and Venus are full-fledged watery planets, while Mercury and Jupiter are called watery only when they occupy watery signs. They are not generators of water. The rest are called dry. So the Sun and Mars produce loss of rain; Mercury and Jupiter cause meagre rainfall; and the Moon and Venus plenty of rain, especially immediately in respect of a query. If the querist's word begins with the 4th letter (aspirate) of a consonant class, a vessel or a long vowel, there will in all probability be rain immediately. Should the first letter be the 1st. 2nd, or 5th of a class, there would be little rain; and 'no rain' should be predicted in the case of other letters.

If a non-watery planet be posited in a watery sign at a query, there would be rain after some time; while if it is otherwise, i.e. a watery planet be posited in a non-watery sign, there would be rain. Similarly, should a watery planet occupy a watery sign, there would be splendid rain.

If either the 2nd or 3rd house at a query be a watery sign, there would be heavy rain within 20 days, which would make the rivers flooded.

If the ascendant of query be a watery sign with Jupiter, Mercury, Venus and the Moon posited in *kendras*, receiving benefic aspect, there would be excellent rainfall. If these planets be aspected by malefics or conjoined with them, there would be scanty rainfall. If the *Ārūḍha* or *Chatra Rāśi* be a watery sign, occupied by watery planets, there would be plenty of rain. An explanation is needed here for the *kendras* mentioned above. The 4th house from the *lagna* speaks of water beneath the earth; the 7th, water flowing in the rivers and the 10th house, rainfall. In spite of planetary configurations standing for rainfall, sometimes as soon as rain starts rain clouds are driven away by strong winds. Why is it so? If the ascendant has Mercury's aspect or association or his *decanate* or *Navāṁśa* rising, the above contingency arises. The same result occurs when the *kendras* are occupied by Mercury, Mars, Saturn and Rāhu. However, should these planets be associated with benefics, some amount of rain might be expected.

Good rain is to be foretold when the *lagna*, *Ārūḍha* and the *Chatra Rāśi* are in signs that are *Pṛṣṭhodaya* or rise with their hind part. Similar result could be expected, if Venus and the Moon be in their exaltation (or own house?).

Should Saturn and Rāhu be posited in watery signs, they would lead to good rains; but if they be aspected by the Moon and Venus, there would be heavy rains.

Watery Signs

According to the author of the *Praśnamārga* the following are watery signs: (1) Pisces, (2) Cancer, (3) the latter half of Capricorn, (4) Taurus, (5) Libra, (6) Scorpio, (7) Virgo and (8) Aquarius. However, I feel that the gradation given by others about this matter is more logical and acceptable.

CHAPTER XIV

WATER RESOURCES

THE IMPORTANCE OF water in the life of human beings, nay of all living beings (including even inanimate objects like rocks, minerals, mountains, hills and dales) cannot be over-emphasized, as it is one of the basic necessities of life on earth like food and air. For cooling the earth which gets heated by the Sun's rays and activities of all beings, the Creator has kept it amidst water, whose volume is three times that of the earth. When the population of the world is increasing by leaps and bounds, the peoples and governments are hard put to the task of finding out new sources of water to slake the thirst of peoples and animals in the developing and undeveloped countries of the world. Since ancient times people have been depending on water that has been available in nature easily in plenty in rivers, lakes and ponds. In some countries people who had no other means or source of water, had to depend entirely on rain water, which they collected in artificial tanks, while others sank wells in congenial places near their residences and got brackish and rarely potable water. In ancient Āyurvedic works like the *Suśruta-Saṁhitā* the properties and sources of water are treated of in great detail. Of the two kinds of water viz. terrestrial and celestial (*Bhauma* and *Āntarikṣa*) the latter is superior in quality and utility, according to *Suśruta*. Even among the water varieties available on the earth is replete with the element of *ether* (*Ākāśa*) and so odourless, colourless and tasteless, is the best in the absence of celestial water, which is said to be possessed of properties that conduce to intellectual powers, physical energy like a tonic, and cure of troubles born of the three humours (*doṣas*). Manu, the great ancient law-giver, declares appropriately that the Creator created water in the beginning, which received the seed for further creation. Lord Nārāyaṇa is closely connected with *Nāra* (water) as He is resting on the Milky Ocean. Nowadays people and rulers in their thirst for water resort to making bore-wells and desalination of sea-water. In this connection, the world of scholars owes a great debt of gratitude to Ācāryapravara Varāhamihira for his pioneering work in the field of water divination.

Query About Wells

People, often seek the help of diviners or dowsers to ascertain the proper place for a well and the depth at which water may be obtained, whether the well would prove beneficial to the family and trees, and such other matters. If a site is fixed for a well, then the querist would ask for the best time for beginning the work. The examination of the site for a well is generally done when the Sun transits any of the four signs beginning with Capricorn; sometimes even the four signs from Pisces are accepted.

Site-Test

The indications of underground water are invariably some trees growing nearby like *Vetasa* (rotang tree), Jamlū, Udumbara (Indian fig tree), Arjuna, *Nirguṇḍī*, Jujube combined with *Palāśa*, *Bilva* as well as anthills along with or nearby the trees. The direction, depth and distance from the trees as well as the directions of the water-veins are given by Varāhamihira, sage Sārasvata and Manu. In this connection they distinguish three types of place viz. *Anūpa* (water-laden), *Jāṁgala* (forest land) and *Maru* (desert land) each having its own indications and depth of the water-vein. The decision arrived at after this test should be confirmed by *Praśna* or query. The site must be selected in such a way that there may not be any danger of the walls of the well to be sunk caving in and of rain-water rushing into the well and spoiling it. The omens observed at the place of query, the words uttered by the querist, limbs touched by him, articles brought by chance by others, the *Ārūḍha* and position of planets—all these are to be carefully weighed by the diviner before declaring the prospects of water in the proposed well.

Some Auguries

(1) The sudden arrival of a *Caṇḍāla*, courtesan, *Brāhmaṇa*, hunter or one who is almost in tears because of the theft of his wealth, or appearances of a rainbow suggests good water in the proposed well.

(2) Should the querist touch his neck or face (mouth), water

could be predicted in the well. On the other hand, should he touch his ear, there would be an accidental death in the well. So to ward off the calamity, the querist should perform propitiatory rites before commencing the work.

Planetary Configuration

(1) There would be water in the well, should the Moon occupy the ascendant along with Rāhu, provided the *lagna* is a movable sign.

(2) The same result could be pronounced, if Jupiter be posited in the 4th house or the Sun in the 10th house from the ascendant at query.

(3) The Moon in the ascendant, and both the *Ārūḍha* and *lagna* being watery signs, would confer success.

(4) Even if the 4th house be occupied by a malefic, success could be expected, if the *Ārūḍha* be posited by the Moon.

(5) Water would be available, if the *Ārūḍha* be Virgo, aspected by Jupiter and Venus, and the Moon be in Pisces (or the Moon in Pisces be aspected by Jupiter and Venus).

(6) Virgo should be the *Ārūḍha* flanked by the Moon and Venus. Then success can be expected.

(7) Should Capricorn be the *Ārūḍha* and Cancer, Libra and Pisces be occupied by their respective lords, there would be success.

(8) If Mercury and Rāhu be combined and the Moon be in Gemini, the result would be good.

(9) If the Moon and Venus be exalted and aspected by debilitated planets, there would be success.

(10) Should the *Ārūḍha* be Taurus occupied by the waxing Moon, plenty of water could be got in the well.

(11) If the ascendant be a fixed sign, and Venus and Saturn be together, or if the Moon be in Leo and the *Ārūḍha* a watery sign, one could expect a small amount of water in the well.

(12) Should Pisces, Virgo and Gemini be occupied by *Ārūḍha*, the Moon and Jupiter respectively (either together or separately), water could be expected in the well.

Even if the Moon be in Taurus, the well would be without water, in case the 7th house be occupied by Rāhu.

Direction of Spring

If the querist touches one of the limbs on the left side, the water spring would be in the south-western corner of the well; if it be in the upper part of the body, it would be in the north-western corner of the well; and if it be below the neck on the right side, the spring would be in the north-western corner of the well.

If the querist touches some part with prominent bones, the result is unfavourable. On the other hand, if it be a fleshy part, it is an indication of a rich spring. If it is a very fleshy limb, the water would be full of silt. If the forehead be touched, a rocky surface without much water would be met with. In this manner the diviner should find out the proper place for a well by means of query and auguries. The exact spot of the well, however, should be pinpointed by means of the *cakra* (circle) called *Candra-Gupti*, "Moon's Protection". The diagram for this, no doubt, is not circular, but rectangular with 28 compartments, the longer sides being 7″ in length and shorter ones 4″ long. It is got by drawing 8 vertical lines with one inch interval between the lines, crossed by 5 horizontal lines with the same interval as before. The 28 compartments are filled with numbers from 1 to 28 starting with the north-eastern corner, in the following manner: Go straight from 1 to 5 and then go down one step and turn backwards and go three steps up to 9th number; and therefrom go down one step and proceed to the right four steps up to 14. Stop there and proceed upwards two steps until you reach number 16. From thence turn to the right and take one step, i.e. 17 Thence you go down three steps until you reach the number 20. Then go to the left taking six steps until you reach 26. Thence go two steps upwards and that completes the *circle*.

East

N.W.	1	2	3	4	5	16	17	S.E.
North	28	9	8	7	6	15	18	South
	27	10	11	12	13	14	19	
N.W.	26	25	24	23	22	21	20	S.W.

West

This figure represents the circle called *Candra-Gupti*. In this figure the 28 asterisms including *Abhijit* are represented as explained below:

This chart is to be used as it is, if the query is made in the fore-noon, i.e. from Sunrise to midday; then onwards till sunset the chart is to be turned clockwise and then the number 1 will be placed in the S.E. compartment and the rest of the numbers put in the order mentioned in this scheme; from Sunset to midnight turn it clockwise and begin the numbers from the S.W.; and lastly if the query be made after midnight and before sunrise, turn it again towards the north and begin the numbers starting with the N.W. as number 1. With regard to the four quarters of the whole day there is some speciality to be noted. In the first part you have to consider always the third star from *Aśvinī* as the rising star, which happens to be *Kṛttikā*; in second part it is the third from the first star viz. *Puṣya*, i.e. *Maghā*; in the third part the first star is *Svātī* and the third, *Anurādhā*; and in the fourth, the first being *Abhijit*, the third comes to be *Dhaniṣṭhā*. This is the speciality of this school of interpretation. On account of this, you will have to draw three more charts afresh for the other quarters of the day with entirely new numbers. So it is not enough if you simply turn the original chart. For, when you begin with S.E. the first star would be *Puṣya*; when with S.W. begin with *Svātī*; and when with N.W., begin with *Abhijit*.

From one sunrise to the next it is one full day of 60 *Ghaṭīs*. This period is to be divided equally among the 28 asterisms, which is equal to 60 *Ghaṭīs* divided by 28. This comes to 60/28 = 15/7 *Ghaṭīs*. Find out the star that rises at the time of the query at the rate of 15/7 G. per star, according to this scheme. Put this star in the place of number 1. This star is called rising star (*Udayarkṣa*). Now find out the star of the day of query from the Almanac or Ephemeris. The first star, *Aśvinī*, cannot be expected to occupy the number 1 at the N.E. corner. For, it depends on the time of query. Let us take an example. Let the time of query be 8-30 A.M. on the day when the sunrise was at 6-22 A.M. So what is the time elapsed from sunrise to the query time? It is 8-30 minus 6-22 = 2 hr-08 mt (2 hours 8 minutes) = 5 *Ghaṭīs* 20 *Vighaṭīs*. Now to find out the star that rises at the time, you have to divide the elapsed *Ghaṭīs* etc. by 15/7 *Ghaṭīs* = 31/3 – 15/7 = 16/3 × 7/15 = 112/45 = 2.49 stars, i.e. it is the 3rd star from *Aśvinī* viz. *Kṛttikā*, which should be written in the compartment of number 1. So you have to prepare a new chart where the numbers representing the stars have to begin with 3 instead of 1 and the last number will be 2 instead of 28. So in the first or topmost horizontal line you will be writing the numbers of stars as 3, 4, 5, 6 and 7 in the places of 1, 2, 3, 4 and 5 respectively. Follow the above rule for writing the other numbers. We have seen the rising star as *Kṛttikā*, but this is not the lunar mansion of the day. It is *Revatī*, called *Candrarkṣa*, which is the 28th star that goes to the north-western corner of the new *cakra*. Hence there should be a very good spring of water in the north-western corner of the well, as it is occupied by the Moon, a watery planet. Similarly, prediction may be made about the location of a well in one's farm or garden. Similarly, locate Mercury, Jupiter and Venus in their respective stars. Of course, the strongest of planets would give the clue to the location of a well.

Second Method of Candra-Gupti

According to another view the numbers should not be changed, and *Aśvinī* and other stars are permanently located in the 28 compartments as shown in the figure. The rising star should be found out by calculation as shown already and located in its proper place in the fixed chart. Likewise the planets are to be located in their respective stars. There is no place in this scheme for the star of the day. You have to predict water in the direction signified by the stars occupied by the strongest of watery and semi-watery planets. In our example the star *Kṛttikā* that rises at the time, should be placed in the compartment numbered 3. Locate other planets also in their respective asterisms. Then the Moon would be in 28 which is very close to the north-east; Mercury in *Hasta*, i.e. 13 which is near the S.W.; Jupiter in *Rohiṇī*, i.e. 4 which is exactly in the centre of the east; Venus in *U. Phālguṇī*, i.e. 12, which is near the West; Saturn in *Mūla*, i.e. 19, which is almost in the centre of the south; and Rāhu in *Śatabhiṣak*, i.e. 25 that is near the N.W.

According to the third method the rising star is permanently placed in compartment 3; and the rest is as before. The prediction is made through the stars occupied by the watery planets and their directions in the chart.

There is yet another method: Here the stars start from *Aśvinī*. Locate the Moon in the number corresponding to the asterism she is in. Count the number of stars from *Aśvinī* to this star. Now count the number of the lunar mansion ruling the day in question from *Aśvinī*, and locate it in the compartment bearing that number. Again add this number to the *Dinarkṣa* which (sum) will give a new compartment with its own number. Treat this new place as that of *Udayarkṣa*. Next find out the distance (in stars) of the Moon's star from the *Udayarkṣa*. Add that number to the *Dinarkṣa*. Mark the place where this resultant number is located. That place or direction will have plenty of water underneath. Let us make the above idea clear through an example: Let the *Dinarkṣa* of the day in question be *Mṛgaśīrṣa*. So locate the Moon in the compartment number 5. Now add this number, i.e. 5, to the *Dinarkṣa*, which comes to 5+5=10. This star No. 10, i.e. *Maghā*, should be treated as the *Udayarkṣa*. Next count the distance from *Maghā* (10) to *Mṛgaśiras*, which is 24 stars away from the former. So count 24 stars from the *Dinarkṣa*, which brings us to *Revatī* (28). Hence in the locality of No. 28, i.e. near the north-eastern corner, there will be plenty of water.* Similarly, the places indicated by the stars occupied by Jupiter and Venus also would have rich springs of water. In our example Venus and Jupiter are posited in *Kṛttikā* and *Rohiṇī* respectively. Hence there must be plenty of water in the east corresponding to the No. 3 and 4.

Water Vein

Should the ascendant at query be a movable sign, there would be only one vein in the well; if an immovable one, many veins of water; and if a dual one, there would be two water veins.

Old Wells

How could we know if there be an old well buried underneath, being completely covered with mud?

*The above explanation of the fourth method is based on the commentary, entitled *Uparatnaśikhā* by the great scholar viz. Punnaśśeri Nīlakaṇṭha Śarmā who was a successor disciple of the original author of P.M. vide preface page 9 for the line of succession.

(1) Should the *Ārūḍha* be an immovable sign, and the Moon in Taurus, the astrologer should declare that there is an old well buried under the earth.

(2) If the *Ārūḍha* be Taurus occupied by Venus, the querist's land would be having an old well. Should Rāhu be in the 10th house and the Moon and Venus in the 4th house, there would be two old wells in the querist's farm.

(3) If the Moon and Venus be exalted, there would be two old wells very deep in the earth. If the Sun be in the 7th house from the *Ārūḍha*, and the Moon in the 7th house from the ascendant, there would be an old well in the place.

(4) If the ascendant be occupied by both Rāhu and the Moon, there would be an old well. The same result should be declared, if the *Ārūḍha* be Aquarius occupied by the Moon and Venus.

(5) If the Moon and Venus occupy together an immovable ascendant, there would be an old well. The same result would be indicated by Jupiter and Venus joined together in the 4th house.

(6) Should the Moon be in the 10th house and Venus in Virgo, there would be an old well in the place. The same is the case with Venus in the 7th house and the Moon who is encircled by a halo, in the 4th house.

Caving-in of Wells

The disappearance of a well occurs as a result of the sides of the well having caved in owing to heavy rains entering the well and its walls being of loose mud. Its place might be hidden by the growth of bushes etc. (1) When both the ascendant and *Chatra* sign are watery signs, and the Moon is posited in the *Ārūḍha*, the above contingency must have taken place in the intended place. The same effect would take place, should the Sun along with Rāhu or Ketu occupy the ascendant which is a watery sign.

(2) Existence of old wells is indicated in the following conditions: (a) Saturn in the *lagna*, and the Moon in the 10th house. (b) Jupiter in the 4th house, Rāhu in the 7th, and the Sun in the 10th house. (c) Rāhu, the Sun and Moon joined together in the 4th house. (d) At the time of query the Sun having a halo around. (e) The ascendant, *Ārūḍha*, and *Chatra* sign being watery, and the *lagna*, an immovable sign.

(3) Arrival of a *Caṇḍāla* etc. (already mentioned) or appearance of a rainbow.

Taste of Well-Water

For this purpose the astrologer should be able to assess the qualities of the soil, taste of the water and such other details by concentrating his attention of the 4th house and the planets that aspect and occupy that house. It may also be surmised from the lord of the *Navāṁśa* of the *lagna*. The six tastes viz. sweet, sour, bitter, salt, pungent and astringent, are ruled in order by Jupiter, Venus, Mars, Moon, Sun and Saturn. Mercury owns mixed taste. It may be found out from the first letter of the words uttered by the querist. There are eight groups of letters of the alphabet as *Avarga*, *Kavarga* (*Guttural*), *Cavarga* (*Palatal*), *Tavarga* (*Cerebral*), *Tavarga* (*Dental*), *Pavarga* (*Labial*), *Yavarga* (*Semi-Vowel*) and *Śavarga* (*Sibilant-Palatal*), which are ruled in order by the Moon, Mars, Mercury, Jupiter, Venus, Saturn, Rāhu, and the Sun. Since the *Ya-group* of four letters viz. *Ya*, *Ra*, *La* and *Va*, is owned by Rāhu, it stands for tasteless water.

The symptoms of water are read from the behaviour and movements of the querist, and the details of the well, taste of water, terrain, depth etc. from the Moon's transit.

Place for Well

First of all the diviner should survey the plot of land in which the well is to be sunk, and imagine the being presiding over the site (*Vāstu-Puruṣa*) to be lying down on the ground with his head lying in the north-eastern corner, left arm in the south-east, right arm in the north-west, and legs in the south-west. Then he should find out carefully and mark the place where his eyes and face fall. A well in the direction of the south-eastern corner should never be sunk on the advice of the science of architecture as well as *Āyurveda*. It should be sunk in the place where one could locate the being's eyes or face.

The best direction for sinking a well is the one signified by the sign Aquarius; moderate are the directions suggested by Pisces and Aries, while the worst is the one indicated by Capricorn. A well sunk in the direction of Virgo would ring a knell for the owner.

ROCKY SURFACE

Should the ascendant at query be occupied by the Sun, water would be found at very great depth; if by Mars, there would be some water in the midst of rocks; if by Saturn or Rāhu, there would not be any water.

COLLECTION OF WATER

If the Moon and Venus be in the *lagna*, there would be good springs and the water inexhaustible; if Mercury and Jupiter be there, supply of water would be pretty good; if Mercury and the Moon, there would be water mixed with sand; and if Mars and the Sun, there would be rocks below, and if they are broken, a little water may be obtained.

If Venus be in the *lagna*, the water that is got would be quite good and clear; if Jupiter, pretty good; if Saturn a small amount of water that is astringent (or brackish), and if Rāhu, only a will-o-the-wisp.

DEPTH OF THE WELL

The depth of the well should be calculated on the basis of the number of letters constituting the querist's words; or it may be equal to the number of rays (*raśmis*) of the planets or *Rāśis*. The depth should be determined through the rays of the planet or planets posited in the *lagna* or the 4th house. Generally 1 ray is equal to 1 cubit. This is in a place called *Anūpa* or water-laden; in a *Jaṅgala* or forest area, the standard unit should be 1 *daṇḍa* measuring 24 digits; and in a *maru* (desert) area, a *Puruṣa*, which is 5 cubits or 120 digits.

RAYS OF PLANETS ETC.

They are 16, 4, 10, 9, 7, 5 and 21 respectively for the seven planets headed by the Sun. The *Rāśis* to have their own Rays. They are for the 12 *Rāśis* from *Meṣa*: (1) 7, (2) 8, (3) 12, (4) 11, (5) 12, (6) 6, (7) 9, (8) 7, (9) 13, (10) 7, (11) 8, and (12) 27. In respect of the planets the rays are to be corrected on the basis of their strength. These two types of rays are used in queries of thefts, loss etc. and their number, distance, depth etc.

There are many points of similarity in the subjects discussed in this and the previous chapters, as their subject-matters are very similar, being well-water and rainfall. In a query about well, importance is given to the consideration of the ascendant and the 4th house, while about rainfall, the *lagna* and the 10th house. Similarly, with regard to river-journey, the ascendant and the 7th house are specially looked into. If dry planets occupy the concerned houses that are watery signs, is one case the prediction would be, "Water will be available very deep in the well", while in the other case it would be, "Rainfall will be poor". In the case of a query as to when water would be flowing in the river, the answer should be that rains would be delayed and so water would be flowing in the river after sometime, i.e. a little late. Suppose the *Rāśis* occupied are waterless and the occupying planets watery, you have to predict that there would be not much water deep down in the well; and in respect of rain and rivers, the answer should be "After some delay". In the case of dry planets in dry *Rāśis* the prediction should be "No rain; no water". If watery planets and watery signs happen to be in *Kendras* etc., the answer should be, 'plenty of water at a little depth in the well', 'plenty of rain very early', and 'Soon the rivers would be flowing with rising waters'. Similarly, the diviner should make use of the first letter of the words uttered by the querist in the present case too. In other words, if the first letter of the words of the querist be the 4th of any of the consonantal groups or a long vowel, there would be plenty of good water in the well at moderate depth.

Current Day's Asterism

Unlike the star that is occupied by the Moon on the day in question, this is one that is got by calculation as follows:

Take the time of query in *Ghaṭīs* etc. from sunrise and multiply it by 28. Divide the product by 60.

The quotient will reveal the number of stars elapsed from *Aśvinī* and the balance the star of the current day. (*Note*: In connection with the *Candragupti* circle two *Ṛkṣas* (asterisms) viz. *Udayarkṣa*—Rising Star—and *Dinarkṣa*—Star of the day—have been mentioned. Here a new method of getting at the star of the day is given.)

CHAPTER XV

LOST ARTICLES

PEOPLE SEEK the help of soothsayers, diviners and others in tracing missing, lost or stolen articles. They want to know the whereabouts of missing or abducted persons or animals too. Our ancient sages have bequeathed a rich store of knowledge that is enshrined in ancient literature bearing on this subject. What is required for a querist and astrologer is unflinching devotion to God, who is the source of all knowledge, an observant mind and eye, unclouded intellect and timely intuition.

When a person approaches an astrologer, the latter should be able to say from the *Ārūḍha*, ascendant and the planetary positions as well as the person's facial expression, gesticulations, words and the omens occurring at the time, whether he has come on a pleasant errand or otherwise. The following information has been culled from my *Praśnajñāna*. When the lord of the *Ārūḍha* or ascendant is posited in the 3rd, 6th, 8th or 12th, the astrologer should declare that the query pertains to a stolen article. It is said that Lord Śiva has ordained that the query should be judged to be about the theft of some articles, if the lord of the 7th house from the *Ārūḍha*, Mars or Saturn be posited in the 3rd, 6th, 8th or 12th house.

The following details are culled from a work entitled, *Naṣṭapraśnadīpikā*.

(1) Should Saturn occupy the 7th, 8th or 12th house from the *Ārūḍha*, ascendant or the Moon, the query would be about a stolen article, provided there is no aspect or association of Jupiter.

(2) The lords of the three untoward houses being posited in the same house or in (mutual?) *kendras* would compel the astrologer to give the same result.

(3) So is the case with the lords of the 2nd and 12th houses being posited in the 6th house.

(4) If Mars or Saturn be posited in the 7th house from the

Ārūḍha or *lagna*, or if the two malefics (or one of them) be debilitated, eclipsed or posited in an inimical house, one could come to the same conclusion.

(5) The following three *Yogas* lead to the finding of loss: (a) The lord of the 7th house being posited in 12th house; (b) the lord of the 12th house being in the 7th house; and (c) the two lords being in *kendras*.

QUERIST'S BEHAVIOUR

If the querist be found with his fist clenched, appears as if he has forgotten something, or looks at the sides, it should be presumed that he has lost something.

With the help of the above-mentioned information the diviner comes to the view that the querist's purpose is to find out the whereabouts of a lost article. There upon he should try to find out the nature, form, type, make, number, time, place and such other details as well as identification of the thief, his name etc. He should also be able to assess the possibilities of recovering the lost article.

The *Navāṁśa* of the *Ārūḍha* or ascendant would give the clue to the nature of the object lost, and the decanate to the identity of the thief and the *Rāśi* to the time and place of theft as well as the place of concealment of the stolen object, and the lord of the *lagna* (and/or *Ārūḍha*) to the age, caste, colour, stature etc. of the thief. Regarding the object that is lost distinction is made in respect of its nature, whether it is mineral, wooden or animal. If the ascendant is a movable sign, it would signify a mineral object (*Dhātu*), if immovable, a wooden (tree, plant) article, and if common, an animal or living being (*Jīva*). In this context, it should be borne in mind, the signs of the Zodiac viz. the movable, fixed and common signs, are termed respectively *karma* (action), *Bhoga* (enjoyment), and *Nāśa* (destruction). According to another system of classification, (1) Action, (2) Enjoyment, (3) and (4) Destruction, (5) Action, (6) and (7) Enjoyment, (8) Destruction, (9) Action, (10) Destruction, (11) Action and (12) Destruction.

This three-fold distinction as mineral, wooden and animal, is made also in respect of the *Navāṁśas* of each Zodiacal sign, of the 27 asterisms, and of the planets as explained below:

(1) *Navāṁśas*—The first *Navāṁśa* of each *Rāśi* is brought under *Dhātu* or mineral; the second, under *Mūla* or Tree, and the third, under *Jīva* or animal. This process is repeated thrice in each sign. Similarly, these three divisions are to be severally grouped together with *Karma* or action, *Bhoga* or enjoyment, and *Nāśa* or destruction.

(2) *Asterisms*—There are altogether 9 sets of three stars each as *Aśvinī-Dhātu*; *Bharaṇī-Mūla*; *Kṛttikā-Jīva*. These also should be clubbed with action, enjoyment and destruction in order.

(3) *Planets*—(a) The Moon, Mars, Saturn and Rāhu are assigned to *Dhātu*; (b) the Sun and Venus to *Mūla*; and (c) Mercury and Jupiter to *Jīva*.

There is some difference of opinion among scholars regarding the allocation of *Dhātu* etc. among the *Rāśis* and *Aṁśas*:

In an odd sign the order is as given in the beginning, but in an even sign it is *Jīva*, *Mūla* and *Dhātu*.

With regard to Navāṁśas proceed thus: If the *Navāṁśa* belongs to a movable sign in an odd *Rāśi*, it should be taken as *Dhātu*; on the other hand, if it be a fixed *Navāṁśa*, take it as *Mūla*; and if a common *Aṁśa*, as *Jīva* for a movable sign; if a fixed sign, take *Mūla*; and if a common sign, *Dhātu*.

Method of Finding the Article

First find out if the *lagna*, its *Navāṁśa*, its constellation and the planets posited in the *lagna* all point to the conclusion that the article belongs to the *Dhātu* (mineral) category; then decide whether the lost article is made of iron, bronze, copper, silver, gold, lead, stone or mud. On the other hand, if the ascendant is of *Dhātu*, but its *Navāṁśa*, asterism, and planets posited therein are of *Mūla*, then it should be considered as an article buried under the earth, that has been stolen; or it may be a hidden treasure kept undergound. If the *lagna* alone be *Dhātu* and the rest *Jīva*, take it as an idol made of some metal like gold or silver.

If the *lagna*, its *Navāṁśa*, its star and the planet in it all come under *Mūla* (root) category, one should think of fruits and vegetables (growing on the earth) like carrot, cabbage, ground-nut, sweet potato, ginger, turmeric etc. as the stolen articles. On the other hand, if the ascendant be *Mūla* and the rest belong to the *Dhātu* group, the article lost or stolen would be clothes, dry timber, jaggery or cooked dishes. If the *lagna* be *Mūla*, and the other three, animal (*Jīva*), it would point to loss of cattle, birds, animals or idols made of wood.

If all the four factors viz. *lagna*, its *Navāṁśa*, its asterism, and the planet in it, belong to the *Jīva* group, it would suggest living beings being kidnapped such as a *Mahout*, a child or a pregnant woman. Should all the four factors be biped, it would be a case of a missing or kidnapped person. On the other hand, if all of them be of animal (quadruped?) group, the loss must be of domestic animals. Now how is one to pinpoint the particular class of living beings—human, animal or bird—among the vast groups of living beings? It is possible to do that by means of the following method:

Let the *lagna* be of *Jīva* (animal) group, and the remaining three factors of *Dhātu* (mineral) group; then it would point to the loss of burnt materials, corpse, or articles made of bones (ivory products). Likewise, if the last three factors be of *Mūla* (root) category, it should be considered that the loss is of materials made of tiger's claws, animal hides, clothes made of wool, elephant's tusks, horns of antelopes etc.

So far we have seen only general principles to guide the students of this science to be able to distinguish the subgroups of the various classes. So the following information is given as a better tool:

Let us take Gemini as the ascendant and its *Navāṁśa*; and the *lagna-star* as *Kṛttikā**, and the planet posited in the *lagna* as Jupiter. Then, since Gemini is a human sign, Jupiter, a human planet, and *Kṛttika*, a *Jīva* star, and since the *lagna* is in *Vargottamāṁśa*, one should predict that couple is missing. However, due attention should be paid to other factors viz. planetary positions, as aspects and conjunctions, so that the prediction may be fairly accurate.

Likewise, if the *lagna* and its *Navāṁśa* be Aries, and *lagna-star* *Āśvinī*, and the occupying planet Saturn, the lost article would be one made of iron or steel. If in this case the planet be Mars instead of Saturn, the loss is of gold; if it be the Moon in the

*As sign Gemini stands for *jīva*, so does star *Kṛttikā*.

lagna, the loss is of pearls. In this manner, the lost articles may be identified on the basis of the planets' significations. However, special aspects and positions of other planets should be taken into consideration. For example, a planet situated in the same house as another, exchanges half of its powers or properties with the other; those posited in mutual trines similarly exchange a third of their strength; those in opposition, 1/7th of their power; those in the 4th and 8th houses from the ascendant, a quarter; and lastly those that occupy the same *Horā*, a quarter of their strength. In the light of this amendment, the characteristics and significations of the planets undergo some changes.

Planets in Aries, sign and *Navāṁśa*, denote the following articles: gold, gold coin, silver, copper, lead etc., lamp, vessel, iron etc. If Mars is associated with Aries, gold is to be predicted; if Venus, silver; if Mercury (with the Sun), a lamp, if Saturn, iron; if the Moon, a vessel; if the Moon and Mercury combined, a coin; if Rāhu, lead. If Taurus be the *lagna* and its *Aṁśa*, the lost articles may be among the following: A cloth, armour, sandalwood, helmet (turban or crown), cotton products, bed, pillow etc.

If Gemini be the *lagna* and *Navāṁśa*, living beings, reptiles, wild animals like hyena, poisonous insects, hornets, honey bees, bandicoots and such other pests are to be predicted.

The significations of Cancer *lagna* and *Aṁśa* are the following: minerals, axe, sword, bow and arrow, weapons, saw etc. These are common to Cancer and Capricorn.

For Leo *lagna* and *Aṁśa* the following are the articles: tubers, cereals, bananas, jack-fruit, mango, roots, blackgram, yams, betel leaves, green gram and Sūraṇa bulbs. Here care should be exercised in giving prediction, taking into consideration planetary aspects on the ascendant. If the Sun or Mars aspects it, materials grown above the ground are to be predicted; if Venus or Mercury should aspect it, the articles would be grown neither above, nor underneath the ground; if Jupiter or the Moon should aspect it, things grown on the ground; and if Saturn or Rāhu aspects it, the items would be those grown below the ground level. The taste of the produce mentioned above may also be predicted with the help of the aspecting planets.

For Virgo *lagna* and *Aṁśa*, the following are indicated: living beings (whose meat is used for food), eatables, all types of animals.

For Libra ascendant and *Aṁśa*, they are: butter-milk, milk, curds, hides, blankets and minerals. For Scorpio similarly they are: liquor, narcotics, roots, fruits, pepper and heroin and such other intoxicating agents.

For the first half of Sagittarius the following are to be thought of: human beings, and for the second half elephants, horses, mongoose, poultry etc.

For Aquarius *langa* the prediction is the same as for Leo.

For Pisces *lagna* and *Aṁśa* the following are to be stated: reptiles, fish and other living beings, especially aquatic ones.

Another Method of Sub-Division

The signs of the Zodiac are divided into four equal parts; and they are called in order (1) *Dhātu* (mineral), *Mūla* (roots), (3) *Jīva* (living being), and (4) *Mṛta* (dead). Here the last part stands for a dead body. Hence if the *Ārūḍha* or *lagna* happens to be the last part of the concerned sign, the astrologer should declare that the subject of query is a corpse.

According to Mādhavācārya, the three decanates of the ascendant represent in order (1) *Dhātu*, (2) *Mūla*, and (3) *Jīva*.

If a planet denoting mineral be posited in a human sign, it would point to chains, anklets, bracelets, small bells and the like. On the other hand, a planet standing for mineral, posited in a watery sign, would suggest a *Kamaṇḍalu* (water vessel), and a cooking utensil etc.

I have already drawn the reader's attention to the importance of omens in the form of sights seen and words heard as well as the limbs touched by the querist in determining lost objects. The following paragraph gives some guidance in this regard:

If the querist touches his nail or teeth, the lost article must be something belonging to the *Dhātu* (mineral) group; and should he touch a depressed or lower part of the body, it would be of the *Mūla* (root) variety. Similarly, if he touches a mirror, lamp or a living thing, the lost thing would be a domestic animal.

No Theft

Should a planet posited in his own *Rāśi* or *Aṁśa*, aspect the ascendant (or *Ārūḍha*), the missing article has not been stolen, but only misplaced. If the planet, posited in an inimical house, should aspect the *lagna*, the article lost would be found in his enemy's house; if it be a friendly house from which the planet aspects the ascendant, the article would be in a kinsman's house. If the house occupied by the aspecting planet be his exaltation house, the article would be in a noble person's house, while if it be his debilitation house, it would be in the house of a menial. The nature of the stolen object could be inferred from the *Aṁśas* of the *lagna* and *Ārūḍha* (or from the strength of the planet posited in the *Navāṁśa* of either).

Direction

The stolen property may be declared to be in the direction of the *Ārūḍha*. If this is occupied by any planet, the article is likely to be in the direction assigned to that planet. Should the *Ārūḍha* be a movable *Rāśi*, the article must have been carried to a distant place; if it be a fixed sign, it would be in the same house; and if a common sign, it would be near the house, or in the same village or town. The directions ruled by the Sun, Venus, Mars, Rāhu, Saturn, the Moon, Mercury and Jupiter are in order the east, S.E., south, S.W., west, N.W., north and N.E.

Direction of Signs

The *Ārūḍha* being one of the Zodiacal signs, the stolen article would be found hidden in a place having these qualities:

Aries: A place where goats and sheep roam about, a forest.
Taurus: Where cattle graze, a pasture, a field.
Gemini: A lonely place, bed-chamber, village.
Cancer: A pond or pit with water.
Leo: Mountain cave, forest.
Virgo: Land with water and luxuriant vegetation.
Libra: Market-place, busy town.
Scorpio: A cave, burial or cremation ground, anthills.
Sagittarius: Battle-field, capital city, king's court.
Capricorn: Forest on river-banks, dwelling place of foresters.

Aquarius: Kitchen, potter's abode.

Pisces: Banks of rivers, ocean, holy waters, pilgrim centre, temple, brahmin house.

The stronger of the two viz. *Ārūḍha* and *lagna*, would give the clue to the place where the stolen article is hidden.

According to Kṛṣṇācārya when the *lagna* is aspected by Jupiter, divide the *lagna* into four equal parts and see in which part the rising degree falls. If it be in the first part, the stolen object would be kept in a cattle-shed; if it be in the second part, in the house of a priest (*purohita*), if in the third part, in a temple, and if in the last part, in a nunnery.

In the case of Venus's aspect on the *lagna*, the latter should be sub-divided into six equal parts, and as before these parts are allotted in order to (1) a dormitory, (2) garden, (3) tank, (4) house of a danseuse, (5) a house where scents, incense, jars, sticks etc. are stored, and (6) where flowers are kept.

When Mars aspects the *lagna*, the latter is divided into two halves, which represent in order (1) the place where a furnace is kept, and (2) workshop of a blacksmith.

If the Sun be the planet that aspects the *lagna*, the latter is to be divided into two equal parts, which stand for the house of a quarrelsome woman, and the doorstep of a house respectively.

If the Moon aspects the ascendant, it should be divided into three equal parts and the place of the stolen article delineated appropriately: (1) Near the water reservoir or tank, (2) Under water, and (3) a house where nicely dressed courtesans dwell.

In the case of Mercury's aspect on the *lagna*, the stolen article would be found hidden in a bungalow where a number of young charming women bedecked with rich garments and ornaments live.

If Saturn be the aspecting planet, divide the ascendant into three equal parts and declare the place as (1) a place occupied by tale-bearing, quarrelsome or aged women, (2) inside broken pots, and (3) a corner where broomsticks or vessels containing condiments are kept or a slushy place, according to the rising part.

If the Sun possessed of complete strength aspects the rising decanate, the stolen article would be found in chasm (according to the commentator, vicinity of a town). The same result could be declared for the Moon as well as Venus, if they are bereft of strength.

In the above discussion importance has been given to the planets aspecting the ascendant, while determining the place where the stolen article is kept. We have not thought of the planets occupying the *lagna*. Should Jupiter occupy the *lagna* which is a quadruped sign or decanate, the concerned place should be declared as cowshed or grazing ground. If the lord of the 9th house also aspects it, it should be 'teacher's house'. If the Sun or lord of 10th house aspects it, the place of concealment would be a temple or its surrounding. If the Moon posited in a benefic house aspects Jupiter posited in a common sign, it would be a place meant for holy ladies.

Should Saturn, occupying the *lagna* which is a biped sign, be aspected by Mars, the article would be hidden in the graveyard. If Venus or the Moon should aspect Saturn, it would be a pleasing, charming place; if Jupiter aspects Saturn, a sacrificial house; if it be the Sun, near a palace (Govt. building), temple or dairy farm; and if Mercury, near a place meant for music and dancing.

Should the full Moon posited in a watery sign, aspect the ascendant, which too is watery, the article would be under water. The same prediction is to be made, if the Moon be in the 1st, 4th or 10th house.

If Saturn be posited in the 12th house from the *Ārūḍha*, ascendant or the Moon, and be aspected by a malefic, it would be the prison or its vicinity. It would be a chasm or cave, should Saturn be in the *lagna* which is either Cancer or Scorpio, aspected by the moon.

If the moon be in the *lagna* receiving a malefic's aspect, and Mars be in the 7th house, the article is not stolen, but dropped unawares, and it cannot be recovered. The same result would have to be given, if Mars and Saturn be in the 11th house under the above condition. If a benefic aspects the Moon in the above *Yoga*, the article is in the possession of a cultured person. On the other hand, should a malefic aspect the Moon, the missing article would be in the possession of a wicked person, and be irretrievable.

When the consultant comes to the conclusion that the querist's property has been stolen, he may be able to say whether the theft took place during the day time or at night. If the *Ārūḍha* be a diurnal sign, the article must have been stolen during the day; while if it be a nocturnal sign, the time would be night.

If the Sun in a theft—Yoga be very strong, the article would be hidden near the house of the querist's father; if the Moon be very strong, it would be near his mother's house. The same rule should be applied to Mars, Mercury, Jupiter etc. and to the relations signified by these planets.

If the benefics be powerless, the article might be found underneath trees or by the side of compound walls. On the other hand, should not a single planet aspect the *lagna* or the Moon, the article is likely to be lying in a dense forest.

When the *Ārūḍha* or the *lagna* is a *Garbha* (central) *Rāśi*, i.e. a dual sign, the article would be lying hidden inside the house. If it be a *Dvāra* (door) *Rāśi*, i.e. movable sign, it would be near the house; and if a *Bāhya* (external) *Rāśi*, i.e. immovable sign, it must be kept in a far away place. There is some speciality about the signs getting the nomenclature as *Ābhyantara* (*Garbha*) or *Bāhya* (external). When the *Ārūḍha* or *lagna* is occupied by its lord, it is always called *internal* or *Garbha*, irrespective of its nature as movable, immovable and common. Otherwise the general rule will prevail.

When the astrologer makes sure that the theft took place from within the house, he should proceed to discover the method by which the thief got entry into the house. The following information would provide the necessary guidelines: (1) Should the Sun and Mars be found to represent the thieves, i.e. they happen to be the thief planets, it would show that the thieves got entry into the house by jumping over the walls or by removing the tiles on the roof. (2) If it be Mercury or Venus, entry was effected by means of burglary, i.e. by cutting a hole in the wall. (3) If it be the Moon and Jupiter, they must have entered by the main door. (4) Lastly, if it be Rāhu and Saturn, it must have been through an underground tunnel. These predictions are based on the principle that these four pairs of planets possess upward, sideways, forward and downward looks by nature.

Number of Thieves

The number of thieves that have taken part in the robbery

can be gathered by noting the number of planets that are posited in between the Moon and the *lagna*. Among these planets find out how many are in the visible and invisible halves of the Zodiac respectively. As many thieves as are the planets in the invisible half must have actually taken part in the crime by entering into the house, and the rest of them remained outside the house. (The visible part of the zodiac consists of the actual portion of the ascendant that has risen and the houses 12th, 11th etc. up to the part of the 7th house that has not yet set in. The remaining signs belong to the invisible half, i.e. those signs that are below the horizon.)

Description of the House

The type of house from which articles were stolen can be inferred from the nature of the planets concerned. If it be Saturn, the house must be old but renovated; if Mars, it must be one that was damaged by fire, or kitchen; if the Moon, a new house; if the Sun; it must be one constructed with a good deal of timber, yet not strong; if Mercury, one that is full of masonry and wood work carried out by many artisans; if Venus, it is a house newly constructed with beautiful artistic designs; if Jupiter, a strong nice house. It is to be remembered that in this connection the planets posited in the 4th house also should be taken into consideration.

Number of Articles

The number of articles stolen may be determined by using the following details:

Numbers of signs: The twelve signs from Aries are allotted the following numbers in order: (1) 7, (2) 5, (3) 12, (4) 6, (5) 8, (6) 6, (7) 4, (8) 7, (9) 13, (10) 10, (11) 5, and (12) 15. The number assigned to the sign that happens to be the *Ārūḍha*, would give the number of articles stolen.

Colour of the articles: Each sign has been alloted a particular colour as follows: Aries—Red; Taurus—White; Gemini—Green; Cancer — Pink; Leo — Smoke coloured; Virgo — Variegated; Libra—White; Scorpio—Black; Sagittarius—Golden; Capricorn —Coppery hue; Aquarius—Black; and Pisces—Light blue.

The strongest of the three viz. the *Ārūḍha*, *lagna* and the 4th house, would show the colour of the lost article. However, in addition to this aspects of planets should also be taken into account.

In the last chapter we have seen the rays of signs and planets. However, there are different accounts of the same in different works. One such list of planetary rays is given here: They are 30, 28, 8, 6, 9, 7, 3 and 2 for the Sun and others ending with Rāhu or Ketu in order. Planets posited in the *Ārūḍha* or *lagna* influence their rays. Moreover, a planet in exaltation or retrogression gets three times its usual number of rays, for one in *Vargottamāṁśa* it is twice the normal number; while one in debilitation gets its quota reduced to a third; and one in inimical house gets only a half.

This is one way of finding out the number of stolen articles. There is another way of getting at it: That is through the number of degrees risen in the ascendant. Similarly, it can be determined through the rays of the aspecting planets or those posited in the *lagna* or their *Navāṃśas*. In fine, the final results of all these calculations would lead us to determine the number of stolen articles.

In horary astrology special attention is paid to the ascendant, *Ārūḍha*, the Moon, and the 4th, 6th, 7th and the 10th houses from the strongest of these three, especially one posited in the *Navāṁśa* of Cancer, Scorpio or Pisces, in the matter of theft. Similarly, if the 10th house from the strongest of the three be occupied by a malefic, it would lead to the conclusion of theft. The planets posited in the Kendras and the 6th house are designated as 'Coragrahas' (thief planets), especially when the 10th house is occupied by a malefic. Among these *Coragrahas*, the strongest would represent the thief. Should there be more than one planet with equal strength, it may be declared that there are many thieves. However, the 6th house would generally give some clue to the characteristics of thieves.

Description of thief: The physical features of the thief correspond to the description of the rising decanate, provided it is strong. In the event of the *lagna* being weak, the planet occupying the 7th house or the strongest among the planets in the angles would help the astrologer in assessing the thief's characteristics.

If many planets be found in the angles in strength, there would be an equal number of thieves involved in the crime. Such planets would provide the physical characteristics of the thieves. The number of thieves should be doubled trebled or if the concerned planet occupied its own house, exaltation or *Vargottamāṁśa.**

The physical features of the Sun and other planets should be taken as those of the thieves, provided the planet is posited in the 7th house.

The Sun's features: His eyes are honey-coloured, his body square and well built, nature bilious, and hair on the head sparse.

The Moon's features: Her body is tender and round, full of wind and phlegm, with sweet and prepossessing speech and attractive eyes, and great wisdom and intelligence.

Mars' features: He has cruel looks, youthful personality, generosity, bilious nature, slender waist and lack of steadiness.

Mercury's characteristics: He speaks using a good deal of puns, is fond of humorous talks, and has all the three humours in his constitution.

Jupiter's features: He has a gigantic body, eyes and hair tawny, an exalted mind and phlegmatic constitution.

Venus' features: He is ease-loving, a handsome personality and attractive eyes, black and curly hair, and has phlegm and wind in his constitution.

Saturn's characteristics: He is lazy, has brown eyes, lean, tall body, big teeth, coarse hair on the head and body, and windly nature. The seven planets from the Sun preside over bones, blood, marrow, skin, fat, semen, and muscles respectively.

Sex of thief: If a new-born child's horoscope were given to you, how would you proceed to find out its sex? That method should be adopted here too: This matter has been already treated in the chapter on 'Progeny'. Generally we could say that the person concerned is a female, if among the seven *Vargas* a large number of *Vargas* of the *Ārūḍha* belong to the female class, and female planets aspect it. Should Saturn be posited in an even house from the *lagna*, it would be a female. Similarly if the 7th house be occupied by the Moon, Mercury or Venus (or even Rāhu), it would be a woman. Should Saturn be in the ascendant,

*Vide chapter XVII for descriptions of decanates.

it would vote for the female. Another condition is the following: (1) The ascendant, the Sun, Moon and Jupiter should be in even *Rāśis* and *Aṁśas* and be strong. (2) The Moon, Venus and Mars must be in even *Rāśis* and *Aṁśas*. (3) The *Coragrahas* and the *Ārūḍha* should be in even *Rāśis* and *Āṁśas* as well as in female decanates. The star of the *Ārūḍha* or *lagna* or those posited by the thief planets should be female. In the realm of asterisms female population is larger than that of male. For, 15 stars are called female, and only 9 male and the rest eunuch. What do we mean by 'female decanates'? It means two things: The decanate *Rāśi* may be an even sign, and may be aspected by or conjoined with a female planet. Secondly, if you look at the description of the 36 decanates, you will observe that 12 are female, can every *Rāśi* except Leo and Libra has at least one female decanate. The sex of the thief may be guessed from the limb touched by the querist. You know that the limbs are divided as male, female and eunuch. The chapter 1 of the *Saṁhitā* of Varāhamihira gives a fund of information on this subject.

The Horā gives descriptions of different parts of the body. The same information may be applied to the description of the thief's limbs too. In the case of theft the *Taskara-graha* (thief planet) should be treated as the *lagna* and the limbs are to be treated on the basis of the decanate occupied by that planet. The first decanates of the *lagna* and other houses represent the head, the eyes, ears, nostrils, cheeks, jaws and mouth. The second decanates of the 12 *bhāvas* correspond to the neck, shoulders, arms, sides, heart, chest and navel. The third decanates suggest the pelvis, the genital organ and anus, testicles, thighs, knees, calves and legs. When Mercury is combined with three other planets in the same decanate, that part of the body indicated by the decanate would invariably get an ulcer or wound or some mark like a mole, according as the planets coming together are benefic or malefic. A malefic in the 6th house produces wounds. When one of the planets in the group happens to be in his own *Rāśi* or in conjunction with Saturn, the ulcer, wound or mark must have been in the limb indicated by the decanate from the very birth. If Saturn be the planet to cause such ulcer, it would be due to a stone or some rheumatic ailment.

If Mars be the planet to cause the trouble, it would be caused by fire, a missile, poison or snake-bite. Should the planet be Mercury, the injury would be caused by a fall from a height, or by blow received from a clod or some earthy substance. If it be the Sun, the injury would be inflicted by a piece of timber or a quadruped. If it be the Moon, the hurt would arise from a horned animal or by liquids such as acids.

Thief's caste, complexion etc: The thief's caste, complexion, profession and such other details should be probed through the planets viz. the lord of the 6th house, one that aspects the 6th, one that is posited therein, or those planets that get the appellation, *Taskara graha* or thief planets.

Thief's dress: If the thief planet happens to be the Sun, the thief was wearing saffron-coloured clothes: if it be the Moon, white dress; if Mars, red clothes; if Mercury, green dress; if Jupiter, yellow dress; if Venus, colourful garment; if Saturn, black dress. In this manner prediction is to be made of the thief's dress through the *Taskara* planet posited in an angle or the 11th house, whichever is stronger.

From another point of view, the clothes worn by the thief may be coarse, if the planet in question be the Sun; if it be the Moon, new cloth; for Mars half-burnt cloth; for Mercury unwashed cloth; for Jupiter cloth that is neither old nor new: for Venus strong cloth, and for Saturn old and tattered one.

Injuries on the thief's body: If the *Taskara* planet be the Sun, the thief would be having a wound on his body. The part of the body in which the injury appears is to be deduced by the rule of decanates that are related to the three parts of the body viz. upper, middle and lower. If it be Mars, it is similar to the Sun's effects; if it be Jupiter, the thief would be having bleary eyes; if Saturn, he has a wound or scar on his left foot; if it be Venus, he has a black mole of the size of sesamum; if it be the Moon, the mole is of the size of blackgram; and if Mercury, he will be full of veins.

More features of the thief: If the 5th, 7th or 9th place from the Sun at a query be owned by a malefic and occupied by Mars and Saturn, the thief's father must be in captivity. This event may be due to (1) his underground or treacherous activities, in case the Sun or the 9th house be strong, or (2) bankruptcy, if the Sun or the 9th house be weak. If the 9th house be a movable sign, the imprisonment mentioned above must have taken place in a far-off country. If it be a fixed sign, it must be in a nearby place or town. These results may be declared on the basis of the lord of the 9th house and his *Navāṁśa* too. Similarly the imprisonment of other relatives of the thief may be predicted on the basis of the respective significators.

By this rule, treat the house occupied by the Sun as the *Taskara* ascendant and then the thief's captivity at the time of query may be predicted in the following way: See if this new ascendant is a movable sign, stable or dual one. If it is movable, imprisonment of the thief must have taken place in a distant place; if immovable, in a nearby town; and if dual, midway.

If at query all the malefics be in the 12th, 5th, 2nd and 9th houses, the thief must be suffering a term of imprisonment. The kind of imprisonment suffered will depend upon the nature of the rising *Rāśi*. For example, if the ascendant be Sagittarius, Taurus or Aries, the captivity would be through the person being bound by means of ropes; if it be Gemini, Virgo, Libra or Aquarius, it is by means of fetters; if it be Cancer. Leo or Pisces, it would be imprisonment within a fort; and if Scorpio, in a subterraneon dungeon. Again, if the rising decanate happens to be a serpent, fetters or weapon *Drekkāṇa*, and if the sign owning the decanate be also aspected by malefics, the thief would surely be suffering imprisonment. It is to be noted in this connection that the 9th house stands for character, reputation and honour. So if the house be occupied by malefics, the person's reputation is tarnished by being imprisoned for a criminal offence. On the other hand, if malefics are in the 2nd and 5th houses, his credit will be affected by his imprisonment in a civil jail. Similarly, if the thief planet is in a serpent, fetters or noose decanate, and if powerful malefics aspect the planet, the imprisonment must be quite certain. When the thief-planet is situated in Saturn's decanate, or in a serpent one, which is aspected by the Moon or Saturn, the above prediction may be made. The same result may be declared, when Saturn be in a malefic sign which is the 4th, 5th, 7th, 8th or 9th house from the *Taskara* planet, and be aspected by malefics.

Now let us try to determine the duration of the fellow's imprisonment: When Saturn occupies a movable sign, the thief's captivity was terminated soon after; if Saturn be in a fixed sign, it was for a pretty long period; if he be in a dual sign, it was for a moderate period. While determining the duration, the astrologer should take into account the portion of *Navāṁśa* already covered by the thief-planet and multiply it by the time elapsed since the beginning of the current solstice. This duration of time will have to be modified according to the planet's being in exaltation, retrogression, debilitation etc.

Sex of Planets

Mercury and Saturn are considered as eunuch, the Moon and Venus as feminine in character; and Mars, the Sun and Jupiter as masculine.

Elements of Planets

Mars, Mercury, Jupiter, Venus and Saturn are governed by fire, earth, ether, water and wind respectively.

If male planets are posited in female signs and female *Navāṁśas*, aspected by female planets, the prediction should be relating to females. On the other hand, should female planets be posited in male signs and *Aṁśas*, being aspected by male planets, the prediction would have to be about men. In the case of Mercury and Saturn who are considered as eunuchs, one ought not to construe the sex literally, but say that it refers to a woman who does not possess feminine characteristics in full; and in the case of Saturn, one should consider a man who does not possess masculine characteristics completely. However, the following distinction should be made on the basis of the nature of signs, *Aṁśas* and the aspecting planets. For example, if Mercury be posited in Aries in the third quarter of *Aśvinī* (Gemini *Navāṁśa*) and aspected by Jupiter or Mars, we have to infer a male instead of an eunuch. On the other hand, if Mercury be posited in a fixed sign and *Aṁśa*, being aspected by female planets, we have to infer a female.

Class of Planets

The Sun represents a brahmin king or a Śudra Governor; the Moon, a Brahmin or a Vaiśya; Mars, a twice-born or a Śūdra; Mercury, a Śūdra or a Vaiśya; Saturn, a Śūdra or one of low caste; Jupiter, a brahmin; Venus, a Śūdra, a Brahmin or a woman. Rāhu stands for one of mixed caste (Saṅkara). If the concerned planets be debilitated, in inimical houses or in combustion, they would point to low-class persons.

Note: If the Sun has the strength of exaltation and own house, we have to infer a king. Similarly, if the Sun occupies a brahmin sign (Cancer, Scorpio or Pisces), or is aspected by a Brahmin planet, a Brahmin alone should be thought of. If he be posited in a friend's house or *Aṁśa*, a Governor or Śūdra community is indicated. If the Moon be very powerful, aspected by Jupiter and posited in a jovian sign, a brahmin is to be understood. If she is posited in her own house or in a friendly sign or *Aṁśa*, a Vaiśya is to be inferred. A strong Mars aspected by Jupiter represents a brahmin. If he is weak, a Śūdra is indicated. A strong Mercury would indicate a Vaiśya, and a weak one, a Śūdra. A strong Saturn represents a Śūdra, while a weak one, a person of the depressed class. In this manner distinction of castes has to be made on the basis of the sign posited by the concerned planets and their strength.

Particulars of Thief

We have already seen who the *Coragrahas* (thief planets) are. Whichever house is occupied by this planet, is to be declared to be related to the thief. For example, if the planet is situated in the *Ārūḍha*, the querist himself or herself is to be declared as the thief. If the planet be posited in the 2nd house, the thief should be one among the family members. If it is the 3rd house, the culprit should be none other than his own brother or sister. In case the thief planet is posited in the 6th or 8th house from the *Ārūḍha*, the theft must have been committed on account of enmity. Taking the house occupied by the thief planet as the *lagna*, the twelve *bhāvas* should be delineated for finding out the thief's appearance, complexion, family, brothers and other relations and profession.

Thief's Residence

The thief's residence and locality are to be assessed by the astrologers through the thief planet and the zodiacal signs:

Planets Locality: Jupiter and Mercury have their residence in a village; the Moon and Venus, near lakes or rivers; and the Sun, Mars and Saturn are residents of forests.

Places of signs: Virgo, Libra and Sagittarius represent urban area; Aries, Taurus, Gemini and Aquarius, village; Leo and the first half of Capricorn stand for forest area; and lastly Cancer, Scorpio, latter half of Capricorn, and Pisces denote an area surrounded by water or near a lake.

The area allotted to the thief-planet stands for the thief's birth-place, while the sign tenanted by that planet points to his present residence. In this manner the birth-place and present residence of the thief are to be determined through the *Cora-graha* and the *Rāśi* occupied by it. In case the area of residence allotted to the planet and *Rāśi* happen to be identical, then the thief should be residing in the same place as that of his birth.

Movements of planets: Should the *Coragraha* be the Moon, the thief should be said to be moving from a village to the woods; while Venus indicates the thief's movement from the forest to a village. Venus also indicates a thief moving across shallow waters (wading through a shallow river). In the case of the Moon, the thief moves across the ocean (i.e. he must be a notorious thief with inter-continental connection). Rāhu would suggest one who moves amidst anthills, pits, caves, pools, marshy land etc. (like the dacoits of the Chambal Valley). The Sun would betoken movements in forests, while Saturn, in a cremation ground or dense, impenetrable forests. Mars' movements would be amidst bushes or bowers of creepers on hills or mountains.

Thief's Name: The Sun governs the vowels.

The Moon—Semi-vowels, i.e. *Ya*, *Ra*, *La* and *Va*.

Mars—Gutturals, i.e. *Kavarga*.

Venus—Palatals, i.e. *Cavarga*.

Mercury—Linguals, i.e. *Tavarga*.

Jupiter—Dentals, i.e. *Tavarga*.

Saturn—Labials, i.e. *Pavarga*.

Rāhu—Sibilants, i.e. *Śa*, *Ṣa*, *Sa*, *Ha* and *Ḻa*.

Rāśis and *letters*: Aries governs *a*, *ā*, *i*, *ī*, *Śa* (5)

Taurus—*u*, *ū*, *ṛ*, *Ṣa* (4)

Gemini—*ṛ*, *ḷ*, *ña*, *Sa* (4)

Cancer—*e*, *ai*, *ha* (3)

Leo—*O*, *au*, *ḷ* (3)
Virgo—*aṁ*, *aḥ*, *Kṣa* (3)
Libra—Gutturals—K*avarga.*
Scorpio—Palatala—*Cavarga.*
Sagittarius—Cerebrals—*Tavarga.*
Capricorn—Dentals—*Tavarga.*
Aquarius—Labials—*Pavarga.*
Pisces—Semi-vowels—*Ya, Ra, La, Va.*

(*Note*: The *Akṣara-kośa* of Yavaneśvara deals extensively with this topic. According to him the Moon owns the eight letters beginning with *Ya*. See *Bṛ. Saṁ. XCVI* as well as *Praśna-mārga X*-41.)

The first letter of the thief's name corresponds to the planet that aspects the ascendant, or is posited in it. If there are many such planets, then the strongest among them will give the first letter. It may also be deduced from the *Ārūḍha*, its lord, the sign occupied by the latter, the lord of *Navāṁśa* of the *Ārūḍha*, the lords of *Dvādaśāṁśa* (1/12 part) and *Triṁśāṁśa* (1/30 part of a sign).

The first letter may also conform to the lord of the 6th house, (if weak), or that of the sign tenanted by the lord of the 6th house, or to the lord of his *Navāṁśa*, or the planet that aspects or occupies the 6th house. (This rule may with advantage be applied to derive the name of the article thought of or held in the closed hand, or lost.)

Now we must proceed to discover the method for determining the letters constituting the thief's name or of the lost article. First of all we have to consider the lords of the *Navāṁśa*, *Dvādaśāṁśa* and *Triṁśāmśa* of the lord of the 6th house from the *Ārūḍha*. If the planet contributing its letter is posited in his own *Varga*, we need to consider that letter alone. On the other hand, if it is posited in another's *Varga*, we will have to take the latter's contribution also and thus have a conjunct consonant for the first letter.

If the planet contributing to the name occupies a fixed sign, the thief's name would consist of four letters; if a dual sign, it would have three letters; and if a movable sign, it would be having only two letters. Further, for dual signs, in addition to the actual name, the felon would have a surname also or a compound name.

His Natal Star: For this purpose proceed as follows:

First find out *Māndī's* longitude on the day of query. Then note the time in *Ghaṭīs* and *Vighaṭīs* yet to be covered in the particular *Navāṁśa*. Convert that time into *Vighaṭīs* and divide that number by 100. The quotient would reveal a planet beginning with the Sun. The remainder will refer to the next planet. The constellation ruled by the planet will be the thief's natal star. Further, the *Vighaṭīs* (to be covered by *Māndi* in the *Navāṁśa*) should be divided by 75 and the result will represent the Zodiacal sign beginning with the *Navāṁśa Rāśi*. The remainder will denote the particular *Rāśi*, on the basis of which the first letter of the thief's name should be determined.

Let us work out an example: Assuming the longitude of *Māndī* to be 7^{s}-10°-25′, the time yet to be covered in the *Navāṁśa* (4th) is 2°-55′. This is equal to 2 *Ghaṭīs* 55 *Vighaṭīs* which is equal to 175 *Vighaṭīs*. Dividing this by 100 we get 1.75, where the number 1 represents the Sun and the remainder, the Moon, and the constellations ruled by the Moon (in this Kerala system) are *Rohiṇī, Hasta,* and *Śravaṇa*. (Now we have to declare the felon's natal star to be one of these three. Next we have to fix the first letter of the name. For that, take the same number of *Vighaṭīs* mentioned above and divide it by 75. The result will be 2.33. This represents the third *Rāśi* from *Māndī's Navāṁśa Rāśi*, i.e. Libra. The third from Libra is Sagittarius, whose letters are those of the cerebral class or *Tavarga*. This is the method to be employed for finding out the first letter of the thief's name. This does not exhaust the subject. For, it is necessary to fix other letters of the name. According to Yavaneśvara the number of letters constituting a name is to be deduced from the rising decanate. In an odd sign, the numbers would be 3, 5 and 7 respectively for the first, second and third decanates; and in an even sign they would in order be 2, 4 and 6. They are also ascertained from the strength of the aspect of planets. It is well-known to students of astrology that there are four kinds of planetary aspects as quarter, half, three-fourths and full. If the *Vargottamāṁśa* of a sign be signified by an even and movable one, the name would consist of two syllables; if by an even and fixed sign, four syllables. If the *Vargottamāṁśa* be an odd and movable sign, there would be three letters. If it be fixed as well as odd sign, five syllables. If the *lagna* be a dual sign, the name would consist of as many letters, as correspond to the nature (odd or even) of the sign. When the planet is posited in his highest exaltation, the letter is repeated; and the name will have a strong syllable (Guru) in the particular place signified by the rising *Navāṁśa*. The length and shortness of the syllables are derived from the long and medium or short signs respectively rising at the time.

The letters of the name are derived from the *Navāṁśas* of the signs that are the 1st, 4th, 7th and 10th houses. A malefic situated in an angle destroys a syallable, while in a *Koṇa* he destroys only a *Mātrā* (syllabic instant). His aspect too produces the same result. Among the four lords of angles the strongest will give the first letter. The following letters will be in the order of their relative strength.

Nature of Article

When a querist or his messenger informs the astrologer about a missing or stolen article, he should calculate the longitudes of the Moon for the moment, and *Māndī*, and take the stronger of the two as the *Ārūḍha*. On the basis of this ascendant he should determine the nature of the article as metallic, wooden or animal.

The present position of the thief and the lost object may be predicted on the basis of the sign occupied by the lord of the 2nd house, according to the rule prescribed by Varāhamihira in I-5 of the *Bṛhajjātaka*. The following is according to the *Daśādhyāyī*:

Aries: This represents a person who is fond of wandering, eats quickly, possessed of dirty nails, afraid of water, lustful and village-dweller.

Taurus: He is one of slow gait, of a large face, having excessive appetite and great endurance, and living in a village.

Gemini: He is a villager, proficient in fine arts, like music, dance etc., clever in sexual dalliance, capable of reading others' thoughts, jocular, and fond of eating.

Cancer: One who walks in a zig-zag fashion, fond of water or one who is interested in sinking wells or tanks.

Leo: A man with a broad face, hater of women, hot-tempered, given to meat-eating, habituated to living in a secluded place, suffering from dental and stomach ailments, full of prowess, haughty and troubled by hunger and thirst.

Virgo: One who is fond of sexual union, bashful, sweet-tongued, staying in another's house, and a city-dweller.

Libra: One who is expert in trade and commerce, of a lean and shaky body, living in a town, and opulent.

Scorpio: One who moves secretly, is full of venom in thought and speech and cruel deeds.

Sagittarius: (First half) represents one of a short stature, stands in need of others' help, and fond of fighting, and a city-dweller. (The second half) represents one with a long face, heroic, with big teeth, generally staying near the king's palace.

Capricorn: This shows one who has lean lower limbs, charming eyes and is sprightly.

Aquarius: One who takes very little water, is corpulent, capable of carrying heavy responsibilities, and is a dweller in a rural area.

Pisces: It is one having an attractive personality and eyes and a big head; he eats fish and such other aquatic food.

Present Locality of Stolen Goods

If the lord of the 2nd house from the *Arūḍha* be in a movable house, the stolen article has been carried to a distant place, while if it be a fixed sign, it should be in a nearby place; and if it be a dual sign, it would be in a place which is neither very near nor very far.

Thief

He is of two types viz. internal and external. The lord of 3rd house points to an internal thief, while the lord of the 6th house, to an external one. This has to be judged from the comparative strength of the lords of the 3rd and 6th houses. In case the lord of the 2nd house and the *Coragraha* (thief planet) are in conjunction or mutual aspect, or if the thief planet be posited in the 11th house, the astrologer should declare that the article is stolen. If these two conditions are not fulfilled, the article is not stolen but only misplaced.

RECOVERY OF ARTICLES

The purpose of the querist in seeking the diviner's help is to know if the lost article could be recovered, and allied matters. If the ascendant be a malefic sign, tenanted by another malefic and aspected by yet another malefic, it would be quite clear that the lost property could not be regained. However, in the above condition, if benefics be involved (by aspect or occupation), a portion of the lost property may be recovered, or recovered fully after a long time; or it might be in the form of monetary compensation. If, on the other hand, the ascendant be a benefic sign, occupied or aspected by benefics, the lost articles would definitely be recovered. In case malefics too are involved in the above configuration by aspect or conjunction, the article would not be regained, though the owner may have the chance of seeing it.

The article would be recovered very soon, if the full Moon be posited in the *lagna*, receiving Jupiter's or Venus's aspect. The same effect would follow, if a powerful benefic be posited in the 11th house.

The above effect could be predicted, if a *Śirṣodaya* (rising with head in front) sign be the *lagna*, occupied by the strong Moon or a benefic, and aspected by a benefic.

The *Kṛṣṇīya* that has been already referred to is held in high esteem in Kerala specially in the sphere of horary astrology. Its author has given some interesting points in Chapter XXIX, which I would like to share with my readers: First, he gives the effect of the ascendant being occupied by a particular planet. Next he gives the effect of an ascendant being aspected by different planets, jointly and separately.

When Aries is the ascendant and occupied by the Moon, a child's bracelet would be the article that is lost. If it is posited by Mercury, it would be a gold necklace or a bangle lost in a garden lake.

If it be, by Venus, a gold-embroidered cloth, taken away by the owner's own sister or mother.

If the planet in this *lagna* be Jupiter, it is a gold ornament stolen in a crowd on the occasion of a death or fire-accident by a twice-born of the neighbourhood with golden complexion.

If Saturn be in the same ascendant (Aries), it should be declared that some gold coins that were buried underground were stolen by a servant-woman living next door. A lady, who was of a golden complexion, lost her pearl-necklace, while bathing in a tank. She would find the ornament sparkling by the rays of the midday Sun, on the fourth day.

When Aries ascendant is aspected by Mercury, the querist should be told that his mules are lost, and would be recovered the next day at day-break, when he goes out in search of them.

When Venus aspects the *lagna*, two cows, one of which is carrying, and a bull are missing, and they would be found on the 8th day.

When it is aspected by Saturn, some goats were lost four days previously, but on the 9th day they would be driven home by a friend living in the neighbourhood.

If the *lagna* be aspected by both the Moon and Venus, the querist should be told that an informant would bring the tidings the same night that his head of cattle numbering eighty were abducted along with the cowherd.

If the aspecting planets be the Moon and Mars, twelve she-buffaloes were lost, but only eleven would be brought back the next day by a friend. If Mars and Saturn should aspect it, vessels made of gold and bronze would be lost and be recovered on the 7th day by cowherds.

If the aspectors be Jupiter, Venus and the Moon, the missing objects are bracelets and shawls, lying on the cot and were taken away by the maid servant named horse. It has been kept in a box kept on a coverlet near water in the fourth house in the street. It is kept dangling inside water.

When the ascendant Aries be aspected by Jupiter and Mars, a golden sphere kept in a box was stolen by a hunch-backed maid and transferred to her friend.

When the ascendant be aspected by Mars and Mercury, bronze vessels and gold embroidered clothes were stolen by a clerk (writer), one of the vessels being broken.

If Jupiter and Mars be exalted and Aries be the ascendant, the loss is that of the holy pot meant for the king's coronation ceremony, but it can hardly be recovered.

If the Moon be in the initial portion of the *lagna*, the thief would be a government servant; if the portion be the middle one, a woman, the thief; and if the last, a painter.

The general rule applicable to all ascendants is that Mars posited in the initial portion, the thief is a lad; if in the middle, a poet; and in the final part, a servant.

Venus posited in a quadruped sign points to a cow; Saturn, to bulls; Jupiter in the 7th house, to a horse.

If the ascendant be aspected by planets of reptilian nature, posited in similar signs, it would suggest ornaments; on the other hand, if they be posited in Leo, it would betoken bronze and gold.

If the ascendant be Taurus, the lost object would be a quadruped; if it be aspected by Venus, clothes; if by Jupiter, Copper; if by Mercury, a gem-set vessel; if by Saturn, black iron; if by the Moon, a woman; if by the Sun, a crest-jewel; and if by Mars, a girdle.

If aspected by Jupiter and Saturn, the ascendant would point to gold and glass; if by Mars and Saturn, ornaments worn by women on their face; and if by the Moon and Venus, gold-studded clothes.

Sex Distinction

The Sun and Mercury, if posited in male *Rāśis*, are males; if in female *Rāśis*, eunuchs; and the Sun, Mars and Jupiter, being posited in male signs, become undoubtedly males.

The Moon and Venus are always feminine in the discussion of all houses. If posited in the initial portion of a movable sign, they rule ponds, wells and rivers.

Gemini Ascendant

When this ascendant is aspected by Mercury, music, messenger or ambassador, writer, woman, door-keeper, architect, and couple as well as ornaments, are indicated.

If it be aspected by Venus, garments; if by Mars, gold; if by Saturn, iron; if by Jupiter, gold; if by the Sun, an animal; and if by the Moon, clothes.

Cancer Ascendant

If Cancer be rising at query, the owner who had gone to the

garden for a stroll, lost his (or her) gold ornament (ring or bangle) near a lake. It was picked up from that place and taken away by a female servant. Should the ascendant be aspected by the Moon, the ornament had fallen into the water of the lake, when a party of picnic friends was busy with its lunch in the flower garden. If it be posited by Venus, the lost ornament was stolen by a woman; if by Saturn, by a servant woman; if by the Sun, by a brahmin; if by Jupiter, by a friend; and if by Mercury, by the cook. If the ascendant be occupied by Venus, it was lost in a tank; if by the Sun and Mars, in a waterless tank; if by Mercury, in a garden; and if by the Moon, in the bath-room.

Leo Ascendant

If the initial part of the sign Leo be rising, the article lost would be gold; if the middle part, gold; and if the last portion, a coverlet, provided there be no planet in the ascendant. In case there be the Sun, Mars, Jupiter, Mercury, Saturn, Moon and Venus in the *lagna*, the respective articles lost would be (1) Gold, (2) Copper, (3) Silver, (4) Gem, (5) Iron vessels, (6) Bronze vessels, and (7) Lead articles. Different articles or metals are indicated for the aspects of the Sun, Saturn, Mercury, Venus, the Moon, and Mars. viz., gold, pearl-necklace, emerald ornament, gold, coverlet, gold and a collection of gold ornaments.

Sagittarius Ascendant

If this *lagna* be posited by none, the following articles would be suggested: Some work of art, a quadruped, pearls, gold, gems, diamond and gold.

If the Sun be posited in the ascendant (i.e. Sagittarius) the article missing or stolen would be gold or weapons; if by Saturn, a treasure. If Rāhu be in the ascendant, the person concerned would be an old woman or slave. If Mars be there, it would be an armour, ivory, gold, bow and shield.

When Capricorn rises, gold, ornaments, bed, lead, garments, iron, bronze, tin and brass. If it is posited by Mercury and Saturn, it would be some drink; if by Venus and Saturn, eating plates or kitchen utensils. If Saturn be in the *lagna*, it would be black iron; if the Moon, diamond; if Mercury, a gem jar; if

Venus, scents; if Mars, lac; and if the Sun, gold. Should the Moon be posited in her highest exaltation, a woman of an aristocratic family.

In treating the sign, Aries and Scorpio should be taken as equal; similarly Taurus and Libra; Virgo and Gemini; Sagittarius and Pisces; and Capricorn and Aquarius.

If the planets aspect their own *Aṁśas* in the *lagna*, they would suggest appropriate articles as shown below:

(1) The Moon—Gold; (2) The Sun—Copper; (3) Jupiter—Gold; (4) Venus—a Woman; Saturn—Bronze. If Venus' *Aṁśa* is aspected, a man and a woman are indicated; if by the Sun, copper; if by Mercury, a carriage; if by the Moon clothes or silken robes; if by Saturn, a wooden *Kamaṇḍalu* (water-pot).

CHAPTER XVI

LOST HOROSCOPES

THERE ARE MANY persons in society whose horoscopes or birth-data were not noted at birth. Later in their life they may wish to know their birth stars and such other details, when they find that their business activities do not run smoothly. Some of them who have faith in the sayings of the ancient sages wish to propitiate the divine planets, gods and other deities that had been worshipped in their families by their ancestors, in order to win their favours for warding off obstacles in their way and to achieve progress and prosperity. To this end they repair to the astrologers who, they think, would be able to deliver the goods.

BIRTH STAR

In this connection certain basic numbers are assigned to the 12 signs of the Zodiac as follows:

Aries—12; Taurus—5; Gemini—10; Cancer—3; Leo—8; Virgo—1; Libra—6; Scorpio—11; Sagittarius—4; Capricorn—2; Aquarius—9; and Pisces—7. These numbers are utilized when these Zodiacal signs happen to be the *Ārūḍha*. There is a basic group of 49 in this scheme. Now the number allotted to the *Ārūḍha* sign should be deducted from the basic group, i.e. 49. The balance should be multiplied by 7 and divided by 27. The remainder will give the star from *Āśvinī*.

Let us take an example: Let the *Ārūḍha* be Leo whose basic number is 8. So $(49-8)\times 7 \div 27 = 10\frac{17}{27}$. Hence the natal star of the querist must be the 17th from *Āśvinī*, i.e. *Anurādhā*.

DETERMINATION OF PLACES OF ASCENDANT, JUPITER AND SUN

First of all the astrologer should fix Jupiter's place in the chart. Then take a new group number as 42, which will help you in determining Jupiter's position. For fixing the Sun's position the Group Number is 35; and for the ascendant, it is 28. Now let us work out Jupiter's star at the querist's nativity: $42-8=$ (which is the deduction of the number allotted to the *Ārūḍha*)

$34 \times 7 \div 27 = 8\frac{22}{27}$, i.e. the star occupied by Jupiter is *Śravaṇa*. Similarly, work out the star occupied by the Sun as follows: $[\{(35-8)/27\}7=7]$ and no balance. In other words, the balance is 27 $=$ *Revatī*. For the natal ascendant proceed thus: $[(28-8)/27]\times 7$ $=5\frac{5}{27}=$ the 5th star viz. *Mṛgaśirṣa*.

Another Method for Natal Star

First of all work out the Moon's longitude for the query time. Let us take it as 6ˢ-5°-54′-22″. This is the second *Navāṁśa* of Libra, i.e. the 4th quarter of *Citrā*. Now find out the expired portion of this second *Navāṁśa*, which is 2°-34′-22″. Convert this into minutes and seconds. It comes to 154′-22″. Multiply this by 9, which comes to 1389′-18″. Divide this by 5, and you get 277′-52″, i.e. 278′. This should be divided by 27 and the remainder would give the querist's natal star. By dividing 278 by 27 you get 8 as the remainder, which means it is the 8th star from *Āśvinī* or *Puṣya*.

Similarly, the same process may be repeated with the expired portion of the *Lagnāṁśaka*.

Omens for Fixing Natal Sign

Aries: The following omens indicate the birth sign to be Aries: sight or mention of Cactus, *Arka* leaf, bleating of sheep or goats, blanket etc.

Taurus: Bull, cow, its hide, lowing, ghee, plough, grass etc.

Gemini: A lute, couple, max, bed, betel etc.

Cancer: Fish, nice clay, crab, dry leaf, water etc.

Leo: Pictures of lions, tigers, elephants, deer, their horns etc.

Virgo: A young girl, boat, lamp, paddy (*Kalamā*), a burning torch etc.

Libra: Arrival of a hawker, trading, measure, weights, balance; business talk etc.

Scorpio: Insects, snake, one who treats persons for snake-bite, scorpion, etc.

Sagittarius: A bowman, arrow, horse, its picture etc.

Capricorn: Antelope, its horns, skin etc.

Aquarius: A pot, potter, water-vessel etc.

Pisces: Sea, fishing net, heap of fish, water, boat etc.

Another Method

Calculate the ascendant at this query and note the comparative strength of the three trines. The strongest of these *Rāśis* may be adopted as the querist's natal sign. In case all the three *Rāśis* are of equal strength, see which part of the body the querist touches. The *Rāśi* corresponding to that limb may be taken as the required natal sign. If he does not touch any part, note the direction he occupies or faces; and that *Rāśi* can be accepted. Another alternative is the first letter of the sentence spoken by the querist. The words *Gaṅgā*, *Rudra*, Ramā, *Maṇi*, Mama, *Vṛṣa* and such other words are said to point to Aries and other *Rāśis*. According to the *Kṛṣṇīya* the querist's natal sign will be that owned by the strongest of the planets that aspect the direction (i.e. sign) occupied by the querist. In the case of such planets as own two houses, except the luminaries, the nature, as odd or even, of the *Rāśis* will be determined by the *Rāśi* occupied by the aspecting planet. If there be no planet aspecting the *Ārūḍha*, take the strongest of the four *kendras*, as the natal sign. Similarly, the natal ascendant of the querist should be fixed on the basis of the strongest of the planets that aspect the ascendant at query. The counting of odd and even signs should be done for the sake of accuracy of the result, from Aries as well as from the sign of the *Ārūḍha*. If both the results be in agreement, you could conclude that the final judgment is perfect.

Another method: Count the number by which the ascendant at query is separated from the *Ārūḍha*. Let it be x. Multiply it by 2 and subtract 1 from the product. That is $=(2x-1)$. Now count from *Aśvinī* the number of stars to the star of the day in question. Let it be y. Add this to $(2x-1)=(2x-1)+y$. Subtract 27 from the latest result, which is$=2x-1+y-27$. Now count from *Aśvinī* so many stars as revealed by this number. That will be the natal star of the lost horoscope.

Count the number of persons including the astrologer and querist at the session. Multiply it by 3 and divide the product by 27. The remainder will give the required star at his birth, from *Aśvinī* or *Maghā*, or *Mūla* on the basis of the ascendant at query being a movable *Rāśi*, or immovable *Rāsi*, or a dual sign, as the case may be.

Solar month: If the Sun is posited in one of the six signs beginning with the *Ārūḍha*, it will be *Uttarāyaṇa* (beginning with the Sun's entry into Capricorn); and if the Sun be in one of the six signs counted from the 7th house, it would be *Dakṣiṇāyaṇa* (beginning with the Sun's entry into Cancer). Should the Sun be posited in the *Ārūḍha*, the Sun at the birth of the querist must have occupied Gemini. That means the querist must have taken his birth in the solar month of Mithuna. If the Sun at query be in the 12th house from the *Ārūḍha*, he must have been born in the month of Karka or Cancer. If he be in the 11th house, the person's birth must have been in the month of Siṁha or Leo. The counting must be done in this manner, i.e. in the opposite direction. If the Sun be in the 2nd house, the birth must have been in the month of Taurus.

If the ascendant at query be in the first half (Horā) of the sign, the querist's birth must have taken place in the *Uttarāyaṇa*; while in the second half, it would be *Dakṣiṇāyaṇa*. If during the query session the person touches some part on his right side, his birth solstice would be the winter one, while if it be on the left side, summer solstice. If the querist touches a limb on the same side as the nostril through which the astrologer's breath flows, the solstice would be determined by the side of the body touched by the querist.

Multiply the number of the *Ārūḍha* sign by 9 and divide the result by 27. The remainder will give the natal Star of the querist.

Birth Ascendant

If the ascendant at query be an odd sign, the person's natal *lagna* would be in one of the first six *Rāśis*. On the basis of the rising decanate at query, the natal ascendant is determined. Here a decanate extends only for 5 degrees. So in the rising sign up to 15° there will be three decanates called *Vṛṣabha*, Mithuna and *Meṣa*. From 15° to 20° it is Leo decanate, then up to 25° Virgo decanate, and up to 30° Cancer decanate. When at even sign rises, the natal *lagna* would be one of the six signs from Libra. In this the order is—the first 5° portion is *Vṛścika*, the next 5° portion, Sagittarius, the next, i.e. up to 15° it is Tulā *lagna*; then up to 20°, it is Kumbha *lagna*; then up to 25° it is Mīna; and up to 30° it is Makara *lagna*.

Aṣṭamaṅgala Method

The *Aṣṭamaṅgala* methodology has been already explained. There 108 cowries are divided into three heaps; and each is divided by 8. So each will yield some remainder. Add these three remainders and keep the sum in two places. The sum kept in one place should be divided by 8 and the remainder to be kept separately. Now we have the first sum of three remainders kept apart and this final remainder-altogether four numbers. Now take the first remainder and multiply it by 64 and divide by 225. Keep apart the quotient, and multiply the remainder by 12, 30 and 60 in order and divide the results separately by 225. The result will be in signs, degrees and minutes respectively. And this will be the longitude of the querist's natal Moon.

Next take the number kept in the 2nd place and multiply it by 48 and divide the result by 225. Keep the quotient apart and take only the remainder. Treat this as in the previous case by multiplying by 12, 30 and 60 severally and dividing the sums by 225. The resulting figure will be in signs, degrees and minutes. And this will be the Sun's longitude at birth of the querist.

The third number also should be treated in a similar manner. Multiply it by 32 and divide the result by 225. Keeping the quotient apart, multiply the remainder alone severally by 12, 30 and 60 and divide the results by 225. The resulting figures in signs, degrees and minutes would represent the longitude of Jupiter at birth.

The fourth number should be multiplied by 16 and the sum divided by 225. As before keeping the quotient apart, treat the remainder as before. The resulting figures will represent in signs, degrees and minutes the longitude of the ascendant at querist's nativity. This procedure is named *Catussādhana* by astrologers.

There is still some correction to be applied to the four longitudes given above. You remember that the 12 signs are divided into diurnal signs (ruled by the Sun) and nocturnal signs (ruled by the Moon). Now if both the *Ārūḍha* and the ascendant at query be nocturnal signs, take the quotient kept aside in the four places severally and add that number to the minutes. This will be the correct longitude. If, on the other hand, the above two *lagnas*, be diurnal signs, then the figure of quotient kept aside should be deducted from the minutes. In case one is nocturnal and other diurnal, the Moon being strong, add only ½ the figure; if the Sun be strong, deduct only ½ the figure from the minutes. Now you have the accurate longitudes of the above four entities.

Another View

Keep the Moon's longitude at query in two places. Deduct the longitude of the *lagna* from the Moon's longitude kept in one place. Add this result to the Moon's longitude kept in the 2nd place. This, they say, would represent the person's lunar longitude at birth.

In case the ascendant at query be Pisces, then the same figures represent the natal Moon's longitude, according to some scholars.

Month of Nativity

Should the *lagna* at query be Aries, the month (lunar) of birth would be *Vaiśākha*; if it be Taurus, the month of birth, *Jyaiṣṭha*; and so on without break. For Pisces *lagna*, the month would be Caitra. How to distinguish the two fortnights? If the *lagna* be an odd sign having the aspect of a male planet, it would be bright fortnight; on the other hand, if the *lagna* be an even sign, and has the aspect of a female planet, it is dark fortnight. In case the sign is odd, and the aspecting planet female, judgment will have to be done on their comparative strength.

Natal Sign and Ascendant

Find out the sign posited by the lord of the exaltation sign of the *Ārūḍha*-lord. The sign occupied by the lord of the above sign should be considered as the sign of the natal Moon of the querist.

Let us make this statement a bit clearer through an illustration: Let the *Ārūḍha* be Taurus, whose lord Venus' exaltation sign being Pisces, is owned by Jupiter, who is posited in the *Ārūḍha*, itself. Its lord is in Virgo. So this sign viz. Virgo should be taken as the querist's natal sign. Now the debilitation sign of the lord of the *Ārūḍha* is Virgo. Its lord Mercury is in Libra, whose lord Venus, is in Virgo. So, that sign again becomes the person's ascendant at birth. Hence we find that both the natal Moon and natal ascendant find their place in Virgo itself.

Mars 6	—	R. Jupi. 12 *Ārūḍha*	—
Rāhu 12.	Illustration 1988-11-10		—
—			Ketu 6
Saturn 2	Moon 4	Sun 3 Mercury 10	Venus 3 N. S. N. Asct.

ANOTHER METHOD

Some speak of another method for determining the ascendant at birth: Should the querist be seated while putting the question, the 7th sign from the ascendant at query would be the natal *lagna*; should he be standing, it would be the 10th house from the *Ārūḍha*; should he be just getting up, the *lagna* itself is the natal ascendant; and should he be lying down, the 4th house.

For this we require the sign rising at query. Let the time of query be 8-30 A.M. The ascendant for this time and place is 7^s-21°-31′-57″, whose *Navāṁśa* sign is Capricorn. So this should be adjudged as the natal ascendant.

According to another interpretation of the original word of Varāhamihira, it is not the same sign, but one similar to that. Hence as Capricorn is the 3rd *Rāśi* from the query *lagna*, the natal *lagna* should be the 3rd from the *Navāṁśa Rāśi*, i.e. Pisces.

Find out the sign representing the rising decanate. Now count the number of decanates from this rising decanate to the Sun's decanate. Count so many *Rāśis* from the ascendant at query to get the ascendant at birth. Now the rising decanate is the third of Scorpio. What is the distance between this rising decanate and the decanate occupied by the Sun? It is exactly 33 decanates. As the number is more than 12 and its multiple 24, deducting 24 you get the remainder 9. Count 9 signs from the *lagna*, i.e. Scorpio, which is Cancer. Call this the natal ascendant.

JUPITER AT BIRTH

If the rising decanate at query be the first one, then Jupiter's position at birth should be in the same place as he is found at query; if the decanate be the 2nd, Jupiter would be in the 5th place from his present position at birth; and if the decanate rising be the 3rd he would be in the 9th place from his present position. Now applying this rule to our example, as the query ascendant is in the 3rd decanate, we have to locate Jupiter in the 9th house from Taurus, i.e. Capricorn.

Find out the *Dvādaśāṁśa* sign of the rising sign. That would be the sign occupied by Jupiter at birth. Hence 1/12 *Aṁśa Rāśi* of the *lagna* happens to be the 9th from the ascendant, i.e. Cancer. This should be taken as the position of Jupiter at the person's birth. But Jupiter completes one round of the circle of the Zodiacal signs in about 12 years. For finding out the number of rounds completed by him we have to make use of the years of the *Nisargadaśā* (natural Daśā) of the planets posited in the *lagna*. For the Moon it is 1; for Mars, 2; for Mercury, 3; for Venus, 4; for Jupiter, 5; for the Sun, 6 and for Saturn, 7. If there be more than one planet, the *Nisargadaśā* figure of the strongest planet should be taken as the number of rounds completed by Jupiter. For example, if the ascendant at query be occupied by the Moon, the person is a boy or girl who has not yet completed 12 years of life. If Mars be there, Jupiter must be in his 2nd round of the Zodiac. Should Saturn be in the ascendant, Jupiter must be doing his 7th round, i.e. the person must be past 72 years and not more than 84 years in age. The age of the querist may also be guessed approximately from his appearance.

There is a method for fixing Jupiter's place at a person's birth on the basis of a 12th division of the decanate of the ascendant at query. You know that a decanate consists of a 10° portion. When that is cut into 12 equal parts, each part has a portion of 50′. Now find out the *Rāśi* of the *Dvādaśāṁśa* of the particular decanate of the ascendant. Count the number of the *Rāśi* from the ascendant. That would show the position of Jupiter at the person's birth.

Natal Asterism on the Basis of Indications

If the querist touches different parts of his body, his natal star may be one of the stars beginning with *Kṛttikā* as shown below:

Part Touched	*Natal Asterism*	*Part Touched*	*Natal Asterism*
Head	Kṛttikā	Tooth	Āśleṣā
Fore-head	Rohiṇī	Neck	Maghā
Brows	Mṛgaśiras.	Right shoulder	P. Phālgunī
Ears	Ārdrā	Left shoulder	U. Phālgunī
Temples	Punarvasu	Hands	Hasta
Chin	Puṣya	Fingers	*Citrā*
		Nail	Svāti

Part Touched	*Star*	*Part Touched*	*Star*
Chest	Visākhā	Navel pit	Śravaṇa.
Heart	Anurādhā	Hips	Dhaniṣṭhā.
Nipples	Jyeṣṭhā	Privities	Śatabhisaj.
Stomach	Mūla	Right thigh	Pūrvābhādra
Right side of abdomen	P. Āṣāḍhā	Left thigh	U. Pūrvābhādra
		Knees	Revatī
Left side of abdomen	U. Āṣāḍhā	Shanks	Aśvinī
		Feet	Bharaṇī

If the querist's touching of limbs is not quite clear, this rule will not be of much use. In that case other methods are to be made use of.

Ṛtu of Birth

There are six *Ṛtus* or seasons in India as Spring, Summer, Rainy, Autumn, Dewy and Winter. The *Ṛtu* of birth should be determined by the ruler of the rising decanate or by the planet occupying the *lagna*, whichever is stronger. The rulers of these seasons are in order Venus, Sun and Mars, Moon, Mercury, Jupiter and Saturn. If the season thus found does not fit in with the solstice (*Ayana*) of birth, but belongs to the other *Ayana*, the correct *Ṛtu* should be predicted on the basis of solar transits. In case there is disagreement between the season (*Ṛtu*) and solstice (*Ayana*), what you have to do is to exchange the Moon, Mercury and Jupiter for Venus, Mars and Saturn respectively. The rising decanate determines the first or second month of the *Ṛtu* according as the first or second half of the decanate is rising.

To determine the lunar day (*tithi*) of the month, proceed thus; convert the degrees, minutes etc. of the decanate that is rising into minutes. If the result is more than 300′, then subract 300. From the remainder find out the *tithi* at the rate of 10′ per *tithi*. According to others the *tithi* is exactly equivalent to the number of degrees, minutes etc. covered by the Sun. If a diurnal sign rises at query, then the birth was at night and vice versa. Similarly the degrees rising on the *lagna* indicate the *Ghaṭikās* after sunrise or sunset as the case may be.

Natal Star

The 8 directions beginning with the east have their own numbers assigned to them as follows: east = 2; S.E. = 3; south = 14; S.W. = 10; west = 15; N.W. = 21; north = 9; and N.E. = 8. Note the direction the querist is facing. Multiply the number of that particular direction by 15 and add the number of persons facing the same direction at the time. Deduct 27 from the result. The remainder will represent the number of star at birth, counting from *Dhaniṣṭhā*.

Chapter XVII

DECANATES AND STARS

Aries: First Decanate

It is a man wearing a white cloth round his waist, black in colour, able to protect many, fierce in appearance, with an axe in hand lifted up, and of reddish eyes. He is generous, but taking things by force, brilliant, fond of fighting, getting up quickly and punisher of his kinsmen ruthlessly.

Second Decanate

It is a woman clad in red garments, fond of ornaments and eatables, round like a pot in appearance, possessed of a face like that of a horse, exceedingly thirsty and standing only on one foot. It represents a woman who is very ambitious for power, ornaments etc., unsettled in life, with an unsymmetrical body.

According to the *Sārāvalī*, it is a romantic man, fond of women, interested in a jolly life, high-minded, lover of music, good-looking, having many friends and plenty of wealth.

Third Decanate

A man who is cruel, skilled in fine arts, of brown colour, active but disappointed in achieving his ambition, with a raised hand holding a rod. He is very angry and wears red garments. This is also of the nature of weapon. It is a man who is not successful in spite of his talents. The *Sārāvalī* represents this as a man serving his king, virtuous, but not very learned, doing harm to others and fond of his spouse and kinsmen and interested in meritorious deeds.

Taurus

The first decanate of this is a woman with her hair curly and cut, with a pot-like body, wearing clothes that are partly burnt, thirsty and hungry and fond of ornaments. She is pining for her lover, being clad in fine clothes bedecked with jewels. She is youthful and engaged in her own duties.

Second Decanate

This is represented by a man who is well-versed in wet-land cultivation (husbandry), cereals, architecture (housemanship), dairy-farming and fine arts; he possesses the expertise in the manufacture and use of the plough and chariots. His neck resembles that of a bull; he is hungry and possesses the face of a ram and is clad in dirty clothes. He appears quite gentle and attractive to the members of the fair sex; he has a thick lower lip; he is endowed with both personal charm and wealth. He is high-minded, firm and loved by greedy women.

Third Decanate

This is a man having a huge body like an elephant, with white teeth, feet like those of a camel and of brown colour. He is fond of sheep and deer, with his mind perplexed. This decanate is both a male and a quadruped. According to the *Sārāvalī* it is a clever person, but without luck, though heroic, slovenly; he extracts money from others but later repents.

Gemini

First decanate is a woman fond of needle work, charming, with raised hands; she is interested in decorative work. Though she has come of age she has no children. According to *Sārāvalī* it is a male, tall, rich, with a big head; though a good man, yet he is a gambler, accustomed to a luxurious life; he gets honour from the king and is a good speaker.

Second Decanate

It is an armed decanate. It is a man standing in a garden, wearing armour, and armed with a bow; he is valiant, a professional warrior. He has an aquiline face. He loves sports and children. He is always thinking of ornaments and wealth. He is famous, of a short stature and small face, gentle-looking, of short hair, happy and very intelligent.

THIRD DECANATE

It is a man decked with ornaments, rich in jewels, fastened with a coat of mail and a quiver, and carrying a bow. He is skilled in the arts of music and dance, and is a poet. According to the *Sārāvalī* it is a tall, handsome man, a misogynist, with a big head, having many enemies, stubborn, with dry nails, feet and palms, and a shaky body.

CANCER: FIRST DECANATE

It is a man holding leaves, roots and fruits and having an elephantine body, stationed in a forest of sandalwood trees, and having feet like those of a camel. His face resembles that of, a hog and neck similar to that of a horse. According to the other work, it is a fair-complexioned man, who is unsteady but devoted to God and Brāhmaṇas, intelligent, handsome having a good wife and helping others.

SECOND DECANATE

It is a woman with her head decorated with lotus-flowers, and carrying a snake with her. She is rough in her behaviour and is crying aloud in a forest. She is resting on a branch of the *Palāśa* tree. The other authority says that it is a man who is greedy, speaking sweetly, fond of sleeping, hen-pecked, conceited, having brothers, ease-loving, unsteady and afflicted by many ailments.

THIRD DECANATE

This is a man who has started on a voyage to procure ornaments for his wife. He has a serpent coiled round his body. He is flat-nosed, and is wearing gold ornaments. This man is very much attached to women, wealth, going abroad, gentle, fond of liquor, forest and water, of poor eye-sight, and wearing garlands.

LEO: FIRST DECANATE

This is of the form of a vulture and a jackal sitting on a silk-cotton tree and resembles a dog as well as a man with dirty garments. He is crying aloud owing to separation from his parents. The other says: It is a leader who is intent on vanquishing enemies, is a charitable person, friend of rich ladies, possessed of great prowess and serving many kings.

Second Decanate

It is a man with the shape of a horse, wearing on his head garlands of whitish colour. He covers himself with deer skin and a blanket. He is unassailable like a lion. He carries a bow, and his nose is slightly bent at the tip.

The other says: It is a man who is generous in gifts, does noble deeds, is firm, handsome, anxious for warfare, happy, interested in scriptures and meritorious deeds; and very intelligent.

Third Decanate

This is represented by a man having the face of a bear; he behaves like a monkey; he carries a stick, fruits and meat in his hands. He has a long beard and curly hair. He is greedy for others' wealth, youthful, stubborn, of lofty mind, a gambler, efficient, short in stature, having many children.

Virgo: First Decanate

It is a young damsel holding a pot full of flowers, clad in dirty clothes. She longs for good clothes, wealth and union and wishes to go to her father's residence. The other says: It is a handsome, tall man, who is polite, eloquent, of tender limbs. He has a long head, eyes like honey and is intent on getting money from women.

Second Decanate

It is a man holding a pen in his hand; he is dark in colour and has his head tied with a cloth. He spends and earns money. He carries a large bow, and his entire body is covered with hair. He is courageous, expert in the narration of scientific stories, skilled in warfare, very talkative, learned, friend of forest-dwellers and travelling in foreign lands.

Third Decanate

It is a woman, golden in complexion, with her body covered by fine, clean garments; she is tall and holds in her hand a pot and a ladle. She is pious and going to the temple. According to the other view it is a person who is keenly interested in singing; he is a protégé of a king. He is short and has big eyes and a big head.

Libra: First Decanate

It is a man who has entered a shop on the way with a balance in hand. He is clever in measuring and weighing, and holds a weight in hand. He is thinking of his wares and their prices. He is a traveller, clever and very handsome. He is very wise, an obedient worker and looks after his wares.

Second Decanate

It is a man with a vulture's face; he is hungry, thirsty and wishes to go out with a pot in hand. He is thinking of his wife and children. The man has large eyes like the lotus; he is good-looking, of sweet speech, and an adventurous spirit. He is well-ornamented and famous. He follows in the foot-steps of the elders of his family.

Third Decanate

It is a man fully adorned with gems, who is carrying a quiver and a coat of mail made of gold. He is like a monkey in appearance and carries fruits and meat, and stands frightening the deer in the forest. He is fickle-minded, roguish, ungrateful, ugly and of crooked limbs. He has lost all his friends, wealth and reputation. He is not intelligent.

Scorpio: First Decanate

It is a beautiful woman bereft of garments and ornaments. She has lost her position. She is coming out of the great ocean to the shore with her feet tied up with a serpent. According to the *Sārāvalī* it is a man of golden complexion, firm, fierce, and an adept in warfare. He is a quarrelsome person with large eyes and a corpulent and tall body.

Second Decanate

It is a woman wishing for all kinds of comforts and a refuge. She has a serpent coiled round her person for the sake of her husband. She has a body similar to that of a turtle, or a pot. The other says it is a man fond of good and sumptuous food and drinks. He is handsome, possessed of arts and virtues. He has fleeting looks. He has a golden complexion. He is enjoying others' wealth.

THIRD DECANATE

It has a leonine form with a face broad and flat like a turtle. It scares away dogs, deer, hogs and jackals, and guards the sandal-wood regions. According to others, it is a man without beard and hair, cruel, murderous, with pink eyes and a big belly. He has lost his brothers. He has stout arms and a courageous heart.

SAGITTARIUS: FIRST DECANATE

It has human face with the body similar to that of a house, and holding a long bow in his hand. He stays in a hermitage and guards the ascetics as well as the materials required for sacrifice. He is a man with round eyes and face; he is a leader of many gro ups; gentle and devoted to the practices of righteous men.

SECOND DECANATE

It is a beautiful woman with golden complexion, seated on a throne. She is of medium stature and separating the gems got from the ocean. Others say that he is a teacher, well versed in the scriptures; he performs many sacrifices, is the foremost of Vedic scholars, and visits very many sacred places and pilgrim centres.

THIRD DECANATE

This is represented by a man with long hair and beard, as well as golden complexion. He is seated on the throne with the sceptre in hand. He wears silk garments as well as deer-skin. According to the other, he is a clever man and leader of his kinsmen; he is a refuge of the virtuous, is meritorious, but passionate, addicted to other women, successful and possessed of personal charm and fame.

Capricorn: First Decanate

It is a man full of hair, with teeth similar to those of the crocodile and with a body like that of a hog. He carries a rope and a net. He is frightful to look at. He is a rogue, dark in colour, with long arms, great fame and physical charm. He speaks with a smile. He is subjugated by women, rich, and has a leaping gait.

Second Decanate

It is a woman skilled in arts, with eyes broad like lotus-petals, dark blue in colour, seeking curious objects; she has metallic ears adorned with ornaments. The *Sārāvalī* makes it out as a man with a small face and shaky waist. He takes away other's women and wealth. He is clever, knowing the actions of the noble, and charitably disposed. He has deformed feet.

Third Decanate

It is represented by a man resembling a Kinnara (a mythical being with a human body and the head of a horse), wearing a blanket. He is ready with an armour, bow and quiver. He carries on his shoulder a pot inlaid with precious stones. Others say that he is a talkative man, slender and slovenly with long limbs. He is separated from his parents. He is very fond of foreign tours.

Aquarius: First Decanate

It is represented by a man, who is anxious and troubled about procuring oil, liquor, water and food. He carries a blanket. He is clad in silken robes and has deer-skin. He has an aquiline face. He is also a tall person, devoted to his duty, wealthy, a king's employee, of high pedigree, and noted for his self-respect, reputation, riches and spouse.

Second Decanate

This is represented by a woman, seated in a half-burnt carriage, with *Śālmalī* wood in it. She is gathering metals in a forest. She is dressed in dirty garments, carrying pots on her head. According to the other authority it is a man who is greedy, efficient, sweet-mannered, of golden complexion, pink, raised eyes and loud laughter. He is rich, intelligent, haughty in speech and has many friends.

Third Decanate

It is a man, black in colour, having lot of hair on his ears, wearing a turban or crown. He is carrying pots containing barks, leaves, fruits gum and shaking them well. He is tall, powerful, lean, of short arms, having sons and riches. He utters lies too much, wicked at heart, having enlarged eyes and erotic.

Pisces: First decanate

It is a man wearing ornaments, handling several articles consisting of ladles; pots, pearls, gems and conch shells. He crosses the ocean (or a river) by boat for the sake of getting ornaments for his wife. He is polite, enjoying pleasures of life, intelligent, wise and devoted to meritorious deeds. His complexion is golden and eyes honey-coloured.

Second decanate

If is a young lady sailing with her retinue to the other side of the ocean in a boat with a banner mounted aloft, and with facial colour resembling the Campaka flower. According to the other authority, it is a man who is adept in serving women's interests, i.e. a gallant, fond of sumptuous food, eats well towards the end of the dinner, an orator and very friendly with women and good men.

Third decanate

The last decanate of Pisces is a man, standing naked near a chasm in the forest, with a serpent coiled round his body. He is weeping, being agitated in mind by the presence of thieves and fire. The *Sārāvalī* describes it as a man who is pretty dark in colour, well versed in fine arts, with large feet, spending money on his friends, a good eater, fond of drinks, and humorous.

The qualities, nature, complexion, mental attitude etc. of these decanates are to be adjudged from the strength of the particular signs, aspects, associations etc. and those of their lords, while examining a natal chart as well as one at a query regarding missing persons, articles and thieves.

SIGNIFICATIONS OF LUNAR MANSIONS

1. *Aśvinī*: Horses, horse-riders, those who steal horses, army commanders, physicians, servants, traders, attractive persons, ostlers and those who keep horses.

2. *Bharaṇī*: Those that consume flesh and blood, terrorists, those that are notorious for murders, smashing and binding and such other crimes, minor grains, weaklings, menials and men of low birth.

3. *Kṛttikā*: White flowers, those that are devoted to worshipping the sacred fire, well-versed in Vedic lore and the *Bhāsyas* (great commentary) on the *Brahma-Sūtras* (and others), makers of dolls, barbers, twice-born, potters, priests and astrologers.

4. *Rohiṇī*: Observances of religious vows, merchandise, rulers, rich men, Yogins (ascetics), cartmen, cow, bull, aquatic beings, and prosperous and fortunate persons.

5. *Mṛgaśiras*: Fragrant objects, clothes, lotus flowers, fruits, gems, hunters, birds, wild beasts, those that drink the *Soma* juice at a *Soma* sacrifice, musicians, libidinous persons and messengers (postmen etc.)

6. *Ārdrā*: Those that are engaged in crimes like murder, imprisoning, torturing, binding with ropes, uttering falsehood, taking away others' property and wives, tale-bearing and roguery, cereals, poisoning, sorcery, black-magic, *Vetāla Vidyā* etc.

7. *Punarvasu*: Persons noted for truthfulness, generosity, purity, noble family, fine personality (or dignified bearing), intelligence; fame and prosperity, superior grains, merchants, architects, artisans and servants.

8. *Puṣya*: Barley, wheat, rice, sugarcane, forests, ministers, kings, fishermen, those who live by water, ascetics, and those that are engaged in big and small sacrifices.

9. *Āśleṣā*: Artificial or crooked means for achieving one's ends, bulbs and roots, fruits, insects, snakes, poison, those that are habitual thieves, cereals, husks and physicians (or those curing snake-poison).

10. *Maghā*: Those that are with money and food crops, store houses, mountaineers, those that are devoted to their parents, merchants, heroes, carnivorous beasts and (haters of women) misogynists.

11. *Pūrva-Phālgunī*: Actors, young damsels, gallants, musicians, artists, merchandise, cotton, salt, oils, honey (or honey-like mineral) and young men.

12. *Uttara Phālgunī*: Those noted for their tender heart, cleanliness, politeness, heresy, charity and interest in the pursuit of *Śāstras*, superior grains, very prosperous ones, pious men and kings.

13. *Hasta*: Thieves, elephants, car-owners, ministers, artisans, commodities, cereals, sneezing persons, traders, and astrologers.

14. *Citrā*: Various ornaments, decorative materials, gems, cosmetics, writing materials, music, perfumes, mathematicians, weavers, surgeons, capitals, royal enjoyments etc.

15. *Svāti*: Birds, animals, horses, traders, corn, windy places, short-time friendship, low stamina, ascetics and expert business-men.

16. *Viśākhā*: Red flowers, fruits, trees, sesamum-seeds, green gram, Bengal gram, black gram, cotton, devotees of Indra and worshippers of sacred fire.

17. *Anurādhā*: Heroes, adventurers, leaders of clans, ascetics, saints, all grains of the autumnal season.

18. *Jyeṣṭhā*: Great warriors, those noted for their noble family, wealth and respectability, those that usurp others' wealth, conquerors, king and army commanders.

19. *Mūla*: Medicines, physicians, leaders of corporate bodies, flowers, roots, fruits and leaves, seeds, rich lords and herbalists.

20. *Pūrvāṣāḍhā*: Tender objects, waterways, voyagers, truthful persons, pure ones, wealthy persons, those who are employed in bridge maintenace, tax-collection and forts, fishermen, fruits, flowers, pearls and such other marine products.

21. *Uttarāṣāḍhā*: Ministers, wrestlers, elephants, horses, devotees of Gods, stationary objects, soldiers, enjoyers of life and powerful persons.

22. *Śravaṇa*: Magicians (or hypocrites), engaged always in work (in training for warfare), efficient workers, enthusiastic men, devoted to *dharma*, God, and truth.

23. *Dhaniṣṭhā*: Men without self-respect, eunuchs, unreliable friends, those that are shunned by women, those that are engaged in charity, very wealthy persons and peace-loving people.

24. *Śatabhiṣaj*: Marine products, aquatic animals, hunters, fishermen, anglers, lotus flowers, those who keep piggeries, washermen, liquor vendors, fowlers etc.

25. *Pūrvābhādra*: Thieves, cowherds, murderers, mean fellows (or misers), despicable persons, rogues, those that are strangers to the moral code, wrestlers etc.

26. *Uttarābhādra*: Brahmins, those that are engaged in penance, sacrifice and charity, very rich persons, dwellers of hermitages, heretics, kings and superior grains.

27. *Revatī*: Aquatic products, fruits, flowers, gems, pearls, conch shells, lotus flowers, fragrant flowers, scents and perfumes, merchants, sailors and boats.

CHAPTER XVIII

TRANSITS

IN THE LIFE of human beings there are many ups and downs which are caused by the movements of planets and the progression of *Daśās*. The *Daśās* show the range of good and bad effects that the native is destined to experience in life. The overall effects of a particular *Daśā* and *Bhukti* are slightly modified or changed by the transits of major planets through certain *Rāśis* counted from the lunar sign at birth of the native. The best example of these transits is that of Saturn through the native's natal sign (lunar), the 2nd and 12th therefrom, which is popularly known as $7\frac{1}{2}$ years or '*Sāḍhe Sāth*', of Saturn, which is generally dreaded by people. Invariably this transit is unfailing in its effect, especially when the current *Daśā* too is unfavourable. In this connection scholars remember the verse meaning—"When Saturn. the Sun, Mars and Jupiter transit the 12th, 8th and 1st houses counted from the *Janma-Rāśi* (natal Moon), they produce danger to life, loss of position and destruction of wealth". In the light of this famous rule, it can be safely concluded that the last period of the $7\frac{1}{2}$ years of Saturn is not that serious.

The *Sun* causes the following effects when the transits the 12 houses counted from the natal sign of the Moon:

1. Physical ailment, destruction of one's wealth or power, journeys strain and tension.
2. Loss of money, eye-disease and becoming the victim of fraud.
3. Acquisition of a position, destruction of enemies and rivals, increase of wealth and good health.
4. Obstacles to one's conjugal happiness, grief and illness.
5. Trouble from enemies and ailments.
6. Removal of diseases, enemies and sorrows.
7. Poverty, journeys, stomach complaints etc.
8. Misunderstanding with women, illness, and trouble from the king.

9. Troubles, wretched condition, serious disease, breach of approved conduct etc.

10. Success in all undertakings and all-round progress.

11. Promotion in service, increase of wealth, freedom from diseases, good and profitable business transactions.

12. Failure of undertakings, loss of money and journeys.

The *Moon* produces the following effects in the 12 places:

1. Sumptuous food, comfortable bed, good clothes etc.
2. Obstacles to one's good deeds, loss of honour and wealth.
3. Conjugal happiness, and gain of good clothes and money.
4. Fear or danger.
5. Illness, all kinds of sorrow, and obstacles during journey.
6. Gain of wealth happiness and destruction of enemies and sickness.
7. Good food, honour, conjugal happiness and gain of money.
8. Danger from fire.
9. Stomach trouble, danger and bondage (imprisonment).
10. Political activities or benefit from the ruler.
11. Meeting with one's kith and kin and increase of wealth.
12. All kinds of troubles, loss, wandering.

Mars produces the following effects in the 12 houses:

1. Wounds in the body, and obstruction to work.
2. Trouble from the king, thieves, fire and enemies, weakness, worries and illness.
3. Gain of gold, wealth and grace of Lord Guha, and destruction of enemies etc.
4. Association with the wicked, stomach trouble, fever, bleeding and the like.
5. Trouble from enemies and ailments and sorrow on account of children.
6. Gain of copper, gold etc., absence of enemies and fear of quarrels.
7. Quarrel with one's wife, illness in the eyes and stomach.
8. Profuse bleeding, wounds, breaking of limbs, disgrace and mental agony.
9. Ailments, failure in work and loss of wealth.
10. Acquisition of wealth from various sources.
11. Position of head of a village and happiness.

12. Drain of money, calamities, diseases caused by the vitiation of bile, eye-disease, and others caused by impure blood.

Mercury produces the following results in the 12 houses:

1. Quarrel with relatives, loss of money, and trouble caused by talking against rulers, long journeys.
2. Increase of income and fortune, and fine speech.
3. Threat from rulers and enemies.
4. Acquisition of wealth, prosperity of kinsmen, and increase or growth of family.
5. Continuous quarrels with one's sons and wife.
6. Success in work, increase of personal charm and promotion in job.
7. Disputes and quarrels.
8. Accomplishment of undertaking, progress of children or birth of a son or daughter, gain of good garments, growth of wealth, mental happiness and energetic pursuits.
9. All kinds of diseases.
10. Destruction of enemies, inflow of wealth, conjugal felicity, splendid and attractive speech, plenty of money and property, and all-round happiness and joy as well as success.
11. Happiness, success in undertakings, happy life in the company of one's wife and children, and good income.
12. Defeat at the hands of enemies, loss of money, great suffering on account of ill-health.

Jupiter gives rise to the following effects while he transits the 12 *Rāśis* from the natal sign:

1. Loss of position and wealth and quarrels with learned men.
2. Gain of money, victory over rivals and enemies, and conjugal happiness.
3. Loss of position, obstruction to one's projects etc.
4. Troubles and worries arising out of one's relatives, and utter lack of happiness and mental peace.
5. Acquisition of horses, bullocks, vehicles, gold, gems, a young damsel (or marriage), fine clothes and a new house as well as birth of a son.
6. Loss of happiness in spite of all requisites as well as disappointments and obstructions to work.
7. Wise and cogent arguments, intellectual acumen, success in

all undertakings, plenty of income, family happiness, mental cheer, and pilgrimage.

8. A great calamity, ailments, imprisonment, loss of freedom, constant journeys, and great exhaustion.

9. Increase of wealth and fortune, happiness of wife and children, efficiency and skill in work, success in all work and in getting one's orders executed.

10. Loss of position and wealth, and lack of success in work undertaken.

11. Achievement of all objects and getting a superior position.

12. Travelling long distances, terrible calamity, loss of position (or retirement), danger to life and loss of money.

Venus causes the following effects while transiting the 12 houses from the lunar sign at birth:

1. Sumptuous food, union with one's spouse, getting musk and other fragrant things and scents, conjugal felicity, gain of cots and such other articles; silken robes and luxury articles.

2. One comes by wealth, grains, flowers, gems and ornaments, gets honour from the king, lives happily with one's family members, enjoying pleasures and wealth as one pleases.

3. Destruction of enemies, respect for one's words, increase of wealth, honourable position, and costly garments.

4. Meeting with one's kinsmen and friends, great power to rule etc.

5. Happiness through children, wealth, friends, elders, teachers etc.

6. Defeat, humiliation, trouble from enemies etc.

7. Getting into trouble on account of women or urinary diseases such as diabetes.

8. Furniture etc. for one's house, union with a woman, gain of gems and other luxury items.

9. Engagement in meritorious and religious activities, gain of money, happiness, conjugal felicity etc.

10. Quarrels, humiliation etc.

11. Sumptuous food, scents, fragrant articles, happiness in the company of kinsmen.

12. Acquisition of wealth from many sources, increase of clothes, ornaments etc.

Saturn produces the following effects during his transit through the 12 houses from the natal Moon:

1. Danger from poison and fire (it might be *Viṣānilabhayam* meaning tragedy from poisonous gas like the one at Bhopal and Chernobyl), death or murder of a relative, going away from home, separation from one's wife, children and kinsmen, destruction of wealth and travelling long distances.

2. Loss of money, health, happiness and personal appearance and disinclination towards pleasures of the body and mind.

3. Ingress of money, buffaloes, elephants, health, happiness and other desideratives of life.

4. One becomes crooked in one's ways, and gets separation from one's family, wealth and kith and kin.

5. Quarrels, separation of one's children etc.

6. Relief from diseases and enemies (debts etc.).

7. Travelling long distances, and cohabitation with a woman servant.

8. Poverty, humiliation and separation from one's family and kinsmen.

9. Hatred for others, one's incarceration and loss of one's *dharma* or excommunication.

10. Heart disease, destruction of learning, reputation and success in work.

11. Cohabitation with another woman, income and increase of power.

12. A series of sorrows and troubles as well as continuous plunging into water and coming up.

As described above these planets including Rāhu and Ketu, who are similar to Saturn or to Saturn and Mars respectively, conduce to good and bad results, in certain places transited by them. Rāhu causes the following effects while transiting the 12 houses from the natal Moon: (1) Death or serious illness. (2) Loss of wealth. (3) Happiness. (4) Sorrow. (5) Loss of money. (6) Happiness. (7) Loss. (8) Danger to life. (9) Loss. (10) Gain. (11) Happiness and (12) Loss.

The following point also should be borne in mind in connection with the transits of the Moon, Mars, Rāhu, Venus, Jupiter, the Sun, Saturn and Mercury: When the Moon passes through the 8th house, Mars through the 7th, Rahu through the 9th, Venus through the 6th, Jupiter through the 3rd, the Sun through the 5th, Saturn through the 1st and Mercury through the 4th house, there is every likelihood of loss of wealth and honour, and even death. According to the directions of ancient sages, whenever the planets appear to be unfavourable during their major and minor periods as well as in their transits people should perform proper remedial religious work for appeasing the deities presiding over the divine planets and securing their grace which results in removing the evil effects of sinful acts of previous life and bestowing health, happiness and proper guidance in their daily life.

Time for Effects of Transits

The Sun and Mars, produce their good or bad effects specially, when they transit the first decanate of the concerned sign; Jupiter and Venus, when they transit the middle decanate; and the Moon and Saturn, in the last decanate. Mercury, on the other hand, causes the effects throughout the period of transit. A planet that is expected to yield very good effects, may not do so, if it is aspected by a malefic. Similarly, a planet that is expected to produce evil effects, would not give entirely bad effects, provided it is aspected by a benefic.

Mode of Worship

The planets are to be worshipped by prayers, *Homas*, Vedic recitations, offerings of water (*Tarpaṇa*), feeding, gifts etc. The planets should be worshipped with flowers, clothes, food offerings etc. with appropriate colours. The Sun and Mars should be worshipped with red flowers; the Moon and Venus, with white flowers; Saturn, with flowers that are mixed with black or blue colour; Jupiter, with yellow flowers; and Mercury, green flowers. Similarly, for propitiating planets one should wear gems and clothes and live in a house with colour-paintings appropriate to them.

The following are the gems that should be worn by people to receive the beneficent and balmy cosmic rays from the respective planets, when they are ill placed: Ruby, pearl, coral, emerald,

Puṣyarāga or topaz, diamond, *Nīla* or Sapphire, *Gomedhika* or Agate, and *Vaidūrya* or *lapis lazuli* respectively for the nine planets beginning with the Sun.

Gifts for Planets

In order to get the grace and blessings of the Sun and other planets the following gifts should be made: For the Sun a brown coloured cow should be given away to a worthy recipient; for the Moon, a conch shell; for Mars, a red-coloured bull; for Mercury, gold; for Jupiter, yellow silk cloth; for Venus, silver and a white horse; for Saturn, a black cow; for Rāhu, iron article, or goat; and for Ketu, elephant or goat.

By engaging oneself in worshipping gods and brāhmaṇas, by getting the blessings of teachers and elders through proper service and carrying out their holy advice, by serving daily ascetics and holy men and listening to their holy words, by recitation of the Vedas or listening to it, by listening attentively to the narration of the lives of ancient heroes, heroines, incarnations etc., by performing *Homas* (sacrifices), participating in big sacrificial sessions, by developing a pure and pious heart filled with noble thoughts, by doing *japa* (repetition of holy Vedic hymns), by giving gifts and doing such other things like *Iṣṭa* (sacrifice) and *Pūrta* (noble deeds for the good of humanity and dumb animals), one gets the blessings of the planets, who being pleased with the devotion and good intentions of their devotees, never torment them. On the other hand, they grow very kind-hearted and do utmost good. Hence it is said—"The divine planets are always kind and do benefactions to those who do no harm to others, who are self-controlled, who earn wealth by fair and approved means (dharma), and whose life is ever well disciplined."

Other Methods

One should also take daily bath accompanied by Vedic mantras; also bath on special occasions such as one in a *Tirtha* (sacred river or lake), during an eclipse etc., bath with the medicines (herbal) prescribed for the planets these remedial measures too help in moving the divine powers to do good to helpless human beings.

Prohibitions

When planets are found adverse in transit, a person especially a king, is forbidden to undertake the following works: Movements in odd places and periods, hunting expedition, adventures, journey to a distant place, riding a horse or elephant, and visiting other houses.

There are some special points to be remembered in connection with planetary transits: They are *Vedha* (piercing) and *Viparīta Vedha*. If a planet's transit in a place from the lunar sign is said to be good, the good effects of this transit may be nullified by the *Vedha* (hurting). This rule holds good in the case of evil transits as well. There is no *Vedha* in the case of the Sun and Saturn as well as the Moon and Mercury. You have understood that the Sun's transit through the 3rd, 6th and 10th houses from the natal Moon is beneficial.

The 11th place is good for all planets in transit. Now each place has a *Vedha* place. If the latter is occupied by some other planet, the effect of transit, good or bad, will not take place. For example, the Sun's transit in the 3rd house is beneficial, but its *Vedha* is the 9th house. So if there is some other planet except Saturn, in the 9th house, the good effects of this transit will not be reaped. Now let us see what is *Pratīpavedha* or counter *Vedha*. We have taken the Sun's transit in the 3rd house and its *Vedha* viz. the 9th house. Here the former is called *Vedhya* (that which is pierced) and latter, *Vedhaka* (that which pierces). The counter *Vedha* takes place when the *Vedhya Rāśi*, i.e. the 3rd house, is transited by another planet, which counteracts the effects of the *Vedha*. In fact, the *Vedha* which tries to undo the good effects of the Sun's transit through the 3rd house, is nullified by the arrival of another planet at the 3rd house. The Sun is favourable in transit through 3, 6, 10 and 11. The Moon is good in places 1, 3, 6, 7, 10, 11. Mars and Saturn in houses 3, 6 and 11. Jupiter's places are 2, 5, 7, 9 and 11.

Mercury is favourable in 2, 4, 6, 8, 10 and 11.

The following table gives the *Vedha* places of the planets:

Houses Planets	I	II	III	IV	V	VI	VII	VIII	IX	X	XI	XII
Sun	1	2	9	3	6	12	7	8	10	4	5	11
Moon	5	1	9	3	6	12	2	7	10	4	8	11
Mars	1	2	12	3	4	9	6	7	8	10	5	11
Mercury	2	5	4	3	7	9	6	1	8	10	12	11
Jupiter	1	12	2	5	4	6	3	7	10	9	8	11
Venus	8	7	1	10	9	12	2	5	11	4	3	6
Saturn	1	2	12	3	4	9	6	7	8	10	5	11

The *Vedha* places of Rāhu and Ketu are the same as for Saturn.

Transit of Stars

When we are speaking of transits of a planet, we have to remember a slightly different kind of transit which is called *Nakṣatra Gocara.* This is resorted to in order to find out if a particular period is beneficial to the native on the basis of his or her natal asterism. This is done by noting the relationship between the natal asterism and the one transited by the Sun at the required period. In this scheme there are some other stars that are harmful to the native's star. For this purpose a diagram is needed, which is called the *Saptaśalākā-cakra.* In this figure you should draw 7 horizontal lines crossed by 7 vertical ones as shown in the chart below: The first star is *Kṛttikā* located in the north-eastern corner and the last is *Bharaṇi*. There are 28 stars in this chart including *Abhijit*.

East

North

Bharaṇī	*Kṛttikā*	*Rohiṇī*	*Mṛga*	*Ārdrā*	*Punar*	*Puṣya*	*Āśleṣā Maghā*
Aśvinī							*P. Phālgunī*
Revatī							*U. Phālgunī*
U. Bhādra							*Hasta*
P. Bhādra							*Citrā*
Śatabhiṣak							*Svātī*
Dhaniṣṭhā							*Viśākhā*
	Śravaṇa	*Abhijit*	*U. Aṣāḍhā*	*P. Aṣāḍhā*	*Mūla*	*Jyeṣṭhā*	*Anurādhā*

South

West

The mode of using this diagram is: You see here some stars being placed along the same line, horizontal and vertical. For example, *Kṛttikā* and *Śravaṇa*; *Āśleṣā* and *Anurādhā*; *Bharaṇī* and *Meghā*; *Dhaniṣṭha* and *Viṣākhā* are along the same line. This means that there is mutual affiliation or *Vedha* between the stars of each pair. The idea is that if your natal star is *Dhaniṣṭhā*, and if the Sun at the time is transiting the star *Viśākhā*, you have to conclude that there is trouble in store for you. You also must be knowing the designations of the nine stars beginning with your own natal star. Among these the 3rd, 5th and 7th are respectively called *Vipat* (danger), *Pratyak* (obstruction) and *Nidhana* (death). Similarly, the 10th, 19th and 23rd stars are called in order *Karma* (Action), *Ādhāna* (depositing) and *Vaināśika* (destructive). So these stars too might be involved in *Vedha* or affiliation. Now take *Mṛgaśiras*, *Citrā* and *Jyeṣṭhā*, which happen to be 10th, 19th and 23rd stars from your natal star taken above. According to this rule, if the Sun be transiting *Mṛgaśiras*, you should not undertake any new project under the star *Uttarāṣādhā*. Similarly, you are called upon to avoid certain other stars for beginning any progressive work: If your natal star happens to be one in which the Sun changes his course from one sign to another which is called Solar-*Saṁkrānti*, that month may be bringing sufferings and disappointments to you. So you have to perform proper *Śāntis* that are recommended by the ancient seers, on such occasions. All the remedial measures are meant to purify man's heart and lead him from unreality to reality, from darkness to light, and from death to immortality. The same effect is said to be produced, if one's natal star or its trine happens to synchronize with the change of sign of any other planet, or with an eclipse, planetary war, falling of meteors or with any other extraordinary event.

Please bear in mind the following point also in this connection: Even if a planet be found to be capable of yielding unfavourable results on account of its transit, the bad effects would be nullified by the aspect of a benefic on that planet. The same argument holds good in the case of a planet supposed to produce excellent results, but aspected by a malefic. Similar is the effect of a planet that is aspected by its enemy. Similarly, see if a planet occupies a very bad house in transit. Even here it cannot give bad effects, provided it occupies its own house or its exaltation. On the other hand, it will produce excellent results. If a planet in transit be in its debilitation, inimical house or combustion, bad effects would be greatly enhanced.

Chapter XIX

MISCELLANEOUS

Kāla Horā

The word *Horā* means hour, which is got by joining the last syllable of the first word and the first syllable of the second word of the compound *Ahorātra*. You know that an hour forms a 24th part of the entire period of day and night. From the chart given on pp. 402-3 you would be able to discover the rationale of the weekdays. The first hour in each weekday is presided over by its own lord. So on Sunday the first hour beginning with Sunrise is ruled by the Sun himself; the second hour by the planet that is 6th from the lord of the day, i.e. Venus, in other words it is the 3rd weekday-lord counted backwards. Continue this process until you reach the 24th hour. On Sunday the 24th hour is ruled by Mercury (*Budha*). Hence the first hour of the very next day is ruled by the Moon. Thus we call it Monday. Similarly on Monday the last, i.e. 24th, *Kāla-Horā* is presided over by Jupiter. In this manner the last *Horās* are ruled in order by Mercury, Jupiter, Venus, Saturn, Sun, Moon and Mars on the weekdays beginning with Sunday. This shows that the last *Horā* on a particular weekday belongs to the planet that is the 4th from that planet presiding over the weekday.

Effects of Horās

These *Horās* can be made use of in electional astrology or *Muhūrta*. Suppose you have to attend a court case on a Tuesday. Then select a good *Kāla-Horā*, provided the lord of that *Horā* is strong and unafflicted, and the *Horā* free from *Viṣa Ghaṭī*. In this case you can elect conveniently the third *Horā* of Venus. It would be excellent, if you could elect Jupiter's *Horā*, if the planet is strong.

Kāla Horā

S. No.	Kāla Horā Sunrise	Sunday	Monday	Tuesday
1	1st Hour	Sun	Moon	Mars
2	2nd Hour	Venus	Saturn	Sun
3	3rd Hour	Mercury	Jupiter	Venus
4	4th Hour	Moon	Mars	Mercury
5	5th Hour	Saturn	Sun	Moon
6	6th Hour	Jupiter	Venus	Saturn
7	7th Hour	Mars	Mercury	Jupiter
8	8th Hour	Sun	Moon	Mars
9	9th Hour	Venus	Saturn	Sun
10	10th Hour	Mercury	Jupiter	Venus
11	11th Hour	Moon	Mars	Mercury
12	12th Hour	Saturn	Sun	Moon
13	13th Hour	Jupiter	Venus	Saturn
14	14th Hour	Mars	Mercury	Jupiter
15	15th Hour	Sun	Moon	Mars
16	16th Hour	Venus	Saturn	Sun
17	17th Hour	Mercury	Jupiter	Venus
18	18th Hour	Moon	Mars	Mercury
19	19th Hour	Saturn	Sun	Moon
20	20th Hour	Jupiter	Venus	Saturn
21	21st Hour	Mars	Mercury	Jupiter
22	22nd Hour	Sun	Moon	Mars
23	23rd Hour	Venus	Saturn	Sun
24	24th Hour	Mercury	Jupiter	Venus

Chart

Wednesday	Thursday	Friday	Saturday
Mercury	Jupiter	Venus	Saturn
Moon	Mars	Mercury	Jupiter
Saturn	Sun	Moon	Mars
Jupiter	Venus	Saturn	Sun
Mars	Mercury	Jupiter	Venus
Sun	Moon	Mars	Mercury
Venus	Saturn	Sun	Moon
Mercury	Jupiter	Venus	Saturn
Moon	Mars	Mercury	Jupiter
Saturn	Sun	Moon	Mars
Jupiter	Venus	Saturn	Sun
Mars	Mercury	Jupiter	Venus
Sun	Moon	Mars	Mercury
Venus	Saturn	Sun	Moon
Mercury	Jupiter	Venus	Saturn
Moon	Mars	Mercury	Jupiter
Saturn	Sun	Moon	Mars
Jupiter	Venus	Saturn	Sun
Mars	Mercury	Jupiter	Venus
Sun	Moon	Mars	Mercury
Venus	Saturn	Sun	Moon
Mercury	Jupiter	Venus	Saturn
Moon	Mars	Mercury	Jupiter
Saturn	Sun	Moon	Mars

The *Sun* would create in his *Horā* (especially in journey) the sight of a single brahmin, a single water pot and a widow. It would also produce troubles and strain.

The *Moon*: Gain of wealth, sight of an eagle (*Garuḍa*), lizard's cries from the left side as well as sight of a pot of milk, toddy, umbrellas and chowries.

Mars: Grief and illness; and sight of an empty pot, butter-milk, a lame person, one with white leprosy etc.

Mercury: The sight of cows, young girls, pots of curds, blazing fire, and flowers and fruits, and acquiring money and learning.

Jupiter: All kinds of prosperity, authority and sight of mirror, music, both instrumental and vocal, a group of Vedic scholars, auspicious women and other holy things.

Venus: Conjugal felicity and meeting with two brahmins, auspicious women holding flowers and fruits in their hands, getting happy tidings and such other auspicious omens.

Saturn: Destruction of wealth and all undertakings as well as sight of a widow and oil-monger and hearing bad news. (*Note*: The special effects pertain to journeys, according to the *Mārkaṇḍeya Jyautiṣa*.)

Query About Food

If a person were to ask an astrologer as to the type of food eaten by him, the latter proceeds thus to answer his query: It is well-known that the seven planets from the Sun onwards preside over the tastes viz. pungent, salt, bitter, mixed taste, sweet, sour and astringent respectively. The querist must have enjoyed those dishes during his meal whose tastes belong to the strong planets posited in *kendras*, or to those that aspect the *lagna*, or to the one that is posited in the *lagna*. Moreover, if the planet mentioned above occupies the sign of a benefic, the food eaten should be very delicious and wholesome, whereas if the planet occupies a sign of a malefic, it must be dry and insipid. Should the planet be retrograde, the querist could not have eaten even the food that was placed before him.

When the Sun be strong and posited in one of the above-named positions, the food eaten would be mixed with sesamum-seeds; when the Moon, a fine rice-meal; when Mars, it would consist of *Masūra* (a kind of pulse or lentil) and Bengal gram;

when Mercury, it is mixed with green-gram and *Rājamāṣa* (a kind of bean or *Alasaṇḍe* in Kannaḍa); when Jupiter, the food consists of wheat and other things; when Venus, it is barley, it is *Vājarikā* and *Yugandharā*; when Saturn, it is horse-gram, black-gram etc., and when Rāhu or Ketu, it is mixed with husk or chaff. If there be benefic aspect on the above planets, the food would be eaten with pleasure. Again, should the Sun be strong in any of the above positions, the curry would be made of roots; should it be the Moon, of flowers; should it be Mars; leafy vegetable, branches and greens; should it be Venus, or Mercury, it is of several varieties; and should it be Saturn, Rāhu or Ketu the preparation is of meat.

In queries about food, if the ascendant be an immovable sign, it should be said that the querist has eaten only once; if it be a dual *lagna*, twice; and if a movable one, several times.

When the Moon is aspected by the lord of the sign she occupies, the querist must have had a happy meal; otherwise a wretched one or a meal obtained with great difficulty.

If Saturn or Rāhu be posited in the *lagna* and aspected by the Sun, the querist would be invited to a dinner by his enemy and be wounded by weapons; and if the Moon and Mars, posited in the *lagna*, be aspected by Saturn, then too he would receive blows.

If Jupiter and Venus, possessed of strength, be conjoined with the Moon, or if the Moon and Mercury be posited in a *kendra* and associated with benefics, malefics being posited in *Upacaya* houses, he would have (already had) a hearty and delicious dinner leading to mutual love and purging of all traces of animosity.

The lord of the ascendant represents the host at a dinner; that of the 4th house, the food served; that of the 7th house, hunger or appetite; and that of the 10th house, the guest. Should the 1st and 11th houses be associated with or aspected by benefics, the dinner should be declared to be excellent.

So far the views of the *Praśnajñāna* have been given. The following are the explanations found in the *Praśnamārga* on the topic of food:

The 12 houses from the query ascendant represent in order (1) the eater's physical features, condition etc.; (2) plates or leaves used for eating; (3) dishes or eatables; (4) drinks etc.; (5) the host; (6) subsidiary dishes or articles; (7) liquid preparations like Rasam, Sâmbhâr etc.; (8) rice, chappatis and such other articles; (9) guests who sit together for meal; (10) satisfaction of eaters or otherwise; (11) talks during dinner; and (12) rest or sleep.

Planetary Tastes

Venus represents sweet taste; the Moon, cold liquids and tender articles; Jupiter and Mercury, dry things; the Sun, salt, and astringent; Saturn, sour and pungent; and Mars, bitter.

According to others the tastes for the 7 planets from the Sun are in order (1) pungent, (2) salt, (3) pungent, (4) astringent, (5) sweet, (6) sour, and (7) bitter.

Sumptuous Food

The food eaten would be excellent, if the ascendant be a benefic sign or occupied by benefics. If it is an odd sign, the food will be dry and insipid; and if it is an even *Rāśi* or a watery sign, it will be full of liquids, ghee, oil etc.

In case the Sun and Mars be posited in dry signs, the food served would be hot and dry; if they be in watery signs, it would be full of liquid curries; and if Saturn and *Rāhu* be in watery signs, it would be cold and insipid.

If the Moon and Venus be posited in watery signs, the food would be full of cold liquid preparations; if, on the other hand, Mercury and Jupiter be in dry Rāhu, it would consist of hard preparations.

Meat Preparations

At a query about food containing meat preparations, the Sun and Mars would suggest venison; the Moon, crabs and fish; Jupiter, meat of elephants and horses; Saturn, meat of bisons and hogs; Mercury, birds' meat; and Venus, meat of buffaloes and bulls.

So far we have deduced the animals from the planets themselves. Similarly we should think of goats and other animals, vegetables, fruits etc. on the basis of the signs occupied by the planets. Think of aquatic animals and products through watery

Rāśis and planets; domestic animals, vegetables etc., through rural *Rāśis* and planets; forest products such as bulbs and roots as well as fruits and hunted animals, through forest *Rāśis* and planets.

Malefic signs and planets point to food consisting of gruel with a little of the grain allotted to them, while benefics suggest good food along with a dish of the particular meat or vegetable assigned to the planets. The Moon represents gruel with plenty of water; Mercury, gruel with curry; Jupiter, rice with ghee; Venus, gruel with butter; and the rest, gruel with oil.

When the 7th house happens to be Aries, or Mars be posited in the 7th house, goat's milk should be inferred; if it be connected similarly with Venus or Taurus cow's milk; if connected with Saturn, buffalo-milk; and in the case of other planets, other liquids should be inferred on the basis of the type of quadruped *Rāśis* occupied by them.

If Mars be in the 7th house, one should predict meat-curry; if Mercury be there, a green-coloured drink; if Venus and Mercury be there, a number of curries as well as *Citrānna* (rice coloured with turmerie and spiced); if Saturn be there, a heap of rancid rice and curries with dead flies in them. The Sun in that place leads to the eating of the curry prepared from the stick of the green leafy vegetable. It is said that after food the querist would have the pleasure of the couch.

Malefics in this context suggest carnivorous animals; while benefics, animals that live on grass and green leaves; Mercury, both classes of animals; Jupiter, those that live on grass and grains; the Moon, worms, fish etc.

Anothhr Classification

Through Aries one should infer goat's meat; from Taurus, beef; from Sagittarius, Leo and Gemini, fish, meat etc; from Capricorn, Scorpio, Cancer and Pisces, ripe fruits; and from Libra, Virgo, and Aquarius, pure food consisting of rice and wheat preparations. Jupiter stands for a meal consisting of rice, ghee, and milk porridge; and Venus, for good food with ghee, *Apūpa* (a soft sweet), milk and curries.

Another point to be remembered in this connection is that the planets stand for different things: The Sun suggests a quadruped;

the Moon, daughter; Mars, thief; Mercury, disputation; Jupiter, money; Venus, woman, and Saturn, departed spirit. These details are to be given when the planets are connected with the *lagna*, by aspect, occupation etc. When you are called upon to find out the place where the querist had his previous meal, if the planet connected with the ascendant be the Sun, you should state that food was served near a manger; if it be the Moon, you have to say that the person who has served food to the guests, is the host's daughter; if it be Venus, it is the host's wife; if it be Mars in the 9th house, the querist took food in the company of a thief; if it be Mercury, there was some disputation between the querist and another person. If Jupiter is connected with the 11th house, the querist must have got some money as *Dakṣiṇā* in addition to a sumptuous meal. If Saturn be the planet concerned, the food eaten was one prepared for *Śrāddha* ceremony.

Query About the Return from Abroad

When the ascendant at the query is a movable sign, and benefics be in 2nd, 3rd, 4th or 8th house, the person will return home. If the lord of the 10th house should arrive at the 9th house during his retrograde motion, the traveller intending to go far would retrace his steps in the middle of his journey. Should the lord of the *lagna* be posited in the 5th or 6th house, it should be declared that the person who was on his way back home has not yet arrived there.

The traveller would not return home, if the lord of the query ascendant be posited in one of the houses between the 4th and 10th houses, i.e. 11th, 12th, 1st, 2nd and 3rd houses. The same prediction should be made, if malefics be posited in the angular houses.

Should the *kendras* be devoid of malefics, but the Moon be in the 8th house, still the traveller would return home without any trouble. The result would be definite, if the *kendras* be occupied by benefics, in the previous case.

Should the *lagna*-lord and the lord of the 10th house be posited in the houses viz. 11, 12, 1, 2 and 3, the person intending to go on a tour would not be able to do so.

The tourist would come back home, should the *lagna*-lord be in his exaltation or *Mūlatrikoṇa*, or any planet that is retrograde be posited in the 7th house.

Should the lord of the ascendant be retrograde, and Jupiter being strong, be in a *kendra*, the traveller would return.

The speed of return of the tourist would be slow, moderate or fast according as the motion of the *lagna* lord or the planet that is responsible for his return is slow, moderate or fast, as the case may be.

Should the *lagna*-lord be in a human sign or *Aṁśa* (Gemini, Virgo, Libra and Aquarius), the ascendant, being strong, the traveller who is far away from home, would return home along with some companions.

Should the *lagna*-lord be in a quadruped sign, the traveller would return making use of carriages such as buses. If the lord be in a *Pakṣi* (bird) decanate, he would return by plane; and if the sign be a watery one, he would travel by ship. If it be a land-sign, the journey would be by road or rail. In the same manner the decanate occupied by the *lagna*-lord may be *Śakaṭa* (carriage), or his *Rāśi* or *Aṁśa*, an Aerial (*Ākāśa*) one (Sagittarius or Pisces). In such cases appropriate modes of conveyance should be predicted. In case the planet responsible for the traveller's return is weak, he would inform his people that he was returning home, but would not be able to do so. If there be benefics in the 9th house, the traveller would be happy during his sojourn abroad; while malefics in that house would make the person unhappy. Likewise at the start of a journey if benefics be in the 8th house, the tour would be successful and happy, while malefics therein would make his life miserable. Similarly, prediction should be made for the return of the traveller on the basis of benefics and malefics in the 7th house.

States of the Moon

There are three states of the Moon known as (1) *Candrakriyā* (Moon's action), (2) *Candrāvasthā* (Moon's condition) and (3) *Candravelā* (Moon's period). A knowledge of these three elements would help the astrologer in assessing the Moon's strength. For the Moon's strength is the very foundation of the horoscope, natal, horary and electional. The three are respectively 60, 12 and 36.

The following is the method for calculating the *Candrakriyā*: First of all we must know the Moon's exact longitude at birth or query: Let us take the following longitude of the Moon at a birth = 8ˢ-4°-57′-28″. This is the second quarter of *Mūla*. You know that a whole star contains 13°-20′ or 800′. If this is divided by 60, you get the value of one *kriyā*, which is 800′/60 or 800 seconds. In our example 4°-57′-28″ is equal to 17848 seconds. By dividing this by 800 seconds, you get $22\frac{31}{130}$ or the 23rd *Candrakriyā* which is "belonging to a famous family".

They are given below:

Candra-kriyās	Effects		
1.	One falls from position.	27.	Conquered by enemy.
2.	Becomes an ascetic.	28.	Wanders away from country.
3.	Runs after other women.	29.	A servant.
4.	Becomes a gambler.	30.	Loses wealth.
5.	Rides an elephant.	31.	Courtier of a king.
6.	Is seated on the throne.	32.	Good Counsellor.
7.	Becomes ruler of men.	33.	A Governor.
8.	Destroys enemies.	34.	Has a wife.
9.	Commands an army.	35.	Frightened by elephant.
10.	Becomes virtuous.	36.	Cowardly in fight.
11.	Dead or exhausted.	37.	Always timid.
12.	One with head chopped off.	38.	Remains incognito.
13.	Whose hands and feet are wounded.	39.	Giver of food.
14.	A prisoner.	40.	Falls into the fire.
15.	Spoilt or missing.	41.	Oppressed by hunger.
16.	Becomes a king.	42.	Eats food.
17.	Vedic scholar.	43.	Wanders aimlessly.
18.	Addicted to sleeping.	44.	Flesh-eater.
19.	One of good character.	45.	Wounded by weapon.
20.	Performs meritorious deeds.	46.	Married.
21.	One of noble birth.	47.	Holds a ball in hand.
22.	Getting a treasure.	48.	Plays at dice.
23.	Belongs to a famous family.	49.	Becomes a king.
24.	Expounds the scriptures.	50.	Distressed.
25.	Destroyer of foes.	51.	Lies on bed.
26.	Sickly.	52.	One served by enemies.

Candra-kriyās	*Effects*		
53.	Accompanied by friends.	57.	Drinks milk.
54.	A *Yogin*.	58.	Does meritorious deeds.
55.	In the company of his wife.	59.	Healthy or self-possessed.
56.	Eats sumptuously.	60.	Lives happily.

The second element is *Candrāvasthā* consisting of 12 conditions. Now divide the total duration of a star viz. 800 minutes by 12. The quotient gives you the value of one *Avasthā* in minutes. So 800′/12=200′/3. Now divide the elasped part of the star converted into minute, i.e. $297\frac{7}{51}$, by 200′/3=297.47× (3/200)=4.462. So it is the 5th *Avasthā*, whose effect is "interest in the merits befitting one's family". The following are the effects of the 12 conditions:

(1) Going abroad; (2) becoming a great favourite of a great king; (3) loss of life through service; (4) kingship; (5) interested in the merits befitting one's family; (6) sickness; (7) holding a royal durbar; (8) fear; (9) tormented by hunger; (10) marriage with a young lady; (11) attachment to a cosy and lovely couch; and (12) eating sumptuous food.

CANDRAVELĀ

There are 36 periods of the Moon. So divide the total longitude of a star viz. 800 minutes by 36. The quotient gives you the value of a single *Velā*. This comes to 200/9. Now divide the elapsed part of the star viz, $297\frac{7}{15}$ by 200/9. Then you get 13.385, which is the 14th *Velā* whose effects are "sport in water, merriment and drawing of pictures". Their results are given below in order.

(1) Disease of the head; (2) Joyousness; (3) Performs sacrifices; (4) Lives happily; (5) Eye-trouble; (6) Happiness; (7) Amusement in the company of women; (8) High fever; (9) Gold ornaments; (10) Sheds tears; (11) Drinks poison; (12) Sexual union; (13) Stomach ailment; (14) Sports in water, merriment and drawing of pictures; (15) Anger; (16) Dancing; (17) Drinking ghee; (18) Sleeping; (19) Giving gifts; (20) Tooth-ache; (21) Quarrel; (22) Journey; (23) Lunacy; (24) Swimming in or crossing water; (25) Hostility; (26) An enjoyable bath; (27) Hunger; (28) Fear; (29) Acquisition of scriptural knowledge; (30)

Wantonness; (31) Assembly; (32) Fighting; (33) Doing meritorious-deeds; (34) Committing sins; (35) Perpetrating cruel acts; and (36) Great joy.

PREVIOUS EXISTENCE ETC.

According to the ancient Indian culture, which has stood the test of time, we are not strangers to the world of mortals. For, the souls repeatedly go away from this world, spend sometime in another world and return to the earthly abode for the purpose of experiencing the fruits, good and bad, of their previous *karmas* and perform more *karmas* for future benefit or sorrow, as the case may be. If it be a fact that the souls had lived somewhere on the earth or in another world in their previous lives, it stands to reason that they will have future lives also elsewhere after they depart from the mortal stage. At this juncture, the sacred science of Astrology bequeathed to posterity by the divine sages, comes to our aid in giving us proper guidance in this matter. We have to read one's previous existence from the lord of the 9th house in the natal or query chart, and the next life from the lord of the 5th house. All the information about the country or world, class, longevity etc. of the souls could be gathered from the places occupied by the concerned planets, their aspects, strength etc. in the chart. Should the lord of the 12th house be hemmed in between malefics, the soul after death would repair to hell and stay there for sometime and suffer the consequences of its sins committed during its sojourn on earth. If that lord be surrounded by benefics, the soul would go to heaven. If the 12th house itself be a malefic *Rāśi* or if it be occupied or aspected by a malefic, the soul would go to hell, all the same. On the contrary, should it be a benefic sign, or be occupied or aspected by benefics, it would be transferred to heaven.

(1) Should the Sun be posited in the 12th house, the soul would repair to the holy Kailāśa, after its physical death.

(2) Should the Moon and Venus be the 12th house, its departure would be to heaven.

(3) Should Mars be posited in the 12th house, the soul would take birth in this mortal world itself.

(4) Should Saturn be in the 12th house of the query chart, the soul would repair to the world of Yama—God of Death.

(5) Rāhu in that place would take the soul to another continent and make it reborn as a follower of another faith.

(6) Ketu would lead it to the worst type of hell.

(7) Mercury would take it to *Vaikuṇṭha,* the world of Lord *Mahā-Viṣṇu.*

(8) Jupiter would take it to the world of brahman. Venus and Mercury belong to the *Rājasa* (active) class: Jupiter, the Sun and Moon, to the *Sātvika* group (pure); and Mars and Saturn, to the *Tāmasa* (dark) class. Their *Rāśis* too are said to have the same qualities.

Asterisms and Geographical Divisions

India is divided into 9 regions on the basis of three stars per division:

(1) *Kṛttika, Rohiṇī* and *Mṛgaśīrṣa* rule and central region of India.

(2) *Ārdrā, Punarvasu* and *Puṣya* rule the eastern region.

(3) *Āśleṣā, Maghā* and *Pūrvaphālgunī*—south-eastern region.

(4) *U. Phālgunī, Hasta* and *Citrā*—southern region.

(5) *Svātī, Viśākhā* and *Anurādhā*—south-western region.

(6) *Jyeṣṭhā, Mūla* and *Pūrvāṣāḍhā*—western region.

(7) *Uttarāṣāḍhā, Śravaṇa* and *Dhaniṣṭhā*—north-western region.

(8) *Śatabhiṣak, P. Bhādra* and *U. Bhādra*—northern region.

(9) *Revatī, Aśvinī* and *Bharaṇī*—north-eastern region.

Whichever asterism is transited by benefics, the region ruled by it would enjoy good rains, good harvest, and prosperity as well as peace and amity among the people of that region. Contrary results would be the lot of the people of the region whose asterisms are transited by malefics.

Query About Sexual Congress

This procedure is resorted to in probing both clandestine and legitimate connections.

The following conditions lead to the conclusion that no sexual union took place the same day:

(1) The Sun be posited either in the *Ārūḍha* or the 7th house.

(2) The Sun should aspect or be conjoined with the lord of the *Ārūḍha* or the 7th house.

In the absence of the above *Yogas* it should be declared that the union has taken place.

(3) If there be associated or aspect of benefics for the 7th house, the union must have taken place with much rejoicing. On the other hand, malefics in such positions would lead to a union full of bitterness.

(4) If the 7th house be bereft of the presence or aspect of the Moon and Venus, but possessed of the presence of malefics, the appointed union did not take place.

(5) If the 7th house be posited by a benefic, and aspected by the Moon and Venus, it must have taken place.

(6) It should be said that the woman is attached to the man, if the *Ārūḍha* be aspected by the Moon and Venus, who themselves should be aspected or joined by benefics and the Sun.

(7) In the above case if there be other malefics along with the Sun, who are either with the Moon and Venus, or aspect them, the union should have taken place without the woman having any love for the man.

Love or Its Absence

If the *lagna* be aspected by benefics, the woman had love for the man during their union, while if it be aspected by malefics, she had no love for him.

If the Moon be conjoined with malefics, the man must have done it by force. On the other hand, if the Sun be in the company of malefics, the woman, being his superior, forced him to satisfy her.

Description of Partners

Should the Moon have the Sun's *Vargas*, aspect or association, the male partner of the union was handsome and of prepossessing features and manners; while the Moon, having benefic aspect, association and *Vargas*, would lead to the conclusion of the woman's excellence in all respects.

Woman's Relationship

If the planet that aspects the *Ārūḍha* be posited in his own sign and own decanate or *Navāṁśa* etc., the man's union took place with his own wife and in his own house. On the other hand, if the above-mentioned planet has a majority of the *Vargas* of other planets, he cohabited with another's wife in another's house. If the aspecting planet be in his exaltation, the woman in the act was his master's wife.

Similarly, prediction will have to be done about the woman on the basis of the *Vargas* such as belonging to an enemy, fiiend etc. If the *Varga* be that of an inimical planet, the woman must be his enemy's wife; if it be that of a friendly planet, it is a friend's or relative's wife. In case the *Varga* belongs to a debilitated planet, he must have cohabited with a wretched woman. If the woman's caste is required, it should be that of the aspecting planet.

The Woman's Status

Should the Sun, Venus and Mars be posited in the 7th house from the *Ārūḍha*, she would be another's wife; if it be Jupiter there (7th) she is his own wife; if it be Mercury or the Moon, he had sexual union with a courtesan; and if Saturn, the woman belongs to another community. The age of the woman should be deduced from the *Avasthā* or condition such as childhood, girlhood etc., of the Moon.

Her Age

If the waxing Moon or Mercury be in the 7th house, the female partner in the union must be a young girl; if it be Saturn, an old woman; if the Sun or Jupiter, one who had a child-birth; and if Mars and Venus, a coarse (or uncivilized) woman. In the same manner the man's age too should be adjudged.

Rendezvous of Lovers

If the *Ārūḍha* be a village *Rāśi*, it was in a village; if a forest sign, in a jungle; if an Urban *Rāśi*, in a town. If the *lagna* be a *Varga* of the Sun, the union took place during the day; and if it be one of the Moon, at night.

Private Life

(1) If the Moon and Mars be joined together in the ascendant, 5th, 7th or 9th house, the man and woman must have spent the night in quarrels.

(2) If the Moon and Venus be joined together in one of the above-mentioned houses, they must have spent a good deal of time in secret talks.

(3) Should the Moon and Jupiter be together in one of these houses, the querist must have had sexual union with a pregnant woman, or the union must have led to pregnancy.

(4) If the planets be the Moon and Mercury, he must have cohabited with another's wife.

(5) If Mars and Saturn (be in the 1st and 7th houses, Mars being strong, there was no union owing to a fire-havoc; Saturn being strong, the same result owing to the fear of thieves. The same result would be predicted, should Mars and Saturn be in each other's house.

House of Union

The type of house is to be deduced from the planet that is posited in the 1st or 7th house, as in the case of eating, child-birth and theft. In case there be no planet connected with these two houses, the result should be declared on the basis of the quality of the sign of the *Ārūḍha* and its lord. For example, if the *lagna* be either Aries or Libra, the house used for the union must be one that is assigned to the lord of that ascendant. For the signs, Taurus, Gemini, Virgo, Sagittarius and Pisces, it is that which is allotted to Mercury viz. study room, dance hall etc. For Leo it is a cow-shed; for Scorpio, as for the Moon, i.e. worship room or office room; for Cancer as for Jupiter, i.e. a strong, decent house; for Capricorn a circular house; for Aquarius, a *Nāgavana* (a holy wood where serpents are worshipped in idols). For Virgo ascendant, it is the granary situated in the south-eastern corner of the house; for Sagittarius, the room where rice and other grains are pounded and where pestles etc. are kept, in the north-western corner; for Pisces, kitchen in the north-east.

Foreign Travel

(1) At a query about foreign tour see if any of the following planets viz. the Sun, Mercury, Jupiter and Venus, is posited in the 11th house from the *Ārūḍha*; and if it is so, the querist would soon go abroad. On the other hand, if some of these planets

be in the 11th and others in the 12th house, he would return home even after going halfway.

(2) If the *lagna* be an immovable sign, there would be no movement from home; and if be a movable *Rāśi*, foreign travel would certainly materialize. If it be a dual sign, there would be a chance for tour after sometime, provided the ascendant fell in the second half of the sign.

(3) Should one of the planets viz. the Sun, Mercury, Jupiter, Venus and Saturn, be posited in a movable ascendant, he would go abroad without delay, but if a retrograde planet be in the *lagna*, he would have no chance of going abroad in the near future.

(4) If the 2nd decanate of Virgo rises at query, or if the strong Moon transiting the star *Anūrādhā*, be in the 11th house; or if Cancer or Pisces be the *Ārūḍha*, the 7th or 9th house, then too the querist would succeed in going abroad.

Marriage

(1) At a query of marriage if the Moon be posited in the 7th, 2nd or an *Upacaya* house, and be aspected by Jupiter, the person would get a damsel as his life-partner very soon. On the other hand, if she be in the 4th, 5th, 9th, 8th, 12th or 1st house, and aspected by or combined with malefics, there would be many obstacles to his securing a bride.

(2) When the Moon is posited in 7th, 6th, 3rd, 10th or 11th house, which is owned by a benefic and aspected by the Sun, Mercury or Jupiter, the person is sure to get a damsel whom he loves most.

(3) The same result would follow, if the lords of the ascendant and the 12th house, or of the 1st and 7th houses, exchange their places. So too when the Moon and Venus are posited in their own houses or exaltation signs.

(4) The same effect should be predicted, if the *lagna*, owned by the Moon or Venus, be occupied or aspected by a strong benefic.

(5) Should the Moon be posited in the ascendant, 6th or 8th house, and a malefic in the 7th house, the girl would become a widow within 8 years.

(6) Should a malefic occupy the 5th house, being aspected by

its enemy, and be debilitated, the wife would become unchaste or barren.

(7) The querist would have no marriage, if the waning Moon. posited in an even sign identical with the 6th or 8th house, be aspected by malefics. The same effect should be predicted when the Moon and Venus are conjoined with malefics in the above case.

Loss of Wife

If the lord of the 7th house be conjoined with malefics and posited in the 1st, 12th, 9th or 6th house, or be in depression, the person would lose his first wife.

Paternal Property etc

1. How are we to find out if one's son would be obedient and dutiful towards him? If the son's natal Moon be in the 9th, 11th or 2nd from the father's *Candra Rāśi,* the answer is in the affirmative.

2. Now start from the son's natal Moon and see where the father's Moon is posited from the former. If it be in the 11th house or in a trine, the son would inherit his father's property. The same result could be predicted in case the father's lunar sign happens to be in trine to the lord of the son's natal ascendant.

3. Should the lords of the 9th house counted from the native's ascendant and lunar sign, be posited in their respective 11th houses, the person would delight his father's heart, both here and hereafter, by serving him and by performing with devotion all the obsequial rites according to the scriptural injunctions.

4. The native would have the same education and profession as the father, if the lord of the ascendant be posited in the 9th house or conjoined with its lord, or with the Sun.

5. If the native's birth be in the asterism ruled by the lord of the 12th house from the father's natal sign (according to the *Pārāśarī* system), he would displease the father by going away from home. He would be inimical to the father's interests, if the native's natal asterism be one that is occupied by the lord of the 6th house, in the father's chart. The same result would follow if the son's natal Moon be in the 6th *Rāśi* from the father's.

6. The son would be burdened with the father's debts, if the

lord of the father's natal sign be conjoined with the lord of the son's 12th house; or if the above planet be posited in the son's 12th house.

7. Should the 9th house or its lord be in a movable sign, and the Sun or the 9th lord be either in the 8th or 12 house, the native would not be by the side of his father at the latter's death; if the 9th house be a dual sign, or its lord in a similar house, he would get the tidings of his father's demise on his way back.

If it be a fixed sign, and its lord similarly placed, and if the 9th house or its lord be associated with or aspected by benefics, or if the Sun be similarly situated, the person would be at home at the time and perform all the rites for the departed soul.

8. A person may approach an astrologer for an answer to his query whether he would be able to perform the last rites for his parents. The following conditions would lead to an answer in the affirmative:

(a) The lord of the 9th house and the Sun should be in their own houses or *Aṁśas*, identical with movable signs or *Aṁśas*.

(b) The above two planets are either posited in or aspect the 12th house.

(c) The same two should be posited in *kendras* in *Rāśi* or *Aṁśa*. If at least one of these conditions be satisfied, he could hope to perform his father's last rites.

Regarding the mother substitute the 4th house and the Moon for the 9th house and the Sun in the three conditions mentioned above.

9. Should the 9th house from the ascendant at query suffer from malefic association or aspect, the person would not be able to observe the last rites for his father on account of some obstacles. If the 9th house has both benefic and malefic connections, find out which planet, benefic or malefic has greater longitude. In case the malefic be less advanced than the other, though the observance might be hindered in its initial part, the querist might take over the charge of the rites after some delay, and then complete them successfully. Should the benefic be less advanced, the rites would be commenced in right earnest, but later they would be abruptly marred by the person's illness or incapacity.

10. (a) If the son be born in the ascendant that is 8th from the

father's natal Moon, or if the lord of the 8th of the latter, be posited in the former's ascendant, he would have opportunities to perform the father's obsequial rites.

(b) If the star occupied by the lord of 8th house from the father's natal Moon or its trine, be the son's natal asterism, the latter would perform the father's last rites and other seasonal *Śrāddhas* properly, being blessed with good children and great grand children as well as health, happiness and longevity.

(c) If the son's natal ascendant happens to be the 10th sign from the father's natal sign (lunar), and if the lord of the 10th sign be posited in the son's ascendant, the son would be much more illustrious than the father.

Aṣṭakavarga

It is not my intention here to explain everything connected with the *Aṣṭakavarga* system which you will find expounded clearly with illustrations in my work *Fundamentals of Astrology* (Chapter XXII). However, I shall content myself by showing some special applications of this system, according to the *Praśnamarga*.

Vittāya

Take the *Samudāya Aṣṭaka* chart, where the benefic dots of all the planets in all the *Rāśi* are totalled up, and added up the benefic dots in the six houses viz. 1, 2, 4, 9, 10 and 11. This is called *Vittāya* or acquisition of wealth. If the sum is more than 164, the native will be blessed with the gain of wealth and be very prosperous. If it is equal to or less than 164, his income will be equal to or less than his expenditure, as the case may be.

Tirtha

Similarly, add up the benefic dots in the three houses viz. 6, 8, and 12; and if the sum be less than 76, his income would be very high. On the other hand, if it be more than 76, his expenditure would be more than his income.

Benefic Dots in the 12 Bhāvas

The ascendant should have 25 benefic dots; II house-22; III-29; IV-24; V-25; VI-34; VII-19; VIII-24; IX-29; X-36;

XI-54; and XII-16. The respective *Bhāvas* would grow or lose, as the case may be, if they have more or less than the given number of benefic dots, provided the houses have no malefic associations.

(i) *Bandhuka* is the sum of the benefic dots in the three houses viz. 1, 5 and 9; that of the dots in 2, 6 and 10 is termed (ii) *Sevaka*; that of the dots in 3, 7 and 11 is (iii) *Poṣaka*; and that of the dots in 4, 8 and 12, is known as (iv) *Ghātaka*. There mean friendly, servant, nourisher and injurious respectively. The third sum should be greater than the fourth one, if one should become wealthy. Similarly, if the first (friendly) be greater than the second (servant), he would enjoy the company of his kinsmen as well as their prosperity. On the contrary, the person would eke out his living as a servant.

Internal and External Parts

The total of the benefic dots in the *Samudāya Aṣṭakavarga* chart in respect of the six houses viz. ascendant, 4th, 5th, 7th, 9th and 10th houses, is called the internal division; while the sum of the benefic dots in the other houses is termed external division. The effects of the former being greater than the other are mental equipoise, self-control, good education, truthfulness, piety, faith in God and devotion to elders and teachers. Should the external division be greater than the other, the person would be a victim of mental worries, showiness, faithlessness, dishonesty and the like.

Dangers Through Malefics

Should Rāhu be posited in an untoward house, the native or querist would suffer from snake-bite or drinking poison at the age indicated by the total number of benefic dots found in the house occupied by Rāhu in the *Samudāya* A.V. Chart. Similarly, in the case of Mars, the number of benefic dots in the house occupied by him would indicate the age at which the person might get wounded by weapons or suffer fracture of bones. In the case of Saturn, the person would be afflicted by serious illness grief of bereavement and the like at the age denoted by the number of benefic dots in the sign occupied by Saturn.

Bad Day from Saturn A.V.

Find out the sign that has very few benefic dots in Saturn's A.V. When that sign rises daily, one might have some trouble or the other during that period. Similarly, when the Sun traverses the above mentioned sign, the person concerned is likely to get into troubles during that month.

Venus in Aṣṭakavarga A.V.

Take the *Śodhya Piṇḍa* (aggregate of the benefic dots that remain in the A.V. Chart of the particular planet after the two corrections for trines and lordship being the same) of Venus and multiply it by the number (before corrections) of dots in the 7th house from Venus. Keep this product in two places separately. Divide the first product by 27 and treat the remainder as the asterism beginning with *Āśvinī*. Similarly divide the product kept in the second place by 12 and treat the remainder as the Zodiacal sign counted from Aries. Now use the asterism and the sign for finding out the approximate time of the person's marriage through the transit of Jupiter. The event may also take place during the *Daśā* and *Bhūkti* of the lord of the *Rāśi* obtained.

Saturn in A.V.

Take the benefic dots that remain after the two corrections in the two houses viz. the one occupied by Saturn and the other that is 7th from that sign in his A.V. Chart. Should both these houses be bereft of benefic dots, the person is likely to meet with his end in a lonely place in tragic circumstances. In case these two houses contain benefic dots contributed by friendly planets, his death would take place in the midst of friends and relatives. Should the contributing planets be inimical to Saturn, the end would be in the midst of enemies.

Saturn and Exit

In Saturn's A.V. find out the *Śodhya Piṇḍa* and multiply it by 7. Divide the product by 27 and take the remainder as the star counted from *Aśvinī*. The period of Saturn's transit through that star may be dangerous to the native's life. Now multiply by the benefic dots (before corrections) in the sign occupied by Saturn, the figure of the *Śodhya Piṇḍa* and divide the product by 27.

The remainder should be added to the previous remainder. This sum will give a star from *Āśvinī*. When Saturn transits that star, the native is likely to make his exit from the world.

यदि मयात्र कृत्री करुणाकरा द्युमणिपूर्वखगा मनसार्चिताः ।
मिहिरसत्पदवी च समादृता सुमनसो मुदिताः स्युरदोऽर्चया ॥ ४ ॥

श्रीमत्सिद्धिविनायकोरुकरुणाधारासुपुष्टा मम
प्रज्ञासल्लतिका ग्रहेश्वरनति स्फीतावृतिः सत्फलम् ।
प्रासूतार्थपदानवद्यसुरसं शिष्टोप भोग्यं महा-
भाग्योदर्कमिदं च प्रश्नपदवीनामोदितं श्रेयसे ॥ ५ ॥*

। ओ३म् तत्सत् ।

*च प्रश्नेत्यत्र चकारः पिङ्गलमतेन पक्षे लघुर्भवति ।

Appendix

SLEEP

Sleep is a synonym of rest. It consists of the means and instruments of rejuvenating human activities.

Young infants spend greater part of the day in sleep. In North America there is a species of squirrel that spends 3/4 years in sleep. Scientists say that plants too sleep. Hippocratus says, "When the external limbs get tired, the internal parts gets rejuvenated. This is called sleep."

Sleep is the laboratory for studying the activities of the brain. Hypothelamus, a part of the brain, controls the physical activities of man during sleep. Sleep also helps us in the investigation of the various ailments that trouble the human body.

In Soviet Union there is an Institute for Research on Sleep in Georgia Republic. Prof. T. Oniyani is the Head of the Sleep Research Laboratory in Tsilisi. Dr. Prof. Heark and others have written exhaustive reports on this. They have explained in this to how the brain works, how it collects through the five senses the necessary information. For this purpose brain is the chief source. During the course of sleep the activities of the different parts of the brain and their power clearly manifest. It is also the aim of these scientists to analyse sleep in the cycle of waking and sound sleep (*jāgrat* and *suṣupti*).

Sleep is not of uniform occurrence. Slow sleep has four stages viz. (1) noddying; (2) slow but deep sleep; (3) slow but not deep sleep; and (4) rapid eye-movement (REM). These four stages are found to be in consonance with the fixed bio-electric activities of the brain. In this slow type of sleep body sinews become loose; breathing also becomes slow; activities of the heart too become steady. In 3/4 of sleep an individual enjoys the pleasure of such sleep. The next stage, however, appears strange and full of contradictions. All of a sudden the body becomes more active: blood pressure and heart-beats increased. The active biological elements are discharged to the blood; and the mysterious activities called dreams are experienced. During the stage of rapid eye-movement (REM) of sleep, every individual sees dreams. But they are rarely remembered afterwards. Scientists have not yet been able to solve the riddle—where and how do the dreams originate?

It is said that the stage of sleep called REM is the most important part of sleep. But Prof. Oniyani has found after experimenting on animals that if the REM pleasure is denied, there is not much change in their behaviour. This has helped medical science. In sick persons at this stage of sleep are found fluctuations in the involuntary development of the body. If by medicines duration of this part of sleep could be altered, it may help in preventing diseases.

In man's life sleep itself is the first stage rather than waking state. Prof. Karmanova has done extensive research on the ramifications of sleep. Dr. Mukhametova has experimented on Dolphins' sleep. During sleep their right and left brains work in turn. It is not clear whether Dolphins actually sleep or not.

The researches of Western scientists have tended to establish the close relationship between sleep and man's individuality. They say that there is close resemblance between sleep and man's mental attitude. The challenges and problems that we meet with in daily life do influence our sleep. If physical exhaustion and pressure is great, slow sleep period is lengthened. Its intensity also increases. In replenishing energy and strength this part of sleep plays a significant role. This sleep is indeed a measuring rod of our capacity to endure pressures.[1]

Prof. P. Deva Rao, who has done research on *The Gāyatrī Mantra* and growth of the human brain has dealt at length with the seven layers of consciousness, conscience, telepathy, sleep, dream etc.[2]

He shows that dreams are mainly telepathic in origin. He says that according to psychologists' dreams are self-originating

1. This information has been culled from an article by *Aruṇa* in the Kannaḍa Digest called *Kastūri* (A Monthly) for Sept. 1988.

2. Vide "*The Gāyatri Mantra and a Thesis on the Growth of the Human Brain*" by Prof. P. Deva Rao, AL-14 Srinivasanagar-574157, South India.

phenomena. But he has found that his dreams consist mostly of non-self-originated components.

In his opinion dreams are powered by sensations caused by and as yet unidentified sense organ which makes possible the phenomenon of telepathy, just as the five main senses do their respective sensations. Analysis of his dreams and his mental processes during the awakened state leads him to believe that telepathic sensations are bottled up when a human being is active in the conscious state, but when certain areas of the brain are dormant as in sleep, the energy of the telepathic impulses relaxes causing dreams to arise. "The ancient Indian seers recognized seven kinds or levels of consciousness in the human brain and three traits which shape human activity. If these are correlated with modern advances of knowledge...we can derive for the human brain a useful working model which can explain to a very large extent its growth and functioning." According to some scientists dreams are hallucinatory experiences during sleep. Psycho-analytic interpretations suggest that "dreams reflect one's own personal needs and wishes in summarized form". Hence a dream generally comprises "several components, each of which is the reflection of a physical state (a particular neuron circuitry)".

Dreams of a normal human being may be analyzed for its telepathic content by the 'Resonance Method'.

BIBLIOGRAPHY

Praśnamārgam, Kannaḍa edn. Pub. Jyotirvijñānaprakāśana, Udupi.

——, Malayālam edn. K. Govindan, Palluruthy.

—— Vol. I, English edn. B.V. Raman, Bangalore.

Praśnajñānam, Tr. V.S. Sastri and M.R. Bhat (1949).

Bṛhajjātakam, Tr. V.S. Sastri and M.R. Bhat (1929).

Jātakāpārijātaḥ, Tr. V.S. Sastri and M.R. Bhat.

Jātakādeśamārgaḥ, Tr. V.S. Sastri and M.R. Bhat (1942).

Kṛṣṇīyam, Trivandrum Sanskrit Series No. 243 (1951).

Daśādhyāyī (*Naukā*), Shri Venkateshwara Press, Bombay (1912).

Ahorātra-Daśādhāyī, Malayālam Tr. Dr. N. Gopala Panicker, Pettah, Trivandrum (1988).

Bṛhat Saṁhitā, 2 Vols, Tr. M.R. Bhat, Motilal Banarsidass, Delhi.

Fundamentals of Astrology, Tr. M.R. Bhat, Motilal Banarsidass, Delhi.

Sārāvalī, Nirnayasagar Press, Bombay (1928).

Vidyāmādhavīyam (3 Vols.), Ed. R. Shama Sastri, Mysore (1923).

Naṣṭa-Praśnadīpikā, (Malayalam) Pub. K.G. Parameswaran Pillai, Quilon.

Caraka-Saṁhitā, Motilal Banarsidass, Delhi.

Suśruta-Saṁhitā, Motilal Banarsidass, Delhi.

Āyurvedasāra (Kannaḍa 2 Vols). P. Ramakrishnaiya, Govt. of Karnataka (1987).

Vīrasiṁhāvalokaḥ, Shri Venkateshwara Press, Bombay.

Yuvabhārati, Monthly for Aug. 1988, Vivekananda Kendra, Triplicane, Madras.

"*The Gāyatrī Mantram and a Thesis on the Growth of the Human Brain*", by P. Deva Rao, Srinivasanagar (1984).

Sudhā (Kannaḍa Weekly, Bangalore) 2-8 Oct. 1988, on "Bākkalada Śāstrokta Sasyodyāna".

Kastūri, (Kannaḍa Monthly) for Sept. 1988 on "Secret of Sleep"

INDEX